The NCAA and the Exploitation of College Profit-Athletes

The NCAA and the Exploitation of College Profit-Athletes

An Amateurism That Never Was

Richard M. Southall,
Mark S. Nagel,
Ellen J. Staurowsky,
Richard T. Karcher,
and Joel G. Maxcy

THE UNIVERSITY OF
SOUTH CAROLINA PRESS

Published by the University of South Carolina Press
Columbia, South Carolina 29208

uscpress.com

Printed in the United States of America

Library of Congress Cataloging-in-Publication Data
can be found at http://catalog.loc.gov/.

ISBN: 978-1-64336-377-6 (hardcover)
ISBN: 978-1-64336-378-3 (paperback)
ISBN: 978-1-64336-379-0 (ebook)

To Jason, Crystal, EJ, & Deb. To my family and friends, thank you for your enduring love and support. I love and cherish each of you. To my current and former students, thank you for the honor of learning with you. To my mom and dad.—Richard S.

To my loving family who constantly provides support and understanding.—Mark

To my students, former students, and colleagues at Ithaca College and Drexel, I am so humbled to have the opportunity to work alongside you. To my family, for your enduring support. And to Dr. Becker, my surgeons and guardian angels from Penn Medicine for extending my shelf life. This book is possible because of you.—Ellen

To all of the profit-athletes who sow but do not reap.—Rick K.

CONTENTS

Preface
The NCAA's Scholarly Colloquium: An Aborted Attempt at Purchasing College Sport Research ix
Richard M. Southall and Mark S. Nagel

Acknowledgments xv

Introduction: Big-Time College Sport Is Big Business 1
Ellen J. Staurowsky, Richard M. Southall, and Mark S. Nagel

PART I
College Athletes Have Always Been Paid

An Amateurism That Never Was 17
Ellen J. Staurowsky, Richard M. Southall, and Mark S. Nagel

Some College Athletes Are Employees: Lessons Learned from Professional Sport Labor 37
Mark S. Nagel

Power Five Football and Men's Basketball: At the Center of It All 68
Richard M. Southall

Challenging the NCAA's Collegiate Model Paradigm 86
Richard M. Southall and Mark S. Nagel

PART II

Legal and Economic Realities of Big-Time College Sports

The Legal Status of College Athletes as Employees under Workers' Compensation and Labor Laws 113
Richard T. Karcher

Northwestern Football, Unionization Efforts, and the NLRB's Decision Not to Exercise Jurisdiction 146
Ellen J. Staurowsky

Title IX, College Athlete Employment, and the Politics of Destruction 189
Ellen J. Staurowsky

College Sport Workplace Economics: Suppressing Player Compensation to Increase Profits 227
Joel G. Maxcy

PART III

Power Five College Sport Today

The Exploitation of Power Five Profit-Athletes: Paternalism, Patriarchy, and Racialization 261
Richard M. Southall

The End of the Beginning of the End? 290
Richard M. Southall and Mark S. Nagel

Contributors 327
Index 329

PREFACE

The NCAA's Scholarly Colloquium: An Aborted Attempt at Purchasing College Sport Research

Richard M. Southall
and Mark S. Nagel

In 2002 higher education researcher John Thelin noted there had recently been "a groundswell of excellent scholarly works dealing with intercollegiate athletics. The topic has both endurance and significance now that such disciplines as history, economics, law, literary analysis, and political science have been brought to bear on the serious study of college sports" (Thelin 2002). He also recognized a dichotomy that "as the scholarship on college sports gets better, the educational and ethical problems of college sports get worse" (ibid.). In 2006, apparently unaware of the almost one hundred years of inquiry as well as the increasing depth and breadth of college sport research, Dr. Myles Brand, president of the National Collegiate Athletic Association (NCAA), and the NCAA leadership decided to sponsor an academic conference to encourage scholars to study college sport and treat intercollegiate athletics as a subject matter for serious research.

In contrast to the way it announced the March Madness brackets of the Division I Men's Basketball Tournament that same month, in March 2006 the NCAA announced with little fanfare that it would host a 2007 Conference on Intercollegiate Athletics and Higher Education in America in conjunction with its centennial 2007 convention. The conference was intended to summarize recent scholarship related to college sport and examine the role of college sport in American higher education and popular culture. Two of the authors of this book were contacted by an NCAA staff member and asked to serve on the conference abstract review board. Quietly, a call for papers—a standard operating procedure in which conference organizers solicit the submission of research abstracts—was sent out and a webpage for online submissions put in place. As is the norm for an academic conference, the peer-review process would play out, with review board members performing blind reviews of submitted abstracts (evaluating them without knowing the identity of authors) in order to determine which abstracts would be accepted and included in the conference program.

As months went by, the status of the conference remained in limbo, with no one on the review board having received an abstract to review. In addition, several authors who had submitted abstracts contacted review board members and the NCAA national office to inquire on the status of the review process. Time was running out. After several months, the NCAA quietly postponed and then cancelled the inaugural conference. No formal announcement, no press release on the NCAA website, nothing. And more interestingly, no one on the review board ever received an abstract to review. After a few phone calls and email exchanges, an NCAA staff member responded that the conference had been postponed because of a "lack of interest" on the part of scholars.

In November 2006, *Inside Higher Ed* reported that NCAA president Brand—citing a lack of "quality" submissions—had unilaterally cancelled the conference:

> The reason for the postponement was simple. . . . The papers received . . . "were not of the quality one would expect for a scholarly conference, or at least there weren't enough of them to put on a conference." Brand said that the NCAA staff members and others who had been involved in planning the original meeting were not familiar enough with higher education to fully understand what an academic conference was all about, and that when Brand himself got involved and saw the nature of the abstracts that had been submitted, he realized the conference was ill-fated.
>
> "Rather than put on a mediocre conference, and get off to a bad start," Brand said, the association decided to start from scratch. It has lined up a group of what he called "leading academicians" to meet at the NCAA's annual convention in early January to plan a new conference, scheduled for January 2008. (Lederman 2006)

Brand commented that having been in the academy for forty years, he could tell the difference between a good abstract and one that was not high-quality. He expressed confidence the 2008 symposium, with the theme "College Sports: A Legitimate Focus for Scholarly Inquiry," would comprise "invited scholars of international repute." Notably, abstract submissions would not be welcome.

After this inauspicious beginning, and for several years, the NCAA did sponsor an annual scholarly colloquium and published a peer-reviewed academic journal, the *Journal of Intercollegiate Sports*. The colloquium's format evolved from just invited speakers to a combination of invited speakers, sponsored panels, and several peer-reviewed research presentations. In many ways it came to resemble a legitimate academic gathering, with a variety of theoretical perspectives and data-driven presentations making up the program. It seemed the NCAA had overcome its initial reticence and now supported academic freedom and serious inquiry into college sport. Then came the winter of 2012 and the demise of the NCAA's scholarly colloquium.

Apparently the more the colloquium became an opportunity for open academic dialogue related to issues in intercollegiate athletics, the more uncomfortable the NCAA became. As reported in the *Chronicle of Higher Education,* by 2012 "several top NCAA administrators apparently were concerned that the last couple of colloquia had 'primarily included ideologues intent on criticizing the NCAA.' As a result, one top NCAA leader told [a member of the colloquium's executive board], the colloquium 'runs the risk of no longer being funded' " (Wolverton 2012). According to reports, "At least one top NCAA executive [was not] happy with the tone of recent conferences and raised questions about whether the association would continue to back the forum" (ibid.). "Some [NCAA] leaders apparently [felt] that the forum [had] turned into too much of an NCAA-bashing" (ibid.). Indeed, 2013 was to be the last NCAA-sponsored colloquium. The 2012 meeting—which concluded with board members "breaking bread" and enjoying a well-appointed buffet—was to be the NCAA's scholarly colloquium's last supper.

As far back as 2006, Brand had dismissed any criticism of the NCAA and/or college sport by utilizing the offhand comment that critics "have their facts wrong." Such a tactic is all well and good, and expected as part of the NCAA's lobbying efforts, but with the scholarly colloquium, the NCAA had ventured into the field of academic and scholarly inquiry. It titled its colloquium as "scholarly," just in case anyone didn't know what a colloquium was.

The most often-quoted characterization of hegemony is Italian journalist Antonio Gramsci's: "the 'spontaneous' consent given by the great masses of the population to the general direction imposed on social life by the dominant fundamental group; this consent is 'historically' caused by the prestige (and subsequent confidence) which the dominant group enjoys because of its position and function" (Gramsci 1971: 12).

A dominant group, which Susan Strange refers to as the hegemon, can be either strong or weak. A strong hegemon functions to produce a semblance of order and stability. However, as Strange (1987: 555) notes, "hegemonic power is a necessary, but not always sufficient, condition for order." Hegemonic order and stability can also be more subtly achieved through Gramsci's spontaneous consent.

Such consent is not only achieved through force but also manufactured using example setting, persuasion, and coercion (Snidal 1985). When hegemony is exerted only through example and persuasion it is characterized as "beneficent" (ibid.). However, hegemony may also be exercised through subtle or overt coercion. It may cease to be beneficent when it is achieved through coercion or results in the exploitation of subordinates or nonruling groups.

Without notions of domination, hegemony has little meaning. Both force and consent are utilized by a hegemon to achieve dominance. If the existing hegemon is also a monopolist and/or monopsonist (as is the case with the NCAA and Power Five conferences), the instruments of coercion and exploitation are much more effective. A hegemon prefers to be seen as beneficent, relying on moral authority exerted through the creation and perpetuation of legitimating symbols and the adoption of institutional logics by dominant and subservient group members (Southall et al. 2008). However, the threat of officially sanctioned force always remains implicit. Fundamentally, a ruling group seeks to achieve hegemony through gaining the consent of subordinate groups to the "correctness" of the existing social order.

One way in which the NCAA's beneficent status is maintained is by the perpetuation of the NCAA's formation mythology. This mythology singularly frames the NCAA's creation and development as a paternalistic response by university presidents to football deaths, prodded by a benevolent President Teddy Roosevelt. Consistent with this narrative, through its use of language the NCAA has sought to establish itself as a quasi-governmental moral authority. The NCAA seeks to foster this hegemony by consistently referring to its bylaws and policies as legislation and the NCAA president's annual convention speech as a "State of the Association" address.

In hindsight the NCAA cartel—not satisfied with sponsoring athletic championships and seeking to monopolize the big-time college sport market—through its scholarly colloquium had attempted to purchase the academic research and discussion surrounding college sports. When it couldn't successfully do so, the NCAA simply withdrew its funding for the colloquium and journal, divesting itself of products that no longer supported its corporate interests. Wishing to characterize itself as an educational association, the NCAA sought to use its scholarly colloquium to support NCAA hegemony. When challenged by a group of academicians, the NCAA simply took its ball and went home.

In many ways, this long-standing tension between the NCAA and the academy—reflected in the historical arc of the NCAA's college sport colloquium—is the genesis for this book. Having spent decades researching big-time college sport, the authors of this book intend it to be a response to attempts by NCAA and Power Five conference administrators to marginalize and/or purchase the dialogue surrounding big-time college sport. We hope you find our response thoughtful and thought-provoking.

References

Gramsci, Antonio (1971). *Selections from the Prison Notebooks.* Edited and translated by Quintin Hoare and Geoffrey Nowell-Smith. New York: International.

Lederman, Doug (2006). "NCAA Sidelines a Scholarly Conference." *Inside Higher Ed,* November 22. https://www.insidehighered.com/news/2006/11/22/ncaa-sidelines-scholarly-conference.

Snidal, Duncan (1985). "The Limits of Hegemonic Stability Theory." *International Organization* 39, no. 4: 579–614.

Southall, Richard M., Mark S. Nagel, John M. Amis, and Crystal Southall (2008). "A Method to March Madness: Institutional Logics and the 2006 National Collegiate Athletic Association Division I Men's Basketball Tournament." *Journal of Sport Management* 22, no. 6: 677–700.

Strange, Susan (1987). "The Persistent Myth of Lost Hegemony." *International Organization* 41, no. 4: 551–74.

Thelin, J. R. (2002). "Academics on Athletics." *Journal of Higher Education* 73, no. 3: 409–19. https://doi.org/10.1353/jhe.2002.0031.

Wolverton, Brad (2012). "NCAA's Tolerance for Dissenting Views at Its Academic Forum Appears in Doubt." *Chronicle of Higher Education,* December 11. https://www.chronicle.com/article/ncaas-tolerance-for-dissenting-views-at-its-academic-forum-appears-in-doubt/.

ACKNOWLEDGMENTS

To this book's coauthors. I am honored to have worked with you. A special thanks to Ellen and Mark for believing in this project and helping make it a reality. Both of you have challenged and inspired me for twenty plus years. I am fortunate to have worked with wonderful colleagues and students throughout my career. Each stop along the way has been a unique and life-altering experience. I wouldn't change a thing. I want to acknowledge some fellow travelers: Billy Hawkins, Fritz Polite, Victor Kidd, Chris Corr, Crystal Southall, Deb Southall, Jon Ericson, Allen Sack, Matt Brown, Peter Han, Doug Wells, Linda Sharp, Gerry Gurney, Woody Eckard, Rick Johnson, Jimmy Adams, Dusty Lawson, Drake Wallick, Rick Karcher, and Kim Boone. To Sonny and Pam Vaccaro, thank you for being not only my heroes but also dear friends. To Drs. Eitzen and Sage, thank you for inspiring me. To former, current, and future college athletes, I hope I have helped further your best interests. To the many colleagues, friends, and students who have believed in the College Sport Research Institute (CSRI) and the *Journal of Issues in Intercollegiate Athletics* (JIIA), thank you. Finally, I must acknowledge my entire family—all fifty-six and growing. Each of you has a special place in my heart.—Richard S.

I am honored to have worked with such amazing coauthors on this project. A special thanks to Ellen for pushing to get this book in motion and to Richard for diligently working to get it completed. I also have the great privilege to work with amazing colleagues and students in the Department of Sport and Entertainment Management at the University of South Carolina. My initial activities in the college sport environment, which spurred continual questions about how the industry operates, would not have been possible without the opportunity to work with the men's and women's basketball teams at the University of San Francisco many years ago. Dan Rascher, Andy Schwarz, and others at OSKR permitted me to not only see but also play a very small role in shaping how the NCAA's operations would be scrutinized in important legal proceedings. Over my many years in academe, a list of other supporters far too long for this limited space has also provided invaluable assistance and insights that I will always appreciate. Finally, my family has been consistently supportive of this project and many others even when that meant many days and nights of researching and writing.—Mark

A publication effort of this kind draws upon a lifetime of work influenced by far too many to acknowledge here; please forgive omissions due to the need for brevity. For the current and former college athletes who have stood up to challenge an exploitative system, I pray that I have served your interests and aided your cause in some small way. A special thank you is reserved for Sonny Vaccaro and his wife, Pam, who have modeled what it means to seek social justice with an open heart, fierce determination, unrelenting will, and generous spirit. To my intellectual inspirations, Drs. George Sage, Harry Edwards, Carole Oglesby, Linda Carpenter, Michael Sachs, Allen L. Sack, Don Sabo, Richard Southall, Joseph Cooper, and Ron Smith, I am grateful beyond words to have learned from you. To US senators Chris Murphy (D-CT) and Cory Booker (D-NJ), thank you for your willingness to try to balance the scales on behalf of college athletes. And to Ramogi Huma, thank you for your enduring example of fortitude, purpose, and humanity.—Ellen

I'd like to thank my colleagues Richard Southall and Mark Nagel for including me in this important project. I'd like to acknowledge all of my former students—I hope you've learned as much from me as I've learned from you.—Rick K.

Introduction

Big-Time College Sport Is Big Business

Ellen J. Staurowsky,
Richard M. Southall,
and Mark S. Nagel

At a foundational level, it is important to understand the "college sport" to which we refer in this book is the industry segment that has come to be known as "big-time" college sport, practiced within Power Five conferences and among other NCAA Division I universities that sponsor men's basketball and football. It does not refer to NCAA Division II and III or "loss sports" in Division I, where the direct commercial value of the players is much less and college athletes largely exist within an educational system as students. Though many people contextualize college athletes as a homogenous group who "go pro in something other than sports,"[1] this belief has largely been crafted and cultivated by a specific NCAA marketing plan designed to prevent meaningful financial and educational reform.

The NCAA's assertion that its principle of amateurism serves to shield athletes from the corrupting forces of professionalism and commercialism is unsupported by the facts. College sport properties directly compete with professional leagues for advertising revenue, media rights income, and audience share. While big-time college athletes are commodified in the same manner as professional athletes, they are denied free-market compensation. While the NCAA's preferred term of art for the enterprise is the "collegiate model," a term designed to highlight the sought-after "clear line of demarcation" (NCAA 2022: 12.01.2) between college and professional sports, other than the players' ability to negotiate their conditions of employment, there is little to distinguish the massive commercialization of big-time collegiate sport from that found within the professional sport industry.

Power Five college sport has adopted business practices that mirror those of professional sport organizations. Much like professional leagues around the world, the NCAA's business focus is global, with international marketing deals consummated daily. Hedlund and Naylor (2020: 17) concluded that "when you combine the NCAA as a whole and the largest money-making universities' revenues together (approximately USD$10.21 billion), college sports in the US would be the second largest 'sport league' in the world."

In the twenty-first century, most Football Bowl Subdivision (FBS) college athletic departments employ the same business practices as professional sports franchises and have increasingly turned to companies such as the Aspire Group, Collegiate Consulting, Learfield, and Legends for ticket sales and marketing expertise. For example, in December 2020, Georgia Tech announced a partnership with Legends that is expected to yield more than $400 million in revenue over the span of eleven years (Carp 2020). As Legends does for its other clients, including professional and Olympic sport properties, it will handle Georgia Tech's business intelligence, corporate hospitality, data analytics, e-commerce, fundraising, multimedia rights, premium seating, and ticketing (ibid.). Legends is a joint venture recently valued at $1.3 billion and is led by global investment firm, Sixth Street Partners; Yankee Global Entertainment Holdings (YGE), an affiliate of the New York Yankees; and Jones Concessions LLP, a company owned by Dallas Cowboys owner Jerry Jones (Bassam 2021). The Disney Institute, a professional development company that is an affiliate of the Walt Disney Company, provides training in enhancing the game-day experience for professional teams as well as teams throughout the college sport sector (Disney Institute 2022).

Just as have their professional peers, Power Five football and NCAA Division I men's basketball programs have sought to expand their international footprint by scheduling overseas events. Modeled after the National Football League's (NFL) International Series games played in Mexico City and London and the National Basketball Association's (NBA) preseason games in China and Europe, in October 2019 Irish American Events Limited announced the launch of the Aer Lingus College Football Classic, with five games scheduled between 2020 and 2025 (*Business Wire* 2019). In 2019, more than sixty NCAA Division I men's basketball teams traveled abroad to at least seventeen different countries (Goodman 2019).

Big-time college football and men's basketball are attractive to corporate brand partners that view these sport properties as equivalent to or, at times, better alternatives to professional sport entities such as the NFL or NBA. Power Five college football and NCAA Division I men's basketball (due to their extensive viewership and audience reach) were among the top five TV sports franchises in terms of postseason advertising along with the NFL, NBA, and Major League Baseball (MLB) (Daniels 2018; Young 2021). According to hookit, a brand valuation and sponsorship analytics platform, some of the nation's biggest brands align with college football (Mosher 2019). As a measure of magnitude, "between July 1, 2016, and June 30, 2017, the SEC alone generated almost $967 million in revenue and the 2017–18 college athletics season saw $1.24 billion spent on sponsorship with football leading the way" (ibid.).

The National Football Foundation (NFF) reported an average audience of 1,742,000 during telecasts of 247 2019 regular season college football games (NFF 2020). ESPN's *College GameDay Built by the Home Depot* show reached nearly 2 million viewers per show and a total of 35,900,000 for the season (ibid.). For the 2019–20 season, college football ranked second in core fans behind only the NFL (ibid.).

The Nielsen Company reported that "while NCAA Men's Basketball is not quite as popular as professional basketball or college football, it still has a large following in the U.S. with 58 percent of the adult population interested" (Nielsen Company 2019). A 2020 review of NCAA and College Football Playoff (CFP) corporate sponsors revealed nearly all are ranked among the Fortune 500 and/or Global 500.

NCAA Division I basketball is among the top forty-five leading global sport leagues as rated by engagement on social media. The list includes such diverse properties as the NBA, La Liga, English Premier League, World Wrestling Entertainment (WWE), Formula One, and NASCAR (Hookit 2021). Just as in big-time college football, major corporate brands want to partner with the NCAA Division I Men's Basketball Tournament. According to Kantar Media (2019), March Madness ($1.3 billion) went toe-to-toe with the NFL ($1.6 billion) in terms of 2019 advertising spending.

While the NCAA's television contract is not the most lucrative in sports, it is the most profitable among postseason properties (Ozanian 2019).[2] Between 2014 and 2019, advertisement revenue for the tournament steadily increased by 3 to 5 percent per year (ibid.). In 2018 the NCAA March Madness generated $1.32 billion in advertising revenue for its media partners, compared to the NFL postseason at $1.68 billion, the NBA playoffs at $970 million, and MLB playoffs at $468 million (ibid.). Consistent with the assertion that NCAA Division I men's basketball is a global sport property, 100 million people from 180 countries were expected to watch the tournament in 2020 before the COVID pandemic led to its cancellation (Lisa 2020).

In a report published by the American Gaming Association (2019a), Division I college football and men's basketball rank alongside the NFL, MLB, and the NBA as leagues in which core sport bettors have the most interest. There is no discernible line of demarcation between professional and college sport properties for those betting on sports in the United States. The NCAA's showcase of men's college basketball, March Madness, inspired an estimated 47 million people to wager $8.5 billion. In speaking about the interest in wagering on men's college basketball, American Gaming Association CEO Bill Miller stated, "During this year's tournament—the first in post-PASPA America—sports fans are expected to bet 40 percent more than they did on this year's Super Bowl" (American Gaming Association 2019b).[3]

Since 2017 at least 86 percent of athletic programs in the Power Five conferences have employed the services of companies to help expand the brand identities of college athletes. When asked about developing individual college athlete brands and allowing college athletes to earn money from them, Brad Underwood, University of Illinois men's basketball head coach, said, "A new era is coming in college sports, and we are excited that our players will have the opportunity to maximize the NIL opportunities that await them" (University of Illinois Athletics Communications Staff 2021). Similarly, University of Iowa athletic director Charlie Taylor touted that Iowa's athletic program was "excited to tell the next chapter of the Hawkeye story while growing both the student-athlete and Iowa brands together through the INFLCR platform" (Stephens 2019). Richard Pitino, the former men's head basketball coach at the University of Minnesota, commented, "I do think [players] should be able to profit off their individual brand" (Seligman 2019).

Show Me the Money!

In the world of sport entertainment, the terms *professional* and *college* are references to properties, not distinct business models. Today the lifeblood of the sport entertainment business is television/livestreaming and multimedia rights agreements. Programming in college football and men's basketball rivals that of their economic peer properties, the NFL and NBA. Indeed, in the permanent "MyESPN" banner at the top of the ESPN.com website, the categories from left to right read as follows: NFL, NBA, Soccer, NCAAF (for NCAA football), NCAAM (for NCAA men's basketball), and MMA (Mixed Martial Arts). Viewers must search to find other sports they wish to follow.

Former Big Ten commissioner Jim Delany's rationale as to why the Big Ten had created its own television network was identical to those offered by professional leagues (e.g., NFL Network, MLB Network, NBA TV): brand repetition, messaging, and an ability to tell a unique story. The similarity of NFL and college football television rights was reflected in comments made by former Pacific-12 commissioner Larry Scott when he explained that the NFL sets the market for television deals and major college conferences adopt similar approaches to maintain competitive position within that market (Wilner 2020). Emblematic of how valuable college football is to media companies, the Southeastern Conference (SEC) negotiated a record-breaking contract during the COVID-19 pandemic. With their existing contract with CBS coming to an end in 2023–24, the SEC entered into a $3 billion, ten-year contract with ESPN to air all their games (Draper and Blinder 2020). With this new deal, the SEC is expected to earn $300 million per year, which represents a nearly sixfold increase from their previous contract with CBS (ibid.). According to Wilner (2020), the magnitude of the agreement reflects that it is an all-in partnership between the most powerful conference in college football and the most influential media company in sports.

When the College Football Playoff (an arrangement that as of 2022 includes a four-team playoff along with four other major bowls) was created in 2012, there was an expectation that it would generate $400–500 million annually (Schroeder 2012). For the 2019 college football season, the total conference-by-conference payout for NCAA Division I football programs was more than $674 million (Dosh 2019). In June 2021, a subgroup of the College Football Playoff's Management Committee presented a proposal to change the current four-team format to a twelve-team event. The proposal was the first step in the expansion process. While, as of this writing, a timetable for expansion has not been formally approved, on February 18, 2022, Bill Hancock, executive director of the CFP Management Committee, reported that "the Board of Managers has accepted a recommendation from the Management Committee to continue the current four-team playoff for the next four years, as called for in the CFP's original 12-year plan. . . . At the same time, the Board expects the Management Committee to continue its discussions of a new format that would go into effect for the 2026–27 season" (Harrison 2022). When the current twelve-year CFP contract expires after the 2025–26 season, expansion is inevitable. There is simply too much demand for expansion and too much money to be made.

The University of Notre Dame has its own contract and received a base distribution of $3.19 million. The Group of Five conferences (American Athletic Conference, Conference USA, Mid-American Conference, Mountain West Conference, and Sun Belt Conference) received $90 million that they dispersed according to different conference formulas. FBS independents, including Brigham Young University, the University of Massachusetts-Amherst, and the United States Military Academy, shared a pool of $1.56 million. A pool of $2.43 million was distributed to NCAA Football Championship Subdivision (FCS) institutions. The University of Memphis was selected for the Cotton Bowl, and the $4 million payout was dispersed to the AAC (College Football Playoff 2021; Dosh 2019).

Similarly, due to its expansive audience, unique combination of local, national, and international reach, and its ability to draw viewership and generate advertising revenue, the NCAA Division I Men's Basketball Tournament occupies a valued place in the constellation of sport properties, that includes the Super Bowl (a single-day event), World Cup (quadrennial event), Olympics (winter and summer quadrennial events), NBA Championship (multiday event), and the World Series (multiday event). According to reporter Andrew Lisa (2020), "The 15-day, 14-city event dominates the news and pushes all other sports onto the back burner—and it's a very big business. Between media, marketing, broadcasting, ticket sales, gambling and the rest, billions of dollars change hands." The

2019 tournament earned a record $933 million in television advertising revenue and is poised to generate over a $1 billion per year in the years to come (Lisa 2020). The NCAA's fourteen-year contract, signed in 2010 with CBS Sports and Turner Broadcasting, was originally worth $10.8 billion. An eight-year, $8.8 billion contract extension was negotiated in 2016 and is set to end in 2034 (ibid.).

March Madness itself has an impact on stockholders in major corporations. As senior investment analyst Luke Lango (2019) reported, "The fact that the stock market tends to perform really well during March Madness isn't up for debate. Stocks often tend to rise during the March Madness tournament, which spans throughout all of March and spills into April. They also tend to rise during that stretch by more than any other stretch during the year."

Though the College Football Playoff and March Madness media rights dollars are staggering, individual Power Five conferences have also secured lucrative media partnerships. Those contracts dwarf the amounts earned by the Group of Five conferences, though those conferences also generate millions of dollars in revenue each year. The proliferation of lucrative conference television agreements has resulted from an incessant desire for fans to consume football content. Much like the NFL has become a year-round sport, so too has Division I football become a sport with something "important" happening nearly every month of the year, not just in the fall when regular season games are played.

There is also a lucrative market for NCAA digital footage. In January 2012 Thought Equity Motion (TEM), a leading provider of cloud-based video management and licensing services, extended its exclusive licensing contract with the NCAA. Taking over the NCAA digital archives in 2010, TEM amassed a digital library of three hundred championship games and four thousand searchable "moments" (Van Riper 2012). Footage is sold to sports networks that wish to air such content. The contract positioned TEM as the sole source to license NCAA content, including fully produced games, video clips, photographs, and radio calls for all eighty-nine (at the time) championships in twenty-three sports across all three NCAA divisions, with some of the footage dating back to 1921. TEM, which has undergone several company name changes during the past decade, most recently becoming Wazell Digital, was acquired by Veritone in 2018.

In 2020, in response to the COVID-19 pandemic, Veritone Digital Hub launched a site to encourage fan engagement in the NBA draft. Ryan Steelberg, the president of Veritone, explained:

> As the exclusive licensing partner for many collegiate and professional sports properties, Veritone has one of the largest collections of iconic sports content in the U.S. Since March Madness was cancelled this year and sports fans haven't seen their favorite college basketball players in action for a long time, we're thrilled to offer a portal where fans can easily

> access and relive thousands of highlight and analysis clips. (SVG Staff 2020)

In addition to full-game broadcasts and game footage, the NCAA and its members have created an extensive and expanding market in college sport merchandise. Learfield, with a client list of over 550 of the nation's top colleges and universities as well as bowl games, athletic conferences, the Heisman Trophy, and the NCAA, has returned, by conservative estimates, $2 billion in royalties to its clients (Hedlund and Naylor 2020: 18). In February 2021, with fans of video games playing in record numbers and fueling a $175 billion industry, Electronic Arts (EA) Sports announced it would be bringing back its college football video game franchise. EA Sports paused the franchise in 2013 after the NCAA declined to renew its contract, citing ongoing legal disputes over the rights of college athletes (former and current) to compensation for the use of their names, images, and likenesses (NIL). After reaching a $40 million settlement with respondents (See *O'Bannon v. NCAA*, 2009), who alleged that their right to be compensated for the use of their NILs had been violated, EA Sports was willing to compensate athletes moving forward, but the NCAA, a codefendant in the case, resisted, and the college football and men's basketball video games were put on hiatus (Sweeney 2021). At the time of the 2021 EA announcement, NCAA players were still not able to participate, and the game was not going to include college football players' NILs (*Business Wire* 2021). However, the expansion of NIL rights in summer 2021 left many fans anticipating that upcoming college sport video games would once again include players who were being compensated for their intellectual property.

Sports apparel companies have also significantly invested in college sports. The increased value of footwear and apparel company agreements has corresponded with the growth in the televising (and now livestreaming) of big-time college sport. The annual cumulative value of Adidas, Nike, and Under Armour's Power Five athletic department contracts is estimated at much more than $212 million. Footwear and apparel companies are drawn to these agreements because of the high visibility that televised Power Five football and men's basketball broadcasts provide.

Ohio State's contract with Nike included a $20 million cash payment when the agreement was executed in 2015 (Duffy 2018). The contract also covers several situations where bonuses are given to coaching staff members and to the overall program (ibid.). In Illinois's contract there is a stipulation that outlines a three-to-one-dollar conversion rate from product allowance to cash (ibid.). Some schools, like Indiana, have a stipulation in their contract that provides a specified amount of money for marketing. In Indiana's case that amount is $300,000.

According to Ryan Brewer (2019), a finance professor at Indiana University–Purdue University of Indianapolis, FBS football programs are worth millions, and in some cases billions, of dollars. In determining a program's value, Brewer considers revenues and expenses along with cash flow adjustments, risk assessments, and projections of future growth. By those metrics the top three Power Five football programs in 2018—Texas, Ohio State, and Alabama—had valuations of more than $1 billion each. Among the top thirty programs, valuations ranged from a high of $1.1 billion for the University of Texas to a low of $270 million for Oklahoma State. Putting these figures into perspective, the Buffalo Bills, an NFL franchise, sold for $1.1 billion in 2014 (Rauf 2017).

"We Eat What We Kill": Where the Money Goes

As the revenues generated by big-time college football and men's basketball have grown, athletic departments have used the new money to pay coaches, build palatial athletic facilities and amenities, and expand recruiting activities. Spared by the NCAA rules from having to share any significant revenue with the athletes whose efforts produce it and essentially forced by laws affecting tax-exempt educational institutions to spend the money generated each year, athletic departments pay more and more for the best coaches and the best facilities, trying to lure the best players so that they can field even better teams—and make even more money. In their analysis of the college sport industry, economists Craig Garthwaite and his fellow researchers concluded that "while intercollegiate sports are often described as student activities undertaken by amateurs, the economic reality is that athletic departments have developed into complex commercial enterprises that look far more like professional sports organizations than extracurricular endeavors" (Garthwaite et al. 2020: 7).

In their book *The System: The Glory and Scandal of Big-Time College Football* (2013), Jeff Benedict and Armen Keteyian describe the Alabama football program as the NFL's thirty-third team, with a roster that is filled with future NFL players and has coaches and staff members resembling an NFL front office. As of February 14, 2021, the Alabama football program's roster as listed in the school directory had grown to a staff of forty, with nine "football analysts," two special assistants assigned to the head coach, and an additional fifteen positions from other areas of the athletic department (e.g., communications and strength and conditioning) with specific football assignments.

The markets for college and professional football coaches are also intimately connected to each other, as illustrated by the career trajectories of current NFL head coaches. In 2019 twenty-two of the thirty-two NFL head coaches had started their coaching careers as a college football coach. Three got their starts as a high school coach, while only seven began in the NFL (ESPN 2019). Historically, while some NFL head coaches migrate from the college level to the NFL and remain there, many others move between college and professional positions throughout their careers. Like their peers in football, NCAA men's basketball coaches earn substantial salaries. As far back as 2013, NCAA Division I men's basketball coaches whose teams took part in March Madness earned on average $1.47 million (average derived from sixty-two of the sixty-eight teams with six salaries unavailable) (Brady, Berkowitz, and Upton 2013). The median increase from the previous year was 8.2 percent.

While college head coaching salaries have increased dramatically, in part due to the athletics arms race and the effects of the professional coaching market, expenses associated with profit-athletes' compensation from Power Five athletic departments have been collectively restrained by NCAA members to no more than a "full ride" grant-in-aid (GIA), which currently consists of room and board, tuition and fees, cost of attendance expenses, and required books. In contrast to college coaches' compensation, especially in the big-time programs, who rely on agents to negotiate on their behalf, the terms and conditions of college athlete compensation are predetermined before players are even recruited. Unlike their coaches, profit-athletes are denied the opportunity to take part in compensation negotiations with their potential university athletic department. Also lost in the discussion is that, in reality, a GIA has never been a "full ride." (Interestingly, in the 1960s athletes received "laundry money" if on full scholarship, though the NCAA rescinded that compensation in the 1970s.) In some cases athletes can access additional compensation through academic scholarships and Pell grants, but they largely remain woefully underpaid given the value many of them provide to their universities.

As the litany of professional and commercial intersections between college and professional sports lays bare, NCAA officials' assertions that profit-athletes are truly amateurs is—simply put—a lie based on propaganda (Southall and Staurowsky 2013). The hypocrisy has been part of college sport since its beginning. One of the enduring icons of college sport, famed Notre Dame football coach Knute Rockne, was a professional football player when he played for the Fighting Irish. He did so for a simple reason: he needed the money. The following anecdote makes clear the longstanding professionalization of college football:

> In the pre-NFL days, the independents or "pros" of that era would hire a college star to play in a particular must-win game or some area championship contest. The use of college ringers was prevalent, and many a college star would play sub rosa on a Sunday afternoon using an assumed name and picking up some extra cash. Knute did just that.
>
> Chet Grant, who spent almost a lifetime with intermittent and diverse stints at Notre Dame, was a field reporter for the *South Bend Tribune* in his pre-Notre Dame days. He covered everything from funerals to weddings

> and anything else assigned to him or come-upon by him. Sunday was Chet's day off, but on one Sunday, he decided to make the trip with the South Bend Huebners when asked to do so by his friend, John Gruber, the manager of the Huebner team. He remembered Rockne catching a pass from Kaz Boinski to set up the only score. Chet didn't know how much Rockne got paid for his afternoon of work, but he thought it was more than any of the other Huebner players had received. Chet wasn't sure but he thought the opponents were either Ft Wayne or Wabash.
>
> One other verifiable appearance of Rockne playing as a ringer in a game for the pros while attending Notre Dame was in 1913. George Greenburg, a South Bender, was playing for a Michigan team against the Fort Wayne Friars and during the pregame warmups saw a Friar whose movements seemed familiar to him. George wanted to get a better look, so he went up close to the player and sure enough, it was Rockne.
>
> "Rock!! What the hell are you doing here?" Greenburg asked in a surprised and loud tone of voice.
>
> "Sheeesh . . . I'm doing the same thing you are George, but try to remember—my name is Jones . . . okay?" Rockne replied. (Klosinski 2022)

The amateurism of college football has always been a myth:

> Notre Dame was a poor man's school in the Rockne days, and it took a lot of players many years to earn their degree. They would drop out in alternate years to earn enough to come back and hopefully finish. Rock as an assistant coach at ND had more than one offer per year to "moonlight" coaching a South Bend pro team. South Bend was a growing industrial city and there were more than one pro team anxious to be a winner. Rockne would usually recommend some of the active Notre Dame players so that they could earn some extra money. Coaching the pros was not prohibited by Notre Dame, only playing pro ball was. (ibid.)

Rockne's professional football career exposes the hypocrisy at the core of what the NCAA calls amateurism. If Power Five football and NCAA Division I men's basketball are not amateur endeavors, then how can the athletes who participate in them—and generate billions of dollars through them—be amateurs? Commercial interests are at the root of the college sport enterprise. The clear line of demarcation between the collegiate model and the professional model that the NCAA claims to protect is one that the NCAA, its members, and their business partners consistently and brazenly violate. Nobody who participates in Power Five football and NCAA Division I men's basketball is an amateur. This is not inherently a bad thing. What is immoral is the lie that is amateurism.

The Reality Is . . .

This book is grounded in the sociohistorical reality that profit-athletes are governed and controlled by a system of rules and regulatory schemes developed by the NCAA and Power Five conferences to support and protect a multi-billion-dollar entertainment industry. This power structure has been unilaterally and collectively imposed upon the athletes whose performances form the basis for the industry itself.

Written from a multidisciplinary perspective by academic researchers who have studied college sport for decades, this book traces the historical roots of the perennial problems that create controversy and charges of corruption in college sport, with emphasis on academic capitalism within higher education that encourages (in many ways demands) continuing efforts to monetize and commercialize the college sport industry; the legal foundations for the assertion that college athletes are not employees but amateurs; the racial and social implications of denying college athletes their rights and their worth; and the consequences of the acceptance by society of an economic cartel that controls the college sport industry. The authors do not advocate reforming big-time college sport. We advocate a new model of college sport that no longer tolerates and relies on the fiction that "amateur defines the participants, not the enterprise" (Brand 2006: 11). Rather we argue for a system that begins with a foundational belief that profit-athletes are human beings deserving of basic human and worker rights. In the coming chapters, we will reexamine the roots of systemic issues that have plagued college sport from the beginning, reconsidering its history as a 120-year labor negotiation in which the employees have had little voice.

In part 1 we offer a tutorial on big-time college sport, outlining the historical landscape that has resulted in the current exploitative collegiate model of athletics. One of the basic premises of part 1 and the entire book is that college athletes have always been paid. "An Amateurism That Never Was" traces the development of the lie that is amateurism and how and why the NCAA and member universities have perpetuated that lie. "Some College Athletes Are Employees: Lessons Learned from Professional Sport Labor" uses examples from professional sport to propose that profit-athletes should most accurately be viewed as employees. "Power Five Football and Men's Basketball: At the Center of It All" places those marquee sports at the center of the college sport revenue–generating universe. "Challenging the NCAA's Collegiate Model Paradigm" offers a rationale for abandoning the current exploitative system.

Part 2 explores legal and economic realities present in big-time college sport. The first chapter in the section focuses on the legal status of college athletes under workers' compensation and labor law. "Northwestern Football, Unionization Efforts, and the NLRB's Decision Not to Exercise Jurisdiction" is a case study in which we examine the 2014–15 Northwestern University football team's failed unionization efforts. "Title IX, College Athlete Employment, and the Politics of Destruction" debunks arguments that provisions of the gender-equity law Title IX prohibit recognition of profit-athletes as employees. "College Sport Workplace Economics: Suppressing Player Compensation to Increase Profits" chronicles how suppression of player compensation results in an increase in profits accruing to the NCAA and Power Five conferences and athletic departments.

In part 3 we take a clear-eyed view of the immorality and exploitation inherent in the current NCAA collegiate model of athletics. In "The Exploitation of Power Five Profit-Athletes: Paternalism, Patriarchy, and Racialization," we examine the racialized exploitation of profit-athletes through the lens of critical race theory. And finally, in "The End of the Beginning of the End?" we offer thoughts on where college sport fans, Power Five coaches and administrators, members of Congress and state legislatures, and relevant stakeholders should or can go in the future. This reenvisioning of college sport seeks to extend the advantages of the free market currently enjoyed by those who control college sport to those who labor within it.

Notes

1. This NCAA PSA tagline was originally announced in a March 13, 2007, press release: http://fs.ncaa.org/Docs/PressArchive/2007/Announcements/.

2. Not surprisingly, the profitability of March Madness is in large part due to the NCAA members' not having to share a percentage of the generated revenues with the players, which contrasts with professional sport postseason playoffs and tournaments, where owners share those revenues with players.

3. The Professional and Amateur Sports Act (PASPA) of 1992 barred wagering on sports in the United States except in a select few states. In 2018 the US Supreme Court declared that PASPA was unconstitutional and that individual states could decide what gambling would be permitted in their jurisdiction.

References

CASE

O'Bannon v. National Collegiate Athletic Association, no. C 09–3329 CW (N.D. Cal. Dec. 11, 2009).

SECONDARY SOURCES

American Gaming Association (2019a). "Sports Betting Consumer Study." March 29. https://www.americangaming.org/.

———. (2019b). "Americans Will Wager $8.5 Billion on March Madness." March 18. https://www.americangaming.org/.

Bassam, Tom (2021). "Legends Valued at 'US$1.35bn' Following Sixth Street Investment." SportsPro, January 12. https://www.sportspromedia.com/.

Benedict, Jeff, and Armen Keteyian (2013). *The System: The Glory and Scandal of Big-Time College Football.* New York: Doubleday.

Brady, Erik, Steve Berkowitz, and Jodi Upton (2013). "Pitino, Calipari among Highest-Paid College Basketball Coaches." *USA Today*, April 3. https://www.usatoday.com/.

Brand, Myles (2006). "Brand Charts Course for Collegiate Model's Next Century." Speech delivered to the NCAA Convention, January 7. https://mylesbrand.com/wp-content/uploads/2006/01/2006-NCAA-State-of-the-Association.pdf.

Brewer, Ryan (2019). "College Football Value Rankings." *Wall Street Journal.* https://graphics.wsj.com/table/NCAA_2019.

Business Wire (2019). "Aer Lingus College Football Classic Series continues to expand with 2021 game announcement and ESPN College GameDay to be part of 2020 game." October 14. https://www.businesswire.com/.

———. (2021). "Electronic Arts & CLC to Bring Back College Football Video Games." February 2. https://www.businesswire.com/.

Carp, Sam (2020). "Georgia Tech Brings Revenue Streams under One Umbrella in Legends Deal." SportsPro, December 8. https://www.sportspromedia.com/.

College Football Playoff (2021). "College Football Playoff Revenue Distribution." https://collegefootballplayoff.com/.

Daniels, Tim (2018). "NCAA Surpasses $1 Billion in Annual Revenue for 1st Time in Association History." Bleacher Report, March 7. https://bleacherreport.com/.

Disney Institute (2022). "About Disney Institute." https://www.disneyinstitute.com/ (accessed July 11).

Dosh, Kristi (2019). "College Football Playoff Payouts for 2019 Season." *Forbes*, December 28. https://www.forbes.com/.

Draper, Kevin, and Alan Blinder (2020). "SEC Reaches $3 Billion Deal with Disney, Drawing CBS Ties toward an End." *New York Times,* December 10. https://www.nytimes.com/.

Duffy, Clare (2018). "Exclusive: See the Top NCAA Apparel Deals for 2017–18." *Portland Business Journal,* April 27. https://www.bizjournals.com/portland/news/2017/08/31/.

ESPN (2019). "How It Started: First Jobs in Football for All 32 NFL Head Coaches." July 18. https://www.espn.co.uk/.

Garthwaite, Craig, Jordan Keener, Matthew J. Notowidigdo, and Nicole F. Ozminkowski (2020). "Who Profits from Amateurism? Rent-Sharing in Modern College Sports." Working Paper 27734. National Bureau of Economic Research, working paper 27734. https://www.nber.org/papers/w27734.

Goodman, Jeff (2019). "Comprehensive List of Every 2019 College Basketball Foreign Tour." *Stadium*, May 6. https://watchstadium.com/.

Harrison, Phil (2022). "College Football Playoff Provides Update on Timeline of Expansion." *Buckeyes Wire,* February 18. https://buckeyeswire.usatoday.com/.

Hedlund, David P., and Michael E. Naylor (2020). "Determinants Impacting Why College Sports Fans Purchase Merchandise." *Journal of Contemporary Athletics* 14, no. 1: 17–35.

Hookit (2021). "Top Rankings: The Leaders in Social Engagement." https://www.hookit.com/ranks/.

Klosinski, Emil (2022). "Knute Rockne's Pro Football Roots." Professional Football Researchers Association. http://www.footballresearch.com/ (accessed July 14).

Lango, Luke (2019). "7 March Madness Stocks to Consider for the Big Dance." *Investor Place,* February 28. https://investorplace.com/.

Lisa, Andrew (2020). "The Money behind the March Madness NCAA Basketball Tournament." Yahoo! Finance, March 9. https://finance.yahoo.com/.

Mosher, Garrett (2019). "How Brands Can Properly Identify Social Influencers." Hookit, August 9. https://www.hookit.com/.

National Collegiate Athletic Association (2022). "12.01.2 Clear Line of Demarcation." LSDBi. Indianapolis, IN. https://web3.ncaa.org/.

National Football Foundation (2020). "2019–20 Report: Amazing College Football Popularity Highlighted by Impressive Ratings and Attendance Data." May 28. https://footballfoundation.org/.

Nielsen Company (2019). "Communal Celebration: NCAA Men's Basketball March Madness." March 6. https://www.nielsen.com/.

Ozanian, Mike (2019). "March Madness Is Most Profitable Postseason TV Deal in Sports." *Forbes,* March 19. https://www.forbes.com/sites/.

Rauf, Brian (2017). "Here's the Purchase Price of the Last 10 NFL Franchises Sold—and Who Bought Them." Chat Sports, December 18. https://www.chatsports.com/.

Schroeder, George (2012). "College Football Playoff Revenue Distribution Set." *USA Today,* December 11. https://eu.usatoday.com/.

Seligman, Andrew (2019). "Changing College Landscape Front and Center for Big Ten." ABC News, October 2. https://abcnews.go.com/Sports/wireStory/.

Southall, Richard M., and Ellen J. Staurowsky (2013). "Cheering on the Collegiate Model: Creating, Disseminating, and Imbedding the NCAA's Redefinition of Amateurism." *Journal of Sport and Social Issues* 37, no. 4: 403–29.

Stephens, Tim (2019). "Iowa Joins INFLCR Team." INFLCR, September 11. https://www.inflcr.com/.

SVG Staff (2020). "Veritone Uses Digital Media Hub, aiWARE as Backbone for New DraftClips.com Site." SVG SportsTech Blog, October 21. https://www.sportsvideo.org/.

Sweeney, Kevin (2021). "Why Did EA Sports Stop Making NCAA Football Video Games?" *Sports Illustrated,* February 2. https://www.si.com/college/2021/02/02/.

University of Illinois Athletics Communications Staff (2021). "Illinois Launches INFLUENCE to Prepare Athletes for NIL Changes." February 18. https://fightingillini.com/.

Van Riper, Tom (2012). "Selling March Madness Memories." *Forbes,* March 15. https://www.forbes.com/.

Wilner, Jon (2020). "Hotline Newsletter: Pac-12 in Danger of Getting Boxed out as the SEC Goes All-in with ESPN." *Mercury News,* December 11. https://www.mercurynews.com/2020/12/11/.

Young, Jabari (2021). "With $1 Billion on the Line, March Madness is Ready for its Comeback." March 16. https://www.cnbc.com/.

PART I

College Athletes Have Always Been Paid

An Amateurism That Never Was

Ellen J. Staurowsky,
Richard M. Southall,
and Mark S. Nagel

On October 10, 2017, Mark Emmert, president of the National Collegiate Athletic Association (NCAA), did something his predecessors had routinely done since the organization's founding in 1905. He formed a commission (Emmert 2017). The formation of the Commission on College Basketball was the NCAA's public-relations response to the dramatic announcement two weeks before by the acting US attorney for the Southern District of New York, Joon K. Kim, that an FBI probe had resulted in conspiracy and bribery charges against four NCAA Division I men's basketball coaches, three athlete advisers, and a senior executive, as well as two other individuals affiliated with the athletic apparel company Adidas in two related fraud and corruption schemes (*United States of America v. Chuck Connors Person and Rashad Michel,* 2017; *United States of America v. Lamont Evans, Emanuel (Book) Richardson, Anthony (Tony) Bland, Christian Dawkins, and Munish Sood,* 2017; *United States of America v. James (Jim) Gatto, Merl Code, Christian Dawkins, Jonathan Brad Augustine, and Munish Sood,* 2017). The FBI assistant director in charge of the investigation, William F. Sweeney Jr., stated that the charges involved steering top basketball recruits to business deals with agents, advisers, and Adidas. These actions allegedly created a pay-to-play culture, with player access facilitated through bribery (US Department of Justice 2017).

Many observers anticipated that others would be implicated and charged in the federal probe. Soon after it was revealed that Brian Bowen Sr. (the father of Brian Bowen II, a highly touted five-star recruit) had purportedly been offered $100,000 if his son (known at "Tugs") enrolled at the University of Louisville (an Adidas-sponsored school). As part of the deal, at the end of his collegiate career, Tugs would sign an endorsement agreement with Adidas (Masisak 2017). Even before public disclosures of this particular alleged payment, Bowen's decision to attend Louisville had generated significant attention. Bowen Sr. admitted he had accepted cash in exchange for his son's basketball play for years: "for playing for an A.A.U. [Amateur Athletic Union] team sponsored by Adidas, for playing for a different A.A.U. team sponsored by Nike, for playing for an Indiana prep school and for playing for Louisville" (Tracy 2018). In April 2017, in an interview with the *Lexington Herald-Leader,* Tugs commented he had not yet determined where he would play in college, identifying six schools he was considering, none of which was the University of Louisville. Five days after that interview, he signed with Louisville, leading then head coach Rick Pitino to say that in his forty years of recruiting, this was the "luckiest" he had ever been at landing a top prospect (Roberts 2017).

Subsequently, the Department of Justice (DOJ) allegations resulted in Louisville's suspending Bowen and Pitino's being fired for cause. During a month-long investigation, Bowen's attorneys denied that their client had any awareness of the alleged activities and insisted that Tugs had not in fact violated any NCAA bylaws. The attorneys further claimed it was unfair to punish Bowen or any other athlete for "actions of others who are not in their control" (Cato 2017). Despite no charges being filed against Bowen and his being cleared of any wrongdoing by the FBI, the University of Louisville would not permit him to play. The school did honor his grant-in-aid, however, allowed him to remain in school at Louisville for the year, and gave him permission to transfer elsewhere.

Louisville's actions suggest that administrators did not want to risk playing Tugs in the event it was later determined he had violated an NCAA bylaw. Having been placed on probation by the NCAA in June 2017 for providing escort and prostitution services to men's basketball players and recruits at parties held at an on-campus residence hall (NCAA Committee on Infractions 2017), the men's basketball program considered playing a "potentially ineligible" player too great a risk to tolerate. The fact that Louisville could bar Bowen from playing even when he had not been found to have violated any NCAA rule and had been cleared of federal allegations reveals how trapped players can be in the NCAA system.

The stark and serious nature of the charges was evident. At the time of their indictment, the defendants faced eighty to two hundred years in jail if convicted (US Department of Justice 2017).

In one of the three announced complaints (*United States of America v. Chuck Connors Person and Rashal Michel,* 2017) written by FBI special agent John Vourderis, the broad parameters of the alleged criminal acts were outlined. Defendant Chuck Person, a former National Basketball Association (NBA) player who—until the indictment—was an associate men's basketball coach at Auburn University, was accused of accepting money in exchange for "encouraging"

Auburn players to make use of financial and management services brokered by Rashan Michel. Michel was a former NBA and college basketball official turned clothier for several prominent professional football and men's basketball players (Forde 2017). In addition, Person was accused of facilitating payments directly to an athlete.

In an overview of the investigation, Vourderis (2017: 9) noted that as part of the business of college basketball, and in its intersection with professional basketball, "agents and other athlete advisors attempt to recruit student-athletes early in their NCAA career, in violation of NCAA rules, including by paying bribes to the athletes' coaches and athletes and/or their families." Along with the athletes involved, Person was accused of perpetrating fraud against Auburn University by falsely attesting to following NCAA rules regarding eligibility, which preclude accepting payments from agents or advisers. According to the complaint, Auburn University was harmed since they allocated athletic scholarships to players who they believed were eligible under NCAA bylaws. Since the players were ineligible as a result of Person's actions, Auburn was harmed, since it was required to return funds received through conference and NCAA basketball tournament profit-sharing distributions. However, what was never an issue in the complaint was the fraud perpetrated on the players, since Person and other coaches took money from the shoe companies and agents and then steered the athlete to certain agents without the athlete knowing. In this case the player was surely defrauded.

The complaint included a section titled "Background on the NCAA and Relevant NCAA Rules." In the complaint there is a reference to the NCAA's Principle of Amateurism, most specifically the expectation that athletes will be "amateurs" in their sports (bylaw 2.9) and that they are barred from being represented by sports agents (bylaw 12.3). The complaint also referred to a statement in the NCAA's Principle of Compliance that threatens corrective and disciplinary action should institutions violate NCAA bylaws (bylaws 2.8 and 2.8.3) (National Collegiate Athletic Association 2017). In addition, the complaint summarizes NCAA prohibitions against payments or compensation "not approved by the Association" to athletes or family members and further restrictions against interactions with agents and advisers. According to NCAA bylaws, if association rules are violated, athletes are no longer eligible. The bylaws also outline that representatives of athletic programs' interests (coaches, athletes, administrators, and others so designated) will have engaged in "unethical conduct" if they knowingly furnished others with or influenced others to provide false or misleading information about NCAA rules (bylaw 10.1).

In a press release issued by the DOJ, the case was presented as one where coaches and advisers exploited college athletes. As DOJ officials put it, "The defendants' alleged criminal conduct not only sullied the spirit of amateur athletics but showed contempt for the thousands of players and coaches who follow the rules and play the game the right way" (US Department of Justice 2017).

This case is a fitting starting point for this book since it is a culmination of NCAA hegemony, with the DOJ added to the list of supporters and enablers who give spontaneous consent to the NCAA and its collegiate model of athletics, in which "amateur defines the participants, not the enterprise" (Brand 2006: 8). With these indictments, the historically accepted view that certain payments (above or under the table) to college athletes for their work and worth are immoral has morphed into a belief—on the part of the United States government (i.e., DOJ)—that such activities are potentially illegal. When former federal prosecutor Ken Wicker was asked why it was illegal for a sneaker company to pay an athlete to go to a certain college or promise to employ them after they left college but not for a tech company to pay a high school graduate who is a whiz at writing code a bonus to attend a particular college or promise that student future employment, he said, "because there are no rules like the NCAA's that prohibit it" (quoted in Wolfson 2017).

Despite the attention the Adidas scandal generated, as will be discussed throughout this book, the real scandal and corruption within college sport is how the NCAA, conferences, universities, and athletic departments have, for more than a century, exploited profit-athletes, that is, athletes whose market value is greater than the value of their awarded grant-in-aid (GIA). According to this definition, profit-athletes are almost exclusively Power Five football and NCAA Division I men's basketball players. This chapter explores the structural roots of player exploitation and examines the key role the myth of amateurism has played in maintaining NCAA hegemony (Sack and Staurowsky 1998). While the college sport enterprise has always limited athlete compensation through ever-changing NCAA bylaws, everyone else involved in the enterprise (e.g., coaches, athletic directors, and college presidents) has unfettered access to a marketplace that allows them to maximize their economic value. In almost any other setting, this denial of college athletes' basic economic and human rights would result in moral outrage and calls from the media, government officials, and business leaders for swift restorative justice. But as a result of NCAA hegemony, historically the rights of profit-athletes have been denied in order to maintain the NCAA collegiate model.

Those Who Control the Marketplace

The NCAA has reserved the right to exploit college athletes, particularly big-time football and basketball players, for its own purposes as far back as 1956 (Sack and Staurowsky 1998; Staurowsky, 2013). Walter Byers, the first full-time NCAA executive director, oversaw the formalization of the association's bureaucracy and its early television contracts. In his 1995 memoir, *Unsportsmanlike*

Conduct: Exploiting College Athletes, Byers wrote that colleges had long exploited football and basketball players, denying them access to a free market readily available to their coaches, administrators, and conference officials. Byers discussed the vast power and resource inequities that exist between college athletes and the professionals who operate the college sport industry: "A historical basis for federal remedies, has been management's exploitation of the isolated and unorganized. The structure of the college's control of their players and the demand that management's pronouncements be accepted as the final word are irresistible targets for redress and correction. Those who control the marketplace are the same as those who define the terms, and preordain the results" (1995: 371). The DOJ's reliance on the NCAA's manual in building its case illustrates Byers's point. Fundamentally, paying someone their worth is neither inherently illegal nor immoral. In a free market, compensating someone according to their market value is rarely—if ever—a criminal act. In fact, it can be argued that in a capitalist system, allowing individuals to be compensated according to their economic value has allowed many people to prosper. In a country built upon capitalism, upon what authority does the NCAA propagate the notion that—only for college athletes—access to a college-sport free market is somehow illegal, immoral, or both?

While many college-sport fans and the general public expressed outrage at the 2017 Adidas scandal that exposed the seamy underbelly of college sport, a critical question remained unasked. Why were athletic apparel company executives, college coaches, financial advisers, sports agents, and athletes and/or their families all willing to blatantly ignore NCAA rules regarding athlete compensation and representation? Notably, few college-sport industry insiders expressed shock at the scandal. Big Ten conference commissioner Jim Delany recalled at least nine occasions since the 1950s when college basketball had been subject to federal investigations (Associated Press 2017). In addition, several college basketball pundits openly questioned why the NCAA and conferences continued to resist changing their business practices to treat athletes more fairly (Bilas 2017; Mellinger 2017).

Among a group of eight basketball coaches interviewed by the *Kansas City Star* (three head coaches, three assistants, and two AAU coaches, who all requested anonymity), "None expressed a drop of shock at hearing about payments from shoe companies to push recruits to specific schools" (Mellinger 2017). One coach commented, "They're acting like they've uncovered a mystery. I read it and I was like, "Are you (expletive) kidding me? That's all they got?" Speaking to the structural inequities in the system and the rules that have produced this problem, another coach stated, "We use these kids and pump them up to the gain for the NCAA or the conferences, so it shouldn't surprise anyone when a parent or middleman wants a piece of the pie" (ibid.).

Admitting that rule breaking is not isolated to the handful of supposed wrongdoers identified in the indictments, another coach commented, "All of us have done something. You might turn your back so that you don't know everything, but you know what's going on. It could be something as small as giving a kid a few bucks for dinner. I mean, c'mon. If I didn't do that, I wouldn't be doing my job" (ibid.). Western Kentucky University head men's basketball coach Rick Stansbury openly admitted, "Everybody acts like it just started. Well, nah, this ain't nothing new in college basketball" (Estes 2017).

Longtime ESPN broadcaster and basketball expert Jay Bilas observed that of the top two hundred high school recruits, very few were "really eligible to NCAA standards of amateurism, and that's on amateurism." He went on to say that "it's not on those players because what they're doing is not illegal. It's not wrong. It violates this NCAA notion of amateurism, which is really a sham" (Wang 2017).

Because college athletes are not NCAA members and, unlike the players in professional leagues such as the NFL and NBA, do not have player unions or associations that represent their interests and provide for collective bargaining over the terms and conditions of their employment, NCAA rules trap profit-athletes in an unjust system, with few mechanisms—apart from laborious and expensive litigation—to meaningfully alter the situation.

The litmus test for two conflicting ideologies is that the college sport underground economy the DOJ sought to prosecute has been in existence, in one form or another, since the founding of the NCAA. If the NCAA's concept of amateurism had true integrity and was truly embraced by everyone involved with college sports, there wouldn't be such an enduring and lasting legacy of corruption associated with the NCAA's collegiate model. (See the following chapter, "Some College Athletes Are Employees," for further discussion of the history of college sport's underground economy.)

Notably, flourishing underground economies existed in both professional baseball and football from the 1910s through the 1960s. Restrictions on player compensation and access to a free market led to many players being enticed by gamblers to throw or manipulate the outcomes of games (Eschner 2017; Lyons 2010). Since players were not compensated accurately for their value, they were vulnerable to such economic or financial appeals. If they were not going to be paid what they were worth by owners, some players were open to filling that gap by other means. These incidents occurred before free agency was available to players, who were bound by reserve clauses that gave owners near total control over them (Goodman 2016; Newman 1987).[1] Underground economies in professional football and baseball receded considerably after players organized and systems of free agency were instituted. Since no such adjustments to college sport's control mechanisms have been made, underground economies continue to thrive.

The NCAA's Ever-Changing Principle of Amateurism

The prosecutorial assertion made by DOJ attorneys that the payment of athletes and coaches in this case "sullied the spirit of amateur athletics" raises the question of what the federal government is referring to as "amateur athletics." Contrary to the general perception that the NCAA has been steadfastly committed to amateurism, the term itself has been repeatedly redefined to fit whatever narrative was most useful to the association's current business interests (Staurowsky 2013). As Mike Ingersoll (2015), a former football player at the University of North Carolina at Chapel Hill, pointed out in a law review article about amateurism and the modern college athlete, it is telling that despite the association's proclaimed abiding commitment to amateurism, the concept of amateurism is not identified as one of the NCAA's core values.

At the dawn of the twentieth century, college faculty who created the NCAA drew upon British notions to articulate a workable view of amateurism for college sport. Decidedly classist in orientation, amateurism was designed to separate the privileged and working classes in the cultural space of sport. Privileged amateurs could afford to engage in sporting pursuits at their leisure, without aspiration or prospect of being paid. Conversely, members of the working class, the rough and uncouth, were associated with professional sport (Sack and Staurowsky 1998; Smith 1990). "Those who were rich enough and had the luxury of time could pursue sporting activities for fun, health, and adventure" (Staurowsky 2013: 4). For the privileged classes, to be an amateur meant pursuing sport as a pastime and not as a means of making a living or as an exchange of value (Sack and Staurowsky 1998).

At its first convention in 1905, the founders of the NCAA took a firm stance against practices that violated this early, aristocratic amateur ideal. Officially, offering players financial inducements (whether tied to education or not) based upon their athletic abilities was prohibited. In its 1916 bylaws, the NCAA defined an amateur athlete as "one who participates in competitive physical sports only for the pleasure, and the physical, mental, moral, and social benefits directly derived therefrom" (ibid.: 25). Six years later, in 1922, that definition would be amended to characterize participation on college sport teams as an "avocation" or, in other words, a pastime or activity that athletes did in their spare time (ibid.).

Fears about paying athletes for their athletic ability were connected to concerns about so-called tramp athletes, effectively hired talent who came in to help teams win games but who were either not enrolled in classes or had little interest in attending class. Conceptualizing college sport as an avocation, it was thought that the professionalization of college athletics and the attendant issues that arose from professionalization (e.g., overemphasis, full-time professional coaches, recruiting, sharing of gate receipts) could be avoided. While an intention to adhere to amateur principles was proclaimed, the actions of NCAA member schools demonstrated little unified consensus over how athletic programs should actually be operated on individual campuses. The supposed purity of amateurism played to upper-class affectations; it was much harder to adhere to notions of sport as an avocation in the day-to-day competitive arena.

Operating under a philosophy of home rule, schools were expected to police themselves and adhere to the rules. No effort was made to create an enforcement mechanism or penalty structure to discourage violations of the amateur code. While the notion that athletes should not be compensated for participating in athletics was a cornerstone of the NCAA's public positions, payments to athletes was a common practice in the 1920s. By 1929 the Carnegie Foundation noted that 81 of 112 colleges were reported to have violated NCAA rules against paying athletes.

As Ellen J. Staurowsky (2013: 5) noted, "There was also a strong belief that other schools were likely breaking the rules as well but concealing the subterfuge by paying athletes for doing jobs requiring little-to-no work, providing loans to athletes who were not obligated to repay them, and disbursing money from slush funds through under-the-table payments to athletes." Similar to today's college sport atmosphere, none of these things was particularly surprising. During the 1920s schools invested heavily in football stadiums that served as symbolic reflections of football's position as a big-business enterprise (Schmidt 2007).

Football programs continually maneuvered to gain competitive advantage, realize a return on investment from the building of large stadiums, and respond to the public pressures associated with winning (Staurowsky 2013). As the financial stakes increased, the college sport enterprise developed a business infrastructure to sustain it, eventually hiring professional coaches and often assigning coaches to also serve as athletic directors. Not surprisingly, in this environment talented athletes were recruited and offered increasingly attractive subsidies. The NCAA's commitment to traditional amateur principles was increasingly put to the test.

In response to these inducements, by 1957 the NCAA had almost completely redefined amateurism. No longer arguing that compensating athletes corrupted the principle of amateurism, the NCAA membership voted to allow schools to offer GIAs, or what are colloquially referred to as "athletic scholarships." A full-ride GIA compensation package included a tuition waiver, room and board, books, fees, and laundry expenses. According to Sack and Staurowsky (1998: 32), this decision was an acknowledgment of a decades-long college-sport reality: "Not surprisingly, the first decades of the twentieth century witnessed a relentless professionalism of collegiate sport. In open defiance of amateur rules promulgated by one governing body after another, universities found ways to subsidize talented athletes. The National Collegiate Athletic Association" . . . was unable to reverse this trend. Many of that organization's actions, especially after 1948, can best be understood as rearguard accommodations to professionalism rather than efforts to preserve amateur ideals." When initially introduced, athletic scholarships were four-year renewable awards. Athletes could retain their scholarships whether they continued to play or not. Over the years the terms and conditions of athletically related financial aid awards would be narrowed to allow coaches more control over athletes and to ensure that those receiving athletic scholarships were effectively working for them. The passage of the "fraudulent misrepresentation rule" in 1968 allowed coaches the option of canceling a GIA for a variety of reasons. It also foreclosed players who wished to prioritize their academic careers from choosing to stop playing. They could certainly continue their studies if they left a team, but if they decided to do so, they risked losing funding to continue their education. This rule also gave coaches greater latitude to punish players whose behavior was deemed insubordinate. Such insubordination might include growing long hair or a beard, taking part in antiwar or civil rights demonstrations, or acting in a manner that (by definition) questioned authority.

By 1973 the four-year GIA was replaced with a one-year award, which allowed for funding to be renewed on a year-to-year basis. This provision made it that much easier for coaches to deal with player personnel issues. Athletes faced the prospect of nonrenewal if they were not performing in line with expectations. In addition, if athletes suffered an injury, they could be let go. Having an attitude problem or simply not fitting into the head coach's system were also causes for losing an athletic scholarship. Of course, coaches also saw the value in increasing performance expectations and incentives by creating uncertainty as to who would be invited back for the next year. Each time rules governing athletes' lives changed, the balance of power became increasingly vested in those who supervised the programs (coaches and administrators), with players having less and less control (Sack and Staurowsky 1998).

In addition to altering the GIA structure, in 1973 the NCAA adopted a reorganization plan that resulted in a federated structure. The outcome of this reorganization was the creation of Divisions I, II, and III and the crafting of separate philosophy statements in accordance with each division's stated values and emphases (see the later chapter "Power Five Football and Men's Basketball: At the Center of It All" for more details). This development is critical to understanding the NCAA's path toward ever-increasing commercialism (built almost exclusively on the economic viability of big-time football and men's basketball) and differing definitions of amateurism within each division. This evolution was—and continues to be—neither accident nor happenstance. It is the fulfillment of a strategic expectation embodied in the Division I philosophy statement that schools will "sponsor at the highest feasible level of intercollegiate competition one or both of the traditional spectator oriented, income-producing sports of football and basketball" (National Collegiate Athletic Association 2017: 361). It is a bit ironic that the NCAA defends its business practices by referring to a principle of amateurism but actually operates under three different versions of amateurism that reflect varying degrees of tolerance for professionalism. Rather than abiding by a single consistent principle of amateurism, the NCAA operates within a shapeshifting amateur landscape that allows extreme levels of Power Five profit-athlete exploitation.

In *O'Bannon v. NCAA* (2015), the Ninth Circuit Court ruled the association's rules pertaining to athlete compensation violated antitrust law as a result of unreasonable restraint on competition in the college education market. The NCAA was enjoined from enforcing its rules that prevented athletes in the Football Bowl Subdivision (FBS) and Division I men's basketball from receiving stipends above the regulated terms of a full GIA, which covers tuition, room and board, and fees.

As it has since the 1950s, the NCAA argued in *O'Bannon* that their rules are designed to reflect a steadfast commitment to a principle of amateurism. Judge Claudia Wilken, however, found the historical record cited by the NCAA as evidence of that commitment to be "unpersuasive." She wrote, "This record reveals that the NCAA has revised its rules governing student-athlete compensation numerous times over the years, sometimes in significant and contradictory ways. Rather than evincing the association's adherence to a set of core principles, this history documents how malleable the NCAA's definition of amateurism has been since its founding" (*O'Bannon v. NCAA* 2014: 80).

Despite the NCAA's adamantly asserting that its defining principle is amateurism, when scrutinized closely, the NCAA has always been hard-pressed to advance a single, coherent position on the subject. The NCAA's claim that paying athletes violates its principle of amateurism is undermined by its 1956 decision to compensate athletes by awarding them athletic scholarships (GIAs). From that moment on, the NCAA abandoned the historic notion of amateurism in favor of a tightly controlled professionalism. As college sport has continued to become more commercialized and professionalized, this abandonment of amateurism has become more and more problematic.

The Inconvenient Truth: Power Five Football and Basketball Players Are Employees

Even though the NCAA has consistently identified amateurism as a foundational principle, it has never expressly defined the term. In fact, in the 428-page NCAA Division I manual there is no answer to the question of what makes an athlete an amateur; the term itself appears only as an adjective, not a noun. There are references to amateur athletics, amateur status, amateur teams, and amateur competitions, but there is no definition of what constitutes a college sport amateur.

Moreover, several years ago the NCAA moved away from referring to college sport as "amateur athletics" and began referring to it as "the collegiate model of athletics" because then-president Myles Brand was concerned the public was using the term *amateur* too frequently to describe college sports (Southall and Staurowsky 2013). Brand wanted to emphasize the connection between college sports and education without deemphasizing the idea that college athletes participate in sport as a pastime or avocation, as the term *amateur* suggests. Brand understood that even though the NCAA's bylaws conceptualize college athletics in precisely this manner, the general public knows amateurism is a myth. The shift to the collegiate model of athletics was intended, at least in part, to avoid charges of hypocrisy (ibid.).

If the NCAA could credibly claim that all college football and men's basketball players (regardless of division or conference affiliation) were amateurs because they engage in sport as a pastime, it presumably would have specifically defined amateurism that way, and it would not have sought to deemphasize use of the term. Participation in sport as a pastime is, after all, exactly how the dictionary defines amateurism and is also consistent with the provision in the NCAA's bylaws stating that college athletes are to participate in sport as an avocation (National Collegiate Athletic Association 2017: 4). But for all of the reasons explained above, the NCAA cannot credibly claim that profit-athletes participate in their sports as a pastime or avocation. As a result, when pressed to define amateurism, NCAA officials do not talk about sports as some kind of secondary or diversionary pursuit. Instead they rely on a tautology: all college athletes are amateurs because they do not get paid. The following account of a conversation between former NCAA president Myles Brand and *Sports Illustrated* columnist Michael Rosenberg in 2010 underscores the perfect circularity of the NCAA's current conception of amateurism:

> **BRAND:** They can't be paid.
> **ROSENBERG:** Why?
> **BRAND:** Because they're amateurs.
> **ROSENBERG:** What makes them amateurs?
> **BRAND:** Well, they can't be paid.
> **ROSENBERG:** Why not?
> **BRAND:** Because they're amateurs.
> **ROSENBERG:** Who decided they are amateurs?
> **BRAND:** We did.
> **ROSENBERG:** Why?
> **BRAND:** Because we don't pay them.

Noticeably absent from Brand's explanation of why college athletes are amateurs is any description of what college athletes do or what intrinsic traits they possess that make them amateurs. There is only the fact that the NCAA does not permit them to receive compensation beyond what they wish to allow. The NCAA never offers an affirmative conception of amateurism, saying what amateurism is; it only offers a negative conception, saying what amateurism prohibits or is not. The reason for this is clear: if the NCAA were to adhere to an affirmative conception of amateurism, especially one that incorporates how college athletes themselves are expected to participate in athletics—that is, if it were to adhere to the conception suggested by its own bylaws—it would be forced to concede that Power Five football and men's basketball players are not, in fact, amateurs.

Significantly, even the NCAA's own conception of college sport amateurism as participation in athletics without getting paid is malleable. Historically and currently, the NCAA's position is that "pay is the receipt of funds, awards or benefits *not permitted by the governing legislation of the Association for participation in athletics*" (bylaw 12.02.10, "Pay"; emphasis added). Consequently, a "professional athlete" is "one who receives any kind of payment, directly or indirectly, for athletics participation *except as permitted by the governing legislation of the Association*" (bylaw 12.02.11, "Professional Athlete"; emphasis added). As these two bylaws connote, the NCAA's conception of amateurism does not preclude college athletes from obtaining money (being paid) for participation in college athletics; it only forbids college athletes from being paid under terms and conditions the NCAA does not permit. Based on this exception, money provided to athletes—and only to athletes—through grants-in-aid, stipends covering the full cost of attendance, the Student Assistance Fund, the Student-Athlete Opportunity Fund, the Catastrophic Injury Insurance Program, and the Exceptional Student-Athlete Disability Insurance Program is not pay, since all of these forms of compensation (i.e., pay) are "permitted by the governing legislation of the Association." (See the chapter "Some College Athletes Are Employees" for further details.) Magically these permitted forms of compensation are not pay-for-play and prevent amateur college athletes from being transformed into paid professionals.

In addition, different conceptions of amateurism exist within the structure of the NCAA itself. In the 1990s, because NCAA member institutions were having difficulty certifying eligibility for international athletes who had received compensation for playing at a young age before they sought to attend college in the United States, certain schools sought successfully to loosen NCAA amateurism standards. Schools in Divisions II and III voted to allow athletes from other countries who have received professional salaries and/or competed professionally in their home countries to redeem their amateur standing (Pierce, Kubarakis, and Fielding 2010). Division I schools, however, summarily rejected this reform. The result is that in Division II and III athletics, previously compensated international athletes are not viewed as having been paid and are automatically eligible to compete as amateurs, while the very same athletes are deemed to have been paid and are ineligible to compete in Division I athletics unless they succeed in obtaining what the NCAA calls reinstatement of their amateur status. According to Pierce, Kubarakis, and Fielding (2010: 315), "Division I rejected legislation that would have permitted former professionals from competing in order to avoid negative public relations and legal consequences that may have resulted in the acceptance of those proposals."

This conscious shaping of NCAA amateurism rules for the specific purpose of controlling the revenue generators in the Power Five sports of football and basketball is further illustrated by the fact that athletes in other sports do not jeopardize their eligibility to compete in college or risk violating the NCAA principle of amateurism by receiving pay for their athletic performances. Following the Rio 2016 Summer Olympics, University of Texas swimmer Joseph Schooling, who competed for Singapore, was rewarded for a gold-medal performance with $740,000 (Solomon 2016). Despite NCAA claims that payment for athletic performance is not acceptable under the principle of amateurism, such compensation is acceptable under bylaw 12.2.1.5.2, which allows international athletes on NCAA member teams to participate in government-funded incentive programs that reward athletes financially if they win a medal in international competitions (National Collegiate Athletic Association 2017). This bylaw was passed by the NCAA membership in January 2015, while the association was arguing on appeal in *O'Bannon v. NCAA* that the "sacred tradition of amateurism" precluded athletes from receiving money for athletic performance that was not tethered to their education.

US Olympic athletes who anticipate or are competing on teams sponsored by NCAA institutions are also permitted to receive money from incentive programs offered through the US Olympic Committee and individual sport governing bodies. Following the 2016 Olympic Games, four swimmers received six-figure payouts for medal-winning performances: Stanford's Katie Ledecky, $355,000; University of California's Ryan Murphy, $234,375; Stanford's Simone Manuel, nearly $200,000; and University of Indiana's Lilly King, $134,375 (Brennan and Berkowitz 2017).

In addition players can go pro in one sport and still retain their amateur status in another NCAA-sponsored sport. A high-profile example of this is Denver Broncos quarterback Russell Wilson, who was selected in the fourth round of the 2010 draft by the Colorado Rockies. The Rockies organization thought so highly of Wilson that he was given a $200,000 signing bonus. Wilson played professional baseball on and off in 2010, 2011, 2013–15, and 2018. In 2011 he played sixty-one games with the Asheville Tourists (Class A affiliate of the Colorado Rockies). Having played football at North Carolina State in 2008–10, after his 2011 baseball season ended, Wilson finished his college football career in 2011, leading Wisconsin to a Big Ten championship and a Rose Bowl berth. While a layperson would assume Wilson was a professional athlete as soon as he signed with the Colorado Rockies, according to NCAA rules, he was still an amateur, since Wilson's playing professional baseball did not preclude his playing college football.

In contrast Donald De La Haye, a placekicker for the University of Central Florida, was declared ineligible to play for the 2017 football season after developing a popular YouTube video series titled *Deestroying* that chronicled his personal life, which, as a young entrepreneur, he was able to monetize (Palladino 2017). The NCAA offered to grant him a waiver as long as any of the videos that referenced his athletic career were posted to a site that would not yield him any remuneration (Inside the NCAA 2017). De La Haye declined to accept the waiver's conditions, effectively ending his college athletic career. Notably, as of 2021 De La Haye's actions were permitted NIL activity.

NCAA members themselves lack a firm understanding of what amateurism means and a correspondingly infirm commitment to the principle. In January 2008 NCAA Division I vice president David Berst conducted a study on amateurism among NCAA members. He found that it "was a definition that was not steeped in any sacred absolute principle that had to be preserved. It continues to be a balancing of vocation vs. avocation influences and can be modified as views change while preserving the line between us and the pros" (Staurowsky 2013: 47).

In sum, the NCAA's inability, or unwillingness, to offer a coherent conception of amateurism—in definition, in theory, and in application—is tacit confirmation that big-time college athletes are not amateurs but college athlete employees.

LEAD1 and the Politics of Exploitation

In September 2015, in the same month that the US Court of Appeals for the Ninth Circuit upheld a ruling that the NCAA's amateurism rules violated federal antitrust laws, an organization known at the time as the Division 1A Athletic Directors Association announced the appointment of former US congressman Tom McMillen as its new executive director (*Baltimore Sun* 2015). A college basketball hall of famer who graduated from the University of Maryland in the 1970s with a sport pedigree that includes membership on the 1972 US Olympic men's basketball team, a twelve-year professional basketball career, and ongoing public policy involvement through his role on the Knight Commission, McMillen was hired to assist athletic directors in the most elite tier of college sport in increasing advocacy and lobbying efforts in Washington, DC (Staurowsky 2017).

Within a year of his appointment, the organization underwent a rebranding campaign orchestrated by a Fifth Avenue creative agency, announcing a name change to LEAD1 Association. As part of the organization's overhaul, its stated mission became increasingly political, as evidenced in McMillen's reflection a year after his hiring that "LEAD1 is much, much more active politically than ever before" (Yates 2016a). And with the rollout of the new image came a series of other announcements, among them the formation of a political action committee and a planned College Sports Congressional Gala to be held on the evening of September 26, 2017, at the Trump International Hotel, an event that was intended to draw members of Congress, high-profile public policy makers, and possibly President Trump, a longtime acquaintance of McMillen's who donated to his first run for Congress in 1985 (Yates 2016b, 2016c).

The announced gala at the Trump International Hotel did not happen, perhaps due to concerns such as those expressed by Richard Painter. Having served as the chief White House ethics lawyer for President George W. Bush from 2005 to 2007, Painter noted Lead1's plans were problematic, since they placed a group seeking political influence into a personal business transaction with the Trump Organization (Brittain and Connell 2017). Despite the gala's being canceled, LEAD1 did proceed to court members of Congress by presenting several awards to former athletes and engaging in briefings on Capitol Hill (Yates 2016c).

LEAD1's complete agenda remains an open question. In an interview with *Vice Sports* in January 2017, McMillen stated that LEAD1 had "no position on amateurism" and "zero agenda" and that "we've not spoken to one member of Congress about any issue in college sports. We have never talked about pay for play as a group" (Hruby 2017). While McMillen denied the group has a position, when college football players initiated the All Players United Movement, an undertaking that preceded Northwestern players' efforts to be recognized as employees under the National Labor Relations Act, then president of the DIA Athletic Directors Association Mike Burke stated unequivocally that "pay for play has no part in an amateur setting" following a meeting in September 2013 to address the issue (Carmin 2013). That position was circulated widely in the media and throughout athletic departments.

LEAD1's move into the political arena and its escalation of efforts to push an amateur agenda with lawmakers emphasizing a conception of amateurism that has not existed since the NCAA's founding speaks to the challenges Power Five college football and basketball players face when attempting to be recognized as employees and to effect structural changes that level the playing field for them in terms of negotiating for better and safer work conditions.

As Byers wrote, the ingredients for an exploitative workplace are clearly evident in the unequal distribution of power and money within college sport. The players are controlled by athletic departments, conferences, and NCAA members, who are some of the most politically connected individuals in their states. From a racial perspective, Power Five football and basketball players, the majority of whom are Black, work for coaches, the majority of whom are White, who are often the highest paid employees in their states. The individuals who oversee these programs (athletic directors and conference commissioners) are also primarily White.

The LEAD1 athletic directors have the power to mobilize finances to back political candidates (typically from both sides of the aisle) who will be amenable to taking through the halls of Congress the fight in support of the myth of college-sport amateurism. The same individuals who are members of LEAD1 vote on NCAA bylaws that affect the lives of players, including the terms and conditions under which they work, their level of compensation, restrictions on player movement through the industry, and mandated health care and medical coverage (or lack thereof).

While LEAD1 athletic directors met in Washington, DC, US Attorney Joon Kim was announcing the DOJ's investigation into college basketball. The Justice Department's characterization of attempts by coaches, advisers, athletes, and sneaker company executives to find a way to compensate athletes for their genuine value as "sullying the spirit of amateur athletics" raises a key issue. Why should the United States government be enforcing the rules of a non-state actor (see *NCAA v. Tarkanian*, 1988) sport governing body, especially a body that has demonstrated it has no genuine commitment to the principle of amateurism that it uses to defend its exploitative practices?

While such a question might be dismissed as hyperbolic, a thorough reading of the NCAA Manual reveals no actual commitment to amateurism on the part of the NCAA or its members. On a page that precedes the start of the NCAA Constitution is a section outlining Commitments to the Division I Collegiate Model. Nine different commitments are listed, one of which is 20.9.1.2, "The Commitment to Amateurism." What is notable, however, is the caveat at the beginning of the statement: "These commitments are not binding on member institutions" (National Collegiate Athletic Association 2017: xii). A commitment statement that ends with "but these commitments are not binding" can hardly be called a commitment.

In response to the federal investigation into fraud and corruption in college basketball, NCAA president Mark Emmert decried what he called the silent enablers who did not speak about how the business actually operates. Ascribing blame to the culture of basketball and isolating the wrongdoers as a few bad actors, he said, "We must take decisive action. This is not a time for half-measures or incremental change" (Emmert 2017). In describing the charge for the Commission on Basketball that he appointed to address the problem, he identified the focus of their work as centering on three things: the relationship between the NCAA national office and its various constituencies (member institutions, athletes, coaches, and outside entities); the NCAA's relationship with the NBA; and what he called "the right relationship" between the NCAA national office and member institutions (ibid.).

Speaking before the Knight Commission a month after the DOJ investigation was announced, Emmert admitted that public confidence in the NCAA and its ability to manage college sports had been shaken, citing the results of a poll conducted by the NCAA that found

- 79 percent of people surveyed said big schools put money ahead of student-athletes;
- 69 percent said big universities are more of a problem than a solution;
- 51 percent said the NCAA is also part of the problem. (O'Donnell 2017)

Emmert identified the situation as dire: "We cannot go into the next basketball season without seeing fundamental change with the way college basketball is operating. We need to act. We need to demonstrate that we are, in fact, capable of resolving these issues" (Hobson 2017).

The overall focus of the commission and the commentary expressed by Emmert and other college officials seemed to suggest the time was ripe to reshape the college sport industry into a model for the twenty-first century that acknowledges Power Five college football and basketball players are employees and that amateurism is a myth exercised to suppress the value of players.

However, as Bilas (2017) pointed out, the NCAA has been adept over the years at taking moments of crisis and using them to advance agendas to ensure the profitability of its business model. About Emmert's approach he wrote, "He has never let a good crisis go to waste before, so there is no indication that he will let this one go to waste. To suggest that there is a code of silence in basketball that kept the NCAA in the dark is absurd" (Bilas 2017).

Bilas's skepticism is justified. The central issues that remain off the table include the abandonment of the pretense of amateurism, recognition of Power Five football and basketball players as employees, the racial implications of the future of predominantly Black players being controlled by an overwhelmingly White authority structure, and the creation of a players' association to advocate on their behalf. Fixing the big-time college sport system requires confronting these issues, otherwise the Commission on College Basketball will be relegated, along with all of the other NCAA committees, to the dustbin of history.

What the history of college sport reveals is that it is impossible to fix a concept that never existed. In the chapters that follow, the NCAA's principle of amateurism is revealed to be an elaborate history of labor relations that has been masked for the purpose of maintaining power structures that suppress the value of college-sport's employee-athletes.

Note

1. Reserve clauses gave owners the right to keep or trade a player until they had no use for them; players were effectively forced to sign contracts without negotiation since they had no sport employment alternatives.

References

CASES

NCAA v. Tarkanian, 488 U.S. 179 (1988).

O'Bannon v. NCAA (2014). 7 F.Supp.3d 955 (N. D. Cal.).

O'Bannon v. NCAA (2015). WL 5712106 (9th cir. 30 September 2015).

United States of America v. Chuck Connors Person and Rashan Michel (2017). Complaint # 17 Mag 7118. Retrieved from https://www.justice.gov/usao-sdny/press-release/file/998746/download.

United States of America v. Lamont Evans, Emanuel (Book) Richardson, Anthony (Tony) Bland, Christian Dawkins, and Munish Sood (2017). Retrieved from https://www.justice.gov/usao-sdny/press-release/file/999011/download.

United States of America v. James (Jim) Gatto, Merl Code, Christian Dawkins, Jonathan Brad Augustine, and Munish Sood (2017). Retrieved from https://www.justice.gov/usao-sdny/press-release/file/999006/download.

SECONDARY SOURCES

Associated Press (2017). "Delany: 'Not Shocked' by FBI Investigation of College Basketball." *USA Today*, October 19. https://www.usatoday.com/.

Baltimore Sun (2015). "Ex-Terp Tom McMillen Tapped to Lead Division IA Athletic Directors Association." September 21. http://www.baltimoresun.com/.

Bilas, Jay (2017). "The Bilas Opus: Here to Rescue College Basketball." ESPN, November 9. http://www.espn.com/.

Brand, Myles (2006). "The Principles of Intercollegiate Athletics." State of the association speech delivered at the 2006 National Collegiate Athletic Association convention. January 16.

Brennan, Christine, and Steve Berkowitz (2017). "Katie Ledecky Earned $355,000 in Medal Bonuses from Rio Olympics Performance." *USA Today*, September 9. https://www.usatoday.com/.

Brittain, Amy, and Jonathan O'Connell (2017). "College Athletic Directors Bring Gala Business to Trump International Hotel." *Washington Post*, January 9. https://www.washingtonpost.com/.

Byers, Walter, with Charles Hammer (1995). *Unsportsmanlike Conduct: Exploiting College Athletes*. Ann Arbor: University of Michigan Press.

Carmin, Mike (2013). "Purdue AD: 'Pay for Play Has No Part in the Amateur Setting.'" *Indianapolis Star*, September 26. https://www.indystar.com/.

Cato, Tim (2017). "Louisville Recruit Brian Bowen Can Be Reinstated after FBI Clears Him of $100,000 Bribe." *SB Nation*, November 2. https://www.sbnation.com/.

Emmert, Mark (2017). "Statement from Mark Emmert on the Formation of the Commission on College Basketball." NCAA.org, October 11. http://www.ncaa.org/.

Eschner, Kat (2017). "The 1919 Black Sox Baseball Scandal Was Just One of Many." *Smithsonian Magazine,* September 1. https://www.smithsonianmag.com/.

Estes, Gentry (2017). "WKU's Stansbury on FBI Scandal: 'This Ain't Nothing New in College Basketball.'" *Louisville Courier Journal,* November 7. https://www.courier-journal.com/.

Forde, Pat (2017). "Meet Rashan Michel, the Suit-Making Middleman in the College Hoops Scandal." Yahoo! Sports, October 19. https://sports.yahoo.com/.

Goodman, Noah J. (2016). "The Evolution and Decline of Free Agency in Major League Baseball: How the 2012–2016 Collective Bargaining Agreement Is Restraining Trade." *Sports Lawyer Journal* 23, no. 1: 19–55.

Hobson, Will (2017). "NCAA President Mark Emmert: 'Fundamental Change' Needed in College Basketball." *Washington Post,* October 30. https://www.washingtonpost.com/.

Hruby, Patrick (2017). "Are Athletic Directors Angling for a Washington Bailout of NCAA Amateurism?" *Vice Sports,* January 19. https://www.vice.com/.

Ingersoll, Mike (2015). "Amateurism and the Modern College Athlete." *Elon Law Review* 7, no. 2: 607–35. https://eloncdn.blob.core.windows.net/eu3/sites/996/2019/07/Elon_Law_Review_V7_No2_Ingersoll.pdf.

Inside the NCAA (2017). "NCAA statement regarding Donald De La Haye." Twitter, posted July 31, 4:40 PM. https://twitter.com/.

Lyons, Robert S. (2010). *On Any Given Sunday: A Life of Bert Bell.* Philadelphia: Temple University Press.

Masisak, Corey (2017). "FBI Sting has Louisville in its Crosshairs." *New York Post,* September 26. https://nypost.com/.

Mellinger, Sam (2017). "College Basketball's Overblown FBI Scandal, and Underappreciated Opportunity." *Kansas City Star,* October 20. http://www.kansascity.com/.

National Collegiate Athletic Association (2017). *NCAA Division I Manual.* Indianapolis: NCAA.

NCAA Committee on Infractions (2017). "University of Louisville Public Infractions Report." June 15. https://web3.ncaa.org/.

Newman, Edward (1987). "A Player's View of the NFL's Reserve System." *University of Miami Entertainment and Law Review* 129: 130–77.

O'Donnell, Ricky (2017). "Even the NCAA Is Fully Aware That No One Trusts the NCAA." *SB Nation,* October 21. https://www.sbnation.com/.

Palladino, Valentina (2017). "UCF Kicker Ruled Ineligible, Loses Scholarship after Monetizing YouTube Videos." *Ars Technica,* August 1. https://arstechnica.com/.

Pierce, David A., Anastasios Kubarakis, and Lawrence Fielding (2010). "The New Amateurs: The National Collegiate Athletic Association's Application of Amateurism in a Global Sports Arena." *International Journal of Sport Management* 11: 304–8.

Roberts, Ben (2017). "The Curious Case of Ben Bowen, the Player at the Center of Louisville's Basketball Scandal." *Lexington Herald-Leader,* September 29. http://www.kentucky.com/.

Rosenberg, Michael (2010). "Change Is Long Overdue: College Football Players Should Be Paid." *Sports Illustrated,* August 26. https://www.si.com/.

Sack, Allen L., and Ellen J. Staurowsky (1998). *College Athletes for Hire: The Evolution and Legacy of the NCAA Amateur Myth.* Westport, CT: Praeger.

Schmidt, Raymond (2007). *Shaping College Football: The Transformation of an American Sport: 1919–1930.* Syracuse, NY: Syracuse University Press.

Smith, Ronald A. (1990). *Sports and Freedom: The Rise of Big-Time College Athletics.* New York: Oxford University Press.

Solomon, Jon (2016). "NCAA Prez Concerned by Texas Swimmer Paid $740,000 for Winning Olympic Gold." CBS Sports, September 6. https://www.cbssports.com/.

Southall, Richard M., and Ellen J. Staurowsky (2013). "Cheering on the Collegiate Model: Creating, Disseminating, and Imbedding the NCAA's Redefinition of Amateurism." *Journal of Sport and Social Issues* 37, no. 4: 403–29. http://intl-jss.sagepub.com/.

Staurowsky, Ellen J. (2013). Expert witness report. Submitted in *O'Bannon v. NCAA.*

———. (2017). "The Power Five and Power Politics: LEAD1 Athletic Directors Taking Their Game to Capitol Hill." Paper presented at the College Sport Research Institute Conference, University of South Carolina, Columbia, April 12.

Tracy, Marc (2018). "Brian Bowen II and the Real Victims of N.C.A.A. Scandals." *New York Times,* October 11. https://www.nytimes.com/.

US Department of Justice (2017). "U.S. attorney Announced the Arrest of 10 Individuals, Including Four Division I Coaches, for college Basketball Fraud and Corruption Schemes." Press release, US Attorney's Office Southern District of New York, September 26. https://www.justice.gov/.

Vourderis, John (2017). "Sealed Complaint: United States of America v. Chuck Connors Person and Rashan Michel." September 25. https://www.justice.gov/.

Wang, Gene (2017). "ESPN's Jay Bilas: The NCAA Makes Its Own Rules and the Rules Are Bad." *Washington Post,* October 30. https://www.washingtonpost.com/.

Wolfson, Andrew (2017). "Why Is It against the Law to Give Money to Recruits? Former Federal Prosecutors Explain." *Louisville Courier-Journal,* September 26. https://www.courier-journal.com/.

Yates, Jonathan (2016a). "Interview with LEAD1 Association President and CEO Tom McMillen on His One-Year Anniversary and the Evolving Role of College Athletic Directors." LinkedIn, November 1. https://www.linkedin.com/.

———. (2016b). "LEAD1 Association Announced 2017 Events, Including Annual Meeting and Congressional Gala in Washington, D.C." PRWeb, December 14. http://www.prweb.com/.

———. (2016c). "LEAD1 Association Announces Formation of Political Action Committee. PRWeb, December 22. http://www.prweb.com/.

Some College Athletes Are Employees

Lessons Learned from Professional Sport Labor

Mark S. Nagel

> You go through the Sporting News for the last 100 years and you will find two things are always true: You never have enough pitching and nobody ever made money.
>
> —MAJOR LEAGUE BASEBALL PLAYERS ASSOCIATION EXECUTIVE DIRECTOR DONALD FEHR

> We let it hang out in front of 70,000 fans. We deserve something. If that many people turned out to watch a guy lay linoleum, then he should get a likewise pension.
>
> — SAN FRANCISCO GIANTS OUTFIELDER LEON "DADDY WAGS" WAGNER

> This case is about young men who've grown rich and famous beyond their dreams who have come to malign the system that made them rich and famous.
>
> —ATTORNEY FOR THE NFL

Public debates regarding whether Power Five football and men's basketball players (and potentially athletes in a few other Power Five sports) should be viewed as employees in a free market are often framed in a historical vacuum. However, these debates involve legal, financial, marketing, and ethical considerations that have long histories in various professional sport settings, going back all the way to the 1869 Cincinnati Red Stockings, the first fully professional American baseball team. As is often the case in a discussion of college athletes as employees, what's past is prologue.

Using a historical lens, this chapter traces key developments in US sport entities, including the NCAA, MLB, the NBA, the NFL, the NHL, and other North American sport leagues and associations. Since numerous books have provided detailed accounts of US sport's labor history, key personnel, and legal and political maneuverings, this chapter focuses on how these key developments provide a context to explore various topics, including:

- sport participation versus ownership or governance;
- retaining control over athletes;
- maintaining amateurism in a professionalized sport setting;
- the application of antitrust law in professional and college sport settings;
- economic exploitation in a sport business setting;
- perceptions "neutral" observers' (e.g., politicians and fans) have about sport labor disputes;
- the media's role in shaping public opinion concerning sport business activities;
- athletes' satisfaction with their current marketing and/or financial situation; and
- the role of paternalism in sport governance.

The Origins of North American Professional Sport

In 1789, as the United States emerged from the Revolutionary War, nearly 90 percent of the labor force was engaged in agriculture. As a result of the Industrial Revolution, by 1840 that number had dropped to 69 percent (Growing a Nation 2018). In addition, as survival rates and leisure time increased, so did opportunities for consumption of entertainment. Immediately preceding the Civil War, the most popular sports were horse racing and cricket, but American baseball (initially played in a variety of forms such as "town ball") was becoming popular. As the sport developed, the idea of forming local baseball teams to participate in organized games against teams from neighboring towns took hold.

In 1845 the Knickerbocker Club of New York was formed. It was primarily a social club, and "gentlemen" members had to adhere to strict high-class society standards. Not surprisingly—since only upper-class gentlemen were permitted to join the Knickerbocker Club—just as in the modern incarnation of the Olympic Games as well as in college athletics, members were required to be nonprofessional amateurs (Seymour 1960: 16). Other similar clubs formed soon after, and despite the Knickerbocker's initial place in baseball history, much of the game's development and setting of uniform rules occurred without the club's involvement. In 1857 sixteen New York–based clubs established the National Association of Base Ball Players (NABBP), which prohibited pay for play and prohibited players from gambling on games. During the 1860s the NABBP steadily grew. Just like early college athletic contests, NABBP games were organized primarily by players. While initially all NABBP clubs (just like every NCAA member university since 1906) claimed to adhere to the no-pay rule, under-the-table payments were commonplace.

In 1866 the Red Stockings were formed and participated in regional baseball games under the no-compensation rules established by the NABBP. However, with hidden financial compensation becoming more common, by 1869 the Cincinnati club, under the direction of player-manager Harry Wright, enlisted ten professional players. After an undefeated season of barnstorming around the country, baseball's popularity increased dramatically. Rather than being concerned that professional players were ruining the game, the common perception of baseball executives was that a professionalized baseball workforce would be popular. Recognizing the untenable nature of prohibiting pay for play, NABBP clubs openly embraced professionalism.

In 1871 the National Association of Professional Base Ball Players (sometimes referred to as the National Association) was formed, with clubs in US cities throughout the Northeast and Midwest. Despite attempting to establish standard admission prices and some minimal revenue sharing, the association experienced limited success, primarily because the Boston club dominated on-field competition and there was a lack of a centralized governing body.

In a nascent professional baseball environment in need of a strong organization, the National League (NL) was formed in 1876. In addition to a league office, clubs employed full-time personnel to deal with baseball business issues, ending the era of player-organized activities. This evolution is similar to what occurred within college sport in the late 1880s, which morphed from player-organized extracurricular activities into an enterprise in which paid, full-time athletic-department employees were retained. Seymour (1960: 80) notes the change the new professional baseball structure would create: "The managing end of the game was to be separate and distinct from the playing end, thus allowing the players to concentrate on performance and leave business affairs and promotion to the owners." This same dynamic certainly applies to college sport. By the early 1900s, most colleges participating at the highest level of intercollegiate football had retained full-time coaches, some of whom did not even give the appearance that they were performing any other functions at the school outside of coaching football.

Interestingly, the NL did not initially concern itself with completely controlling player movement. At its onset players could change teams as their contracts expired, which enabled successful players to broker their services to the highest bidder. However, higher player salaries inevitably resulted in lower profits for club owners. Recognizing this, in 1879 NL president William Hulbert declared that if baseball was "to be conserved in its best state," all salaries needed to be decreased (Seymour 1960: 106). To accomplish this, NL team owners secretly instituted a plan to reserve five players from each team from the open marketplace. By 1883 the NL and the recently formed American Association agreed to increase the reserve number to eleven. In 1886 that number was raised to twelve and by 1887 to fourteen, which for most clubs was nearly every player on their rosters. In 1887 owners began to insert formal language regarding reserving players into all employment agreements. Since all teams had agreed to institute and honor these reserve clauses, once current contracts expired, players lost the right to bargain their services with other clubs (Seymour 1960: 106). The reserve clause bound players to a club in perpetuity, though the application of the specific language detailing the reserve clause was later successfully challenged by Andy Messersmith and Dave McNally in 1975 (Korr 2002: 157). Recognizing the reserve clause's threat to the future of player compensation, in 1890 some professional players formed a union known as the Brotherhood and created a "Players League." The new venture failed after one season.

The Intercollegiate Athletic Association of the United States (IAAUS), now known as the National Collegiate Athletic Association, was formally established on March 31, 1906. Since its formation the NCAA implemented and has maintained similar reserve-clause strategies to control players. During the early years of intercollegiate football in the late nineteenth century, players would often switch teams during a season, sometimes changing their names as well. With minimal photographic records and operating within a much less regulated environment, a football player could bargain his services to various teams. In many cases actually enrolling in or attending classes was of little concern. Though from its inception the NCAA banned athletic scholarships (i.e., pay for play), by 1956 such compensation was permitted. As commercialism and potential revenue increased, the NCAA had been forced to allow player compensation (in the form of an athletic grant-in-aid [GIA] or scholarship). The NCAA also began to place limits on player movement, typically preventing athletes who wished to transfer to another school from being granted a release. In what were even then the revenue sports of Division I football and basketball, an athlete had to sit out two years of competition if he transferred to another Division I school (Bilas 2017). If a release was granted, an athlete still had to sit out one year of competition (out of four total years of competitive eligibility). Ironically, recent efforts by the NCAA to permit football and basketball players who have graduated but still have a year of eligibility to transfer have been seen by many in the college coaching ranks as among the worst and most "dangerous" NCAA provisions (Levin 2013). Given the NCAA's stance that college sport is a critical but secondary component of an educational experience, a number of people have correctly noted that coaches criticizing a rule that enables a graduated athlete to pursue an advanced degree marks the highest form of hypocrisy (Bilas 2017).

The establishment of MLB's reserve clause was seen by many as extremely restrictive, particularly in light of the Sherman Antitrust Act of 1890, which was designed to limit control of industries through illegal conspiracies. As noted by many, the reserve clause was at its core anti-American. A fundamental American principle after the Civil War was that all men were free to bargain their services to the highest bidder. Despite this, many baseball fans and stakeholders supported the reserve clause, typically claiming such collusion was necessary for the business of baseball to function effectively. The *St. Louis Globe-Democrat* noted, "The reserve rule is, on paper, the most unfair and degrading measure . . . ever passed in a free country. Still . . . it is necessary for the safety and preservation of the national game" (quoted in Seymour 1960: 111). Countless other baseball owners, executives, and managers vehemently asserted—sometimes under oath while testifying in various legal proceedings—that the game of baseball would be fundamentally and irrevocably damaged if the reserve clause were ever eliminated. The belief in the reserve clause was so strong that when hired in 1966 as Major League Baseball Players Association (MLBPA) executive director, Marvin Miller noted that his interactions with players indicated that many of them believed the reserve clause was a necessary component of preserving professional baseball (Miller 1991: 45). As former player Steve Boros noted, "After all, lots of players never thought about anything other than they were getting paid good money to play a kids' game. . . . It was so ingrained, that they [players] never thought about it [the reserve system]" (Korr 2002: 27).

So, too, many current and former Power Five football and men's basketball players unwaveringly support the current NCAA collegiate model of athletics (Southall and Staurowsky 2013). A key aspect of team sport competition is being able to function in a group setting. Even the greatest football and basketball players must perform on a team, under the guidance of coaches. Rather than fostering individuality, team sports often discourage it. Young players are taught that the current paternalistic sports system is designed with their best interests at heart. Part of this system is the belief that a high school or college athlete should not be paid a salary. While established forms of compensation ostensibly tied to education (e.g., tuition, room and board, etc.) are permitted and valued, any pay in excess of established parameters is unseemly and a bad thing. Within the current system, players with professional options are forced to go along to get along until they make it to the next level—at which point they can enjoy the financial fruits of their labor. The mythology that college players should wait to be paid until they reach the professional ranks is supported by a number of former players, many of whom seem to ignore the exploitative nature of the current collegiate system. Len Elmore, former University of Maryland basketball player and current attorney and college basketball analyst, has argued that college athletes should not be paid above the compensation they are already receiving (Hazell 2017). Charles Barkley, another prominent former college and professional basketball player, also believes college players should not be paid, either in additional salary or via endorsements. In a convoluted exchange with a reporter, Barkley explained it would be impossible to pay only some players:

> **BARKLEY:** The endorsement thing is tricky because only the good players are going to be endorsed. The bad players, think about it, let's say hypothetically the quarterbacks do endorsements. He can't do anything without a running back or an offensive line. So that'd be like only paying the good player on the NBA team.
> **REPORTER:** But that's what happens.
> **BARKLEY:** That's not what happens. The bad players get paid too. It's not the same as in college. The offensive line makes the quarterback and the running back . . . So if I'm an offensive lineman why should I let Johnny Manziel get a big contract and I'm blocking for him? It doesn't help me. (Mandell 2015)

Interestingly, Barkley spent most of his career as the best player on his various professional teams, and most of his endorsements were done individually, not with other players. He may be attempting to discuss some of the group licensing deals established by various professional sport leagues' players' associations that do distribute incoming revenues equally to all the players. However, most of those deals are for large group activities, such as for the licensing of video games. Group licensing deals certainly do not preclude an individual player from securing additional lucrative individual opportunities.

With former NBA players such as Elmore and Barkley (who have made millions of dollars during their careers) expressing doubts about college players receiving greater compensation, it is not difficult to understand why so many current NCAA football and basketball players are reticent about saying they should be paid a market wage. In many cases the public is more apt to listen to those who say that the system should be left as is rather than calling for an end to college sport as we know it. With many current players unwilling to express their feelings, the current college sport system continues largely unchanged.

One of the reasons the exploitative MLB reserve clause was permitted and even supported by so many was the perception that every player was receiving a great deal. Learning from MLB, other North American professional sport leagues (e.g., the NBA, NFL, and NHL) utilized similar reserve rules to control player movement and limit salaries. Historically players competing at the highest level of professional baseball received salaries that exceeded those of the typical American worker. After their formation the other Big Four leagues made similar player salary comparisons to the wage-earning capacity of ordinary (i.e., blue-collar) workers. In some cases players in the minor leagues earned salaries at least comparable to those of industrial workers. The message from owners—often supported vigorously by a compliant media—was that baseball involved eight months of playing a kid's game rather than real work. The sports editor of the *Atlanta Journal,* Furman Bisher, asked, "Why should anyone have sympathy for men who are paid an average of twenty-two to twenty-three thousand dollars a year, get to live in fine hotels, and spend each spring in Florida?" (Korr 2002: 44). Most pundits were either uninformed or unwilling to take a stand against the owners because owners often subsidized journalists' trips to spring training in Florida and provided other perks. In the words of Jackie Robinson, "the owners have the writers in their pockets . . . a player might get a hamburger for a writer . . . but the owners feed them steak" (quoted in ibid.: 8). Former MLB commissioner A. B. "Happy" Chandler once justified the reserve clause by stating, "No major leaguer makes less than $5,000 a year and some make up to $100,000. If you call that peonage, then a lot of us would like to be in on it" (quoted in Seymour 1960: 112).

Those who perceived that MLB players were sometimes paid exorbitant salaries ignored the important fact that baseball owners and management often enjoyed tremendously large salaries that greatly exceeded the typical American wage. Too often the public failed to investigate owners' profits and instead focused on player demands. When Jim "Catfish" Hunter became a free agent in 1975 (because of Oakland A's owner Charlie Finley's failure to adhere to an insurance provision in Hunter's contract), many fans seemed mortified at Hunter's desire to make more money but ignored Finley's profit motives (Miller 1991: 229). Like so many other supposedly greedy players, Hunter was seen as the problem, while owners—who artificially suppressed player wages below what they would earn in an open market—were victims.

A similar public relations situation has occurred in big-time college sport, particularly as current and former players have advocated or even litigated for higher college sport compensation. Among the most vocal arguments against paying college athletes is that they already receive a good deal in the form of athletic GIAs, some of which are the coveted full ride, in which an athlete receives a compensation package that covers many expenses associated with college attendance. Given that 71 percent of 2012 college graduates (totaling 1.3 million students) needed financial assistance to attend college and that the average student loan debt among 2016 graduates was $37,172 (Student Loan Hero 2017), a majority of past, current, and future college attendees are understandably not overly receptive to complaints from Power Five college football and basketball players who are receiving full scholarships. Since many college students work while in school, they often perceive Division I basketball and football players who are excused from classes to travel to exotic locations for games as being spoiled.

Most college students would love to be celebrities seen on television and cheered on by adoring fans. As a result it is no surprise that many college students and fans express little sympathy for athletes' complaints. Ironically, despite usually being on full-ride scholarships, many athletes still secure student loans, often to pay for their own expenses or to support other members of their family. Despite the perception that full-ride scholarship athletes leave college with no debt, a 2014 *Forbes* article detailed that many full-ride athletes left college with significant loan repayment obligations (Heitner 2014).

In addition, since approximately 95–97 percent of all college athletes have much less market value (NCAA 2014), many of these loss-athletes, whose market value is less than the value of their awarded grant-in-aid (GIA), reject the notion that profit-athletes have a legitimate right to be paid a negotiated wage. Even though athletes in the profit sports largely subsidize the GIAs, travel, equipment, and additional academic services loss-athletes receive, there is a concern that paying some athletes is somehow unfair since ostensibly every athlete works just as hard. The "different athlete, same work ethic" mentality is similar to what occurs among various academic departments on a college campus—faculty members may work just as hard as their colleagues in more prestigious departments, but their contributions to the overall success of the institution are not compensated in the same manner. Faculty in medical schools and business schools tend to receive higher salaries than those in the fine arts or social sciences, and most institutions still function effectively despite this disparity. Though some in the lesser-paid academic units certainly desire to be paid more, there is an understanding that the free market is the driver of disparate faculty compensation. As the NCAA notes, in college sports "there are 400,000 NCAA student-athletes, and almost all of them will go pro in something other than sports" (New 2015), which means the vast majority of athletes on campus have no vested interest in helping the roughly thirteen thousand football and four thousand Division I basketball players (and a very small amount of baseball and hockey players) receive additional compensation above a full-ride GIA. Not surprisingly, loss-athletes many times do not want to see profit-athletes compensated according to their market value, since if greater compensation was provided to profit-athletes, the amount of money available to pay for charter flights, four-star hotel stays, and other perks for loss-athletes and coaches might decrease.

Historically, with both professional and college sport ownership and management unwilling to cede control of financial resources and the public largely unsupportive of rescinding restrictive rules, professional and college sport players have turned to the courts in order to affect meaningful change. With this in mind, the following section details some of the significant antitrust and labor litigation that has affected the sport environment.

Reserve Rules Are Adjudicated

At beginning of the twentieth century, the National League contracted from twelve franchises to eight. However, despite this, professional baseball experienced rapidly growing popularity. With numerous non-NL teams increasing their fan bases, in 1901 Ban Johnson formed the American League (AL) to compete with the NL for top players. Locating franchises in some of the recently abandoned NL cities and offering higher salaries than many NL clubs, the AL successfully raided NL rosters. Sensing it was easier to conspire and cooperate rather than compete, by the end of the 1902 season, the two leagues (and the National Association, which represented minor league clubs) signed an agreement honoring each other's right to players under the reserve clause. In 1903 the two champions from each league met in the first World Series, which was formalized as a yearly event in 1905. Though the leagues maintained their own schedules, once merged into Major League Baseball, the fully enforced reserve rule effectively restricted player movement and curtailed salaries, which had risen prior to the merger.

With the AL and NL merger, the next decade was one of relative labor peace. While the sport continued to become more popular, which resulted in much greater revenues, the lack of any meaningful competition for player services limited player compensation. Sensing an opportunity to attract top talent that was underpaid, the Federal League was formed in 1913 and immediately began to offer substantially higher salaries to players, which resulted in increased salaries across the industry. The Federal League encountered significant resistance from the established baseball hierarchy, which caused it to fold shortly after its 1915 season. Most of the owners were permitted compensation, either through direct payments or being permitted to purchase existing MLB teams, but the owners of the Baltimore Terrapins sought redress through the courts against the National League for alleged antitrust violations. Upon appeal, in a landmark decision, the US Supreme Court ruled that baseball was not interstate commerce and therefore antitrust laws did not apply (*Federal Baseball Club v. National League*, 1922).

The *Federal Baseball Club* decision permitted MLB to tightly control all aspects of the baseball business, including restricting player employment rights. Essentially players had one opportunity to negotiate compensation for their services with a franchise. After signing their first contract, players became the property of that organization until their services were no longer necessary. A few players attempted to fight MLB's harsh rules, with limited success. With the conclusion of World War II, a number of established major league players who had fought in Europe and Asia returned to reclaim their prior jobs. A handful of players, including Danny Gardella, Sal Maglie, Max Lanier, and Mickey Owen, sought employment in the Mexican League and were promptly banned from MLB for at least five years. When MLB commissioner Happy Chandler lowered Owen's suspension to three years, Chicago Cubs general manager Jim Gallagher noted that "the spectacle of Mickey Owen languishing on a Missouri farm will do more to keep players from jumping this winter than anything Mr. Rickey [Branch Rickey, the Brooklyn Dodgers' general manager] or the rest of us could do" (quoted in Miller 1991: 177). Gardella attempted to fight his ban through the courts (*Gardella v. Chandler*, 1948). Though his suit was dismissed at the district level due to MLB's antitrust exemption, the appeals court ordered the case remanded for a full trial. MLB officials publicly called Gardella a communist and vowed to press their case, but privately they were concerned about a potential ruling that would upset their labor practices. Commissioner Chandler decided to "temper justice with mercy" and offered former Mexican League players amnesty (Burk 2001: 106). On the advice of his attorney, Gardella accepted a sixty-thousand-dollar settlement and returned to play only one more MLB game. Interestingly, despite apparent precedence regarding baseball's antitrust exemption, MLB was willing to pay a large settlement in order to ensure the Gardella case went away.

In 1953, to the detriment of players, the Supreme Court reaffirmed its prior decision to permit MLB an antitrust exemption (*Toolson v. New York Yankees*, 1953). George Toolson had been a longtime pitcher in the New York Yankees minor league system. While Toolson felt he was capable of playing Major League baseball, he had been unable to move up to the powerhouse Yankees parent club and was also unable (because of the reserve clause) to negotiate with any other franchise. Consequently he languished in the minor leagues, an insurance policy in case a New York Yankees player became unable to perform. Toolson sought redress through the courts, but even though some observers noted his predicament was un-American, the Court cited the precedent that since MLB was not interstate commerce, antitrust laws did not apply. In addition most fans ignored Toolson's plight, feeling he and other players were lucky to have an opportunity to play baseball for a living.

During the 1950s other professional sport organizations sought to affirm their rights to an antitrust exemption, but they were rebuffed, despite being similarly structured and financed. In *United States v. International Boxing Club* (1955), the Court opined that baseball's antitrust exemption was unique to their sport and found that James Norris and Arthur Wirtz violated antitrust laws when they sought to control access to nearly all heavyweight championship boxing matches. In another case (*Radovich v. National Football League*, 1957), in which an NFL player, William Radovich, had been blackballed by the NFL after he completed his Detroit Lions contract and chose to play for the Los Angeles Dons of the

All-America Football Conference, the court deemed the NFL was engaged in interstate commerce despite legal and commonsense arguments that staging baseball and football games are similar business practices. Rather than endure a full trial, the NFL chose to settle with Radovich for $42,500 (Rhoden 1994). In subsequent litigation throughout the 1950s and 1960s, only MLB enjoyed a full antitrust exemption concerning labor activities (Farzin 2015). However, the NBA, NFL, and NHL eventually implemented similar reserve rules to those in MLB.

In big-time college sport, the NCAA has long been recognized as having both monopoly (sole supplier of a good or service) and monopsony (sole buyer of a particular good or the sole employer of a specific class of worker) power. The NCAA has consistently been termed a cartel and is often viewed as wielding as much if not more power over the college sport industry as OPEC has over the petroleum industry (Barro 2002). In particular the NCAA has consistently wielded monopsony power over profit-athletes. As mentioned previously, the NCAA has placed significant restrictions on basketball and football players transferring from one Division I institution to another and only reluctantly lessened some of those restrictions in 2021 (Zagoria and Ingemi 2021). In addition, despite previously allowing four-year GIAs for athletes, in 1973 the NCAA decided to alter its rules and change four-year GIAs to one-year renewable grants, with athletes still tied to the school after the year and the school retaining the ability to not renew the award. The four-year GIA rule was only brought back as a permitted option in 2012 in response to litigation (*O'Bannon v. NCAA*, 2014, 2015) and subsequent media scrutiny that revealed the exploitative nature of college sports (Solomon 2014).

Though for many years the NCAA vehemently argued that their rules were necessary to maintain its amateur collegiate business model, much like MLB in the Gardella case, the organization has been willing to settle with litigants when strategically beneficial. When sued by the National Invitation Tournament (NIT) for establishing postseason tournament rules perceived to be in violation of antitrust law, the NCAA eventually settled out of court for $16 million . . . and then subsequently bought the NIT for $40.5 million (Nagel and Southall 2005). In *Oliver v. NCAA* (2009), the attorney for plaintiff Andy Oliver argued that restrictive rules on high school athletes preventing them from seeking advice from counsel when contemplating career opportunities were a violation of a citizen's rights. The NCAA initially defended their rules and then settled the matter out of court for $750,000 (Nagel and Southall 2009). Despite previously altering the total compensation that a full-ride GIA provided on numerous occasions, in 1975 the NCAA took away the fifteen dollars earmarked as laundry money and steadfastly refused to increase total compensation over the next thirty-plus years. By 2011 a modest increase of two thousand dollars for what was termed "cost of attendance" was proposed for full-ride GIAs, but NCAA members defeated the proposal, even with NCAA president Myles Brand advocating for the increase (Dodd 2015). However, when faced with litigation regarding the matter (*White, et al. v. National Collegiate Athletic Association,* 2008), the NCAA eventually settled for $228 million, with only roughly $20 million of that being new money to be allocated to athletes (Lederman 2008).

As the previous section highlights, prior to the 1970s, players' efforts to utilize the courts to curtail the reserve clause and other restrictive practices of MLB, the NBA, the NFL, and the NHL were largely ineffectual. However, the 1960s was a decade in which tremendous political and social change took place. A significant number of US citizens began to question established rules and cultural norms. While professional athletes believed the times they were a-changin', they also believed significant court-mandated alterations to the established player-compensation model were not likely. Consequently many players felt their only viable option was to collectivize their efforts.

Players Organize

Even though the US court system did not exempt non-baseball North American professional sport leagues from antitrust scrutiny, salaries and playing conditions in all four of the Big Four professional leagues were substandard, mostly because there was limited competition for player services. The NFL had implemented its first draft in 1936, the NBA in 1947, the NHL in 1963, and MLB in 1965. The draft system, combined with a version of the reserve clause that each league enforced, limited any single player's ability to negotiate for better wages or working conditions. The only times salaries dramatically increased was when viable competitor leagues were established. Unfortunately for the players, from 1940 until 1982 the only viable rival leagues—the All-American Football Conference (1946–49); the American Basketball Association (1967–76); the American Football League (1960–69); the World Hockey Association (1972–79)—were often underfunded. Furthermore, in each of these leagues, the most successful franchises were eventually asked to merge with the established leagues, re-creating a monopolistic financial environment. Some players realized the only opportunity to create meaningful change was to organize and attempt to force the owners to collectively bargain.

The first serious effort to galvanize players and address their working conditions occurred on April 17, 1946, when Robert Murphy registered the American Baseball Guild. Murphy planned to establish a union of major league players that could voice their concerns, particularly in the areas of salaries and pension benefits. In early June 1946, Pittsburgh Pirates players, trainers, and coaches took a strike vote. With the threshold to strike being 67 percent, the 20–16 vote in favor of striking fell short. The reaction of the owner of the Pirates preceding the strike vote became a blueprint for future owner/management reactions. If the strike vote were to have passed, the Pirates had a semiprofessional team ready to replace the strikers. The Pirates also utilized the media to shape opinion against the players. However, the Pirates' greatest weapon was sowing mistrust among the players by utilizing one of their own against them. Pitcher Rip Sewell, who had been treated relatively well by the Pirates, was adamantly opposed to the guild and a potential strike. In fact, he was reported to have said that he was "glad the owners had finally told these ungrateful players where to get off. First, they wanted the hamburger, then filet mignon, eventually the cow and the entire pasture" (quoted in Bierne: 2022). Sewell's position was likely a factor in the two-thirds strike threshold not being achieved.

Early efforts to organize NBA players met with similar results. Boston Celtic great Bob Cousy founded the NBA Players Association (NBAPA) in 1954, but the organization went largely unnoticed by the NBA owners until 1964. NBA owners consistently ignored NBAPA's attempts to secure a viable pension plan, gain increases in meal money and medical care, and create a more manageable travel schedule. However, with the first televised NBA All-Star Game scheduled to be played on January 14, 1964, NBAPA pressed its demands (Quinn 2020). Under tremendous pressure to have a successful All-Star Game to promote the fledgling league, owners were forced to negotiate with the players in their locker room up until minutes before game time. Though an agreement was not finalized that evening, NBA commissioner J. Walter Kennedy provided assurances that the owners would formally recognize the players' union and bargain in good faith. The game was played and a labor agreement later signed, which guaranteed many players' demands. It was one of the first times professional players collectively brokered a labor deal (Nagel and Southall 2008).

The NFL players first attempted to collectivize their labor efforts in 1956, but owners were reluctant to bargain. Many player demands were not addressed until the founding of the AFL resulted in competition for player services. While the AFL's aggressive pursuit of top college talent, particularly quarterbacks, forced NFL owners to increase player salaries, it was not until 1968 that the NFL Players Association (NFLPA) was recognized as a bargaining unit. In that same year the first NFL collective bargaining agreement (CBA) was signed, with a short player strike during the summer (no games were missed) helping speed negotiations (Associated Press 2011). The 1968 CBA focused primarily on owner contributions to the players' pension fund and raising the minimum salaries to nine thousand dollars a year for rookies and ten thousand dollars a year for veterans. In 1970 a two-day NFLPA strike occurred with the primary issues being player pensions, minimum salaries, health and dental insurance, and the right to impartial arbitration for grievances (Harris 1986: 194). In this case the players were not as successful in getting their demands met, and though not proven to be in direct retaliation, a number of players instrumental in the CBA negotiations were released by their teams (ibid 218.).

National Hockey League players attempted to form a union in 1957. Led by players Ted Lindsay and Doug Harvey, players were unsuccessful in creating an organization with sufficient clout to demand owners alter the players' pension agreement. Consequently a number of key players involved with the organization efforts were either traded or sent to the minor leagues. (It should be noted that with only six original franchises, jobs at the top level of the sport were scarce.) Lindsay was traded from one of the best situations in professional hockey—playing on the Detroit Red Wings front line with Gordie Howe—to one of the worst with the Chicago Blackhawks. Harvey was traded from the great Montreal Canadiens to the lowly New York Rangers. The Canadiens' disappointment with Harvey's unionizing efforts lasted for decades. Despite being one of the best defensemen in NHL history, he did not have his number retired by the Canadiens until 1985, twelve years after he had been elected to the Hockey Hall of Fame. It was not until 1967 that Alan Eagleson was able to fully organize the players and establish the National Hockey League Players Association (NHLPA) (Mullen 2017). Labor relations between the NHL and the NHLPA mirrored those in other professional sport leagues in the 1960s and 1970s. Low salaries and pension contributions tended to dominate most bargaining discussions, but in the case of the NHL, a few legal differences existed, because hockey teams played in both the United States and Canada, which meant that some labor issues could be litigated in Canadian courts.

Despite failing to effectively organize in 1946, MLB players eventually created what most observers consider the most successful professional players' union in the world. In the 1950s MLB players were able to retain a part-time legal adviser to assist them in discussions with owners. By 1965 the players believed they should form a permanent players association and hire a full-time executive director. The initial choice to assume the new full-time duties was "Judge" Robert Cannon, who had previously worked as the players' part-time legal adviser. Fortunately for the players, negotiations regarding Cannon's duties and office location prevented an agreement being consummated. Cannon believed that most of baseball was in good shape and that players should not endanger the tremendous gains they had achieved over the previous decade. He once remarked that players had a job "that 10,000 men making a lot more money would give anything to do" and that he "was not there to fight ownership. . . . [You] can't do anything to damage the good of baseball. . . . [You] have to make sure that [they] didn't endanger the cash flow of the clubs" (quoted in Korr 2002: 27). Instead of hiring the owner-compliant Cannon, the players instead turned to Marvin Miller, who had considerable experience working for the United Steelworkers.

Almost immediately Miller began to educate players and owners regarding labor law. Miller knew and communicated to players that the new MLB Players Association (MLBPA) must be independent from the owners. He informed the players that their longstanding belief that they "could trust the owners' judgement and instinct to do what was best for everyone" should be stricken from their minds (Korr 2002: 48). It was not until Miller began negotiating the first MLB CBA that owners realized that many of their longstanding policies—such as manipulating television revenues from the All-Star Game and the MLB Game of the Week to maximize owner profits and minimize player payments—would not occur as long as Miller was employed by the players.

Although it is hard to believe today, with the average MLB salary in 2022 being $4.41 million (Poindexter 2022) and one hundred and thirty five players making $10 million or more per year and forty eight making $20 million or more per year (Spotrac 2022), the first few years of Miller's stewardship was focused on increasing marketing opportunities, making small gains in salary, improving the pension, permitting players to retain agents in contract negotiations, and receiving fair compensation for the players' name, image, and likeness from baseball card contracts with Topps (Miller 1991). While the initial 1968 CBA increased minimum salaries from seven thousand to ten thousand dollars, most importantly it established the union as a legitimate bargaining unit. In the second negotiated CBA, a number of provisions were enacted, along with an apparent minor point—the right of players to seek binding arbitration from a neutral chairman for instances of labor matters—that came to be one of the most important clauses in the history of sport business.

Depending on one's point of view, college sport's organized labor movement is either still in its infancy or yet to be born. Though a few vocal critics have been calling for significant big-time college labor reform for many years (Byers 1995; Gerdy 2006; Ridpath 2012; Sack and Staurowsky 1998), the origins of calls for significant change are often ascribed to Ramogi Huma, a former University of California, Los Angeles, linebacker. While a freshman in college, Huma observed that a teammate, All-America linebacker Donnie Edwards, began to receive groceries and small under-the-table compensation from an agent after he had complained he did not have enough money to buy food. Once the NCAA uncovered a $150 payment, Edwards was suspended for a game. At the same time the NCAA was suspending Edwards, UCLA was selling his jersey in the campus bookstore (Nocera and Strauss 2016). Huma was also shocked to hear that while participating in "voluntary" summer workouts, he would be responsible for his own health insurance.

Before Huma left UCLA, he founded the Collegiate Athletes Coalition. By the mid-2000s the organization had changed its name to the National College

Players Association (NCPA), enlisting members at more than 150 colleges and universities and seeking financial support from the United Steelworkers union (Nocera and Strauss 2016). While through the years the NCPA has made small strides, most of the organization's efforts have essentially involved Huma telling the story of college athlete exploitation to sympathetic audiences, as well as to those who choose to ignore the situation. Unlike Marvin Miller and the labor leaders in the NFLPA, NBAPA, and NHLPA, Huma has had a difficult time enlisting and organizing college players, primarily because there are so many Division I football (120+) and basketball (300+) teams and because the four-year eligibility rule makes gaining traction among an ever-changing player population on any of hundreds of individual campuses around the country a huge challenge. However, in 2014 Huma and the NCPA did make a significant impact upon the general sport consciousness.

A Changing Landscape

While the MLBPA under Miller's leadership was making significant inroads as a group, individual players also began to better understand their potential power in the industry. In 1966 Los Angeles Dodgers pitchers Don Drysdale and Sandy Koufax—two of the best players in baseball—began joint holdouts. Each refused to sign a contract unless the other's demands were also met (Bavasi 1967). Everyone in baseball took notice, with the Dodgers' front office being the most concerned. Dodger general manager Buzzie Bavasi had publicly expressed his negotiating style and belief in the limited ability of most players to comprehend the business of baseball: "Some players do not understand money at all, or don't stop to figure things out . . . you could take advantage of them something frightful . . . we don't negotiate by the Marquis of Queensbury Rules . . . as far as I'm concerned, anything goes at salary time. [Bavasi knew before discussions] almost to the penny what each player is going to get" (quoted in Korr 2002: 64).

Bavasi's supposedly enlightened comments reminded some of the late 1800s and early 1900s, when significant progress was made by labor unions. In 1902 George Baer, president of the Reading Railroad, had famously said, "The rights of the laboring man will be protected, and cared for, not by the labor agitator, but by the Christian men to whom God has given control of the property interests of the country" (Holton 1992: 28–29). For both Baer and Bavasi, once the employees began to exert more power, the labor dynamic was altered. Despite his public and private protests, eventually Bavasi signed Drysdale and Koufax to contracts that significantly increased their salaries. The Dodgers won the 1966 National League pennant but lost the World Series. It would be the last time Koufax pitched in the major leagues. In the aftermath of the contract negotiations, Bavasi wrote:

> They said that one wouldn't sign unless the other signed. Since one of the two was the greatest pitcher I've ever seen (and possibly the greatest anybody has ever seen), the gimmick worked. But be sure to stick around for the fun the next time somebody tries that gimmick. I don't care if the whole infield comes in as a package; the next year the whole infield will be wondering what it is doing playing for the Nankai Hawks. (Bavasi 1967)

Though Bavasi never faced another joint holdout with as much star power as Drysdale and Koufax, other players, emboldened by the stance of the two Dodger players as well as efforts of Marvin Miller, began to question the long-held structure that owners insisted was necessary for the sport to prosper.

Curt Flood was one of the best outfielders in baseball during the 1960s. Playing for the powerful St. Louis Cardinals, he was an integral part of two World Series championship teams. At the conclusion of the 1969 season, he was traded to the Philadelphia Phillies. Not wanting to leave a city he had lived in for many years for a city and team that he felt were not good fits, Flood wrote a letter to MLB commissioner Bowie Kuhn explaining his intentions:

> After twelve years in the major leagues, I do not feel I am a piece of property to be bought and sold irrespective of my wishes. I believe that any system which produces that result violates my basic rights as a citizen and is inconsistent with the laws of the United States and of the several States.
>
> It is my desire to play baseball in 1970, and I am capable of playing. I have received a contract offer from the Philadelphia club, but I believe I have the right to consider offers from other clubs before making any decision. I, therefore, request that you make known to all Major League clubs my feelings in this matter and advise them of my availability for the 1970 season. (quoted in Miller 1991: 190–91)

Citing the standard players' contract and its reserve clause provisions, Commissioner Kuhn denied Flood's request for free agency. In response, on January 16, 1970, Flood filed a $1 million lawsuit alleging MLB's labor rules violated federal antitrust laws (*Flood v. Kuhn,* 1972). Despite (or maybe because of) the importance of the trial, no current and only a few former players were willing to testify on Flood's behalf. Fearing potential retribution, no current players even attended any of the trial's proceedings. In addition, despite the enormous ramifications of a rule that was often compared to indentured servitude, few civil rights organizations rallied to Flood's cause. As Brad Snyder (2006: 116) explains, "Maybe civil rights organizations were overwhelmed by the turmoil of the late 1960s and early 1970s and therefore too busy to stand up for Flood's cause. Maybe they lacked sympathy for a small group of athletes perceived to be spoiled and overpaid, rather than subjugated and oppressed."

Though Miller and the MLBPA provided support, the US Supreme Court eventually ruled against Flood. Similar to previous baseball lawsuits, the Court failed to overturn its 1922 decision in *Federal Baseball* and ruled 5–3 against Flood. In its decision the Court mentioned (as it had in previous baseball cases) that if there was concern for the application of an antitrust exemption for MLB, then Congress should address it.

While Flood and the MLBPA lost because of MLB's antitrust exemption, other professional sports unions were—to an extent—winning antitrust lawsuits. In the NFL future Hall of Fame tight end John Mackey headlined an antitrust lawsuit against the NFL questioning the so-called Rozelle Rule, which effectively tied a player to his current team (*Mackey v. NFL*, 1976). Under the Rozelle Rule, Commissioner Pete Rozelle could award compensation to a team that lost a free agent. That compensation came from the free agent's new team, effectively ending free agency as teams did not bother to pursue free agents for fear of what compensation they would lose. When asked about the effect free movement of players might have on the NFL, Mackay remarked, "Some say freedom for athletes will destroy the NFL. I say nonsense" (quoted in Harris 1986: 181). Though Mackey and the NFLPA won, they negotiated away free agency in exchange for a series of other benefits (ibid.). It would not be until the 1990s that collective bargaining impasses and the threat of additional antitrust litigation led to NFL players' achieving true free agency.

In the NBA competition from rival leagues resulted in higher salaries and increased antitrust litigation. In 1970 future Hall of Fame guard Oscar Robertson filed an antitrust suit against the NBA claiming that its reserve rules and player draft were illegal restraints of trade (*Robertson v. National Basketball Association*, 1976). Of particular concern to Robertson and the NBAPA was the potential merger between the ABA and NBA. While both leagues were in competition for players, salaries increased dramatically. The Robertson case delayed a potential NBA-ABA merger until 1976. Without an antitrust exemption, the NBA was not in a position to shield itself from the ramifications of its restrictive rules. The NBAPA and NBA negotiated a CBA that did not fully grant free agency but did address many player concerns.

Though MLB players were unable to use antitrust litigation to obtain free agency, they eventually were able to use the arbitration clause in their employment contract to make significant changes. Baseball's reserve rules were thought to bind a player to his team in perpetuity, but clauses in the standard playing contract going back all the way to the 1880s indicated that an unsigned player was to be renewed for an option year. Essentially teams could renew a player's employment even if that player did not sign a contract. As Miller began to increase player gains, a number of MLBPA officials contended the reserve clause might not actually tie a player to a club in perpetuity. With this in mind, in the early 1970s, a number of players began seasons without signing contracts. Among them Ted Simmons and Sparky Lyle steadfastly refused to sign, and eventually each was rewarded with significant salary accommodations from their clubs, with some believing the owners were scared that if a prominent player ever did complete a contract and was subsequently unsigned during his option year, he could become an unrestricted free agent.

Such a situation occurred in 1975 when star pitcher Andy Messersmith and injured pitcher Dave McNally each completed an unsigned option year and expressed their desire to become free agents. Despite Commissioner Kuhn and other baseball officials publicly declaring that neither player would be declared a free agent, the Dodgers offered Messersmith a significant salary increase, and the Expos offered McNally a large sum of money to play in 1976. The case of McNally was particularly intriguing, because his injury had not healed, and he had actually left the Expos the previous year during the season to work at an auto dealership in Billings, Montana (Miller 1991: 243). Neither player agreed to accept the lucrative offers, and their cases went before an arbitration panel, with arbitrator Peter Seitz being the deciding vote.

At the arbitration hearings, a number of impassioned arguments were made, with Dodgers manager Walter Alston asserting, "If Messersmith is declared a free agent, then baseball is dead" (quoted in Miller 1991: 244). Perhaps no comment was as dramatic as Kuhn's concern for the entire baseball industry if the players won the case: "The reserve system is the cornerstone of baseball. It gave baseball the stability, economic stability, to develop a system where you were able to eliminate the problems of integrity that had been flagrant in the game" (Helyar 1994: 162). When asked about eliminating the reserve rule, Kuhn added:

> What I see is the loss of clubs—some of our clubs would not be able to survive it. You'd have the loss of employment opportunities for our players and other personnel, the elimination of any possibility that in the near term we could expand into cities that have much wanted baseball, the loss of minor leagues—if not all of them, most of them, and, not inconceivably, the loss of a major league. I say that very carefully and very thoughtfully to the chairman. I think the loss of a major league is quite possible. (ibid.: 162–63)

Despite the pleas of Kuhn and other baseball officials, it appeared that Seitz was going to rule in favor of Messersmith and McNally. Seitz later reflected, "I begged them to negotiate. But the owners were too stubborn and stupid. They were like the French barons in the twelfth century. They had accumulated so much power they wouldn't share it with anybody" (quoted in Miller 1991: 251). When Seitz eventually ruled for the players, the owners fired him as an arbitrator, and within a short period of time, Messersmith had signed a three-year, one-million-dollar free agent contract with the Atlanta Braves.

In the aftermath of the Seitz decision, additional players refused to sign their option contracts, and MLB owners had a dilemma. How should they proceed in this new free agent environment? Despite Kuhn's earlier pleas that the entire industry would collapse, the reality was that owners and players negotiated a new CBA that included free agency provisions. Ironically, one of the owners proposed an idea (feared by Miller, who felt total free agency would become a reality) that would have given the owners significant leverage in legally keeping player salaries suppressed. Charlie Finley, the maverick owner of the highly successful Oakland A's, simply advocated that every team sign all players to one-year contracts with the entire roster becoming free agents each November (Miller 1991:370). Finley contended that Miller and the MLBPA, after years of fighting for free agency, would be unable to successfully argue that granting every player the right to seek employment with the club of their choice was unacceptable. What Finley understood was that a system in which every player was a free agent would likely lower demand since position scarcity would never exist (ibid.). Fortunately for Miller and the players, the owners, who had long loathed Finley, ignored his idea. Instead the new CBA contained language that enabled free agency to occur only after a player had accrued a set period of MLB service time. (This stipulation has been included in all subsequent CBAs.)

During the 1970s labor advocates came to appreciate the importance of being able to utilize antitrust laws and maintaining a strong, unified players' association. After the Seitz decision, Miller and the MLBPA continued to press for higher wages and greater player benefits. Despite predictions of total financial ruin, free agency actually resulted in increased year-round interest in MLB. The "hot stove league" of offseason activity that usually centered on potential trades now also included free agent acquisitions. Attendance increased, and fan consumption of MLB content via television and radio also dramatically skyrocketed in the 1980s, particularly with the proliferation of cable television. Far from being a death knell, the new free agency system coincided with one of the greatest decades of MLB growth.

Though other leagues took longer to implement free agency, they also saw dramatically increased fan interest during the 1980s. However, the rapidly changing labor environment in professional sports still experienced significant turmoil as owners attempted to overturn many of the players' financial gains.

Organized Labor in Big-Time College Sport

The only real attempt to collectivize player efforts in big-time college sports occurred at Northwestern University in 2014–15. Quarterback Kain Colter expressed an interest in forming a union after extensive discussions with Ramogi Huma. During the 2013 season, Colter and ten other teammates (and a few players at other schools) had worn wristbands with the hashtag "#APU" (All Players

United) on them. The wristbands received some media attention but were largely ignored by the general public. By the spring of 2014, Colter and his teammates sought an opportunity to form a union. After investigating and then holding hearings with the players, Peter Sung Ohr, the National Labor Relations Board (NLRB) regional director, ruled that Northwestern football players receiving a GIA were employees and had the right to vote to form a union. Northwestern requested a review of the decision.

During the time before the appeal was heard, Northwestern football coach Pat Fitzgerald urged his players not to form a union. Though there is some discrepancy regarding what was stated in certain meetings behind closed doors, it was clear that many Northwestern officials were vehemently opposed to any unionization attempt to and believed Colter was fomenting discontent among members of the team. Colter noted that "the NFL has the NFLPA, the NBA has the NBAPA, and now college athletes have the College Athletes Players Association" (Nocera and Strauss 2016). Interestingly, before the final decision was heard, the Big Ten Conference notified the NCAA of plans to improve medical insurance provided to players and to guarantee multiyear scholarships, two important issues Colter and his fellow players had advocated for in their complaints (ESPN.com 2015). While waiting for the final decision, the players voted regarding their desire to unionize. The vote was sealed, and when on August 17, 2015, the national NLRB declined to exercise jurisdiction over the dispute (Johnson 2015), the ballots were destroyed. Though some have speculated that the vote would have supported a union, no one can know for sure. Certainly from a labor rights perspective, the failure of the NLRB to side with the players created a setback for those who believed profit-athletes should be classified as employees.

The Owners Fight Back . . . and Learn

As the tumultuous 1970s largely ended the owners' omnipotent reign in various North American professional sport leagues, a few owners advocated for a more peaceful working environment. However, most league owners sought to regain their past power. Ironically it was a league experiencing the most turmoil that would find a way to work effectively with its players. In the late 1970s and early 1980s, the NBA was perceived as a league with a dual image problem: too many Black players and too many players using illicit drugs. Several teams had low attendance figures, and even some of the strongest clubs were financially underperforming. In a landmark partnership, the 1983 NBA collective bargaining agreement included a salary cap, a players' licensing guarantee, and a promise that if any team disbanded, their player contracts would be honored by the league (Bradley 2022). The last clause was particularly interesting as there were legitimate concerns that some NBA teams might fold. Even most casual fans know what happened next: the salary cap provided some cost containment, established players Julius Erving, "Magic" Johnson, and Larry Bird continued to play at a high level, the league promoted David Stern to commissioner, and a new crop of dynamic players, led by Michael Jordan, arrived in 1984. Despite his legal background, Stern proved to be a highly effective marketer, helping the league achieve stability and financial success. Though the NBA certainly had more labor pains to endure, it became much easier to find common ground once there were massive increases in revenues.

In the 1980s MLB and the NFL would not have nearly as peaceful labor relationships with their players as did the NBA. MLB owners insisted the new free agency era must involve a Rozelle Rule–like compensation plan. The players vehemently opposed such a proposal, and a strike occurred in 1981 (Miller 1991: 297). On August 9, after 713 games were canceled, the strike ended, and regular season games resumed. While players and owners had reached a compromise, neither side was completely satisfied with the new CBA. The 1981 strike became a prelude for a 1985 strike and 1990 lockout. Though no games were lost in those seasons, the entire conclusion of the 1994 baseball season, including the World Series, was canceled due to another strike. It was not until after the tremendous backlash to the 1994 strike that MLB owners and players found ways to settle their disputes more effectively without labor stoppages.

In the NFL, owners and players had not been able to achieve a true partnership in the 1970s, despite the sport's increasing popularity. By 1982 players demanded a guaranteed portion of overall league revenues. When their demands were not met, the players implemented a fifty-seven-day strike, which canceled seven games for each team. The strike was not a success for the players, as they were not able to maintain their solidarity, and they eventually returned to play having gained some concessions from owners but without getting most of what they had demanded. The 1982 strike set the stage for another strike in 1987 when the CBA expired. The players once again hoped to gain significant concessions from the owners, including a more liberal free agency system. The owners had anticipated the strike and organized replacement players. With NFL games still occurring with "scab" players and the players association split regarding what actions to take, players began to return to work. In some cases Pro Bowl–caliber players lined up with replacement players to play games that counted in the regular season standings. By the third week of replacement-player games, the strike was over, and regular players returned to work. After 1987 the NFL and NFLPA worked more closely, which resulted in few vehement disagreements and a dramatic increase in overall revenues for both owners and players (Easterbrook 2007).

Many of the labor struggles in the NHL occurred in the 1990s and 2000s rather than the 1980s. While considered to be North America's "fourth league," by the 1990s the NHL was still a multibillion-dollar operation, though at times it did not appear to be financially successful. In 1992 a short strike postponed thirty games, but player demands for more compensation and greater control of their marketing activities were essentially met. The lockouts in 1994–95 and 2004–5 were much more damaging to the sport as key issues of free agency and the implementation of a salary cap prevented easy resolutions. The 2004–5 lockout was particularly damaging, as it resulted in the entire season being canceled. Though the NHL has had relative labor peace the last ten years, there is continual concern that upheaval is on the horizon because of the tremendous disparity in franchise revenues. While the league's rapid expansion and relocation into warmer cities in the 1990s created more jobs, it also created a situation where traditional hockey cities often earned much larger revenues than the new locations. Certainly, despite these difficulties, NHL finances are much stronger now than they were in the 1970s and 1980s. The NHL's major problem is as much about how to divide revenues among the owners as how to divide revenues between the owners and the players.

Although there have certainly been tremendous labor disputes in professional sports since 2000 (the NBA lockouts of 1998–99 and 2011–12; NFL player discipline concerns; drug testing across all sports), for the most part, current relations between players and owners are much better than they were from 1960s to the 1990s. Part of that can certainly be attributed to a better understanding of how to negotiate, but thawing labor relations are also the result of there being much more on the table. It is far easier to find solutions to financial problems when there are many millions or billions for a small group of owners and players to divide. Even in the most recent CBA, where several pundits felt NBA owners clearly won the negotiations with the NBA players, the average NBA salary reached $7.7 million a year by the 2019–20 season (Huddleston 2019).

While professional sport leagues were learning how to implement efficient collective bargaining agreements, they were also, more importantly, learning how to maximize revenues. Professional sports have morphed from a sideline passion or hobby for many people into a powerful cultural force in American society. It is not uncommon to see live sporting events on televisions at restaurants that are not sport focused. The 1970s model of three television channels has now morphed into hundreds of channels available on basic cable packages and nearly unlimited access to sports through mobile devices. By 2015 sport-related licensed merchandise sales generated over $14.92 billion dollars in North America alone (Transparency Market Research 2016).

In the 1970s many prominent players in the Big Four sports were largely unknown to the public. It was rare for an athlete to receive a national advertising campaign. However, by the 1980s and 1990s, players such as Joe Montana, Michael Jordan, Wayne Gretzky, Bo Jackson, Charles Barkley, Larry Bird, Deion Sanders, Barry Bonds, and Mario Lemieux had become household names. When Magic Johnson held a press conference in 1991 to announce he had contracted the AIDS virus, it was a worldwide story. Sport's place in society has changed dramatically, with today's players and owners having opportunities to generate tremendous revenues.

In hindsight the arguments made by Bowie Kuhn and other baseball executives predicting a depressed future if free agency were permitted have become comical. Free agency in sport did not destroy leagues; it created an environment where fans research and talk about their team's situation nearly year-round. The thought that free agents might consider signing with another team is a key component of the burgeoning sport talk radio industry. Events like the baseball winter meetings are covered extensively with live broadcasts on site. The growth in sport popularity has even seen an event where names are called become a TV ratings bonanza. The 2019 NFL draft attracted 47.5 million combined viewers over a three-day period; those watching essentially consumed an event where teams phoned in the names of their selections and no real on-field competition occurred (Around the NFL 2019).

Within this dynamic sport marketplace, the NCAA has certainly taken advantage of marketing opportunities. Much like other professional sports leagues, the NCAA increased its television presence and explored new revenue opportunities. At the start of the twenty-first century, one area the NCAA developed was the burgeoning video game marketplace. Like the NBA and NFL, the NCAA partnered with EA Sports to create NCAA football and basketball video games. In many of those games, player names and likenesses could be determined, despite the fact college players ostensibly participate in athletics as an extracurricular, education-focused activity. Among the many people who played the NCAA video games was former UCLA forward Ed O'Bannon. Though O'Bannon had left UCLA in 1995, a video game he was playing had an option to play "classic" teams from the NCAA's past. Concerned about the exploitation of his name, image, and likeness (NIL), O'Bannon sued the NCAA (*O'Bannon v. NCAA*, 2014). At trial various NCAA witnesses offered dire testimony that echoed Bowie Kuhn's predictions many years before. In particular Big Ten commissioner Jim Delany expressed a deep-seated fear about the future of his conference if O'Bannon and other players were to gain access to intellectual property revenue or performance-based compensation. Delany warned the Big Ten, one of the richest conferences, would simply remove itself from an environment where college players could receive additional revenue:

> It has been my longstanding belief that The Big Ten's schools would forgo the revenues in those circumstances and instead take steps to downsize the scope, breadth, and activity of their athletic programs. . . . If a court decided that Title IX is out and players must be paid—I don't think we'd participate in that. I think we'd choose another option. . . . If that's the law

> of the land, if you have to do that, I don't think we would. . . . If that were to happen I think our presidents, our faculties and our boards of trustees would just opt out. . . . I don't know what the opt-out means, whether that's Division III or another model. . . . These alternatives would, in my view, be more consistent with The Big Ten's philosophy that the educational and lifetime economic benefits associated with a university education are the appropriate quid pro quo for its student athletes. (Staples 2013)

At the time Delany made those statements, a number of people noted that he either was completely clueless about the nature of the Big Ten and the importance of big-time college sport to its member universities' marketing efforts, or he was misleading his audience. Later, when testifying under oath, Delaney admitted that he could not completely speak for all of the Big Ten membership, indicating that "some probably would—may be disagreeable" with his earlier thoughts (Vint 2013). Eventually, despite the posturing of Delany and other NCAA witnesses, the court ruled in favor of O'Bannon. However, it capped the compensation college athletes could receive to the cost of attendance (McCann 2015). Though it was a victory for O'Bannon, the capped compensation decree was disappointing, particularly since most Division I schools were already moving toward offering full cost of attendance as part of athletic scholarships once the NCAA had loosened those restrictions at the beginning of the 2015–16 academic year (Kerkhoff 2016).

One other important note from the O'Bannon case that appears to have been quickly forgotten is that the doom-and-gloom scenario did not occur. During the trial Delany was not alone in his assessment that a win for O'Bannon in any form would mean dramatic and unsustainable changes for NCAA member schools. A number of NCAA witnesses offered repeated comments that college sport fans would not support an environment where players could be compensated for their NIL. These arguments are almost identical to those proffered during International Olympic Committee (IOC) debates on whether to allow openly professional athletes to participate in the Summer and Winter Olympic Games. Notably the loss of amateurism in the Olympics has had little impact on the games' overall popularity. The Olympic Games have not only maintained but also strengthened their marketing position since NBA stars and other professionals have begun competing. When Judge Claudia Wilken initially ruled that the NCAA NIL rules were illegal restraints of trade, there was not a mass exodus of college season-ticket holders canceling their football ticket packages. On the contrary the August ruling was released as the new college football season was set to kick off. With the new College Football Playoff (CFP) in place, fan excitement for the playoff system dramatically dwarfed any concern that participating players might soon be able to receive additional compensation.

In the years since the *O'Bannon* ruling, the US Congress has proposed a few college sport NIL bills. In addition, a number of state legislatures have passed rules intended to enhance the intellectual property rights of college athletes. Among the most prominent was California's SB 206, which was signed into law by Governor Gavin Newsome in 2019. The law permitted college athletes to profit from their NIL starting in 2023. Though NCAA president Mark Emmert threatened California schools with postseason bans if they permitted their players to access their NIL rights, others noted that this was likely posturing (Brown 2019). It was highly unlikely that prominent Pac-12 schools such as Stanford; the University of California, Berkeley; UCLA; and the University of Southern California would be banned from bowl games and the NCAA basketball tournaments without significant fan pushback and potential legal proceedings. With the winds of change blowing, other states passed permissive NIL laws, and by 2021 the NCAA—realizing it had no legitimate legal or moral grounds on which to stand—essentially removed itself from the business of policing college players' NIL. However, despite college athletes' gaining a great deal of control over their NIL, the NCAA still refuses to classify profit-athletes as employees and, just as its North American professional sport counterparts, continues to engage in distasteful labor practices.

Conclusion

As one reviews the business history of North American professional sport, it is interesting to note how professional sport owners treated players. In many cases simple, commonsense requests that would have been accepted in nearly every other industry were repeatedly denied professional athletes. Professional sport owners consistently cited collusive rules as necessary to maintaining unique industries. Certainly professional sports are in many ways different from other industries; though teams compete on the field, court, or ice, they are business partners in other matters.

When the MLB players began to exert more control of their working conditions, a paternalistic owner-player bond developed over nearly one hundred years began to fray. Peter Bavasi, the son of former Los Angeles Dodger general manager Buzzie Bavasi, observed that "for years there was this paternalistic relationship between players and management. There was no way [Marvin] Miller could amass any influence unless he destroyed that. So, he stepped in and drove a wedge between them" (quoted in Helyar 1994: 109). This paternalistic relationship, in which owners restricted the freedom and responsibilities of subordinated players, allowed owners to amass huge profits while the players received comparatively minuscule compensation. Many owners justified this relationship, contending that players were incapable of thinking or planning for themselves. Nick Young, the National League's secretary, "saw no point in paying high wages because the players often squandered their money" (quoted in Seymour 1960:

106). Perhaps no other comments express the perception of the players' abilities and place in society as those included in a letter written by Presbyterian minister William R. McGery to Marvin Miller. McGery condemned the players for playing a child's game and mentioned that they "should be thankful for the fame and fortune they had, especially since they performed no useful social function" (quoted in Korr 2002: 117). As appalling and belittling as that comment is, it reflected the mindset of many fans in the 1960s.

When that paternalistic bond broke and the players became freer to engage in an equal business relationship, fans did not suddenly revolt and stop consuming professional sport. In reality the increasing player salaries have had no bearing for most consumers and a small, positive bearing for some who enjoyed following how much players were being paid. In 1980, when Nolan Ryan became MLB's first million-dollar-a-year player, many fans looked forward to who would pass the million-dollar mark next. Ryan's salary (and the subsequent $10 million, $20 million, and $30 million salaries that soon became commonplace) happened because baseball revenues supported it.

The NCAA has taken a similar paternalistic approach to profit-athletes and has failed to discourage fans from condemning entitled, greedy athletes who want to be compensated for their labor. Many message boards are replete with comments that question players' ability to manage any monetary compensation. In addition some fans solely blame profit-athletes for their subpar academic achievements, assigning no culpability to institutions of higher education that recruited and admitted them and then demanded they participate in a highly structured system that includes practice, film study, weight training, travel, community service, and media appearances and that inhibits their ability to succeed academically. Many fans view profit-athletes as kids not satisfied with a full-ride GIA and an educational opportunity. The following comment is indicative of some people's view of profit-athletes receiving a greater portion of overall generated revenues: "There are countless young people who would pay large sums of money to participate in college athletics for the unique advantages it provides to its participants, and yet there are still some people who believe they deserve even more" (Zilinske on Sports 2016).

In addition to fans, some college-sport administrators believe that many profit-athletes are not appropriately appreciative of the benefits provided by Power Five institutions. As University of Texas Women's athletic director Chris Plonsky wrote in a 2009 email to Big 12 commissioner Dan Beebe: "I view these cases as being the result of the entitlement attitude we've created in our revenue sports. We now have threatening (student-athletes)—many of whom, based on grad rates of the 80s and 90s, sucked a whole lot off the college athletics pipe—and now want to buckle the system at the knees at the expense of today's (student-athletes)" (quoted in Trahan 2014).

Another paternalistic argument against classifying profit-athletes as employees is that if profit-athletes are paid a salary, they will have to pay taxes on any wages (Martin 2017). Even though the vast majority of college undergraduates are employed at some point, apparently profit-athletes—who must absorb complex information presented in team handbooks and playbooks and have often also been employees in other jobs—are unable to understand how to file a tax return. Not only does this belittle a profit-athlete's intellect, but it is also offensive to every eighteen-year-old who has made an informed adult decision to join the military and fight for their country, often in hostile areas where death or serious physical injury are distinct possibilities.

Fundamentally the NCAA and supporters of its collegiate model—just as professional sport owners in the past century—do not believe players have a right to fair compensation for their labor. Rather than learning from the past and seeking ways to cooperatively create an equitable system, the NCAA has steadfastly held on to their outdated collegiate model. By refusing to relinquish their power, the possibility of that power being removed without their cooperation greatly increases. Jay Bilas, speaking at the 2012 College Sport Research Institute's 5th Annual CSRI Conference on College Sport, asked the audience to consider what would happen if right before the tip-off of a University of North Carolina–Duke basketball game the players simply walked out of Cameron Indoor Stadium and went to the nearby and much smaller athletic facility to compete. Since the NCAA has repeatedly stated that college athletics is a volunteer activity within the context of an overall educational environment, how could UNC, Duke, the Atlantic Coast Conference, and/or NCAA officials respond to such an action? The players would still be prepared to play, just without the paying fans, television cameras, and other ancillary activities. Would the NCAA say that in order to protect its collegiate model, the players must play at Cameron Indoor in order to generate revenue? With critics, politicians, and members of the media finally asking key questions about the NCAA's business model and its treatment of the players who generate the majority of college sport revenues, any response to such a show of solidarity by the players would likely result in the NCAA losing any credibility regarding its long-proclaimed educational focus. In essence such a show of player unity would likely significantly alter or even end the NCAA's role in commercialized college sport.

References

CASES

Federal Baseball Club v. National League, 259 U.S. 200 (1922).
Flood v. Kuhn. (1972). 407 U.S. 258.
Gardella v. Chandler (1948). 79 F. Supp. 260.

Mackey v. National Football League. (1976). 543 F.2d 606.
O'Bannon v. NCAA. 2014. 7 F.Supp.3d 955.
Oliver v. NCAA (2009). Erie County Court of Common Pleas, State of Ohio 920 N.E.2d 203.
Radovich v. National Football League (NFL), 352 U.S. 445 (1957).
Robertson v. National Basketball Association, 622 F.2d 34 (2d Cir. 1980).
Toolson v. New York Yankees, Inc. (1953). 346 U.S. 356.
United States v. International Boxing Club of New York (348 U.S. 236, 1955).

SECONDARY SOURCES

Around the NFL (2019). "Record Nashville Crowd Hosts Most-Watched Draft." NFL.com, April 29. www.nfl.com/.
Associated Press (2011). "NFL Labor History since 1968." *ESPN.com*, March 3. https://www.espn.com/.
Barro, Robert J. (2002). "The Best Little Monopoly in America." *Bloomberg Businessweek*, December 9. https://www.bloomberg.com/.
Bavasi, Buzzie (1967). "The Great Holdout." *Sports Illustrated*, May 15. https://www.si.com/.
Bierne, Gerald (2022). "Rip Sewell." Baseball Library.com. https://web.archive.org/ (accessed August 17).
Bilas, Jay (2012). Keynote speech, 5th Annual CSRI Conference on College Sport, College Sport Research Institute, Chapel Hill, NC. (April 19).
———. (2017). "Solving the Transfer Problems Is Easy: Let Them Play." ESPN, September 7. http://www.espn.com/.
Bradley, Robert (2022). "Labor Pains Nothing New to the NBA." APBR.org. http://www.apbr.org/labor.html (accessed July 24).
Brown, Matt (2019). "What Happens Next after California's Governor Signed a Bill to Pay NCAA Players?" *SB Nation*, September 30. https://www.sbnation.com/.
Burk, Robert F. (2001). *Much More than a Game: Players, Owners, and American Baseball since 1921*. Chapel Hill: University of North Carolina Press.
Byers, Walter, with Charles Hammer (1995). *Unsportsmanlike Conduct: Exploiting College Athletes*. Ann Arbor: University of Michigan Press.
Dodd, Dennis (2015). "Players About to Get Paid as Money Changes Game in College Athletics." CBS Sports, February 27. https://www.cbssports.com/.
Easterbrook, Gregg (2007). "Tuesday Morning Quarterback Returns!" *ESPN Page 2*, August 10. http://www.espn.com/.
ESPN.com (2015). "Northwestern Football Union Timeline." August 17. http://www.espn.com/.
Farzin, Leah (2015). "On the Antitrust Exemption for Professional Sports in the United States and Europe." *Jeffrey S. Moorad Sports Law Journal* 22, no. 1. http://digitalcommons.law.villanova.edu/.
Gerdy, John R. (2006). *Air Ball: American Education's Failed Experiment with Elite Athletics*. Jackson: University of Mississippi Press.
Harris, David (1986). *The League: The Rise and Decline of the NFL*. New York: Bantam.
Hazell, R. A. (2017). "Len Elmore's Closing Arguments on Paying College Athletes." *Shadow League*, March 23. https://www.theshadowleague.com/.
Heitner, Darren (2014). "College Athletes Are Not Immune to America's Student Debt Dilemma." *Forbes*, June 3. https://www.forbes.com/.

Helyar, John (1994). *Lords of the Realm: The Real History of Baseball.* New York: Villard Books.

Growing a Nation (2018). https://www.agclassroom.org/gan/timeline/farmers_land.htm.

Holton, J. L. (1992). *The Reading Railroad: History of a Coal Age Empire,* vol. 2, *The Twentieth Century.* Laury's Station, PA: Garrigues House.

Huddleston, Tom, Jr. (2019). "These Are the Highest Paid Players in the NBA Right Now." *Make It,* October 22. https://www.cnbc.com/.

Johnson, Angela N. (2015). "NLRB Declines Jurisdiction over Northwestern Football Players—Punts to NCAA to Address Athletes' Grievances." Faegre Drinker, August 18. https://www.faegredrinker.com/.

Kerkhoff, Blair (2016). "They're Not Paychecks, but Major College Athletes Got Extra Scholarship Stipends for First Time This School Year." *Kansas City Star,* June 26. http://www.kansascity.com/.

Korr, Charles P. (2002). *The End of Baseball as We Knew It: The Players Union, 1960–81.* Urbana: University of Illinois Press.

Lederman, Doug (2008). "Settlement raises questions for NCAA." *Inside Higher Ed,* February 4. https://www.insidehighered.com/.

Levin, Josh (2013). "The NCAA Has Truly Lost Its Mind." *Slate,* July 2. Retrieved from http://www.slate.com/.

Mandell, Nina (2015). "Charles Barkley: Paying NCAA Athletes Is 'Crazy.'" *USA Today,* March 10. http://ftw.usatoday.com/.

Martin, Nick (2017). "Check Out an Actually Interesting Debate on Amateurism in College Sports." *Deadspin,* October 24. https://deadspin.com/.

McCann, Michael (2015). "What the Appeals Court Ruling Means for O'Bannon's Ongoing NCAA Lawsuit." *Sports Illustrated,* September 30. https://www.si.com/.

Miller, Marvin (1991). *A Whole Different Ball Game: The Inside Story of the Baseball Revolution.* New York: Carol.

Mullen, Liz (2017). "The Making of a Union." *SportsBusiness Journal,* January 23. http://www.sportsbusinessdaily.com/.

Nagel, Mark (2015). "NCAA Follows Path of MLB History but Fails to Heed Lessons." *Sports Business Journal,* June 1. https://www.sportsbusinessjournal.com/.

Nagel, Mark, and Richard Southall (2005). "NCAA Gets a $56.5 Million Bargain." *Sports Business Journal,* September 12. https://www.sportsbusinessjournal.com/.

———. (2008). "Boycott Might Open Economic Discussion for NCAA Athletes." *Sports Business Journal,* May 12. https://www.sportsbusinessjournal.com/.

———. (2009). "Motivated Plaintiff Could End NCAA's Settlement Game." *SportsBusiness Journal,* November 30. https://www.sportsbusinessjournal.com/.

New, Jake (2015). "A Long Shot." *Inside Higher Ed,* January 27. https://www.insidehighered.com.

Nocera, Joe, and Ben Strauss (2016). "Fate of the Union: How Northwestern Football Union Nearly Came to Be. *Sports Illustrated,* February 24. https://www.si.com/.

Poindexter, Owen (2022). "Average Salaries for MLB Players Increase in 2022." Front Office Sports, April 17. https://frontofficesports.com/average-salaries-for-mlb-players-increase-in-2022/.

Quinn, Sam (2020). "NBA Boycott: How the 1964 All-Star Game Set Stage for 2020 Walk-out in Protest of Jacob Blake Shooting." CBSSports, August 27. https://www.cbssports.com.

Rhoden, William C. (1994). "Sports of the Times: N.F.L.'s Labor Pioneer Remains Unknown." *New York Times*, October 4. http://www.nytimes.com/.
Ridpath, B. David (2012). *Tainted Glory: Marshall University, the NCAA, and One Man's Fight for Justice.* Bloomington, IN: IUniverse.
Sack, Allen L., and Ellen J. Staurowsky (1998). *College Athletes for Hire: The Evolution and Legacy of the NCAA's Amateur Myth.* Westport, CT: Praeger.
Seymour, Harold (1960). *Baseball: The Early Years.* New York: Oxford University Press.
Snyder, Brad (2006). *A Well-Paid Slave: Curt Flood's Fight for Free Agency in Professional Sports.* New York: Penguin.
Solomon, Jon (2014). "Schools Can Give Out 4-Year Athletic Scholarships, but Many Don't." CBS Sports, September 16. https://www.cbssports.com/.
Southall, Richard M., and Ellen J. Staurowsky (2013). "Cheering on the Collegiate Model: Creating, Disseminating, and Imbedding the NCAA's Redefinition of Amateurism." *Journal of Sport and Social Issues* 37, no. 4: 403–29.
Spotrac (2022). "MLB Salary Rankings." August 17. https://www.spotrac.com/.
Staples, Andy (2013). "Delany: Big Ten Could De-emphasize Athletics if O'Bannon Plaintiffs Win." *Sports Illustrated,* March 18. https://www.si.com/college-football/.
Student Loan Hero (2017). "A Look at the Shocking Student Loan Debt Statistics for 2017." September 13. https://studentloanhero.com/.
Trahan, Kevin (2014). "Texas Women's AD Says Athletes Who Want a Cut Are 'Entitled.'" *SB Nation,* June 17. https://www.sbnation.com/.
Transparency Market Research (2022). "Licensed Sports Merchandise Market Insights, 2019–2027." https://www.transparencymarketresearch.com/ (accessed August 17).
Vint, Patrick (2013). "O'Bannon v. NCAA: Jim Delany Admits Division III Claim Was Bluff." *SB Nation,* June 9. https://www.sbnation.com/.
Zagoria, Adam, and Marisa Ingemi (2021). "Rule Change Prompts a Game of Musical Chairs in College Basketball." *New York Times,* April 4. https://www.nytimes.com/.
Zilinske on Sports (2016). "Ungrateful College Athletes Demanding More Pay." April 16. https://zilinskeonsports.wordpress.com/.

Power Five Football and Men's Basketball

At the Center of It All

Richard M. Southall

The NCAA is a multifaceted member organization, which (according to its 2004 strategic plan) has three organizational components:

> The "Association" is the "corporate entity" comprising member institutions, conferences, the governance structure (for example, boards, cabinets, committees) and affiliated entities (for example, coaches associations), as well as student-athletes, coaches and athletics administrators.
>
> The "membership" of the Association is primarily the colleges and universities. It is campus based.
>
> The "national office" represents the employees in Indianapolis who make up the infrastructure of the Association. (NCAA Executive Committee 2004: 2)

As of 2021, the association's membership includes 1,098 athletic departments in 102 athletic conferences across three NCAA divisions, with a diverse range of budgets, revenue sources, and associated expenses. This diversity is celebrated by the NCAA in a public-service announcement that notes the association has "nearly half a million college athletes [who] make up the 19,886 teams that send more than 57,661 participants to compete each year in the NCAA's 90 championships in 24 sports across 3 divisions" (NCAA 2022e).[1]

Historically the NCAA has recognized that this membership diversity includes a range of financial haves and have-nots. While the financial disparities among its members have been apparent since the NCAA's founding in 1906, throughout most of its first fifty-five years these differences were not officially reflected in the NCAA governance structure. In 1973, in response to financial inequities and philosophical differences, the membership divided itself into three divisions, most notably based on differing commercial and professional strategies associated with Division I football and men's basketball programs. Just as in 1973, today's Division I athletic departments by and large exist along a commercial continuum (i.e., revenues and expenses) highly correlated with level of football sponsorship. Division I athletic departments were and are associated with universities that most often have tens of thousands of students and the largest athletics budgets that offer a generous number of grant-in-aid financial packages. Many Division I universities are either a state's flagship or its land-grant university. Almost immediately Division I members recognized that there were marked competitive imbalances in football within the new division. To address this discrepancy, in 1978 Division I was split once again into Division I-A and Division I-AA. Subsequently in 2006 additional modifications to the criteria for membership were instituted, and Division I-A was rebranded as the Football Bowl Subdivision (FBS), while Division I-AA was renamed the Football Championship Subdivision (FCS). Notably, almost all these changes were associated with football: "Schools that participate in bowl games belong to the Football Bowl Subdivision. Those that participate in the NCAA-run football championship belong to the Football Championship Subdivision. A third group [formerly known as Division I-AAA] doesn't sponsor football at all. The subdivisions apply only to football; all other sports are considered simply Division I" (NCAA 2021b). The NCAA recognizes the highly commercialized nature of FBS football. Consequently, FBS teams have to meet minimum attendance requirements (an average of fifteen thousand people in actual or paid attendance per home game), which must be met once in a rolling two-year period (NCAA 2022a, 2022b). Notably FCS teams do not have minimum attendance requirements. Recognizing the growing chasm between FBS and FCS football, FBS conferences have recently limited the number of games versus an FCS opponent that can count toward an FBS team's achieving bowl eligibility at one.

In a recognition of the desire of FBS (and increasingly Power Five) conferences to not share their revenue with non-FBS NCAA members, the bowl system and the variety of national championship formats devised by FBS conferences all have one fundamental purpose: retain control of revenue associated with football. The increased degree of separation between the NCAA and FBS/Power Five conferences has been a constant theme in NCAA governance and litigation since at least the 1980s. The *NCAA v. Board of Regents* (1984) case hinged upon the ability of then Division I-A schools to control television revenue. Subsequently the Power Five conferences achieved significant governance autonomy in 2014. Today this autonomy allows Power Five conferences to enact policies allowing cost-of-attendance stipends and instituting Power Five–specific recruiting rules. In 2014 SEC commissioner Mike Slive made a veiled threat that Power Five conferences might secede from the NCAA: "If we do not achieve a positive outcome under the existing big tent of Division I, we will need to consider the establishment of a venue with similar conferences and institutions where we can enact the desired changes" (Myerberg 2014).

While the NCAA has traditionally sought to brand its collegiate model of athletics (Southall and Staurowsky 2013) as an educational enterprise that helps hundreds of thousands of "student-athletes go pro in something other than sports" (Christianson 2007), a close examination of athletic department and conference governance structures, policies and finances reveals a system in which the economic exploitation of profit-athletes is institutionalized and racialized.[2] In light of this reality, a more appropriate NCAA national branding campaign tagline would be "There are over 480,000 college-athletes, and though most of them do not pursue a professional sports career, all of them benefit from the athletic labor of profit-athletes." While most college sport stakeholders choose to ignore or rationalize the Power Five collegiate model's exploitative nature, this chapter will detail the institutional exploitation inherent in the current college sport industry.

An initial aid to this examination is Sack's (1987) typology of college athletic programs based on the degree of professionalism and commercialization in college sport (fig. 1).

While Sack's (1987) typology is still a useful analytic tool, over the past thirty-plus years, increased hypercommercialization and professionalization within certain college-sport segments necessitate an updated rubric (still with four cells): Cell A, Power Five football, Division I men's basketball;[3] Cell B, Division I women's basketball, Group of Five football, Football Championship Subdivision (FCS) football, and Division I Olympic sports; Cell C, Ivy League sports; and Cell D, Divisions II and III sports (fig. 2).

Cell A reflects the quantitative and qualitative overt differences in hypercommercialism and professionalism in Power Five football and men's basketball, the widening gap between this segment's expenses and revenues and those of all other divisions and sports, and an increased acceptance of hypercommercial,

	Commercialized	**Less Commercialized**
Professional Athletic Scholarships	Cell A Corporate Model	Cell B "Small Time" Corporate Model
Amateur No Athletic Scholarships	Cell C Ivy Model	Cell D Amateur Model

Figure 1. Sack's (1987) typology of college athletic programs.

Cell A Hypercommercialized Professionalized Corporate Model Power-5 FB/MBB	Cell B "Big-to-Small Time" Corporate Model
Cell C Ivy Model	Cell D Corporate— Amateur Model

Figure 2. Updated typology of college athletic programs.

corporatized, and professional management strategies by all segments of college sport (Brand 2006). The updated typology's permeable cell borders signify a core belief among those associated with college sport that the enterprise is fundamentally a sport-entertainment business that should appropriately be conducted in accordance with sound business practices, which include whenever possible maximizing revenues while minimizing labor costs.[4]

The majority of NCAA Division II and Division III athletic departments are still most appropriately placed in Cell D. However, given the NCAA's continual redefinition of amateurism (Southall and Staurowsky 2013), there is no longer a clear line of demarcation between what is amateur and what is corporate. The line is now permeable, with many Division II and Division III athletic departments and/or programs dipping their toes into the "small-time" corporate model (Cell B) whenever feasible. In addition, while Cell C still accounts for the Ivy model, its economic fundamentals have become much more aligned with academic capitalism, which has resulted in an Ivy model that, while genteel and refined, is increasingly commercialized, with associated examples of athletic departments or programs bending the rules, such as Harvard men's basketball throwing caution to the wind and ignoring its long-standing policy against athletic scholarships and making unofficial provisions to provide athletics-related financial aid to its top men's basketball players.

Interestingly membership in Cell B simultaneously expands and contracts, with some NCAA Division II sport programs periodically entering and populating the cell's lower level.[5] Quite often programs aspire to move up within whatever cell they are in and become a bigger small-time program. Cell B contains FCS Division I football, as well as several FBS Division I Olympic sport programs (most notably Division I baseball, hockey, women's basketball, and volleyball). Many programs in Cells B and D offer in-game spectator experiences remarkably similar to those of their professional counterparts (e.g., Minor League Baseball and the Women's National Basketball Association). Significantly, while since 1987 many B and D programs have increasingly adopted a more commercialized, professionalized, and corporatized orientation, they have not (in most cases) generated net positive revenues but have remained dependent on university subsidization and institutional support.

While almost every college-sport program has to one degree or another adopted some elements of a commercial college-sport institutional logic, the hypercommercialism and professionalization of Power Five football and men's basketball programs reflect the pinnacle of a hypercommercial/professional institutional logic antithetical to the NCAA's bylaw 2.9, which articulates the Principle of Amateurism: "Student-athletes shall be amateurs in an intercollegiate sport, and their participation should be motivated primarily by education and by the physical, mental and social benefits to be derived. Student participation in intercollegiate athletics is an avocation, and student-athletes should be protected from exploitation by professional and commercial enterprises" (NCAA 2021c). In an attempt to cope with this conflict, NCAA and athletic department administrators point to Cell D (i.e., NCAA Division III athletics, with more than 190,000 athletes from about 450 colleges and universities who usually play in front of a few hundred close friends and family members) as the exemplar of true amateurism. In this amateur Division III tableau, whistles and muffled cheers echo across college quads, with college students cheering their classmates on in small venues. Winning is important, but (as outlined on the NCAA Division III website)

> academics are the primary focus for Division III student-athletes. The division minimizes the conflicts between athletics and academics and helps student-athletes progress toward graduation through shorter practice and playing seasons and regional competition that reduces time away from academic studies. Participants are integrated on campus and treated like all other members of the student body, keeping them focused on being a student first. (NCAA 2021a)

Division III athletes (according to the NCAA website) "compete not for financial reward, but quite simply, for the love of the game" (ibid.).

In addition, FBS administrators celebrate elite, world-class Olympic sport athletes (Cell B) from the United States and around the world who train and compete at the highest collegiate level in sports such as tennis, golf, water polo, field hockey, fencing, rifle, skiing, ice hockey, swimming and diving, wrestling, track and field, rowing, volleyball, and beach volleyball. While most of these sports attract few spectators, some have become niche sports (e.g., women's volleyball and baseball) drawing several thousand fans. However, most programs still operate at a deficit, since by and large Division I Olympic sports are enormously expensive to finance. Annually nearly 350 Division I colleges and universities sponsor more than 6,000 athletic teams and provide athletic opportunities for more than 170,000 athletes (NCAA 2021b). World-class facilities and highly qualified coaches afford elite athletes unrivaled athletic opportunities and world-class training facilities. Athletes from around the world populate Division I Olympic sport rosters. Each year there are more than 20,000 international NCAA athletes enrolled and competing for universities and colleges in all three NCAA divisions (NCAA 2022c). At least 363 international NCAA athletes competed for their countries in the 2016 Rio Olympic Games. Another 657 athletes represented the United States (NCAA 2022d). The top three sports represented were track and field, swimming and diving, and basketball (ibid.).

The FBS football expenses/revenues continuum reflects the permeable nature of Cells A and B in figure 2 and highlights the substantive differences between Power Five and Group of Five football programs. Even within Power Five there are marked differences in football expenses and revenues.

Not only does the Power Five football and men's basketball market segment have a distinct financial footprint but it also has divergent player sociodemographics; vastly different player, coach, and administrator compensation models; and clearly dissimilar educational outcomes.[6] In addition, while the economic exploitation and resulting racialization vary from segment to segment (being most apparent in market segment 1), the NCAA collegiate model and college sport hegemony is predicated upon spontaneous consent to historic institutional racialization.

Power Five Football and Men's Basketball

While all NCAA divisions and sports are worthy of examination, this chapter's focus is primarily on two sports: Power Five football and men's basketball, whose business models are fundamentally different from those of all other NCAA sports. This difference is evident in the NCAA's Finances of Intercollegiate Athletics Database.[7]

Leaving aside the drastic differences between Power Five and NCAA Division III financial situations, an examination of the Division I finances reveals remarkable differences in revenues. Most notably, for Power Five athletic departments, the top three revenue streams in 2020 were media rights (34.8 percent), donor contributions and endowments (24.0 percent), and ticket sales (18.8 percent). Notably media rights and ticket sales are not in the top three (or even 10 percent of generated revenue sources) for any of the other Division I market segments (Group of Five, FCS, Non FB). Group of Five, FCS, and Division I Subdivision (non FB) departments are all dependent on institution and government supports, student fees, and donor contributions and endowments (see table 1). Not surprisingly, not only do overall revenues decrease from Power Five to other Division I subdivisions, but there is an increasing reliance on institutional

Table 1. Revenue sources

REVENUE SOURCES	D I (P-FIVE)		D I (G-FIVE)		D I (FCS)		D I (NON FB)	
	65		*65*		*127*		*96*	
Inst. & Govt. Support	5.9%	$485,771,501	41.7%	$1,160,047,519	60.0%	$1,675,690,246	64.1%	$1,196,589,596
Student Fees	1.7%	$139,180,748	17.4%	$484,688,621	13.3%	$371,335,944	14.1%	$263,286,124
Media Rights; NCAA/ Conf. Distr. & Bowl Rev.	34.8%	$2,872,554,448	8.1%	$226,195,737	3.9%	$108,308,848	4.2%	$78,756,335
Other Rev.	5.1%	$417,969,573	4.1%	$114,727,833	2.2%	$62,501,816	1.9%	$34,829,016
Ticket Sales	18.8%	$1,551,814,122	7.6%	$211,656,015	4.2%	$116,869,202	3.9%	$72,399,260
Donor Contributions & Endowments	24.0%	$1,981,065,123	11.0%	$304,977,632	10.6%	$295,224,555	7.6%	$141,862,042
Guarantee Rev.	0.6%	$50,003,987	3.8%	$104,824,780	3.3%	$92,484,214	7.6%	$24,811,509
Royalties, Licensing, Advertising	9.2%	$761,188,121	6.2%	$173,400,983	2.5%	$70,290,938	3.0%	$55,306,383
Total	100.0%	$8,259,547,623	100.0%	$2,780,519,120	100.0%	$2,792,705,763	100.0%	$1,867,840,265

Source. See https://www.ncaa.org/sports/2019/11/12/finances-of-intercollegiate-athletics-database.aspx.

and governmental supports, which is the single largest source of revenue for non–Power Five departments.

In addition to marked differences in revenue sources, the drastic difference in the amount of revenues offers clear evidence of the fundamental difference between Cell A (Power Five) and all other cells (Group of Five, FCS, non FB). The difference between Power Five and Group of Five media rights revenues provides a stark snapshot of the haves and have-nots:

- Power Five media rights (2020), $2.9 billion;
- Group of Five media rights (2020), $226 million;
- FCS media rights (2020), $108 million (it should be noted that the FCS has 127 members);
- Division I (non-FB) Subdivision (2020), $79 million.

As can be seen, there are marked differences in expenses and revenues between Power Five college sport and all other Division I levels. In addition the differences between Power Five and Division III revenue sources and amounts are drastic (see table 2). Comparing one specific revenue source is illuminative. The approximate $486 million of institutional and government support in Power Five accounts for only 5.9 percent of Power Five athletic department revenues. By contrast, in Division III sport (with 247 members), this same source of revenue accounts for 87.2 percent of all revenues and is almost $50 million more than Power Five's institutional and government support.

In addition to the marked differences evident in a cursory snap-shot examination of these revenue sources, some brick-and-mortar examples offer evidence

Table 2. Revenue sources/amounts—Power Five vs. Division III

REVENUE SOURCES	DIVISION I (POWER FIVE)		DIVISION III (FOOTBALL)	
	65		*247*	
Inst. & Govt. Support	5.9%	$485,771,501	87.2%	$535,319,710
Student Fees	1.7%	$139,180,748	3.3 %	$20,394,003
Media Rights; NCAA/ Conf. Distr. & Bowl Rev.	34.8%	$2,872,554,448	0.4%	$2,254,035
Other Rev.	5.1%	$417,969,573	2.0%	$12,377,345
Ticket Sales	18.8%	$1,551,814,122	0.5%	$3,319,043
Donor Contributions & Endowments	24.0%	$1,981,065,123	6.1%	$37,199,060
Guarantee Rev.	0.6%	$50,003,987	0.1%	$399,620
Royalties, Licensing, Advertising	9.2%	$761,188,121	0.5%	$2,833,657
Total	100.0%	$8,259,547,623	100.0%	$ 614,096,473

of the fundamental difference between Power Five football and men's basketball and all other levels and types of college sports:

1. Eight of the ten largest stadiums in the world are Power Five football venues (see table 3).
2. Seven of the ten largest college basketball arenas are those of Power Five programs, with capacities that range from 19,000 to 34,616 (see table 4).
3. Twenty-two of the top twenty-five average attendance totals in Division I men's basketball are Power Five programs (see table 5).

In a prescient statement, Sack (1987: 31) noted: "In some schools, football and basketball have become university run businesses [*sic*] which generate millions in revenue and make profit maximization their primary concern." In the

Table 3. Largest stadiums in the world (2020)

STADIUM	CAPACITY
Rungrado 1st of May Stadium (North Korea)	114,000
Michigan Stadium (Big Ten)	107,601
Beaver Stadium (Penn State; Big Ten)	106,572
Ohio Stadium (Ohio State; Big Ten)	104,944
Kyle Field (Texas A&M; SEC)	102,733
Neyland Stadium (Tennessee; SEC)	102,455
Tiger Stadium (LSU; SEC)	102,321
Bryant-Denny Stadium (Alabama; SEC)	101,821
Darrell K. Royal–Texas Memorial Stadium (Texas; Big 12)	100,119
Melbourne Cricket Ground (Australia)	100,024

Table 4. NCAA Division I top ten arenas (2020)

COLLEGE BASKETBALL ARENAS	CAPACITY
Carrier Dome (Syracuse; ACC)	34,616
Rupp Arena (Kentucky; SEC)	23,000
KFC Yum! Center (Louisville; ACC)	22,090
Dean Smith Center (North Carolina; ACC)	21,750
Thompson-Boling Arena (Tennessee; SEC)	21,678
Capital One Arena (Georgetown; Big East)	20,356
Madison Square Garden (St. John's; Big East)	19,812
PNC Arena (North Carolina State; ACC)	19,557
Bud Walton Arena (Arkansas; SEC)	19,368
Marriott Center (BYU; WCC)	19,000

Table 5. 2018 NCAA Men's basketball attendance—Top 25

RANK	SCHOOL	GAMES	ATTENDANCE	AVERAGE
1	Kentucky	18	393,743	21,874
2	Syracuse	19	407,778	21,462
3	North Carolina	15	275,681	18,378
4	Wisconsin	18	310,901	17,272
5	Creighton*	18	306,000	17,000
6	Louisville	22	371,427	16,883
7	Kansas	18	294,206	16,344
8	Tennessee	15	243,148	16,209
9	Arkansas	17	275,084	16,181
10	Indiana	18	280,631	15,590
11	Nebraska	17	263,367	15,492
12	NC State	19	289,807	15,253
13	Missouri	16	240,976	15,061
14	Michigan State	17	251,549	14,797
15	Maryland	18	264,164	14,675
16	Arizona	16	230,947	14,434
17	Purdue	17	243,884	14,343
18	BYU*	16	227,692	14,230
19	Iowa State	16	225,941	14,121
20	Virginia	17	236,703	13,923
21	Ohio State	18	242,196	13,495
22	Alabama	17	227,640	13,390
23	Dayton*	16	207,950	12,996
24	South Carolina	15	189,265	12,617
25	Illinois	18	227,051	12,613

*Non-Power Five university.

Source: http://fs.ncaa.org/Docs/stats/m_basketball_RB/Reports/attendanceYBYtop25.pdf.

institutional field of Power Five college sport, what was some in 1987 has become all. These two sports provide tremendously popular television and live-streaming content for ESPN, Fox, NBC, CBS, and ABC. In addition to these broadcast networks, all Power Five conferences have their own network (ACC Network, Big Ten Network, Big 12 Digital Network, Pac-12 Network, SEC Network). These digital platforms form the economic backbone of the big-time college sport industry. All Power Five football and men's basketball programs

Table 6. NCAA Power Five finances

RANK	UNIVERSITY	CONFERENCE	REVENUE	EXPENSES
1	Texas	Big 12	$223,879,781	$204,234,897
2	Texas A&M	SEC	$212,748,002	$169,012,456
3	Ohio State	Big Ten	$210,548,239	$220,572,956
4	Michigan	Big Ten	$197,820,410	$190,952,175
5	Georgia	SEC	$174,042,482	$143,299,554
6	Penn State	Big Ten	$164,529,326	$160,369,805
7	Alabama	SEC	$164,090,889	$185,317,681
8	Oklahoma	Big 12	$163,126,695	$157,958,270
9	Florida	SEC	$159,706,937	$141,829,002
10	LSU	SEC	$157,787,782	$148,977,880
11	Wisconsin	Big Ten	$157,660,107	$154,621,828
12	Florida State	ACC	$152,757,883	$150,147,316
13	Auburn	SEC	$152,455,416	$139,260,711
14	Iowa	Big Ten	$151,976,026	$146,282,275
15	Kentucky	SEC	$150,435,842	$144,886,246
16	Tennessee	SEC	$143,765,903	$142,976,173
17	South Carolina	SEC	$140,695,659	$136,879,732
18	Michigan State	Big Ten	$140,010,865	$135,655,740
19	Louisville	ACC	$139,955,824	$151,167,940
20	Arkansas	SEC	$137,497,788	$129,620,361
21	Nebraska	Big Ten	$136,233,460	$124,148,206
22	Clemson	ACC	$133,861,515	$131,978,513
23	Washington	Pac-12	$133,792,677	$131,317,636
24	Minnesota	Big Ten	$130,456,454	$129,450,256
25	Indiana	Big Ten	$127,832,628	$114,822,135
26	Oregon	Pac-12	$127,508,498	$128,943,543
27	Arizona State	Pac-12	$121,698,840	$118,404,377
28	Kansas	Big 12	$121,553,307	$108,881,800
29	Illinois	Big Ten	$118,565,501	$120,168,951
30	Mississippi State	SEC	$112,273,809	$ 98,832,615
31	Purdue	Big Ten	$110,844,907	$102,026,477
32	Virginia	ACC	$110,219,117	$112,621,238
33	Maryland	ACC	$108,796,303	$108,785,924
34	Mississippi	SEC	$108,442,428	$113,013,400

RANK	UNIVERSITY	CONFERENCE	REVENUE	EXPENSES
35	UCLA	Pac-12	$108,412,967	$127,339,042
36	North Carolina	ACC	$107,812,619	$110,809,706
37	Missouri	SEC	$106,610,244	$108,398,447
38	Arizona	Pac-12	$105,091,389	$100,565,835
39	Rutgers	Big Ten	$103,251,280	$103,167,344
40	West Virginia	Big 12	$102,680,928	$98,249,890

Source: https://sports.usatoday.com/ncaa/finances/.

generate significant revenues, with at least forty Power Five athletic departments reporting 2018–19 revenues of at least $100 million (Berkowitz, Wynn, and McManus 2019), more than triple the number in 2014 (Table 6). It should also be noted that thirty-eight departments reported expenses of at least $100 million (table 6). Power Five athletic departments clearly eat what they kill, spending most revenues generated. While year to year some departments may set aside a percentage of generated funds, since Power Five athletic departments are ostensibly nonprofit entities, they are not incentivized to practice fiscal constraint.

The Power Five football and men's basketball industry has historically demonstrated a steady rate of growth, of which other industries would be envious (Finkel, Martin, and Paley Foxworth 2013). Every year, Power Five athletic departments (consistent with the revenue theory of costs) fail to practice fiscal restraint in the areas of capital expenditures or coaches' salaries. In spite of the NCAA and Power Five members being found to violate US antitrust laws (e.g., *O'Bannon v. NCAA*, 2014, 2015), Power Five football and men's basketball programs still conspire to limit profit-athletes' compensation, portraying relatively small monthly cost-of-attendance payments (four to six hundred dollars on average) as non-pay stipends and travel awards to conference and NCAA championships (that generate millions of dollars in revenues) as magnanimous gestures that allow athletes' families to "be included in the memories that come from being present in the moment" (Hobson 2016).

Ironically, while Power Five athletic administrators consistently complain that their departments are cash-strapped, over the last ten years Power Five football and men's basketball programs have generated such significant revenues that Power Five haves face a difficult balancing act: consistent with NCAA's Principle of Amateurism, they must protect amateur football and men's basketball players from exploitation by professional and commercial enterprises (i.e., not pay them) while also forestalling a work stoppage by increasing player compensation through cost-of-attendance stipends, extending training-table offerings, constructing opulent football and basketball facilities, paying for family travel to NCAA men's and women's Final Four tournaments, and allowing the CFP to pay travel expenses for families. While holding fast to the NCAA commitment of never paying players, NCAA and Power Five athletic administrators have simultaneously incrementally increased athlete compensation in order to demonstrate that they are "committed to providing student-athletes with the best possible experience" (Hobson 2016). Indicative of this balancing act, Power Five athletic departments often purchase items or enhance facilities with accoutrements (e.g., lazy river, recovery cove, waterfalls, barbershop, slide, mini-golf course) that have little educational value while relying upon the Principle of Amateurism as justification for not paying Power Five football and men's basketball players a negotiated market wage.

The Power Five college-sport industry's pre-COVID-19 fiscal health was reflected in hundreds of millions of dollars in 2019 conference distributions to Power Five members (table 7). The Big Ten led the way, distributing $781.5 million (an average of $55.6 million per member athletic department; Berkowitz 2020, 2021).

Since 2014, the four-team College Football Playoff (CFP) has provided additional millions of dollars in revenue that dwarfs March Madness, which is dominated by Power Five schools.[8] Only the Division I men's basketball championship game, held in a football stadium, has CFP-like attendance (table 8). Amid this growth curve, conflicts between Power Five conferences and the rest of the NCAA membership threatened to paralyze the NCAA governance process.

Table 7. 2019 Power Five conference distributions

CONFERENCE	DISTRIBUTION	PER TEAM
SEC	$721 million	$45.3. million*
Big Ten	$781.5 million	$55.6 million**
Big 12	$439 million	$38.2–42 million
Pac-12	$530.4 million	$32.2 million
ACC	$455.4 million	$27.6–34 million***

*Mississippi did not get a full share because its football team was banned from postseason play for the 2019 season.

**The Big Ten brought in $781.5 million, which resulted in payouts of about $55.6 million to each of the fourteen-team conference's twelve longest-standing members. Maryland and Rutgers received smaller shares, but both schools also received loans from the conference against future revenue shares.

***Notre Dame received $6.8 million.

Table 8. Year-by-year March Madness finals' attendance (2014–19)

YEAR	ATTENDANCE
2014	79,238
2015	71,149
2016	74,340
2017	76,168
2018	67,831
2019	72,711

Source: http://www.ncaa.org/championships/statistics/ncaa-mens-basketball-attendance.

A look at the tournament's financial indicators highlights the scale and scope of March Madness:

- Television contract: $19.6 billion over twenty-two years (avg. $891 million per year);
- Advertising revenue: $1.24 billion in 2017, $1.32 billion in 2018, and $1.42 billion in 2019;
- Ticket sales: $160 million for sixty-eight games in 2018 (Vidovic 2019).

In addition to helping Power Five schools support their Olympic sports, March Madness revenue subsidizes every NCAA-sponsored national championship in Division I, II, and III. The tournament also fuels a number of burgeoning subindustries, most notably gaming, with more than $12.1 billion reportedly wagered on March Madness in 2018 (ibid.).

Markedly, since Power Five profit-athletes are not viewed as employees, do not have a players association, and do not have the ability to collectively bargain for working or living conditions, they eat, train, study, and perform within a tightly controlled, paternalistic, "total institution" system (Goffman 1968), with training regimens that are often more demanding than those of NFL or NBA teams. As a result of their long workday, profit-athletes are cut off from other college students for a good portion of each day (Hatteberg 2018; Southall and Weiler 2014). While the Power Five conferences are not required to collectively bargain with profit-athletes over wages or working conditions, in response to sporadic and aborted attempts by Power Five football players to unionize (e.g., Northwestern University), strike (e.g., University of Missouri), or bargain with athletic departments (e.g., Clemson University), football and basketball programs have increasingly offered profit-athletes a variety of financial inducements and compensation packages (including increased grants-in-aid, cost-of-attendance stipends, and unlimited food, etc.), all the while insisting that granting such benefits does not affect the amateur, nonemployee status of profit-athletes.

While the NCAA insists—for obvious legal and policy reasons—that all college athletes are the same, this book focuses almost exclusively on Power Five football and NCAA Division I men's basketball players. This concentration is intentional, since these profit-athletes generate (through their athletic labor) a disproportionate amount of college sport's revenues. As will become clear, the diversity in budgets, revenue sources, and expenses that is celebrated by the NCAA national office and its members is possible in large part because of the economic exploitation of NCAA profit-athletes. The nearly half-million mostly White and middle- and upper-class college athletes who compete each year in the NCAA's ninety championships in twenty-four sports across three divisions in many ways owe their opportunities, benefits, and privileges to a college sport enterprise that denies profit-athletes access to that enterprise while also disproportionately failing to deliver equal access to the educational opportunities that are college sport's supposed quid pro quo.

Notes

1. As of September 2021, NCAA division membership is as follows: Division I, 351 schools (https://www.ncaa.org/our-division-i-members); Division II, 309 schools (https://www.ncaa.org/our-division-ii-members); and Division III, 449 schools (https://www.ncaa.org/our-division-iii-members).

2. Profit-athletes are college athletes whose market value exceeds the value of their grant-in-aid (GIA). Conversely a loss-athlete's GIA exceeds the athlete's market value. Therefore loss-athletes may appropriately be viewed as college sport consumers. Microlevel or individual racialization involves an individual's actions (discrimination) that are motivated by an individual's beliefs (prejudice) about racial/ethnic minorities. Meso-level institutional racialization in Power Five college sport is reflected in institutional policies, practices, and procedures that result in the economic exploitation of an athletic labor force (i.e., profit-athletes) that disproportionately comprises racial/ethnic minorities (e.g., Black athletes in Power Five football and men's basketball). For a detailed discussion of meso-level racialization in Power Five football and men's basketball, see "The Exploitation of Power Five Profit Athletes: Paternalism, Patriarchy, and Racialization."

3. The Power Five (autonomy) conferences include the Atlantic Coast Conference, the Big Ten Conference, the Big 12 Conference, the Pacific-12 Conference, and the Southeastern Conference.

4. In the NCAA collegiate model, coaches and administrators are management executives, as opposed to players, who are labor.

5. The use of lower and upper levels reflects the amount of expenses and revenues associated with a given department, sport, or program (e.g., lower-level programs have relatively fewer expenses and generate less revenues).

6. See https://www.csri.org/reports.

7. See https://www.ncaa.org/sports/2019/11/12/finances-of-intercollegiate-athletics-database.aspx.

8. Of the sixty-eight bids to March Madness, thirty-two automatically go to the conference champions from the NCAA Division I conferences. In 2019, twenty-six of the remaining thirty-six (72%) bids went to Power Five teams.

References

CASES

O'Bannon v. NCAA (2014). 7 F.Supp.3d 955 (N. D. Cal.).

O'Bannon v. NCAA (2015). WL 5712106 (9th Cir. 30 September 2015).

SECONDARY SOURCES

Berkowitz, Steve (2020). "Power Five Conferences Had Over $2.9 Billion in Revenue in Fiscal 2019, New Tax Records Show." *USA Today,* July 10. https://www.usatoday.com/.

———. (2021). "Southeastern Conference's Revenue Increased Slightly to $729 Million in 2020 Fiscal Year." *USA Today,* February 4. https://www.usatoday.com/.

Branch, Taylor (2011). "The Shame of College Sports." *Atlantic,* October, 80–110. http://www.theatlantic.com/.

Brand, Myles (2006). "Brand Charts Course for Collegiate Model's Next Century." Speech delivered to the NCAA Convention, January 7. https://mylesbrand.com/.

Christianson, Erik (2007). "NCAA Launches Latest Public Service Announcements, Introduces New Student-Focused Website." NCAA Press Release Archive, March 13. http://fs.ncaa.org/Docs/PressArchive/2007/Announcements/.

Farmer, S. M. (2012). "How the University Handles Admissions for Student Athletes." *Raleigh (NC) News and Observer,* November 24. http://academicreview.unc.edu/.

Finkel, Ross, Trevor Martin, and Jon Paley, dirs. (2013). *Schooled: The Price of College Sports.* Makuhari Media.

Gaines, Cork (2017). "The 27 Schools That Make at Least $100 Million in College Sports." *Business Insider,* November 25. https://www.businessinsider.com/.

Gallo, D. J. (2011). "An Athlete's Commencement Address." ESPN.com, May 17. http://www.espn.com/.

Goffman, Erving (1968). *Asylums: Essays on the Social Situation of Mental Patients and Other Inmates.* New York: Penguin.

Gramsci, Antonio (1971). *Selections from the Prison Notebooks.* Edited and translated by Quentin Hoare and Geoffrey N. Smith. New York: International.

Hatteberg, Sarah (2018). "Under Surveillance: Collegiate Athletics as a Total Institution." *Sociology of Sport Journal* 35, no. 2: 149–58.

Hobson, Jackie. (2016). "NCAA to Again Pay Final Four Family Travel Expenses." NCAA.org, October 10. http://www.ncaa.org/.

Hosick, Michelle Brutlag (2019). "NCAA Working Group to Examine Name, Image and Likeness." NCAA.org, May 14. http://www.ncaa.org/.

Infante, Nick (2019). "Big Ten Makes Good (Money)." *College Athletics Clips,* May 19. https://mailchi.mp/collegeathleticsclips/.

Jepperson, R. L. (1991). "Institutions, Institutional Effects, and Institutionalism." In *The New Institutionalism in Organizational Analysis,* edited by W. W. Powell and P.J. DiMaggio, 143–63). Chicago: University of Chicago Press.

McCormick, Robert A., and Amy Christian McCormick (2010). "Major College Sports: A Modern Apartheid." *Texas Review of Entertainment and Sports Law* 12, no. 1: 13–51.

McKay, Brett, and Kate McKay (2022). "When Christianity Was Muscular." *The Art of Manliness.* Accessed July 29. https://www.artofmanliness.com/.

Myerberg, Paul (2014). "Mike Slive Says SEC Must Pursue Separation if NCAA Autonomy Isn't Gained." *USA Today,* July 14. https://www.usatoday.com/.

———. (2007). "NCAA launches Latest Public Service Announcements, Introduces New Student-Focused Website." NCAA Press Release Archive, March 13. http://fs.ncaa.org/.

National Collegiate Athletic Association (2012). "Emmert Cheers on the Collegiate Model." NCAA.org, January 12. http://www.ncaa.org/.

———. (2014). "Division I Steering Committee on Governance: Recommended Governance Model." NCAA.org, July 18. https://www.ncaa.org/.

———. (2021a). "About Division III." NCAA.org. https://www.ncaa.org/.

———. (2021b). "NCAA Division I." NCAA.org. https://www.ncaa.org/.

———. (2021c). "2.9. The Principle of Amateurism." NCAA LSDBi. https://web3.ncaa.org /lsdbi/.

———. (2022a). "Divisional Differences and the History of Multidivision Classification." NCAA.org. http://www.ncaa.org/ (accessed July 29).

———. (2022b). "Football Bowl Subdivision—Membership Requirements." NCAA.org . http://fs.ncaa.org/ (accessed July 29).

———. (2022c). "International student-athlete participation." NCAA.org. https://www.ncaa .org/ (accessed July 29).

———. (2022d). "Putting Rio within Reach." NCAA.org. https://www.ncaa.org/ (accessed July 29).

———. (2022e). "What Is the NCAA?" NCAA.org. https://www.ncaa.org/ (accessed July 29).

National Collegiate Athletic Association Executive Committee (2004). *NCAA Strategic Plan.* Indianapolis: National Collegiate Athletic Association.

New, Jake (2014). "Autonomy Gained." *Inside Higher Ed,* August 8. https://www.inside highered.com/.

Olson, Eric (2019). "Special Admissions Called 'Original Sin' of College Sports." ABC News, March 16. https://abcnews.go.com/Sports/wireStory/.

Phillips, Coretta (2011). "Institutional Racism and Ethnic Inequalities: An Expanded Multilevel Framework." *Journal of Social Policy* 40, no. 1: 173–92.

Plaschke, Bill (2010). "Paying College Players Is an Inherently Bad Idea." *Los Angeles Times,* November 18. https://www.latimes.com/.

Renfro, Wally (2006). "NCAA News Release: NCAA President Delivers State of the Association Address." NCAA Press Release Archive, January 7. http://fs.ncaa.org/Docs/Press Archive/2006/.

Runstedtler, Theresa (2018). "More than Just Play: Unmasking Black Child Labor in the Athletic Industrial Complex." *Journal of Sport and Social Issues* 42, no. 3: 152–69.

Russo, Ralph D. (2019). "NCAA to Consider Allowing Athletes to Profit from Names." Associated Press, May 14. https://apnews.com/article/dc0de44c2f5a46be9a7b1f60a266efb1.

Sack, Allen L. (1987). "College Sport and the Student-Athlete." *Journal of Sport and Social Issues* 11, nos. 1/2: 31–48. https://doi.org/10.1177/019372358701100103.

Smith, Earl (2007). *Race, Sport, and the American Dream.* Durham, NC: Carolina Academic Press.

Southall, Richard M. (2014). "NCAA Graduation Rates: A Quarter-Century of Re-branding Academic Success." *Journal of Intercollegiate Sport* 7, no. 2: 120–33. http://dx.doi.org/10.1123/jis.2014-0134.

Southall, Richard M., M. T. Brown, M. S. Nagel, and C. Southall (2014). "Media March Madness: A Comparative Content Analysis of 2006 and 2011 NCAA Division I Men's National Basketball Tournament Broadcasts." *International Journal of Sport Management* 15, no. 3: 367–83.

Southall, Richard M., and Richard T. Karcher (2016). "Distributive Injustice: An Ethical Analysis of the NCAA's 'Collegiate Model of Athletics' and Its Jurisprudence." *International Sports Law Journal* 15, no. 3: 210–25. https://doi.org/10.1007/s40318-015-0084-6.

Southall, Richard M., Mark S. Nagel, John M. Amis, and Crystal Southall (2008). "A Method to March Madness: Institutional Logics and the 2006 National Collegiate Athletic Association Division I Men's Basketball Tournament." *Journal of Sport Management* 22, no. 6: 677–700.

Southall, Richard M., and Ellen J. Staurowsky (2013). "Cheering on the Collegiate Model: Creating, Disseminating, and Imbedding the NCAA's Redefinition of Amateurism." *Journal of Sport and Social Issues* 37, no. 4: 403–29.

Southall, Richard M., and Jonathan D. Weiler (2014). "NCAA D-I Athletic Departments: Twenty-First Century-Company Towns." *Journal of Issues in Intercollegiate Athletics* 7: 161–86.

Sperber, Murray (1998). *Onward to Victory: The Creation of Modern College Sports.* New York: Holt.

Staurowsky, Ellen J., and Allen L. Sack (2005). "Reconsidering the Use of the Term Student-Athlete in Academic Research." *Journal of Sport Management* 19, no. 2: 103–16.

St. Louis, Brett (2009). "Post-Marxism, Black Marxism and the Politics of Sport." In *Marxism, Cultural Studies and Sport,* edited by Ben Carrington and Ian McDonald, 109–30. New York: Routledge.

Trahan, Kevin (2014). "Texas Women's AD Says Athletes Who Want a Cut Are 'Entitled.'" *SB Nation,* June 17. https://www.sbnation.com/college-football/.

Van Rheenen, Derek (2013). "Exploitation in College Sports: Race, Revenue, and Educational Reward." *International Review for the Sociology of Sport* 48, no. 5: 550–71.

Vidovic, Andrej (2019). "NCAA March Madness Handle Will Go over $12.1 Billion." Real Money Action, March 15. https://www.realmoneyaction.com/.

Vrousalis, Nicholas (2013). "Exploitation, Vulnerability, and Social Domination." *Philosophy and Public Affairs* 41, no. 2: 131–57.

Challenging the NCAA's Collegiate Model Paradigm

Richard M. Southall
and Mark S. Nagel

In 1817 poet and philosopher Samuel Taylor Coleridge suggested readers willingly suspend disbelief about even the most outrageous and implausible story as long as "human interest and a semblance of truth" are skillfully woven into the narrative (Coleridge 2008: 314). Such disbelief is crucial to literature, television, film, politics, and the business of big-time college sport. Almost from college sport's inception, its fans and well-meaning reformers have willingly accepted a mythology that college athletes are simply students engaged in an extracurricular activity—a hobby. They forego critical analysis and tacitly accept legal, financial, sociological, marketing, and educational fictions, which in any other walk of life they would likely vehemently denounce.

Those who work in and those who consume college sport are subject to a range of unconscious biases designed to perpetuate their innate fandom learned at a young age. Yesterday's youngsters, who often went to their first college football or basketball game with a parent, older sibling, or as part of an extended family outing, are today's fans (including students and alumni), as well as athletic department administrators, university faculty, and the corporate partners and sponsors who populate luxury suites and club seats, and form game-day backdrops across the country. These consumers, policy makers, lawyers, doctors, plumbers, truck drivers, and legislators construct a college sport reality in which they are Kunda's (1987) "motivated reasoners," who seek information that reinforces the college-sport mythology they desperately want to believe instead of rationally evaluating the business of college sport. Just as in political campaigns (Redlawsk 2002), in which voters' candidate evaluations are biased toward existing preferences, college sport stakeholders practice biased decision making. They easily assimilate congruent information but ignore and/or deny conflicting data (ibid.). Such motivated reasoning—along with the coordinated use of branding/rebranding strategies by college sport stakeholders—is why college sport reform will not likely derail the NCAA's commercial sport enterprise.

Unable to even entertain the possibility that NCAA college athletes could be employees, the typical college sport fan, sponsor, reformer, legislator, or administrator is M. H. Abrams's (1958: viii) "skilled reader [who] in some fashion suspends his disbelief so as to go along in imagination with express judgments and doctrines from which he would ordinarily dissent." In literature willing suspension of disbelief allows readers to enjoy fictional realities populated by zombies, hobbits, and student-athletes. To one degree or another, most college sport reformers engage in a suspension of disbelief, ignoring decades of contrary evidence as they profess the sanctity of a Platonic ideal of college sport and amateurism to which they hope college sport will return.

The tacit acceptance of the NCAA's expressed college sport paradigm allows fans, sponsors, and reformers to hope that magically college sport can be saved if only athletic programs truly embrace the amateurism mythology (even though the NCAA has not been involved in amateur athletics since at least 1956, when members voted to allow athletic grants-in-aid). Overlooking or ignoring uncomfortable facts to hold tight to their cherished amateur facade requires college sport stakeholders to violate the constitutional and human rights of big-time college sport's labor force—NCAA profit-athletes in Football Bowl Subdivision (FBS) football and men's basketball whose market value exceeds the value of their grant-in-aid—and inflict long-term financial, intellectual, and emotional harm upon these unorganized laborers.

Consistently college sport's stakeholders have held sacrosanct the NCAA's collegiate model of athletics, the mythology of which portrays college athletes as students participating in college sport as a leisurely avocation, balancing their academic, social, and athletic experiences (NCAA 2022a) as they obtain a well-rounded education, replete with guest lectures by well-known authors, concerts by world-renowned virtuosos, and lazy spring days on the quad playing frisbee. When institutional dissonance arises, in the form of academic fraud or bribery scandals in which bogus classes are uncovered or a player being paid for his athletic talents, cries arise to reform or return the collegiate model to its original pure state. Instead of adopting a commonsense professional model, almost universally college sport leaders vow to uphold, reform, and/or protect the collegiate model.

Echoing this point of view, in 2012 NCAA president Mark Emmert vowed to update the model: "So here we are at this curious fork in the road, and we have to decide. Are we going to take the collegiate model, maximize our values, make the changes we need to make, but bring the collegiate model up to the 21st century consistent with our values as academic enterprises? Or are we going to wave the white flag, throw in the towel and say it's too much?" (Emmert 2012: 13). According to this NCAA collegiate-model paradigm, whatever reform efforts are to be undertaken must be based upon "two very simple, complicated, but simple propositions. One, that student-athletes have to be students in all the ways that we mean that, and two, we have to behave with integrity, consistent with our own values and our own rules structure" (ibid.: 10).

From a business perspective, the NCAA paradigm is also a globally recognized, multifaceted institutional brand.[1] The college sport brand represents an NCAA membership that includes 1,121 (and counting) colleges and universities, within several distinct brand categories (i.e., NCAA Divisions I, II, and III), and spanning twenty-four sports and ninety discrete championship products—with traditional blue-collar sports, such as football, wrestling, and basketball, as well as country club sports, including soccer, volleyball, lacrosse, swimming, golf, and tennis. In addition to being significant revenue streams, for many large research-intensive universities their FBS football and Division I men's basketball programs are major marketing and donor-acquisition platforms, as well as important student-recruitment vehicles. As is often expressed, athletics is the front porch of these universities.

In order to present a coherent product to its various stakeholders and consumers, the college sport industry engages in coordinated brand-management decision-making (NCAA 2022c). NCAA member universities, deeply committed to academic capitalism, which Slaughter and Leslie (1997: 11) describe as "market and market-like behaviors on the part of universities and faculty," have tasked their athletic departments with managing their college-sport brands in much the same way as corporations in any other business. This includes athletic departments developing brand positioning strategies, integrating brand marketing plans across conferences and divisions, and continually assessing the brand's performance both on and off the field. In short, athletic department CEOs (i.e., athletic directors) are responsible for growing and strategically managing the university's athletic brand. In addition to wanting to believe big-time college sport's amateur mythology, college-sport stakeholders are encouraged to suspend disbelief and engage in motivated reasoning through a combination of coordinated branding/rebranding and institutional propaganda strategies.

While these branding/rebranding activities are a normal part of almost all markets, in several subtle ways the college sport brand is unique, reflecting a bifurcated college sport landscape in which profit-athletes, who are in almost all ways revenue-generating employees, must be constantly and consistently portrayed not as employees but as students engaged in a mere hobby or diversion. For more than one hundred years, in order to blunt "cynicism over the commercialization of our most visible athletic programs [that] has reached epidemic proportions" (Carter 2001: 64), college sport stakeholders, including the NCAA national office, member universities, athletic departments, and corporate sponsors and partners, have consistently demonstrated "(a) a shared understanding of how individual initiatives should both reflect and connect to the brand, and (b) the discipline to stay on message and on brand" (NCAA 2010b; Nocera 2012). As part of this messaging, college athletes are represented as being just like other college students, fully integrated into the academic community (Hosick 2014; Hosick and Durham 2017). The NCAA national office, member institutions, conferences, and affiliated organizations utilize similar brand-management strategies and elements of institutional propaganda to cope with cognitive dissonance that many college-sport consumers recognize on an intellectual level but emotionally look away from as they celebrate their team's latest victory over their rival. They willingly ignore the sweatshop nature of the college sport product so they can eagerly consume and celebrate the collegiate model. Branding and rebranding college sport to foster motivated reasoning is most difficult for everyone involved in the most lucrative, commercialized, and professionalized level of college sport: Power Five football and Division I men's basketball. The fan avidity and consumption levels of the College Football Playoffs (CFP) and NCAA March Madness rival any professional sport brands. They are the branding linchpins of a multibillion-dollar college sport industry.

While Keller and Lehmann (2006) note that organizations can develop brands that offer consumers a simple choice, promise a particular quality level, and build trust and brand loyalty, it is difficult and demanding for college sport stakeholders to fundamentally alter reality. However, many stakeholders want to be convinced that the NCAA collegiate model they hold so dear is not a myth but real. In addition to the psychological importance of the NCAA brand, Walter Byers, former NCAA executive director, understood the need to brand college sports as an avocation, in order to reduce the legal and financial risks posed by "the dreaded notion that NCAA athletes could be identified as employees by state industrial commissions and the courts" (Byers and Hammer 1995: 69). To achieve these goals, the NCAA national office continues to provide focused brand-strategy leadership, through the consistent use of various terms, including *student-athlete, collegiate model, pre-professional experiences, student-athlete well-being,* and *fairness,* to counter threats to the NCAA brand.

The preeminent example of an NCAA-coordinated brand-advancement strategy was the creation and dissemination of the term *student-athlete.* Over the past half century, *student-athlete* has become a ubiquitous part of the American lexicon, applied not only to college athletes but also high school—and even middle school—athletes.

Consequently, branding/rebranding theory provides a context from which to view the NCAA management and communication decisions.[2] These decisions reflect both branding/rebranding theory and elements of institutional propaganda.

While branding takes place in a marketing landscape, propaganda occurs within a political arena. Since college sport is a consumer product protected by political forces within local, state, and federal legislative settings, both theoretical perspectives are appropriate frameworks from which to examine how college sport stakeholders willingly suspend their disbelief and protect a fictitious collegiate model.

Branding/Rebranding

According to the NCAA, its institutional brand "is a collection of the Association's messages, visual presentation, decisions, actions, behaviors, relationships and experiences" (NCAA 2010b). The NCAA utilizes traditional marketing communication and planning frameworks to transmit its institutional logic: creating and perpetuating legitimating symbols and ceremonial facades agreed upon by both dominant and subservient group members (Southall et al. 2008). Kuhn (2012) referred to these elements as constituting a paradigm. These legitimating efforts figure strongly and explicitly in selling the college-sport brand (Hatch and Schultz 2003). Communicating its professed amateur institutional logic to relevant stakeholders and public policy makers is critical to the NCAA's brand management strategy.

As Merrilees and Miller (2008: 538) define it, branding is the "initial coherent articulation of the corporate brand and can occur at any time." Extending this concept, rebranding is the dislocation and reformulation of a brand, resulting in a new or slightly altered brand articulation. As a market changes, a brand may need to be reimagined or revised. This rebranding often requires—or is a result of—changes to an organization's management processes or leadership. Not surprisingly, developing a coherent institutional brand involves making sure the articulated brand is consistent with expressed institutional logic(s) and ceremonial facades (Southall et al. 2008). Consequently any rebranding necessitates moving an institution—and relevant stakeholders—from one set of logics to another.

This movement occurs along a continuum: minor to intermediate to complete (Ahonen 2008; Daly and Moloney 2004). Minor rebranding involves a makeover—a surface change in a brand's aesthetics. An intermediate rebranding not only is a facelift but also uses internal and external communication techniques to favorably reposition an existing brand to relevant stakeholders (Ahonen 2008). In both minor and intermediate rebranding, there is still an association with the existing brand. Necessarily, in a complete rebranding, ties to the previous brand are intentionally discarded, and no attempt is made to retain any association with the previous brand. In much the same way, Stuart and Muzellec (2004) view rebranding as ranging from evolutionary (e.g., new slogan or logo only) to revolutionary, which incorporates name, logo, and slogan rebranding simultaneously. Successful rebranding involves retaining or reimaging a group of core values, vision, mission, and goals and communicating these to relevant publics (Merrilees and Miller 2008).

The first step in rebranding is identifying the extent to which the brand needs to be changed. Once this has been decided, the following steps can occur: (1) justify the brand revision to relevant stakeholders, recognizing and anticipating potential internal resistance to such change; (2) develop a well-structured change management program that aligns with an institution's core values and alert all institutional members to the forthcoming rebranding; and (3) identify new market segments for which the rebranding will satisfy their needs.

Rebranding occurs in identified phases (Ahonen 2008; Greyser 2009). While the phases have been variously titled, most models have similar attributes (fig. 1):

- Phase 1—Triggers and brand revision,
- Phase 2—Rebranding strategy implementation, and
- Phase 3—Stakeholder buy-in and outcomes.

Throughout its history the NCAA and its members have been embroiled in a series of reputational crises and scandals. One of the NCAA national office's primary responsibilities is to react to reputational triggers and protect the collegiate model. The NCAA president must be a personification of the brand. While various NCAA national office staff units are responsible for specific elements of the association's branding and rebranding strategies, other college sport stakeholders, including athletic conferences, individual athletic departments, corporate partners, and even reform organizations such as the Knight Commission on Intercollegiate Athletics (KCIA) and the Drake Group, are part of continual rebranding efforts.

While rebranding is an ongoing activity, the collegiate model faces a constant barrage of reputational triggers. Some, such as the infamous October 2012 tweet from Ohio State University quarterback Cardale Jones—"Why should we have to go to class if we came here to play FOOTBALL, we ain't come to play SCHOOL, classes are POINTLESS" (Lesmerises 2014)—are fodder for one or two news cycles and then recede into the constant white noise of commercialized college sport. Others take longer to unfold and last for extended periods of

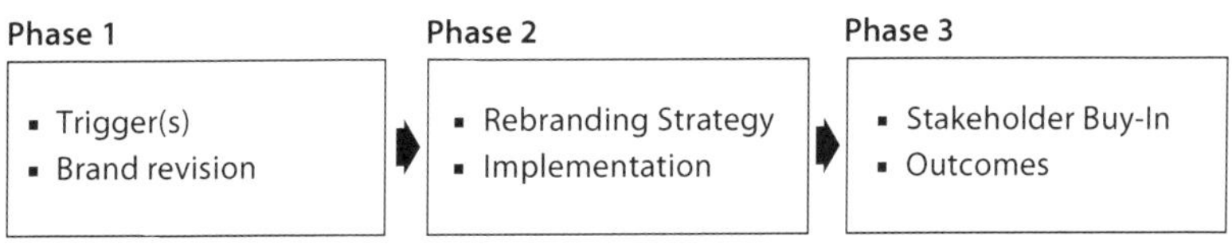

Figure 1. Phases of rebranding.

time. These longitudinal triggers include scandals at NCAA member universities: Penn State, Baylor, University of North Carolina at Chapel Hill, University of Louisville, Oklahoma State, Auburn, and so on. A trigger crisis may involve criminal or violent behavior by athletes, coaches, or fans and/or significant violations of NCAA bylaws (which are often depicted by the media as criminal or illegal in nature). A real or manufactured crisis may subject an athletic department and university to intense media scrutiny, reform or advocacy-group criticism, governmental investigation, disaffected consumer/fan complaints or protests, or general public dissatisfaction, which is amplified by social media.

Some college-sport reputational triggers are portrayed as "life-threatening," with the potential to change college sport as we know it. These existential threats include legal challenges to the collegiate model (e.g., *O'Bannon v. NCAA*, 2014, 2015; *Jenkins v. NCAA*, 2014; *NCAA v. Alston*, 2021; and Northwestern University and College Athletes Players Association [CAPA] 2014). These actions call into question the collegiate model paradigm and have the potential to severely diminish, or interrupt completely, college sport's revenue streams or mandate a reordering of spending priorities (e.g., increased profit-athlete compensation; allowing athletes access to name, image, and likeness; facility construction).

As any marketing firm would do for its clients, the NCAA national office (which functions as big-time college sport's trade and marketing association) has conducted periodic situational analyses and reenvisioned the college sport brand, while retaining the brand's amateur essence. From the NCAA's point of view, it is fundamentally important to maintain the generational tie, now more than a hundred years old, that binds college athletes, students, alumni, and fans. This nostalgic brand association is clearly outlined in the chapter of the KCIA's report "College Sports 101" on "myths and intangibles," in which intercollegiate athletic contests are viewed as positive community builders. As the report notes, "Logos, nicknames, and television appearances brand institutions locally and nationally" (KCIA 2009). As might be expected, many college sport reformers advocate for a return to a more amateur bygone era, in which they imagine educational values were paramount, "practices that [made] academic values a priority" were rewarded, and athletes were treated "as students first and foremost—not as professionals" (KCIA 2010). Many college-sport reformers ignore decades of contrary evidence and believe in the sanctity of an almost Platonic ideal of college-sport amateurism.

Reform groups choose to willingly disbelieve big-time college sport is fundamentally a commercial enterprise that enriches athletic administrators, coaches, sponsors, and media partners and provides predominately middle- and upper-class consumers, including "loss-athletes" (whose market value is less than their grant-in-aid) in NCAA Olympic sports, a subsidized collegiate athletic experience. An examination of reform organization documents reveals narratives replete with NCAA language, customs, and principles that ignore the exploitative nature of big-time college sport. In addition, almost without exception, reformers contend that a priori college sport supports and contributes to universities' educational mission and provides valuable life lessons for athletes and consumers alike.

What seems clear, is that currently reform must occur within the shadow of the NCAA's blue disk. As NCAA president Mark Emmert declared in 2011: "Student-athletes are students. They're not professionals. And we're not going to pay them. And we're not going to allow other people to pay them to play. . . . Behaviors that undermine the collegiate model, wherever they occur, are a threat to those basic values, and we can't tolerate them" (Moltz 2011). Almost without exception reformers do not advocate paying profit-athletes a negotiated market wage. Instead reform consists of either returning to a bygone, sepia-toned era when college sport was pure and players played for love of game and college; having Congress grant a magically reformed NCAA an antitrust exemption to legalize the current illegal cartel behavior; allowing third-party "collectives" to pay athletes for charitable appearances, or permitting college athletes to become entrepreneurs through the monetization of their names, images, and likenesses (NILs)—the economic crumbs of the college sport industry.

The current college sport brand is seemingly sacrosanct, not just to reformers but also to fans, corporate stakeholders, Congress, the courts, and the media. Emmert's statement reflects the NCAA's success in skillfully using institutional propaganda and rebranding strategies to create, embed, and disseminate its collegiate model in order to shape and control college sport reform (Southall et al. 2008; Southall and Staurowsky 2013; Southall 2014; Southall and Southall 2018).

Not surprisingly, most fans and stakeholders unconditionally accept this NCAA collegiate-model paradigm. However, Congress and the US judiciary also ignore the illegality and immorality of the college-sport enterprise, with congressional committee hearings and high-profile legal cases consistently resulting in logically inconsistent responses masquerading as reform. In the initial *O'Bannon v. NCAA* (2014) district-court decision (in which the term *student-athlete* was mentioned at least 256 times in the ninety-nine-page ruling), Judge Claudia Wilken ruled that "this restraint does violate antitrust law" (*O'Bannon v. NCAA*, 2014: 98). However, unlike nearly every other ruling involving an identified antitrust violation, instead of enacting specific measures to remedy the violation the court proposed a modest reform (five thousand dollars deposited annually into a trust fund) while allowing the illegal system to remain intact. The Ninth Circuit appellate court also suspended its disbelief, ignoring clear violations of law in nullifying Wilken's injunction designed to cure identified specific violations and arguing (without legal or logical justification) that any remedies must be educational and consistent with the NCAA's existing collegiate model (*O'Bannon v. NCAA*, 2015).

Coordinated Branding/Rebranding

Consistently, using both mass-media and social-media platforms, the NCAA's national office—through its Brand Strategies and Events (BSE), New Media Strategies and Content Development (NMSCD), and Public and Media Relations (PMR) staff units (NCAA 2010a)—coordinates the chosen brand strategy or series of rebranding strategies with conferences, other associated organizations, and individual colleges or universities. According to internal NCAA documents, its BSE unit "provides full-service integrated communications to advance the NCAA mission. . . . Through partnership with other national office groups and with the NCAA membership, the BSE unit delivers a full range of expertise from brand strategy design to activation. Specifically, the BSE staff shapes the NCAA brand through the development of national television awareness campaigns; cohesive visual identity and messages" (NCAA 2010a).[4]

The staff of the NMSCD, established in May 2009, develops and implements the association's online (e.g., ncaa.org and ncaa.com) and social-media strategies, including on Facebook, Twitter, Instagram, YouTube, TikTok, and LinkedIn (NCAA 2022b). NCAA social media provides leadership and technical advice to other national office groups regarding best practices for online and social-media strategies (NCAA 2010a). In addition to these duties, its public and media relations staff "develops, implements and manages the Association's issues management communication model" (ibid.).

An important element of the NCAA's issues management model is developing "proactive, reactive and crisis-response initiatives and strategies that are specifically tailored to issues, have a desired communication effect, and are supported by research and analysis" (NCAA 2010a; Nocera 2012). Again, as does any good public-relations or media-relations unit, the PMR team provides strategic and practical communication advice to national office senior leadership that allows "the national office, especially senior leadership, to speak with one voice. In addition to its efforts within the national office, PMR also has initiated a variety of outreach efforts to provide communication advice and counsel to the NCAA membership and affiliated organizations" (ibid.).

Successful rebranding must ensure internal brand understanding and consistently execute selected rebranding activities. Understanding the power of nostalgia and the retention of cherished memories, the NCAA most often does not completely sever ties to past brand meanings. Subtly the NCAA national office has deemphasized Walter Byers's 1950s term *student-athlete*, which was "created by the NCAA to convince workers' compensation boards, as well as the general public, that scholarship athletes are students like any others" (Byers and Hammer

1995: 69). Recognizing that the term is so embedded in the American sport lexicon, the NCAA national office no longer mandates its exclusive use but now uses it interchangeably with *college athlete*. While *student-athlete* is the preferred NCAA moniker for both profit-athletes and loss-athletes (i.e., consumers of an NCAA Olympic sport experience), the NCAA no longer mandates the term, since consumers are conditioned to hearing *student-athlete* anyway. Over the past fifty years, the term has become self-reproducing, permanently reshaping our view of college sport. As with any effective advertising jingle, *student-athlete* positions college athletes as amateur kids, not adult employees.

Rebranding College Sport's Mythology

Despite an obvious disconnect between the college-sport enterprise and their educational mission, imaginative and strategic brand management provides Power Five universities with opportunities to reinforce their cherished college-sport mythology. This mythology allows many within the big-time college sport institutional field to believe that the NCAA's business practices are nonexploitative and educational (Huma and Staurowsky 2012; Southall and Staurowsky 2013). While big-time college sport has almost from its inception been criticized for low athlete-graduation rates, questionable academic standards, and athletics programs that operate independently of real university oversight (KCIA 2010), college sport reformers almost universally pledge allegiance to most, if not all, of the NCAA brand's core values. They "firmly believe that—at their best—intercollegiate sports bring enormous benefits to their universities and communities" (ibid.). Despite ample evidence to the contrary, they unilaterally "recognize that intercollegiate athletics have a legitimate and proper role to play in college and university life. Our interest is not to abolish that role but to preserve it by putting it into perspective" (ibid.). The acceptance of the normality of college sport as we know it and the acceptance of the college-sport paradigm is often clearly articulated: "At the nation's most prominent universities, intercollegiate athletics have always played a dual role in campus life. . . . They are managed for the benefit of student-athletes" (KCIA 2010).

Many reformers either do not know, or choose to ignore, the motivation and implementation of the term *student-athlete* as part of the branding of college sport as nothing more than an extracurricular avocation or hobby. Reformers rarely note that the NCAA created the term in the wake of the introduction of athletic grants-in-aid (GIAs), which effectively instituted a "pay for play" system that threatened the NCAA's historic definition of amateurism:

> Student-athletes shall be amateurs in an intercollegiate sport, and their participation should be motivated primarily by education and by the physical, mental and social benefits to be derived. Student participation

> in intercollegiate athletics is an avocation, and student-athletes should be protected from exploitation by professional and commercial enterprises (NCAA 2021).

Byers recalls in his memoir that "we crafted the term 'student-athlete,' and soon it was embedded in all NCAA rules and interpretations as a mandated substitute for such words as players and athletes. We told college publicists to speak of 'college teams,' not football or basketball 'clubs,' a word common to the pros" (Byers and Hammer 1995: 69). Byers and other college sport leaders astutely understood the likelihood that in the wake of athletic GIAs, state industrial commissions and courts would identify college players as employees. The term, designed to differentiate college sport from professional by rebranding college players as students first and foremost, has served the NCAA well for more than sixty years.

Recognizing the term's brand equity, NCAA leaders sought to expand its brand attributes through the articulation of four "key principles that should underlie any adequate strategic plan for reform and advocacy in college sports" (Brand 2003: 1). This strategy was designed to insulate and protect the NCAA's overall sport brand: "The integrity of intercollegiate athletics is and must remain paramount. College sports have their own unique identity. They are different from professional sports" (ibid.: 3–4).

Almost without exception, big-time college sport—as exemplified by Power Five football and Division I men's basketball—is portrayed as a great American subculture (Brand 2008). Consistently the NCAA brand has been positioned as encapsulating cherished American traditions: "There are not many events that are as enjoyable as watching a hard-fought football game on a sunny fall Saturday afternoon, or a basketball game between two teams proud of their university affiliations" (ibid.).

However, as the scale and scope of the business of college sport has increased, NCAA members and associated organizations have struggled to reconcile big-time college sport's rampant and increasing commercialism with the NCAA's historic notion of amateurism: "As the scale of both revenue generation and spending has grown over the past few decades, there is a general sense that 'big-time' athletics is in conflict with the principle of amateurism" (NCAA 2010b; Nocera 2012).[3] In response to these commercialized reputational triggers, college-sport stakeholders have subtly rebranded amateurism. This rebranding was alluded to in NCAA president's briefing documents prepared for incoming NCAA president, Mark Emmert: "Critical for the future of intercollegiate athletics will likely be a better understood definition of amateurism that isolates the principle to the way in which student-athletes are viewed without imposing its avocational nature on revenue-producing opportunities" (ibid.).

In the documents the NCAA conceded it had consistently attempted to "change the way people talked about intercollegiate athletics" (ibid.). In almost every possible context, intercollegiate athletics has been portrayed as a sacred American tradition inextricably tied to the nation's colleges and universities, which have a moral obligation to protect this most American of cultural sport experiences.

The rebranded view of college sport, the collegiate model of athletics, is intended to impart two principles: " (1) Those who participate in college sports are students, and (2) intercollegiate athletics is embedded in the values and mission of higher education" (NCAA 2010c). In addition to Power Five football and Division I men's basketball players being consistently referred to as student-athletes, the professional model—in which players negotiate a percentage of gross revenues—is subtly denigrated while the collegiate model is imbued with distinctly American values: "In the professional model, the athletes are a work force, a commodity that can be traded from team to team. In the collegiate model, the athlete is a student. In the professional model, the goal is to generate revenue through entertainment. In the collegiate model, the goal is to acquire an education, including learning the value of hard work and teamwork, self-sacrifice and self-discipline, resilience and persistence, and the pursuit of excellence" (ibid.). Not surprisingly in this narrative, college football and basketball programs are "enduringly connected to a community through the sponsoring college or university" (ibid.). Meanwhile, in the professional model, "the team is connected to a community only so long as the community supports the franchise through the building and maintenance of facilities and the purchase of tickets" (ibid.). Conveniently, college sport stakeholders ignore the annual outlay of hundreds of millions of dollars on capital projects: new or renovated stadiums, practice facilities, and academic support complexes—most of which are paid for by state taxes and/or issuance of bonds as well as the tax-exempt status of educational donations to athletic associations.

For the past two decades, NCAA national-office senior leadership, as well as university and athletic department spokespersons, has adhered to specific talking points from this collegiate model template in public statements, depositions, and court testimony. From 2002 until 2010, as part of the NCAA's rebranding of amateurism, increased attention was paid to the "460,000 student-athletes going pro in something other than sports," subtly differentiating these Divisions I, II, and III Olympic-sport (i.e., loss) athletes from the 3–5 percent of "pre-professional" athletes who generate the vast majority of the revenue for the college sport enterprise. Whenever possible, non-revenue-generating student-athletes were represented as the rationale for the business of college sport. Since the revenue from FBS football and Division I men's basketball supports all the national championships in all other NCAA sports and often supports many—if not all—of a department's Olympic sports, the narrative has unfolded that if profit-athletes were allowed to receive a market wage, then athletic opportunities for all these deserving Olympic sport athletes would have to be eliminated. In other words, pay for play would end college sport as we know it.

This utilitarian rebranding was on full display during Emmert's 2014 testimony before the US Senate Committee on Commerce, Science, and Transportation, in which he called attention to a core truth of intercollegiate athletics:

> Before I address the challenges, I want to begin by highlighting a core truth of intercollegiate athletics. For the vast majority of those who participate in NCAA sports-more than 460,000 young men and women each year at 1,084 institutions across three divisions and in 23 different sports—the experience is exactly what it is intended to be: a meaningful extension of the educational process that provides the opportunity for students to compete fairly against other students, in an educational environment. (NCAA 2014)

While Emmert admitted college sport has "challenges," he maintained that the 460,000 hard-working amateur college athletes were truly students (NCAA 2014). While the management and execution of some college sports may look a great deal like their professional iterations, even Power Five football and Division I men's basketball players are fundamentally students, just like all the college students who fill the stadiums and help form the backdrop for the annual Michigan versus Ohio State football classic or the Tobacco Road basketball clashes between Duke and the University of North Carolina.

Throughout this long rebranding process, NCAA national office staff members have consistently defended "the presence of commercial activity within the context of intercollegiate athletics" (Renfro 2012: 33). The collegiate model has been described as being "as old as the games themselves and it is growing" (ibid.). According to this line of argument, college sport's commercialism allows colleges and universities to provide opportunities for "participation in college sports, [which] enhances the educational experience of student-athletes and ... is the only rational reason for the continued support of intercollegiate athletics in higher education" (ibid.).

To the NCAA national office and its members, the salient *brand attribute* that distinguishes big-time college from professional sport is not whether college sport is overtly commercialized but rather the amateur status of college athletes, "whose first order of business is acquiring an education" (Brand 2006: 3). College sport's stakeholders have never openly advocated scaling back or abandoning professional sport business practices. However, the possibility that college athletes (specifically profit-athletes) might collectively bargain working conditions, health and disability insurance benefits, and a percent of generated revenue has consistently been viewed as a looming disaster. In 2004 NCAA president Myles Brand warned the membership that "the threat is real, and the consequences devastating. I want to go on record in calling attention to this potential disaster" (Brand 2004: 7). College sport stakeholders have steadfastly vowed to fight being "drawn to the professional model like a moth drawn to a flame" (ibid.).

Fundamentally the collegiate model has been portrayed as a commonsense—albeit idiosyncratic—economic model that is essential for the survival of college sport as we know it. However, to blunt criticisms of out-of-control coaching salaries, bowl payouts, media right's contracts, and nightly game broadcasts, the NCAA—through public service announcements within college-sport broadcasts and on its YouTube channel, as well as infographics packages (such as "NCAA 101") that can be viewed and downloaded as pdf documents from NCAA.org—offers an explanation to the question: "Where does the money go?"

Supporting and Protecting College Athletes

For many years college sport apologists have ignored the rampant commercialism and professionalism in big-time college sports. In response to continuing claims profit-athletes are exploited employees, college sport's supporters have once again subtly rebranded the collegiate model, with an emphasis on positioning the NCAA and universities as kinder, gentler, athlete friendly, nimble, nonauthoritarian, and supportive institutions determined to become less bureaucratic and more responsive to all college athletes' concerns.

The NCAA national office and its members have publicly branded themselves as not exploiting college athletes but actually supporting and protecting them. Messaging consistently highlights how such support has resulted in increased college athlete success on the field, in the classroom and later in life. In addition the college sport landscape is portrayed as one in which academic achievement, well-being, and fairness are priorities. This rebranding strategy involves portraying athletic departments as progressive benefactors that provide athletic and educational opportunities, ensure athletes' physical and mental well-being, and offer multiyear, full cost-of-attendance GIAs:

> The NCAA and its member schools continue to improve how they support student-athletes, by protecting their health and safety, creating more opportunities for them to succeed academically, and involving more students in governance of the Association. . . .
>
> Emmert emphasized the gains made in academic reform, increased graduation rates and higher academic standards for incoming students. He

> also stressed the ongoing commitment to player safety and more recent changes such as cost of attendance, multi-year scholarships and unlimited meals. . . .
>
> The bottom line, Emmert said, is how the NCAA answers an important question: "How are we helping young men and women be successful in life when they leave our institutions?" (Schwarb 2015)

Consistently the NCAA national office's public and media relations team provides NCAA senior leaders with strategic and practical communication advice that allows them to speak with one voice regarding the college sport brand.

Responding to Educational Reputational Triggers

College football and men's basketball players have historically graduated at significantly lower rates than the general student body (NCAA 1991). However, by the mid-1980s the disconnect between educational opportunities and the business of college sport had become so pronounced (Byers and Hammer 1995; *Hall v. University of Minnesota,* 1982; and *Ross v. Creighton University,* 1992), that, as Diana Nyad wrote in the *New York Times* (1989), 76 to 92 percent of professional football and men's basketball players were not college graduates. Many former NCAA and Olympic basketball players believed high school athletes and their parents should have information about the likelihood of graduating from college. A public outcry took place in 1989 when former Oklahoma State University defensive end Dexter Manley testified before Congress that despite playing football at OSU for four years, he had not learned to read until well after he had left college (Jacobson 1992). Subsequently critics and college athlete advocates lobbied members of Congress and secured passage of the 1990 Student Right-to-Know and Campus Security Act (SRTKA). The act included a Department of Education–administered program that requires colleges and universities to collect and disseminate student graduation rates (see National Center for Educational Statistics website: http://nces.ed.gov/collegenavigator/) (Selingo 2012). After initially voicing concerns over the federal graduation rate program, the NCAA acquiesced and agreed to make athlete graduation rates public (ibid.).

In the years before the passage of the SRTKA, the NCAA knew it needed to rebrand academic success, since profit-athletes were clearly not graduating at rates comparable to the general student population. Consequently a series of research projects were commissioned to "inform our member institutions and others" (NCAA 1991: 1) about college athletes' graduation rates. One of these projects was the NCAA Academic Performance Study, which began in 1985 (NCAA 1994). Among the study's first reports, published in 1991, was data on the five-year graduation rates of 3,288 NCAA athletes who "entered NCAA Division-I institutions in the fall semester of 1984 or 1985" (NCAA 1991: 6). The employed methodology was similar to what would be used in calculating the congressionally mandated federal graduation rate: "The graduation rates for the following tables were calculated by dividing the number of graduates after five years by the number of student-athletes who had entered that institution as freshmen in the initial year of the survey" (ibid.). In addition, the study also reported an "adjusted graduation rate . . . calculated by removing all student-athletes who left their institutions in good academic standing from the group of initially entered freshmen" (ibid.).

Athletes expunged from the cohort were initially referred to as "eligible dropouts" (NCAA 1991: 10). This statistical adjustment (see table 1) removed approximately 33 percent of sampled athletes and resulted in an overall adjusted graduation rate of 68.4 percent—an improvement of 22.7 percent (ibid.). For football and men's basketball players, the adjustment resulted in a 20.4 percent jump, from 42.1 percent to 62.5 percent. Tellingly there was no mention of eligible dropouts or an adjusted graduation rate in a subsequent peer-reviewed article (McArdle and Hamagami 1994) or NCAA reports (see http://www.ncaa.org/about/resources/research/academic-initial-eligibility-research). From all appearances it seemed as if the eligible-dropout effect had been forgotten, just another statistical analysis in yet another report.

Graduation Success Rate

However, when the NCAA "launched a major academic reform program in 2003" (LaForge and Hodge 2011: 219), the eligible-dropout adjustment reappeared as the cornerstone of the NCAA's new and improved graduation success rate (GSR). The NCAA justified the removal of a third of athletes because "the federally mandated rate is an inaccurate graduation measure" (Brand 2004). Since the GSR's introduction in 2003, virtually every NCAA document, communiqué, or press release has proclaimed that it was developed at the request of NCAA members, particularly presidents and chancellors, who sought an improved and more accurate metric. The rebranding of academic success was initially unveiled in the NCAA president Brand's 2003 and 2004 state of the association addresses. From its inception the GSR has been hailed as evidence of the NCAA's successful academic reforms (Brand 2003, 2004).

The GSR's branding as a more accurate measure of academic success is now embedded in every press release and news story on the NCAA.org website, in the mainstream media, and on university athletic department websites as evidence that college athletes are overall more successful than regular students. In addition the outdated federal graduation rate is consistently described as divorced from reality: "The NCAA also devised a new metric for measuring graduation in an effort to amend the shortcomings of the federally mandated methodology" (Brown 2014).

Table 1. Five-year graduation rates for 1984–85 NCAA athletes by group

GROUP	PEOPLE	%	ATHLETES GRADUATED	OVERALL GRADUATION RATE, $N = 3,288$	ADJUSTED GRADUATION RATE, $N = 2,198$*
Overall	3,288	100.0	1504	45.7%	68.4%
Group by race					
White	2,453	74.6	1282	52.3%	77.0%
Black	835	25.4	222	26.6%	41.6%
Sex					
Male	2,314	70.4	979	42.3%	63.7%
Female	974	29.6	525	53.9%	79.4%
Sport					
Male, revenue	1,314	40.0	553	42.1%	62.5%
Male, nonrevenue	1,018	31.0	436	42.8%	65.3%
Female, all	956	29.1	515	53.9%	79.5%
Separate groups					
White male, revenue	751	22.8	412	54.9%	78.5%
White male, nonrevenue	895	27.2	407	45.5%	69.3%
White female, all	807	24.5	463	57.4%	83.9%
Black male, revenue	563	17.1	141	25.0%	39.5%
Black male, nonrevenue	123	3.7	29	23.6%	35.8%
Black female, all	149	4.5	52	34.9%	54.2%

Note. All percentages based on sample size listed.

*N for adjusted graduation rate is based on total sample minus eligible dropouts.

Every annual release of NCAA graduation rates highlights the degree to which the NCAA's rebranding strategy has been implemented by NCAA members and other college sport stakeholders. NCAA national office press releases set the stage for athletic department sports information directors to tout the superiority of the graduation success rate:

> The Division I Board of Directors created the GSR in response to Division I college and university presidents who wanted *data that more accurately reflected the mobility of college students than the federal graduation rate.* The *federal rate counts any student who leaves a school as an academic failure,* no matter whether he or she enrolls at another school. Also, the federal rate does not recognize students who enter school as transfer students.
>
> The GSR formula removes from the rate student-athletes who leave school while academically eligible and includes student-athletes who transfer to a school after initially enrolling elsewhere. *This calculation makes it a more complete and accurate look at student-athlete success.*
>
> The rate also allows for a *deeper understanding of graduation success* in individual sports than the federal metric, which provides only broad groupings. (Hosick and Durham 2017; emphasis added)

In many cases athletic departments simply cut and paste text intended to point out the inherent superiority of the GSR. Often these statements, supplied to various stakeholders by the NCAA, athletic conferences, and/or member athletic departments, make their way into media accounts as well as online and television commentary:

University of Alabama–Tuscaloosa

> The NCAA GSR and the Academic Success Rate (ASR) were developed in response to college and university presidents who wanted graduation data that more accurately reflected the mobility among college students today. Both rates improve on the federally mandated graduation rate by including students who were omitted from the federal calculation (University of Alabama 2008).

University of Notre Dame

> The GSR was created to more accurately reflect actual graduation rates by including transfer data in the calculation. . . . College and university presidents asked the NCAA to develop a new methodology that takes into account the mobility among students in today's higher education environment. Research indicates that approximately 60 percent of all new bachelor's degree recipients are attending more than one undergraduate institution during their collegiate careers (Brown and Heisler 2005).

Atlantic Coast Conference

> The Graduation Success Rate was developed by the NCAA as part of its academic reform initiative as a better measure of student-athlete academic success. . . .
>
> The federal graduation rate, which is less accurate than GSR because it counts transfer students as academic failures, is the only rate that allows comparison between the general student body at a school and its student-athletes (Augusta Free Press 2014).

The dates of the press communiques may change, but the messaging remains virtually unchanged. A summary of GSR branding strategies includes the following elements:

- The GSR must demonstrate success: it's right in its name.
- It's more accurate than the FGR, because we say it is.
- Our research indicates that our metric is very successful.
- Even though they measure two distinct outcomes and the GSR by definition must be equal or higher than the federal graduation rate, we will encourage media outlets to report the two metrics as comparable.

By consistently simply asserting that the GSR more accurately assesses the academic success of college athletes and steadfastly referring to GSR rates in all discussions of college athletes' academic success, the NCAA and its member institutions have convinced a sizeable portion of the media and college sports fans that education is big-time college sport's priority. However, the consistent use of the "more favorable" GSR metric confuses the media, fans, and the general public. Using the GSR in touting graduation success and increased academic standards is undoubtedly savvy marketing and public relations, but the GSR's exclusive use rebrands academic success in a light most favorable to the collegiate model. Unfortunately the GSR has resulted in an increased practice of keeping profit-athletes eligible, fostered academic dishonesty, and devalued higher education.

Final Thoughts

It is no surprise that when faced with fiscal, legal, and sociocultural challenges, college sport stakeholders continually rebrand their core products of football and men's basketball to paint themselves in the most favorable (e.g., educational) light possible. Unfortunately for college sport's revenue-producing labor force, many current and former players, as well as some attorneys and advocates who have mounted challenges to college sport's exploitative labor practices, have not sought to dismantle the current system but to effect reform within the NCAA's collegiate model paradigm.

In several previous court decisions, judges have been reticent to completely undermine the core brand of the NCAA and its members. Though it is unknown to what extent NCAA branding and rebranding has influenced court decisions, there is no doubt the NCAA's messaging has played a significant role in the rejection of legal arguments that would have granted profit-athletes greater access to the capitalistic system of big-time college sports. Unfortunately even during oral arguments in *NCAA v. Alston* (2021), which was a unanimous decision in favor of Alston and a repudiation of the NCAA's business model, some of the nine justices continued to utilize NCAA language and gave deference to the NCAA's long-standing collegiate model. At the time of this writing, how much the Court's decision will impact the day-to-day business of Power Five college sport is yet to be seen.

Even the media consistently suspends disbelief when reporting college-sport issues. Despite Judge Wilken's ruling that the defendant NCAA had violated federal antitrust laws, the media largely buried the lede and focused on the ruling allowing Power Five college sport's survival. Concurrently, since many reformers either ignore or misconstrue big-time college sport's exploitative nature, meaningful change never occurs. Trapped within the current collegiate model paradigm, reformers seem satisfied with minor Pyrrhic victories: cost-of-attendance tuition stipends (which are really pay raises), optional four-year GIAs, better training methods and health protocols, and calls for reductions in practice schedules.

In discussing the nature of scientific revolutions, Kuhn (2012: 78) noted: "The decision to reject one paradigm is always simultaneously the decision to accept another, and the judgment leading to that decision involves the comparison of both paradigms with nature and with each other." For the most part, reformers and college athlete advocates have not fully articulated a competing paradigm to the NCAA's collegiate model; they simply offer weak reforms that are easily assimilated and diluted by college sport's stakeholders. What is needed is not reform, which fundamentally serves to perpetuate the status quo, but a paradigm shift in which previously normal beliefs are discarded and replaced with radical new ones (Kuhn 2012). Such a paradigm shift would result in the abandonment of college sport reform efforts that have done little-to-nothing to prevent continual and cataclysmic difficulties in Power Five college sport. As long as the NCAA's collegiate model is the paradigm, meaningful reform is a fiction. The only solution is a revolution in which profit-athletes' employment and educational rights—really their fundamental human rights in a capitalistic system—are recognized and protected. What is unclear is whether college sport stakeholders have the intellectual and moral courage to abandon the familiar and financially successful but morally bankrupt and exploitative collegiate model.

Notes

1. In this chapter references to the NCAA brand include the overall institution (Southall et al. 2008), which comprises the association (i.e., member athletic departments, conferences, governance structure, and affiliated entities), membership (i.e., colleges and universities), and the national office (NCAA 2004: 2).

2. The developed analysis utilizes branding/rebranding theories on corporate or organizational levels, as well as institutional branding/rebranding. Such usage is consistent with the literature, in which similar properties are applied to corporate, organizational, retail, service, and institutional brands (Berry 2000; Birstwistle and Freathy 1998).

3. After a link to the NCAA's president's briefing documents was published on March 30, 2012, in the *New York Times* (Nocera 2012), the NCAA deactivated all URLs associated with the documents. The link currently goes to a page that reads "Entry Page for fs.ncaa.org This page contains no content." The NCAA does not deny the existence of the documents.

References

CASES

Hall v. University of Minnesota, 530 F. Supp. 104 (D. Minn. 1982).
Jenkins v. National Collegiate Athletic Association. No. 14-cv-02758-CW (2014).
O'Bannon v. NCAA (2014). 7 F.Supp.3d 955 (N. D. Cal.).
O'Bannon v. NCAA (2015). WL 5712106 (9th cir. 30 September 2015).
Ross v. Creighton University, 957 F.2d 410 (7th Cir. 1992).

SECONDARY SOURCES

Abrams, M. H. (1958). *Literature and Belief.* New York: Columbia University Press.

Ahonen, Mari (2008). "Corporate Re-branding Process: A Preliminary Theoretical Framework." In *Proceedings of the Conference on Corporate Communication 2008*, 31–38. Madison, NJ: Corporate Communication Institute at Fairleigh Dickinson University.

Augusta Free Press. (2014). "ACC Teams Continue to Set High Graduation Success Rate Standard." October 28. https://augustafreepress.com/acc-teams-continue-set-high-graduation-success-rate-standard/.

Berry, Leonard L. (2000). "Cultivating Service Brand Equity." *Journal of the Academy of Marketing Science* 28, no. 1: 128–37.

Birtwistle, Grete, and Paul Freathy (1998). "More than Just a Name above the Shop: A Comparison of the Branding Strategies of Two UK Fashion Retailers." *International Journal of Retail and Distribution Management* 26, no. 8: 318–23.

Brand, Myles (2003). "State of the Association Address." *mylesbrand.com,* January 20. https://mylesbrand.com/wp-content/uploads/2003/01/2003-NCAA-State-of-the-Association.pdf.

———. (2004). "Brand Address: Fortify Bond between Academics, Athletics." *NCAA News,* January 19. http://fs.ncaa.org/Docs/NCAANewsArchive/2004/Associationwide/brand%2baddress%2b%2bfortify%2bbond%2bbetween%2bacademics%2bathletics%2b-%2b1-19-04.html.

———. (2006). "Brand Charts Course for Collegiate Model's Next Century." Speech delivered to the NCAA Convention, January 7. https://mylesbrand.com/wp-content/uploads/2006/01/2006-NCAA-State-of-the-Association.pdf.

———. (2008). "Give Optimism a Chance." *Huffington Post*, November 20. https://collegeathleticsclips.com/news/point-counterpoint-reality-is-somewhere-between-optimism-and-cynicism-.html.

Brown, Gary. (2014). "NCAA Graduation Rates: A Quarter-Century of Tracking Academic Success." NCAA.org, October 28. http://www.ncaa.org/.

Brown, Dennis, and John Heisler (2005). "Irish Athletes Fare Well in Graduation Success Rate Survey." *Notre Dame News*. December 19. https://news.nd.edu/.

Byers, Walter, with Charles Hammer (1995). *Unsportsmanlike Conduct: Exploiting College Athletes*. Ann Arbor: University of Michigan Press.

Carter, David M. (2001). "Commentary: And You Thought You Were Watching Football." *Business Week*, January 29, 64.

Coleridge, Samuel T. (2008). *Samuel Taylor Coleridge: The Major Works*, edited by H. J. Jackson. Oxford: Oxford University Press.

Daly, Aidan, and Deirdre Moloney (2004). "Managing Corporate Rebranding." *Irish Marketing Review* 17, no. 1–2: 30–36.

Greyser, Stephen A. (2009). "Corporate Brand Reputation and Brand Crisis Management." *Management Decision* 47, no. 4: 590–602.

Hacking, Ian (2012). Introduction to Kuhn 2012.

Hatch, Mary Jo, and Majken Schultz (2003). "Bringing the Corporation into Corporate Branding." *European Journal of Marketing* 37, nos. 7–8: 1041–64.

Hosick, Michelle Brutlag (2014). "Student-Athletes Earn Diplomas at Record Rate: Graduation Success Rate Jumps Two Points, Virtually Every Demographic Improves." NCAA.org, October 28. http://www.ncaa.org/about/resources/media-center/news/student-athletes-earn-diplomas-record-rate.

Hosick, Michelle Brutlag, and Meghan Durham (2017). "DI African-American Student-Athletes Graduate at Record Rates." NCAA.org, November 8. http://www.ncaa.org/about/resources/media-center/news/di-african-american-student-athletes-graduate-record-rates.

Huma, Ramogi, and Ellen J. Staurowsky (2012). "Study: The $6 Billion Heist: Robbing College Athletes under the Guise of Amateurism." NCPA.org. https://www.ncpanow.org/.

Jacobson, Steve (1992). "Manley Finally Gets a Read on Education He Missed." *Baltimore Sun*, October 8. https://www.baltimoresun.com/news/bs-xpm-1992-10-08-1992282145-story.html.

Keller, Kevin Lane, and David R. Lehmann (2006). "Brands and Branding: Research Findings and Future Priorities." *Marketing Science* 25, no. 6: 740–59.

Knight Commission on Intercollegiate Athletics (2009). "College Sports 101." http://www.knightcommission.org/wp-content/uploads/2017/09/college-sports-101-1009-01.pdf.

———. (2010). "Restoring the Balance: Dollars, Values, and the Future of College Sport." http://www.knightcommission.org/images/restoringbalance/KCIA_Report_F.pdf.

Kuhn, Thomas S. (2012). *The Structure of Scientific Revolutions*. 4th ed. Chicago: University of Chicago Press.

Kunda, Ziva (1987). "Motivated Inference: Self-Serving Generation and Evaluation of Evidence." *Journal of Personality and Social Psychology* 23, no. 2: 636–47.

LaForge, Larry, and Janie Hodge (2011). "NCAA Academic Performance Metrics: Implications for Institutional Policy and Practice." *Journal of Higher Education* 82, no. 2: 217–35.

Lesmerises, Doug (2014). "Remembering the 'Famous Tweet' of Changed QB Cardale Jones; Greg Schiano Visits Practice: Ohio State Buckeyes Urban Meyer Quick Hits." Cleveland.com, March 19. http://www.cleveland.com/osu/index.ssf/2014/03/remembering_the_famous_tweet_0.html.

McArdle, John J., and Fumiaki Hamagami (1994). "Logit and Multilevel Logit Modeling of College Graduation for 1984–1985 Freshman Student-Athletes." *Journal of the American Statistical Association* 89: 1107–23.

Merrilees, Bill, and Dale Miller (2008). "Principles of Corporate Rebranding." *European Journal of Marketing* 42, nos. 5–6: 537–52. https://doi.org/10.1108/03090560810862499.

Moltz, David (2011). "NCAA President Answers Critics." *Inside Higher Ed*, January 14. https://www.insidehighered.com/news/2011/01/14/ncaa-president-answers-critics.

National Collegiate Athletic Association (1991). *NCAA Academic Performance Study: Report 91-01.* Overland Park, KS: NCAA.

———. (1994). *NCAA Research Report: Report 91-07.* Overland Park, KS: NCAA.

———. (2004). *NCAA Strategic Plan: NCAA Executive Committee.* Indianapolis: NCAA.

———. (2010a). "Branding and Communications Group Functional Description." President's Briefing Documents. Accessed March 2012. http://fs.ncaa.org/Docs/newmedia/2010/Emmert/Part3/BC/BC1.html.

———. (2010b). "Branding and Communications Major NCAA Challenges from Group Perspective." President's Briefing Documents. Accessed March 2012. http://fs.ncaa.org/Docs/newmedia/2010/Emmert/Part3/BC.html.

———. (2010c). "Protecting the Collegiate Model." President's Briefing Documents. Accessed March 2012. http://fs.ncaa.org/Docs/newmedia/2010/Emmert/Part5/protecting.html.

———. (2014). "NCAA President's Testimony on Value of College Model." NCAA.org, July 9. http://www.ncaa.org/about/resources/media-center/news/ncaa-president%E2%80%99s-testimony-value-college-model.

———. (2021). "2.9. The Principle of Amateurism." NCAA LSDBi. https://web3.ncaa.org/lsdbi/search/bylawView?id=2470#result.

———. (2022a). "NCAA Core Values." Accessed August 20. https://www.ncaa.org/.

———. (2022b). "Digital & Social Media." Accessed August 20. https://www.ncaa.org/.

———. (2022c). "What Is the NCAA?" Accessed July 30. http://www.ncaa.org/.

National Labor Relations Board (2014). Northwestern University and College Athletes Players Association (CAPA), Decision and Direction of Election. No. 13-RC-121359, March 26.

Nocera, Joe (2012). "Orwell and March Madness." *New York Times*, March 30. https://www.nytimes.com/.

Nyad, Diana (1989). "View of Sport: How Illiteracy Makes Athletes Run." *New York Times*, May 28. http://www.nytimes.com/.

Redlawsk, David P. (2002). "Hot Cognition or Cool Consideration? Testing the Effects of Motivated Reasoning on Political Decision Making." *Journal of Politics* 64, no. 4: 1021–44.

Renfro, Wallace (2012). "Amateurism, Professionalism, Commercial Activity and Intercollegiate Athletics: Ambivalence about Principles." *Proceedings of the Santa Clara Sports Law Symposium*, 32–45.

Sack, Allen L., and Ellen J. Staurowsky (1998). *College Athletes for Hire: The Evolution and Legacy of the NCAA Amateur Myth.* Westport, CT: Praeger.

Schwarb, Amy Wimmer (2015). "NCAA's Mark Emmert Reflects on Progress, Looks Ahead to Challenges." NCAA.org, January 16. https://www.ncaa.com/.

Selingo, Jeffrey J. (2012). "The Rise and Fall of the Graduation Rate." *Chronicle of Higher Education,* March 2. http://chronicle.com/article/The-RiseFall-of-the/131036/.

Slaughter, Sheila, and Larry L. Leslie (1997). *Academic Capitalism: Politics, Policies, and the Entrepreneurial University.* Baltimore: Johns Hopkins University Press.

Southall, Richard M. (2014). "NCAA Graduation Rates: A Quarter-Century of Re-branding Academic Success." *Journal of Intercollegiate Sport* 7, no. 2: 120–33. http://dx.doi.org/10.1123/jis.2014-0134.

Southall, Richard M., Mark S. Nagel, John M. Amis, and Crystal Southall (2008). "A Method to March Madness: Institutional Logics and the 2006 National Collegiate Athletic Association Division I Men's Basketball Tournament." *Journal of Sport Management* 22, no. 6: 677–700.

Southall, Richard M., and Crystal Southall (2018). "The National Collegiate Athletic Association's 'Nothing Short of Remarkable' Rebranding of Academic Success." In *Sport in the Neoliberal University: Profit, Politics, and Pedagogy*, edited by Ryan King-White. Piscataway, NJ: Rutgers University Press, 131–52.

Southall, Richard M., and Ellen J. Staurowsky (2013). "Cheering on the Collegiate Model: Creating, Disseminating, and Imbedding the NCAA's Redefinition of Amateurism." *Journal of Sport and Social Issues* 37, no. 4: 403–29.

Stuart, Helen, and Laurent Muzellec (2004). "Corporate Makeovers: Can a Hyena Be Rebranded?" *Journal of Brand Management* 11, no. 6: 472–82.

The University of Alabama (2008). "UA Student-Athletes Post Strong Graduation Success Rate." Accessed August 20, 2022. https://news.ua.edu/2008/.

PART II

Legal and Economic Realities of Big-Time College Sports

The Legal Status of College Athletes as Employees under Workers' Compensation and Labor Laws

Richard T. Karcher

> Athletes on grants are contractual employees of an athletic program. They sell their talents as sports entertainers in exchange for athletic scholarships. They cannot be compared to regular students because the latter are consumers, not sellers. Athletes are like staff members whom the university hires on the basis of their skills to do particular jobs.
>
> —MURRAY SPERBER, *COLLEGE SPORTS INC.*

A person who receives a benefit from another in return for services on a contractual basis is either an employee or an independent contractor. The characterization of the relationship can be agreed upon by the parties prior to the commencement of services. Indeed sometimes the parties expressly agree upon what the relationship is not by including a provision in the contract that states, for example, "The relationship of the parties shall not be deemed an employer-employee relationship." The characterization of the relationship has significant legal consequences, including the applicability of state workers' compensation statutes as well as state and federal labor laws. Employees are afforded various rights and benefits under workers' compensation and labor laws, but independent contractors generally are not.

College athletes do not, technically, receive scholarships (financial aid provided on the basis of academic merit) in return for performing athletic-related services for their universities. Rather they receive a grant-in-aid (GIA). The NCAA (2021a) defines a full GIA variously—but fairly consistently—in several bylaws:

- For purposes of Bylaw 20, a full grant is the value of full tuition and fees, room and board, and required course-related books.

- As defined in Bylaw 15.02.5. The elements of a grant-in-aid are tuition and fees, room and board, books, and other expenses related to attendance at the institution.

College athletes awarded a GIA undisputedly receive a benefit from their universities in return for performing services on a contractual basis. But college athletes receiving GIAs are not designated as either employees or independent contractors in any of the documents forming the contractual relationship with their universities—which includes the National Letter of Intent (NLI), the financial aid agreement, and university publications and brochures—or the entire NCAA 2022–23 *Division I Manual* or Legislative Service Database (LSDBi)—that documents every aspect of the university-athlete relationship. College athletes are not designated as employees or independent contractors because universities, through their voluntary association known as the National Collegiate Athletic Association, collectively and unilaterally characterize the university-athlete relationship on a take it or leave it basis. By designating them as student-athletes, universities have historically avoided both obligations that accompany employee status under workers' compensation and labor laws as well as the connotation that college athletes (especially profit-athletes) perform work deserving of payment as independent contractors.

For more than fifty years, college athletes receiving GIAs have sought compensation and benefits via legal challenges to universities' collective and unilateral characterization of their relationship, specifically by filing workers' compensation claims for sport-related injuries and antitrust claims for universities' conspiring to fix the price for their services at the cost of a full GIA. In 2014 (discussed in detail in the chapter "Northwestern Football, Unionization Efforts, and the NLRB's Decision Not to Exercise Jurisdiction") football players at Northwestern University sought the right to organize as a union under federal labor law. While the unionization of college football players may still seem like a revolutionary idea, it was only half a century ago that labor unions did not exist for professional athletes (Gould, Wong, and Weitz 2014). According to Weiler et al. (2011: 275), "Not until the mid-1960s did players realize that, for all their status in the outside world, if they were to force owners to change the structure of the players' market they would have to engage in full-fledged collective bargaining under real and professional union leadership." The sport industry aptly illustrates "a basic truth about employment (and other) relationships: intense and visible conflicts about how to divide up the available revenues are more likely when the size of the pie is changing dramatically rather than remaining constant or growing incrementally" (ibid.: 274).

As the size of the financial pie in Power Five football and Division I men's basketball grows exponentially in the twenty-first century, player values are being suppressed to increase profits. Thus conflicts are likely to continue to arise between profit-athletes and their universities about how to divide the increasing revenues. The question remains whether profit-athletes will force universities to change the profit-athlete market, as professional athletes did during the second half of the twentieth century.

This chapter addresses the legal status of college athletes (with a focus on profit-athletes) receiving GIAs as employees under workers' compensation and labor law. The first part outlines what these athletes must prove under state workers' compensation laws as well as the historical challenges faced by athletes in seeking rights under such laws. The second part analyzes the application of the National Labor Relations Act (NLRA) to GIA profit-athletes through the employment lens of players in the professional sport leagues. This part examines the historical framework of National Labor Relations Board (NLRB) precedent regarding college students' employment status from the 1970s through the 2016 *Trs. of Columbia Univ. in the City of N.Y.* decision that student assistants are statutory employees, which helps explain why GIA athletes in the revenue-generating sports—and specifically profit-athletes (as defined throughout this book)—should be viewed as statutory employees. The second part will also address profit-athletes' employment status under the Fair Labor Standards Act.

Workers' Compensation Fundamentals

In the 1800s the industrialization and mechanization of US industrial plants resulted in numerous physical injuries to workers that were often severe and left them temporarily or permanently disabled. In response, in the early 1900s, states began enacting workers' compensation statutes and today every state has one. Under these statutes employers are responsible for compensating employees for job-related injuries even if the employer is not at fault. Workers' compensation is, in essence, a compulsory insurance program by which the employer is required by statute to purchase insurance.

Employers benefit from workers' compensation in two primary ways. First, workers' compensation is the employee's "exclusive remedy" against the employer. This means an injured employee is precluded from filing tort claims against the employer for job-related injuries. Second, an employer's liability is limited to compensation for medical needs and wage loss, with fixed amounts expressed as specific amounts for certain injuries or as a percentage of average wages. Therefore the employer is not responsible for common law damages, such as compensation for pain and suffering the employee might otherwise recover in a court of law.

Insurance premiums for workers' compensation are calculated by multiplying the employer's total payroll by the applicable classification rate used by the state. If a state workers' compensation board determined that athletes receiving

GIAs were employees of their college or university, the board could also determine that the value of their GIA constitutes a salary, in which case an institution's payroll would be the total value of the GIAs (Gould, Wong, and Weitz 2014). Calculating the additional costs to colleges and universities of providing workers' compensation benefits for their athletes is complicated because (1) an institution's cost varies depending on the applicable state's workers' compensation classification rate used to calculate the insurance premium, (2) the value of a GIA varies for each sport, and (3) the value of a GIA varies for each athlete (ibid.).

Moreover, states can exclude certain persons from coverage under their workers' compensation statutes, and a handful of states specifically exclude college athletes. For example, California's statute excludes "any student participating as an athlete in amateur sporting events sponsored by a public agency or public or private nonprofit college, university, or school, who does not receive remuneration for the participation, other than the use of athletic equipment, uniforms, transportation, travel, meals, lodgings, scholarships, grants-in-aid, or other expenses incidental thereto" (California Labor Code §3352(k), 2017). New York law says that the term " 'employee' shall not include persons who are members of a supervised amateur athletic activity operated on a non-profit basis" (N.Y. Worker's Comp. §2(4), 2017). Hawaii's statute provides that "employment" does not include "service for a school, college, university, college club, fraternity, or sorority if performed by a student who is enrolled and regularly attending classes and in return for board, lodging, or tuition furnished, in whole or in part" (Haw. Rev. Stat. Ann. §386-1, 2017). Oregon and Vermont expressly exclude college athletes from coverage as well (Or. Rev. Stat. §656.027(13), 2017; Or. Rev. Stat. §656.027(13), 2017).

However, in 2012 California enacted the Student Athlete Bill of Rights, which effectively nullified the exclusion in California's workers' compensation statute for injured college athletes at large revenue-producing universities (e.g., Power Five universities). By doing so it became the first state to mandate financial protections for college athletes who suffer career-ending injuries at one of the four universities that receive more than $10 million annually in sports media revenue—University of California, Berkeley; University of California, Los Angeles; the University of Southern California; and Stanford University (California Education Code §§67450, 2013). The law, which went into effect at the start of the 2013–14 school year, requires universities to provide a GIA for up to five academic years if the athletic program does not renew GIAs of athletes who suffer incapacitating injuries or illnesses from their athletic participation. In addition the university is required to pay for ongoing medical treatment for a minimum of two years after graduation or separation from the university and to cover insurance deductibles and health-care premiums for low-income athletes.

As can be seen from these examples, while college athletes have historically not been viewed as employees, this does not exclude statutory remedies. If some college athletes (i.e., profit-athletes) are more correctly viewed as employees involved in a for-profit enterprise, it is not unreasonable that state legislatures might take steps to address these athletes' employment status.

College Athletes' Claims for Workers' Compensation Benefits

Notwithstanding the theoretical efficacy of profit-athletes being viewed as employees (see Northwestern University), injured college athletes have historically had little success receiving workers' compensation benefits. This lack of success is based upon the manner in which courts have answered the initial question that must be addressed: With respect to these claims, in the absence of a statutory exclusion from coverage, is an athlete an 'employee' of a college or university? In answering this determination, courts have generally used two tests: the economic reality test and the contract test.

The Economic Reality Test

In determining whether someone is a covered employee for workers' compensation purposes or an independent contractor, some courts look into the "economic reality" of the relationship, which takes into account the following factors:

(1) the proposed employer's right to control or dictate the activities of the proposed employee;
(2) the proposed employer's right to discipline or fire the proposed employee;
(3) the payment of "wages" and, particularly, the extent to which the proposed employee is dependent upon the payment of wages or other benefits for his daily living expenses; and
(4) whether the work performed by the proposed employee was an "integral part" of the regular business of the proposed employer. (*Coleman v. Western Michigan University*, 1983, 38)

In *Coleman* the Michigan Court of Appeals applied the economic reality test to deny the existence of an employer-employee relationship between Western Michigan and a football player named Willie Coleman who was offered and received an annual, renewable GIA consisting of full tuition, room and board, and books. Coleman played for three seasons (1972–74) and during his third year suffered a disabling injury that prevented him from continuing to play football. Coleman continued to receive his GIA for the remainder of his third year; however, the following fall semester his GIA was reduced. As a result Coleman sought workers' compensation benefits equivalent to four semesters, the remainder of his college tenure at the time of injury.

The court agreed with Coleman that the third factor, the payment of wages, was satisfied in his situation, noting that "in return for his services as a football player, [Coleman] received certain items of compensation which are measurable in money, including room and board, tuition and books" (39). The court also noted that Coleman was financially dependent on the GIA to meet his living expenses, and when the GIA was not renewed, he was forced to pursue his education elsewhere because he could not afford to stay at Western Michigan.

But the court rather surprisingly concluded that the second factor, the university's "right to discipline or fire" Coleman, was lacking, because even if the university wanted to remove Coleman from the football team during an academic year, it could not revoke Coleman's GIA for that year. According to the court, because the university could not revoke Coleman's GIA at will, it did not have control or disciplinary authority over him. Interestingly the court did not take into consideration that the university did at the time of Coleman's injury have the right to remove players from the team or the extent to which a coach and the university had the right to discipline players, including the ability to suspend them and deny playing opportunities at their discretion.

Applying the fourth factor, the court concluded that Coleman's football playing was not essential to the business of the university, which it found to be "education and research." The court reasoned that the university's academic program could operate effectively even in the absence of the intercollegiate football program. Unfortunately the *Coleman* court's interpretation of the application of the fourth factor inappropriately requires courts to determine on an ad hoc basis which particular job duties and tasks are essential and which are not. What should not be overlooked is that following the court's line of reasoning would entail excluding from consideration as essential anyone who works for a university's athletic program, including coaches, personnel in athletics administration, and janitors and maintenance workers who clean and maintain athletics facilities. Moreover, the *Coleman* court's opinion that athletics is not essential to the business of the university directly contradicts universities' own view that "competitive athletics programs of [NCAA] member institutions are designed to be a vital part of the educational system" (NCAA 2021a: bylaw 1.3.1). In reference to competitive athletic programs, former Harvard president Derek Bok (1985: 124) noted that "few aspects of college life have done so much to win the favor of the public, build the loyalties of alumni, and engender lasting memories in the minds of student-athletes."

The court also deemed Coleman's football duties to be nonessential because the greater part of his school year was devoted exclusively to obtaining a regular college education. However, the court's assessment of the amount of time a college athlete devotes to their sport was—and is—not accurate. McCormick and McCormick (2006) found that the daily demands placed upon college football players are enormous and constant: approximately 240 days per year and as many as 262 days if the team participates in a bowl game. This is almost identical to the 260 days an average American works each year (Symmetry Software 2017).

Most courts today would have little difficulty concluding that intercollegiate athletics, in particular Power Five football and Division I men's basketball, is an integral part of the business model of the universities that sponsor these sports. The 2021 *NCAA v. Alston* decision was a notable example of the shift in how the NCAA collegiate model is viewed (Libit 2021; McCann 2021). Even in the mid-1980s, when *Coleman* was decided, the Supreme Court in *NCAA v. Board of Regents of the Univ. of Oklahoma* (1984) explained that the NCAA and its member institutions "market a particular brand of football—college football. . . . The identification of this 'product' with an academic tradition differentiates college football from and makes it more popular than professional sports to which it might otherwise be comparable, such as, for example, minor league baseball (101–2). In 1983 the *Coleman* court's view that college football was not essential to the business of big-time universities was based upon an outdated view of higher education. Today, when research-intensive universities adjust their academic calendars around not just regular-season football or men's basketball games but also March Madness and College Football Playoff (CFP) schedules, it is clear that college sports is an integral component of the "collegiate experience" (Libit 2021).

Lastly, in addressing the "right to control" factor, the court focused on Coleman's academic as opposed to football activities and concluded that his GIA "did not subject him to any extraordinary degree of control over his academic activities. . . . The degree of [the university's] control over this aspect of [Coleman's] activities was no greater than that over any other student" (*Coleman v. WMU,* 1983, 39). Thus, even though Coleman was recruited for his football playing skills and playing football is what Coleman agreed to do (e.g., it was his job) in return for wages in the form of a full GIA, the court took the view that Coleman was a "student first, athlete second" (38). Tellingly the court failed to identify by what measure it concluded athletes and non-athletes are subject to the same degree of control over their academic activities. It is also curious why the court completely neglected to address the university's extensive control over Coleman's football-related duties and responsibilities.

Waldrep v. Texas Employers Insurance Assn. (2000) is a more recent case that addressed the "right to control" element and, like *Coleman,* held that a college football player was not an employee for workers' compensation purposes. Alvis Kent Waldrep Jr. enrolled at Texas Christian University (TCU) in August 1972 and received a full GIA plus ten dollars per month for incidentals in exchange for playing football. In October 1974 Waldrep sustained a severe injury to his spinal cord during a game against the University of Alabama and was paralyzed below the neck. In 1991 he filed a workers' compensation claim and was awarded benefits by the Texas Workers' Compensation Commission. The Texas Employers Insurance Association appealed the award to the district court, and a jury found that Waldrep failed to prove that he was an employee of TCU at the time of his injury. While the Texas Court of Appeals found that "the record reflects that TCU *exercised* direction and control over all of the athletes in its football program" (*Waldrep v. Texas Employers Insurance Assn,* 2000, 702; emphasis added), like the *Coleman* court, it also found that Waldrep's acceptance of a GIA from TCU "did not subject him to any extraordinary degree of control over his academic activities" (702). It is unclear why the *Coleman* and *Waldrep* courts concluded universities do not exercise direction and control over an athlete's academic activities. For several years, athletic departments have had academic counseling programs, tutoring programs, class monitors, and regularly scheduled study halls (Davis 1991). Participation in many of these programs and/or activities is mandatory. In addition both courts failed to acknowledge the myriad academic standards and requirements set forth in NCAA bylaws that athletes must adhere to in order to maintain their eligibility and retain their GIA.

However, two particularly noteworthy aspects of the *Waldrep* case are highly favorable to college athletes. First, the court of appeals noted that "Waldrep clearly presented evidence that TCU *exercised* direction or control over some of his activities while a student at the university" and that "the jury might have found this sufficient to prove that TCU had the *right* to direct the means or details of Waldrep's activities, but the jury declined to do so" (*Waldrep v. Texas Employers Insurance Assn.*, 2000, 702; emphasis added). Second, in the concluding paragraph of the opinion, the court of appeals highlighted that "college athletics has changed dramatically over the years since Waldrep's injury" and that its decision to affirm the jury's verdict "is based on facts and circumstances as they existed almost twenty-six years ago" (707). The court added: "We express no opinion as to whether our decision would be the same in an analogous situation arising today; therefore, our opinion should not be read too broadly" (ibid.).

The Contract Test

An employer-employee relationship for purposes of workers' compensation law may be created only by contract. Therefore an alternative test courts have used to determine whether a college athlete is a covered employee for workers' compensation focuses on the existence of an express or implied contract of hire.

It is undisputed that the university and athlete have a contractual relationship in which the athlete agrees to participate in athletics for the university in exchange for various benefits provided by the university that have monetary value. The key documents evidencing the express contract between the university and athlete consist of the NLI and the financial aid agreement. Pursuant to the NLI, a prospective college athlete agrees to attend a university in exchange for a promise in writing from the university to provide financial aid for one full academic year. The financial aid agreement provides that the university commits to extending financial aid to the athlete in exchange for the athlete's promise to attend the university and participate in athletics. What is peculiar about the university-athlete relationship is neither the NLI nor the financial aid agreement states whether the athlete is an employee or independent contractor. Instead college athletes are assigned the unique label of student-athletes.[1]

The pertinent question under the contract test for workers' compensation purposes is whether either or both the NLI and financial aid agreement can be construed as a "contract of hire." In answering this question, courts attempt to determine the intentions or expectations of the parties. In the same year that *Coleman* was decided, the Indiana Supreme Court in *Rensing v. Indiana State Univ. Bd. of Trustees* (1983) applied the contract test to deny workers' compensation benefits to a football player who sustained an injury during football practice that left him a quadriplegic. The court said there must be a mutual belief that an employer-employee relationship exists, and it focused on the NCAA's strict rules prohibiting pay (see bylaw 12.2.1), that the Internal Revenue Service does not tax GIA recipients, that Rensing did not hold a regular job for the university in addition to playing a sport, and that he was not considered to be a professional athlete who was being paid for his athletic ability.

Two cases decided prior to *Rensing* applied the contract test and ruled in favor of athletes: *University of Denver v. Nemeth* (1953) and *Van Horn v. Industrial Accident Commission* (1963). Both cases involved a similar fact pattern in which the athlete was employed by the university to perform a job unrelated to athletics (such as maintaining tennis courts or working in the cafeteria) but was injured while participating in his sport. In *Nemeth* the Supreme Court of Colorado awarded compensation because the job unrelated to athletics at the university was dependent, or conditional, on his playing football, noting that Nemeth could not retain his non-athletic job without playing football. The *Van Horn* court focused on whether there was consideration (was Van Horn paid for his services?) and noted that the form of remuneration is immaterial: "Direct compensation in the form of wages is not necessary to establish the [employment] relationship so long as the service is not gratuitous" (464). In response to the threat posed by *Nemeth* that athletes could be identified as employees by state industrial commissions and the courts, Walter Byers (then NCAA executive director) crafted the term *student-athlete* and mandated that it be used in place of such words as *players* and *athletes* (Byers and Hammer 1995: 69; Sperber 1998). In other words, even though athletes are compensated for performing athletic services for their universities, the NCAA created a term of art designed to portray college athletes as primarily students engaged in an extracurricular educational activity (Byers and Hammer 1995: 69).

The *Waldrep* court, in addition to assessing the right to control, examined whether a contract of hire existed and, like the *Rensing* court, focused on the expectations of the parties to conclude that no such contract existed. The *Waldrep* court relied on the following pieces of evidence: (1) the NCAA's strict rules against "taking pay for participation in sports"; (2) Waldrep and TCU did not treat the financial aid as pay or income, as he was never placed on TCU's payroll or paid a salary, no social security or income tax was withheld, and Waldrep never filed a tax return; (3) during the recruitment process the parties never discussed that he would be considered an employee or employed; and (4) Waldrep knew that he had to maintain certain academic requirements in order to play football and thus that his academic responsibilities dictated whether he could continue to play.

Reliance on the Workers' Compensation Cases to Reject College Athletes' Employee Status in Other Contexts

Courts have even relied upon or referenced the workers' compensation cases to conclude that college athletes are not employees in other contexts that require the existence of an employment relationship.

For example, under the doctrine of *respondeat superior,* there must be an employment relationship established in order for an entity to be vicariously liable for the tortious acts of its worker. *Kavanagh v. Trustees of Boston Univ.* (2003) held that the university was not vicariously liable for any torts committed by an athlete while playing for the university's basketball team because an employment relationship was found to be lacking. In reliance on the *Rensing* and *Coleman* decisions, the court said that "the fact that a college or university has facilitated a student's ability to attend that institution by providing a scholarship or other financial assistance does not transform the relationship between the academic institution and the student into any form of employment relationship" (1175). In *Townsend v. State of California* (1987), the court held that a men's basketball player was not an employee of San Jose State University for purposes of the California Tort Claims Act and the applicability of the doctrine of *respondeat superior.* The court referenced the portion of the California's workers' compensation statute that excludes college athletes from the definition of employee to hold that a scholarship athlete was not an employee in other contexts as well.

In addressing whether there was an employment relationship that gives governmental workers immunity from tort claims, an Ohio court in *Korellas v. Ohio State Univ.* (2002) distinguished *Van Horn* and held that a scholarship athlete on the football team was not an employee of the university and therefore not entitled to governmental immunity in civil actions. That same year a California court, in *Shephard v. Loyola Marymount Univ.* (2002), held that a women's basketball player was not an employee for purposes of bringing suit under the California Fair Employment and Housing Act.

College Athletes as Independent Contractors: Removing the Exclusive Remedy Barrier

If athletes who are contractually bound to participate in athletics for a university in exchange for a GIA that has monetary value are not employees, then what are they? The *Waldrep* court curiously noted that in workers' compensation cases, courts have almost uniformly analyzed whether the claimant of benefits is an employee as distinguished from an independent contractor. For example, in *Thompson v. Travelers Indem. Co.* (1990), the court addressed whether a jockey was an employee of a racetrack when he was injured immediately after a race and prior to dismount. The court stated that "the test to determine whether a worker is an employee or an independent contractor is whether the employer has the right to control the progress, details, and methods of operations of the employee's work" (278).

Interestingly the *Waldrep* court also highlighted the fact that "there is no allegation that Waldrep was an independent contractor" (698). Employees are barred from filing tort claims against their employer by workers' compensation's "exclusive remedy" provision—that is, workers' compensation benefits are the injured employee's exclusive remedy. Thus injured workers who are independent contractors are not barred from filing tort claims. However, unlike with workers' compensation, the injured worker must prove that the injury was caused by the employer's negligence. Negligence is conduct that "falls below the standard established by law for the protection of others against unreasonable risk of harm" (Restatement [Second] of Torts §282). In the university-athlete relationship, examples of negligence could be failing to provide supervision and training, failing to provide preventive measures in the event of a medical emergency, failing to diagnose and treat medical injuries, and permitting or requiring an injured athlete to return to a game (*Davidson v. University of North Carolina,* 2001; *Kleinknecht v. Gettysburg College,* 1993; *Lamorie v. Warner Pacific College,* 1993; *Orr v. Brigham Young University,* 1997; *Searles v. Trustees of St. Joseph's College,* 1997).

Universities' insistence that athletes are not employees subjects them to potential tort liability without the benefit of the damage limitations afforded by workers' compensation statutes, and the damage awards and settlements can be quite substantial in tort. For example, a court awarded damages of six hundred thousand dollars due to the failure of a team's coaches to recommend that a softball player see a physician for treatment of her eye injury, which had occurred when she was struck by a ball thrown during practice. Later the player lost her vision as a direct result of the initial injury and the failure to address it properly (*Stineman v. Fontbonne College*, 1981). In 2005 Northwestern University paid $16 million to settle a wrongful death lawsuit. A player who had a known asthmatic condition collapsed during a preseason workout, and the subsequent lawsuit claimed that negligent emergency medical treatment was provided (Mitten et al. 2013).

To avoid tort liability and having to pay injured athletes any compensation, universities have generally defended tort lawsuits by asserting that they owe their athletes no legal duty of care—that is, that the university has no legal obligation to protect athletes from risk of injury while participating in athletics. A court will dismiss a tort claim if it concludes that the university does not owe a duty. If no legal duty is owed and workers' compensation is unavailable, injured athletes whose GIAs are not renewed are left without a remedy.

However, there is substantial precedent that has held a duty of care is owed to college athletes. If the alleged negligence is premised on a university's failure to protect an athlete from a harm that the university or its agents did not directly create, some courts have found that an affirmative duty to act is imposed upon the university as a result of a "special relationship" between the university and the athlete. This special relationship was explained in *Kleinknecht v. Gettysburg College* (1993: 1368):

> There is a distinction between a student injured while participating as an intercollegiate athlete in a sport for which he was recruited and a student injured at a college while pursuing his private interests, scholastic or otherwise. This distinction serves to limit the class of students to whom a college owes the duty of care that arises here. . . . The fact that Drew's cardiac arrest occurred during an athletic event involving an intercollegiate team of which he was a member does impose a duty of due care on a college that actively sought his participation in that sport.

The court in *Davidson v. University of North Carolina* (2001) also concluded that a special relationship existed between the university and a member of the cheerleading squad. First, with an athlete who is a member of a school-sponsored intercollegiate team, there is a situation of "mutual dependence" (927). UNC benefited from the cheerleaders' appearances at games and events, and in such capacity they act as representatives of the school. The cheerleaders received benefits in the form of uniforms, transportation, the use of facilities and equipment for practices, and one hour of course credit that satisfied the school's physical education requirement. Second, and ironically, the *Davidson* court found it significant that universities "exert a high degree of control over many aspects of a student athlete's life" (ibid.), noting that the cheerleaders had to abide by certain standards of conduct such as maintaining a minimum GPA and refraining from drinking alcohol in public.

Even though tort liability may be a mechanism for profit-athletes to pursue, it is not a sufficient remedy for college athletes for three primary reasons. First, even if a legal duty is owed, in order for athletes to recover damages they must prove that an act of negligence caused their injury. Second, lawyers working on a contingency fee basis will typically only take on representation if the athlete has suffered serious injury or is a highly ranked professional prospect whose injury substantially impacts a future athletic career. Finally, depending on the jurisdiction, a public university and its employees may be insulated from tort liability by asserting the defense of sovereign (governmental) immunity, which results in the university owing the athlete nothing even if its employees were negligent (*Harris v. University of Michigan Board of Regents,* 1996; *Lennon v. Petersen,* 1993; *University of Texas at El Paso v. Moreno,* 2005).

Labor Law, the Right to Organize, and the Definition of "Employee"

Section 7 of the NLRA gives workers the right to (1) form a labor organization, (2) bargain collectively through a representative of their choosing, and (3) engage in "concerted activities" such as picketing and strikes (National Labor Relations Act, 29 U.S.C. §157). Section 8(a) prohibits employers from interfering with workers' exercise of these rights (29 U.S.C. §158(a)). The oversight and enforcement of these rights of workers falls under the jurisdiction of the NLRB and the federal courts (Mitten et al. 2013).

In order for a union to become NLRB certified, an organizing drive must result in the right to represent the employees in collective bargaining with their employer. If a union can demonstrate a 30 percent "showing of interest" among the employees, it must petition the NLRB to conduct a secret ballot election (Weiler et al. 2011). To certify a union as the exclusive bargaining representative for all the employees, section 9(a) of the NLRA requires that a simple majority votes in favor of union representation.

Before an election is conducted, section 9(b) of the NLRA provides that the NLRB must first define the "unit appropriate for purposes of collective bargaining" (ibid.: 297). In doing so the NLRB determines whether the union's proposed employee grouping has a sufficient "community of interest" (ibid.). In professional sports it is assumed that the appropriate bargaining unit comprises all active players in the league (i.e., a national league-wide bargaining unit, not local team bargaining units) (ibid.). On the management side, multi-employer bargaining occurs when individual teams in the league band together to negotiate a collective bargaining agreement (CBA) with the players' union that applies equally to all teams. Yasser et al. (2015: 435) notes that the collective bargaining process in professional sports "is necessarily a multi-party phenomenon," and "neither labor nor management is internally monolithic."

A professional sports league "is comprised of several franchises bearing few similarities, economically or otherwise," and club owners have diverse personalities (Yasser et al. 2015: 435). A players' union comprises athletes with vastly different positions, roles, skill sets, and market values. Nevertheless the unique structure and operation of league sports makes a single league-wide unit much more functional for bargaining than multiple single-team units. In *North American Soccer League v. NLRB* (1980), the Fifth Circuit affirmed the NLRB's finding that a single league-wide bargaining unit was appropriate in a joint employer relationship in which the league exercises a significant degree of control over essential aspects of the clubs' labor relations, including the selection, retention, and termination of players; the terms of individual player contracts; dispute resolution; and player discipline.

The NLRA requires employers to negotiate with a union that is duly certified by the NLRB over issues relating to "wages, hours, and terms and conditions of employment"; these issues are considered mandatory subjects of bargaining (29 U.S.C. §158(d)). Thus if college football players in the Big Ten Conference were to unionize as part of a multi-employer bargaining unit, their universities would incur an immediate obligation to bargain with them over these mandatory subjects of bargaining (Edelman 2014). In the late 1960s, initial CBAs in professional sport leagues (e.g., the NFL and MLB) mostly focused on job security, pension plans, minimum salaries, and fringe benefits (Mitten et al. 2013). Since then, with the changing economic landscape of sports, the focus has shifted to issues involving restraints on player mobility (e.g., the draft, free agency, etc.) and salaries (e.g., salary caps, luxury taxes, etc.) (ibid.).

Unlike in many other industries, in North American professional sport leagues management actually favors, and benefits from, a unionized workforce. Club owners need players to be unionized if they want to create and enforce league-wide rules and policies that restrict player mobility and salaries (Masteralexis 2014). Importantly, while agreements among employers that restrict competition in the labor market would normally be subject to antitrust scrutiny, they are immune from the antitrust laws under the "non-statutory labor exemption" when they are the product of good-faith bargaining between unionized employees and their employers (*Brown v. Pro Football, Inc.*, 1996). As Edelman (2014: 2356) notes, if Football Bowl Subdivision (FBS) college football players were unionized as part of a multi-employer bargaining unit, it "would grant the NCAA the benefit of antitrust law's non-statutory labor exemption—thus allowing for collective bargaining over athlete pay without the risk of any further antitrust liability." In other words FBS football players could no longer file antitrust lawsuits against the NCAA. Moreover unionization as part of a multi-employer bargaining unit would also prevent the players from challenging eligibility decisions in court, because collective bargaining would likely lead to an agreed-upon system of final, binding arbitration to resolve eligibility disputes. Ross, Karcher, and Kensinger (2014) argue that implementing a system of arbitration to resolve NCAA eligibility disputes would provide quick, final, and independent review by neutral experts and promote increased privacy, flexibility, and cost-effectiveness.

Masteralexis (2020) explains how the unionized workplaces in professional sports are vastly different than typical unionized settings. For example, with the average career length in professional sports being approximately three years, athletes' careers are far shorter than in other industries. As such there is more short-term pressure for sport union members to negotiate the best possible wages and working conditions. Also, because sport-union member turnover rate is much higher than other industries, players associations are forced to constantly keep new members informed. Moreover, there are logistical challenges for North American players associations with geographically dispersed memberships. And unlike with typical union members, there is great disparity in the talent and compensation levels and little job security. Weiler et al. (2011) note that while a three-year term is the norm in most industries, CBAs in professional sports typically run four to five years.

Although the NCAA insists that college and professional athletes are distinct, unionized professional athletes in North American team sports have much in common with profit-athletes. Specifically both Power Five and NFL football players

- have three- to four-year average careers with a significant lack of job security;
- perform identical job duties and responsibilities with substantially similar game and practice schedules;
- are susceptible to the same career-ending injuries;
- have similar safety concerns regarding play and equipment;
- play for teams that are geographically dispersed regionally and nationally;
- must follow rules that restrict player movement from team to team;
- are subject to disciplinary action in the form of suspension or termination for violating team or league/conference rules;
- have intense competition to secure their services;
- work in an industry with disparate levels of team revenues and profits;
- have licensing value in their names, images, and likenesses (NIL).

Despite these commonalities, in 2014 when Northwestern University was confronted with a unionization effort by its GIA football players, the university relied on the NLRB's decision in *Brown University* (2004), which held that graduate student assistants are not employees because they "are primarily students and have a primarily educational, not economic, relationship with their university" (487). Tellingly, *Brown University* has since been overruled by the NLRB in *Columbia University* (2016). With this in mind, it is important to understand the NLRB's position concerning the employment status of student teaching and research assistants before addressing its ruling in *Northwestern University* (2015).

NLRB Decisions on the Employment Status of Student Assistants

The controversy over the treatment of graduate student teaching and research assistants as employees under the NLRA began at the turn of this century at New York University. In *New York University* (2000), the NLRB reversed its ruling in *Leland Stanford Junior University* (1974) that graduate assistants were statutory employees with the right to engage in collective bargaining under the NLRA. However, the legal status of graduate assistants as statutory employees lasted for only a brief four-year period when the NLRB again reversed its position in *Brown University* (2004).

Brown University

In *Brown University* the United Auto Workers sought to represent a unit of approximately 450 graduate students employed as teaching assistants or research assistants in certain social sciences and humanities departments or as proctors at Brown, a private university. The Region 01 director applied the authority of *New York University* (2000) to find that graduate students at Brown were statutory employees within the meaning of the NLRA and constituted an appropriate unit for collective bargaining. Brown subsequently filed a request for review to the NLRB urging it to reconsider its decision in *New York University.*

On review Brown argued that in *New York University* the NLRB "did not adequately consider that the relationship between a research university and its graduate students is not fundamentally an economic one but an educational one" (486). Brown also contended that "the support to students is part of a financial aid program that pays graduate students the same amount, regardless of work, and regardless of the value of those services if purchased on the open market (i.e., hiring a fully-vetted Ph.D.)" (ibid.). Brown asserted: "Common sense dictates that students who teach and perform research as part of their academic curriculum cannot properly be considered employees without entangling the [NLRA] into the intricacies of graduate education" (ibid.).

The NLRB agreed with Brown, overruled *New York University,* and concluded that "the Board's 25-year pre-*NYU* principle of regarding graduate students as nonemployees was sound and well-reasoned" (487). Relying on earlier decisions from the 1970s, including *Adelphi University* (1972), *Leland Stanford Junior University,* and *St. Clare's Hospital* (1977), the NLRB reversed course and decided graduate student assistants are not university employees but rather "are primarily students and have a primarily educational, not economic, relationship with their university" (ibid.).

In *Brown University* the NLRB highlighted the following factors from *Leland Stanford* that supported the "primarily students" principle:

> (1) the research assistants were graduate students enrolled in the Stanford physics department as Ph.D. candidates; (2) they were required to perform research to obtain their degree; (3) they received academic credit for their research work; and (4) while they received a stipend from Stanford, the amount was not dependent on the nature or intrinsic value of the services performed or the skill or function of the recipient, but instead was determined by the goal of providing the graduate students with financial support. (487)

Notably the NLRB emphasized that graduate student assistants must be enrolled as students at Brown to be awarded teaching assistantships, research assistantships, or proctorships; they spend only a limited number of hours performing their duties, with their principal time commitment at Brown focused on obtaining a degree; and their service as a graduate student assistant is "part and parcel of the core elements of the Ph.D. degree" (488–89). The NLRB also emphasized that the money received by the teaching and research assistants and proctors was equivalent to that received by fellows; therefore the money is not "consideration for work" but rather "financial aid to a student" (488). Moreover, the NLRB explained the "purely academic dimension" embedded in the graduate student assistants' relationship with Brown's faculty:

> Because the role of teaching assistant and research assistant is integral to the education of the graduate student, Brown's faculty oversees graduate student assistants in their role as a research or teaching assistant. Although the duties and responsibilities of graduate student assistants vary among departments and faculty, most perform under the direction and control of faculty members from their particular department. TAs generally do not teach independently, and even teaching fellows who have some greater responsibilities follow faculty-established courses. RAs performing research do so under grants applied for by faculty members, who often serve as the RA's dissertation adviser. In addition, these faculty members are often the same faculty that teach or advise the graduate assistant student in their coursework or dissertation preparation. (489)

The NLRB also expressed a policy concern that imposing collective bargaining would "unduly infringe upon traditional academic freedoms" and "have a deleterious impact on overall educational decisions by the Brown faculty and administration"—decisions over (1) class size, time, length, and location; (2) graduate assistants' duties, hours, and stipends; and (3) who, what, and where to teach or research (490). Nevertheless, even if educational matters are beyond the collective bargaining process due to the NLRB's concerns about the integrity of universities' educational missions, the mere assertion of jurisdiction by the NLRB would not necessitate bargaining over education-related issues, because the NLRB "has the ability to except certain issues from the status of mandatory bargaining subjects" (Gould, Wong, and Weitz 2014: 37).

By relying on the "primarily students" principle and proclaiming that traditional academic freedoms would be unduly infringed by imposing collective bargaining, the NLRB avoided the common-law definition of "employee" that was applied in *New York University* (2000), which "reflects the common law agency doctrine of the conventional master-servant relationship" (1205 [citing *NLRB v. Town and Country Electric,* 1995]). Under the common-law test, an employee is "a person who performs services for another under a contract of hire, subject to the other's control or right of control, and in return for payment" (*Brown University,* 2004, 490n27 [citing *NLRB v. Town & Country Electric*]). Thus the key common law test for employee status is "whether there is both benefit and control" (Gould, Wong, and Weitz 2014: 33).

The dissent in *Brown University* contended that the majority "overstepped its authority, overlooked the economic realities of the academic world, and overruled *NYU* without ever coming to terms with the rationale for that decision" (500). While this may have been the case, it should be noted that the Supreme Court (in *NLRB v. Town & Country Electric*) had acknowledged that the NLRB's interpretation and construction of the term *employee* as it is used in the NLRA "is entitled to considerable deference" unless the court determines that the NLRB's "departure from the common law of agency with respect to particular questions and in a particular statutory context, renders its interpretation unreasonable" (94). Accordingly, Gould, Wong, and Weitz (2014: 41) note that while the NLRB "often resorts to the explicit common-law test, the Board nonetheless retains broader discretion to determine the bounds of the NLRA."

Although the NLRB overruled *NYU,* McCormick and McCormick (2006) argue that *Brown University* did not overrule or eliminate the use of the common-law test for "employee" in *New York University.* Rather the NLRB "found that graduate assistants were not employees by virtue of failing the NLRA's statutory definition of employee" (*New York University,* 2000, 96). *Brown University* is grounded on two core principles: "Students who work for their universities are not employees, first, if their work is primarily educational and, second, if their relationship with the university is not an economic one" (McCormick and McCormick 2006: 95). If this is the case, it must follow that "when a student who works for his university performs services that are not primarily educational or academic and his relationship to the university with respect to those services is an economic one, then the student may be an employee under the [NLRA], provided that he also meets the common law test for that term" (ibid.: 95–96).

The NLRB repeatedly emphasized in *Brown University* that the teaching and research duties of graduate student assistants are an integral part of the educational program: "graduate student assistants . . . for whom supervised teaching or research is an integral component of their academic development" (483); "for a substantial majority of graduate students, teaching is so integral to their education" (488); "a given graduate student may be a teacher, researcher, or proctor for only a portion of his or her tenure as a student. However . . . that task is an integral part of being a graduate student" (489); "the role of teaching assistant and research assistant is integral to the education of the graduate student" (489).

The "integral part of the educational program" language also appeared in *St. Clare's Hospital,* which was directly quoted and relied upon by the NLRB in *Brown University:*

> The rationale . . . is a relatively simple and straightforward one. Since the individuals are rendering services which are directly related to—and indeed constitute an *integral part of—their educational program,* they are serving primarily as students and not primarily as employees. In our view this is a very fundamental distinction for it means that the mutual interests of the students and the educational institution in the services being rendered are predominantly academic rather than economic in nature. Such interests are completely foreign to the normal employment relationship and, in our judgment, are not readily adaptable to the collective-bargaining process. (489 [quoting *St. Clare's Hospital,* 1977, 1002]; emphasis added).

The NLRB's strong pro-academic and anti-economic stance articulated in *St. Clare's Hospital* survived as precedent for a twenty-two-year period from 1977 to 1999 and then became the rationale for *Brown University.*

It is no coincidence the NCAA incorporated language from these decisions in crafting bylaws that set forth as a "fundamental policy" a differentiation between college and professional sports. Article 1.3.1 states: "A basic purpose of [the NCAA] is to maintain intercollegiate athletics as an *integral part of the educational program* and the athlete as an *integral part* of the student body and, by so doing, retain a clear line of demarcation between intercollegiate athletics and professional sports" (NCAA 2021b; emphasis added).

Columbia University

The NCAA may want to rethink its "fundamental policy" in light of a more recent NLRB decision in *Trustees of Columbia University* (2016), in which it flatly rejected the "primarily students" principle and held that undergraduate and graduate student assistants, including assistants engaged in research funded by external grants, are statutory employees entitled to the protections of the NLRA. Applying the common-law test to a research assistant's work, the NLRB found the requisite control and benefit because "Columbia directs the student research assistants' work and the performance of defined tasks is a condition of the grant aid" (18).

In overruling *Brown University,* the NLRB explained: "The fundamental error of the *Brown University* Board was to frame the issue of statutory coverage not in terms of the existence of an employment relationship, but rather on whether some other relationship between the employee and employer is the primary one—a standard neither derived from the statutory text of Section 2(3) nor from the fundamental policy of the Act" (5). *Columbia University* makes it entirely possible that two distinct roles—education and employment—can coexist: "[A] graduate student may be both a student *and* an employee; a university may be both the student's educator *and* employer" (7).

Northwestern University: The Regional Director's Decision

On March 26, 2014, the regional office of the NLRB in Chicago released its decision and direction of election in the Northwestern University case. In 2014 football players at Northwestern University, a private university and member of the Big Ten Conference, petitioned the NLRB for a union election, seeking to organize as the College Athletes Players Association (CAPA). At the time Northwestern's football team had 112 players, 85 of whom received a full GIA, to which Northwestern attached a retail value of sixty-one thousand dollars each academic year (approximately seventy-six thousand dollars if a player enrolled in summer classes) (*Northwestern University,* March 26, 2014, 3).

Application of the Common-Law Test

NLRB regional director Peter Sung Ohr concluded that GIA football players at Northwestern were employees within the meaning of the NLRA, which gave them the right to form a union and collectively bargain over terms and conditions of their employment with Northwestern. Applying the common-law definition of *employee,* Ohr found that "players receiving scholarships to perform football-related services for [Northwestern] under a contract for hire in return for compensation are subject to [Northwestern's] control and are therefore employees within the meaning of the [NLRA]" (Northwestern University, 2014, 14). The regional director articulated three principal reasons for his finding: (1) scholarship football players perform services for the benefit of Northwestern for which they receive compensation (14–15); (2) scholarship football players are "under strict and exacting control" by Northwestern in the performance of their duties as football players (15–16); and (3) walk-ons are distinguishable from scholarship players and do not meet the definition of *employee* because, unlike scholarship players, they do not receive compensation for the athletic services they perform and do not sign a tender or otherwise enter into any type of employment contract with Northwestern (17).

In support of the first reason, Ohr noted that football players perform valuable services for Northwestern; its football program generated revenues of approximately $235 million during the nine-year period from 2003 to 2012 and also has an "immeasurable positive impact" on alumni giving and increase in the number of applicants for enrollment (Northwestern University, 2014, 14). In order to field the most competitive team possible, GIA players are "initially sought out, recruited and ultimately granted scholarships because of their athletic prowess on the football field," making it clear that the GIAs they receive are compensation for the athletic services they perform for Northwestern (ibid.). Although the players "do not receive a paycheck in the traditional sense," the GIAs constitute "a transfer of economic value" in that Northwestern pays for the players' tuition, fees, room and board, and books throughout the four or five years they perform football duties for Northwestern (ibid.). How the university characterizes GIAs is irrelevant: "The fact that the [university] does not treat these scholarships or stipends as taxable income is not dispositive of whether it is compensation" (ibid.).

The regional director explained that there is an extensive degree of employment-type control exercised by Northwestern and its coaches over the players, evidenced as follows:

- During the six-week training camp before the start of the school year, the coaches "prepare and provide detailed itineraries to the players which set forth, hour by hour, what football related activities the players are to engage in from as early as 5:45 a.m. until 10:30 p.m., when they are expected to be in bed," and "the location, duration, and manner in which the players carry out their football duties" (15).
- The football games themselves comprise a large time commitment for the players: "if the team is playing an away game, it is not unusual for the players to have to spend 25 hours over a two-day period traveling to and from the game, attending practices and meetings, and competing in the game" (15–16).
- The coaches "have control over nearly every aspect of the players' private lives by virtue of the fact that there are many rules that they must follow under threat of discipline and/or the loss of a scholarship" (16).
- The players' academic pursuits are even impacted and controlled in that they often are unable to take certain courses due to conflicts with scheduled practices and must miss classes due to conflicts with travel to football games (16).

The tender that GIA football players are required to sign sets forth the type of compensation provided to the players and "serves as an employment contract and also gives the players detailed information concerning the duration and conditions under which the compensation will be provided to them" (14). The regional director noted that "scholarship players are truly dependent on their scholarships to pay for basic necessities, including food and shelter" (14). He also noted that players' GIAs can be reduced or canceled by the head football coach for a variety of reasons and that a GIA "is clearly tied to the player's performance of athletic services," because it can be immediately canceled if the player voluntarily withdraws from the team or violates team rules (15).

Distinguishing GIA Football Players from Graduate Student Assistants

Northwestern argued that its GIA football players are not employees, because they do not meet the statutory definition of *employee* under "primarily students" principle put forth in *Brown University.* Even though the "primarily students" test was declared invalid by the NLRB in *Columbia University* (after the *Northwestern University* decision), it is important to understand why GIA football players are not employees under that test in the event the NLRB reverts to it. Essentially the regional director found that they failed the test because "the players' football-related duties are unrelated to their academic studies unlike the graduate assistants whose teaching and research duties were inextricably related to their graduate degree requirements" (18). The regional director applied the four factors of the "primarily students" test to GIA football players and found as follows:

- Regarding the first factor, the regional director noted that it cannot be said that GIA players are primarily students because they spend fifty to sixty hours per week on their football duties during a one-month training camp prior to the start of the academic year and an additional forty to fifty hours per week on those duties during the three- or four-month football season, which is more hours than many undisputed full-time employees work at their jobs and many more hours than the players spend on their studies and attending classes (18).
- A second factor was that the players' athletic duties do not constitute a core element of their educational degree requirements. Unlike the graduate assistants at Brown, GIA football players "do not receive any academic credit for playing football," and "they are also not required to play football in order to obtain their undergraduate degree, regardless of which major they pursue" (19). The regional director was not persuaded that the players' relationship with their university is primarily an academic one because

they learn "great life lessons from participating on the football team" and "important values such as character, dedication, perseverance, and team work" (19). Rather he found the relationship to be "an economic one that involves the transfer of great sums of money to the players in the form of scholarships" (19).

- Regarding the third factor, unlike the graduate student assistants at Brown, faculty do not supervise or oversee the athletic duties that players perform; rather football coaches who are not faculty members supervise these activities. According to the regional director, "this critical distinction certainly lessens any concern that imposing collective bargaining would have a 'deleterious impact on overall educational decisions' by the [university's] academic faculty" (19).
- Regarding the fourth factor, unlike the graduate student assistants at Brown, the university only offers a GIA to prospective students if they intend to provide an athletic service to the university, which includes playing in games and attending all of the practices, workouts, and meetings. Moreover, players "stand to lose their scholarship if they 'voluntarily withdraw' from the team" (20).

Direction of Election

The regional director ordered an immediate election by secret ballot under his direction among the employees in a bargaining unit consisting of "all football players receiving football grant-in-aid scholarship[s] and not having exhausted their playing eligibility" (23). In April 2014 Northwestern football players voted by secret ballot whether to unionize, which would have required a majority of the ballots cast (McCann 2015). The NLRB directed the ballots to be impounded until it issued a decision affirming, modifying, or reversing the regional director's decision (DeFrancesco 2014).

In addition, the regional director concluded that CAPA is "a labor organization" within the meaning of the NLRA. CAPA introduced sufficient evidence at the hearing to demonstrate that it was established to represent and advocate for the rights of collegiate athletes in collective bargaining with respect to "health and safety, financial support, and other terms and conditions of employment" (23). There was also a "substantial portion" of Northwestern's GIA football players who signed authorization cards seeking to have CAPA represent them for the purposes of collective bargaining.

Northwestern University: The NLRB's "Non-decision" Decision

On April 24, 2014, the NLRB granted Northwestern University's request for review of the regional director's decision and direction of election, saying Northwestern had raised substantial issues that warranted review. The NLRB raised the following six questions that interested parties were invited to brief:

1. What test should the Board apply to determine whether grant-in-aid scholarship football players are "employees" within the meaning of Section 2(3) of the Act, and what is the proper result here, applying the appropriate test?
2. Insofar as the Board's decision in *Brown University*, 342 *NLRB* 483 (2004), may be applicable to this case, should the Board adhere to, modify, or overrule the test of employee status applied in that case, and if so, on what basis?
3. What policy considerations are relevant to the Board's determination of whether grant-in-aid scholarship football players are "employees" within the meaning of Section 2(3) of the Act and what result do they suggest here?
4. To what extent, if any, is the existence or absence of determinations regarding employee status of grant-in-aid scholarship football players under other federal or state statutes or regulations relevant to whether such players are "employees" under the Act?
5. To what extent are the employment discrimination provisions of Title VII, in comparison to the antidiscrimination provisions of Title IX of the Education Amendments Act of 1972, relevant to whether grant-in-aid scholarship football players are "employees" under the Act?
6. If grant-in-aid scholarship football players are "employees" under the Act, to what extent, if any, should the Board consider, in determining the parties' collective-bargaining obligations, the existence of outside constraints that may alter the ability of the parties to engage in collective bargaining as to certain terms and conditions of employment? What, if any, should be the impact of such constraints on the parties' bargaining obligations? In the alternative, should the Board recognize grant-in-aid scholarship football players as "employees" under the Act, but preclude them from being represented in any bargaining unit or engaging in any collective bargaining, as is the case with confidential employees under Board law? (*Northwestern University* 2014).

In its decision on review and order issued on August 17, 2015, the NLRB concluded that it should decline jurisdiction over the petition to unionize Northwestern University's football players because "it would not effectuate the policies of the [NLRA] to assert jurisdiction" (NLRB 2015: 3). The NLRB noted that its decision "is primarily premised on a finding that, because of the nature of sports leagues (namely the control exercised by the leagues over individual teams) and the composition and structure of FBS football (in which the overwhelming majority of competitors are public colleges and universities over which the Board cannot assert jurisdiction), it would not promote stability in labor relations to assert jurisdiction in this case" (ibid.). All but 17 of the 125 colleges and universities participating in FBS football are state-run institutions and thus are not employers within the meaning of Section 2(2) of the NLRA (ibid.: 5). Indeed, given that Northwestern is the only private school in the Big Ten, the NLRB cannot assert jurisdiction over any of the other conference members (ibid.). Therefore *Northwestern University* presented "novel and unique circumstances" (ibid.: 3) that made it an "unprecedented" NLRB case; it was a "single-team bargaining unit," and all previous NLRB cases in professional sports involved league-wide bargaining units (ibid.: 5). The NLRB explained that even if GIA players can be analogized to players for professional sports teams, professional sport league collective bargaining "has never involved a bargaining unit consisting of a single team's players, where the players for competing teams were unrepresented or entirely outside the Board's jurisdiction" (ibid.: 4).

The fact that Northwestern University was a single-team bargaining unit raised practical concerns for the NLRB due to the nature of league team sports. The activity of team sports "must be carried out jointly by the teams in the league or association involved," and "there is no 'product' without direct interaction among the players and cooperation among the various teams" (NLRB 2015: 4). The board noted that a league or association must therefore set common rules and standards governing their competitions and have the authority to police and enforce the rules and regulations that govern eligibility, practice, and competition, all of which are necessary to ensure the uniformity and integrity of individual games and thus league competition as a whole (ibid.). This, the NLRB explained, creates "a symbiotic relationship among the various teams, the conferences, and the NCAA" (ibid.). As such labor issues that involve only one team and its players at Northwestern would have ramifications for the NCAA, the Big Ten Conference, and the other member institutions (ibid.).

McCann (2015) noted this difficulty: "[A] decision by the NLRB that Northwestern players are employees—and by implication eligible for salary and other employment benefits—would have altered Northwestern's recruiting as well as the recruiting of other sports programs at private universities."

The Status of College Athletes as "Employees" after Brown and Northwestern

Perhaps the most significant aspect of the NLRB's decision to decline jurisdiction over the petition to unionize Northwestern University's GIA football players is the NLRB's express statement that it did not decide whether the players were employees within the meaning of the NLRA. Thus the NLRB's decision did not overrule the regional director's determination and finding that the GIA football players were employees; if anything it implies that they are (Birmingham 2015). The NLRB highlighted that GIA football players "do not fit into any analytical framework that the Board has used in cases involving other types of students" and, in this regard, "bear little resemblance to the graduate student assistants" in *Brown University* and *New York University* (NLRB 2015: 3). In a footnote the NLRB even expressed agreement with a key finding of the regional director: "Unlike those graduate assistants, the scholarship players are undergraduates, and—with the potential exception of students seeking undergraduate degrees in physical education—the football activities they engage in are unrelated to their course of study or educational programs" (ibid.: 4). In combination the regional director's decision, the board's decision on review, and *Columbia University* suggest that GIA football players are statutory employees under the NLRA.

The NLRB also clarified that its decision not to assert jurisdiction was limited to the GIA football players in the particular circumstances of this case. The NLRB clearly did not slam the door on any petitions that may be brought by GIA football players in the future:

> We are declining jurisdiction only in this case involving the football players at Northwestern University; we therefore do not address what the Board's approach might be to a petition for all FBS scholarship football players (or at least those at private colleges and universities). The record before us deals solely with Northwestern's football team and, in the absence of any evidence concerning the players and athletes at other schools, we do not decide any issues about them today. As a final note, the Board's decision not to assert jurisdiction does not preclude a reconsideration of this issue in the future. For example, if the circumstances of Northwestern's players or FBS football change such that the underpinnings of our conclusions regarding jurisdiction warrant reassessment, the Board may revisit its policy in this area. (NLRB 2015: 6)

As McCann (2015) highlighted, the NLRB's decision was carefully limited. It is not necessarily a permanent setback for the college-athlete labor movement. Nevertheless, given the multi-conference nature of Power Five football, it is unlikely that GIA football players from private universities will successfully petition to unionize on their own, since the NLRB cannot regulate the substantial majority of public universities within each conference.

On May 27, 2021, the College Athlete Right to Organize (CARO) Act was introduced by Senators Chris Murphy (D-CT) and Bernie Sanders (D-VT).[2] The CARO Act would solve the public university jurisdictional problem by giving the NLRB jurisdiction over public universities in the limited context of employment matters involving college athletes, including the certification of a collective bargaining unit of college athlete employees. The CARO Act would also require the NLRB to recognize multiple schools within a conference as a "multi-employer bargaining unit," which would be the most optimal structure based upon typical factors the NLRB considers in determining appropriate units (business operations, markets, revenue sources and distribution, competition, geography, etc.) and would also be consistent with the historical treatment of the professional leagues under both NLRB and judicial precedent.

Following the board's decision, Northwestern University GIA football players' status as statutory employees was also confirmed in memoranda issued by the NLRB general counsel. In an advice memorandum regarding a charge that limiting athletes' speech and use of social media in Northwestern University's football handbook constituted unfair labor practices, the general counsel stated: "We assume, for purposes of this memorandum, that Northwestern's scholarship football players are statutory employees" (NLRB 2016: 1). The general counsel concluded that the rules were unlawful and required the university to modify or rescind them. In a subsequent memorandum, the general counsel wrote that based on "the record developed in *Northwestern University,* which includes information about NCAA rules that significantly control the activities of Division I FBS scholarship football players; other public information; and the Board's recent decision in *Columbia University,* . . . scholarship football players in Division I FBS private sector colleges and universities are employees under the NLRA" (NLRB 2017: 16). That memorandum was short-lived; it was rescinded in December 2017 by the general counsel, who was appointed by President Donald Trump and confirmed by the US Senate on November 8, 2017 (Wilkinson, 2017). However, on September 29, 2021, the memo was reinstated by the NLRB general counsel in an advice memorandum, which provides updated guidance regarding the general counsel's prosecutorial position that certain players at academic institutions are employees under the NLRA and further provides that, where appropriate, the general counsel will allege that misclassifying such employees as mere student-athletes and leading them to believe that they do not have statutory protections is a violation of Section 8(a)(1) of the NLRA (NLRB 2021: 1).

Employee status analysis under the NLRA and workers' compensation statutes is virtually the same. Thus the NLRB regional director's decision, the board's decision on review, and *Columbia University* support reversing the precedent that GIA football players are not employees under workers' compensation statutes. Indeed the *Waldrep* court highlighted the fact that college athletics has changed dramatically since Waldrep's 1974 injury and left the door open for a GIA football player to prove employee status. One such dramatic changed circumstance is the exponential increase in university revenue generated by GIA football players' activities.

The College Athlete as "Employee" under the Fair Labor Standards Act

The Fair Labor Standards Act (FLSA) is a federal statute that mandates a minimum wage and overtime pay for employees. Unlike the NLRA, an employer under the FLSA includes public universities (29 U.S.C. §203(d)). The FLSA defines an employee as "any individual employed by an employer" (29 U.S.C. §203(e)(1)) and *employ* means "to suffer or permit to work" (29 U.S.C. §203(g)). The term *work*, however, is not defined. Courts have thus determined that "status as an 'employee' for purposes of the FLSA depends on the totality of circumstances rather than on any technical label" and that it requires an examination of "the 'economic reality' of the working relationship" (*Vanskike v. Peters*, 1992, 808).

In assessing whether a college athlete attending a private or public institution meets the definition of *employee* or whether intercollegiate athletics activity constitutes work, the Department of Labor has taken the following position:

> As part of their overall educational program, public or private schools and institutions of higher learning may permit or require students to engage in activities in connection with . . . intramural and interscholastic athletics and other similar endeavors. Activities of students in such programs, conducted primarily for the benefit of the participants as part of the educational opportunities provided to the students by the school or institution, are not work contemplated by [the FLSA] and do not result in an employer-employee relationship between the student and the school or institution. Also, the fact that a student may receive minimal payment for participation in such activities would not necessarily create an employment relationship. (US Dept. of Labor 2016: §10b03(e))

In *Berger v. NCAA* (2016), the US Court of Appeals for the Seventh Circuit held that current and former members of the women's track and field team at the University of Pennsylvania were not employees for purposes of the FLSA. The court said that a "revered tradition of amateurism in college sports" (*NCAA v. Board of Regents*, 1984, 120) is an essential part of the economic reality of the university-athlete relationship (*Berger v. NCAA*, 2016, 291). The court was also persuaded by the Labor Department's position that participation in "interscholastic athletics" is not work and rejected the plaintiffs' contention that "NCAA-regulated sports" should be treated differently from "student-run activities" (293).

Curiously *Berger*'s discussion of the economic reality of the university-athlete relationship avoided an examination of several important elements, including the university's right to control or dictate the athlete's activities, the university's right to discipline or fire the athlete, and the form of payment in exchange for services that benefit the university (albeit athletes at Ivy League schools do not receive athletic scholarships). Instead the court said college athletes are not employees of their university because "participation in collegiate athletics is entirely voluntary" and they "participate in their sports for reasons wholly unrelated to immediate compensation" (293). The court essentially decided that college athletes are not employees under the FLSA because universities have always operated the business of college sports without treating them as employees, yet they choose to participate anyway.

A critical limitation of *Berger* is that the case involved only non-GIA athletes in a non-revenue sport and thus left the employment status of GIA athletes in revenue sports unresolved. The NLRB regional director's findings in Northwestern University and the NLRB's decision on review (declining jurisdiction without explicitly reversing the regional director) suggest that *Berger* may have been decided differently if the plaintiffs were GIA athletes in revenue sports. LeRoy (2012: 1096) argues the FLSA could be applied to find that college football players are employees. He asserts big-time college football is structured as an NFL apprenticeship, and "because the NFL has no minor league system, NCAA football provides the equivalent of an unpaid internship."

State Labor Law Exclusions

Most profitable college football and men's basketball teams are operated by state institutions and are subject to their respective state, not federal, labor laws. This jurisdictional reality presents a unique set of challenges that do not affect unionization in the professional sport leagues. Some states afford broad collective bargaining rights to public employees, while others limit or prohibit collective bargaining in the public sector. As the NLRB noted, "there is an inherent asymmetry of the labor relations regulatory regimes applicable to individual teams" (Northwestern University 2015). The professional sport leagues do not have this patchwork regulation problem, because none of the teams are state-run organizations subject to varying state labor laws.

States can even amend their labor laws to deny GIA athletes at public universities rights as employees. The same year the Chicago NLRB regional director decided GIA football players at Northwestern University were statutory employees and directed an immediate election, Michigan and Ohio, which together operate three universities in the Big Ten conference, enacted laws excluding GIA athletes from their statutes' definition of *employee* (Mich. Comp. Laws §423.201(1)(e)(iii), 2014; Ohio Rev. Code Ann. § 3345.56, 2017). The amendment to Michigan's labor law moved swiftly, without a hearing and without any pending effort to unionize by any athletes at any college or university within the state (Feldscher 2014a). During the "lame duck" session in December 2014, the bill was introduced, passed both the Michigan House and Senate, and was signed into law by the governor (Feldscher 2014a, 2014b).

Conclusion

It is hard to dispute that profit-athletes being paid via a GIA meet the definition of *employee* for purposes of workers' compensation and federal labor laws. Big-time college sport is the only industry in which the legal system allows competitors to collectively and unilaterally characterize the legal status of their labor as something other than employees or independent contractors. Put simply, a college athlete may be both a student and an employee—as profit-athletes clearly are. In addition a university may be both a profit-athlete's educator and his employer.

Notes

1. For a discussion of the genesis of the term *student-athlete,* see Byers and Hammer (1995).
2. The author of this chapter assisted in the drafting of the bill.

References

CASES

Adelphi University, 195 NLRB 639 (1972).
Berger v. NCAA, 843 F.3d 285 (7th Cir. 2016).
Brown v. Pro Football, Inc., 518 U.S. 231 (1996).
Brown University, 342 NLRB 483 (2004).
Coleman v. Western Mich. Univ., 336 N.W.2d 224 (Mich. Ct. App. 1983).
Davidson v. Univ. of North Carolina, 543 S.E.2d 920 (N.C. Ct. App. 2001).
Harris v. University of Mich. Bd. of Regents, 558 N.W.2d 225 (Mich. Ct. App. 1996).
Kavanaugh v. Trustees of Boston Univ., 795 N.E.2d 1170 (Mass. 2003).
Kleinknecht v. Gettysburg College, 989 F.2d 1360 (3d Cir. 1993).
Korellas v. Ohio State Univ., 779 N.E.2d 1112 (Ohio Ct. Cl. 2002).
Lamorie v. Warner Pacific College, 850 P.2d 401 (Or. Ct. App. 1993).
Leland Stanford Junior University, 214 NLRB 621 (1974).
Lennon v. Petersen, 624 So. 2d 171 (Ala. 1993).
NCAA v. Board of Regents of the Univ. of Okla., 468 U.S. 85 (1984).
New York University, 332 NLRB 1205 (2000).
NLRB v. Town & Country Electric, 516 U.S. 85 (1995).
North American Soccer League v. NLRB, 613 F.2d 1379 (1980).
Northwestern University, Decision and Direction of Election, Case 13-RC-121359 (March 26, 2014).
Northwestern University, Decision on Review and Order, Case 13-RC-121359 (August 17, 2015).
Northwestern University, Notice and Invitation to File Briefs, Case 13-RC-121359 (May 12, 2014).
Orr v. Brigham Young Univ., 960 F.Supp. 1522 (D. Utah 1994), *aff'd*, 108 F.3d 1388 (10th Cir. 1997).
Rensing v. Indiana State Univ. Bd. of Trustees, 444 N.E.2d 1170 (Ind. 1983).

Searles v. Trustees of St. Joseph's College, 695 A.2d 1206 (Me. 1997).
Shephard v. Loyola Marymount Univ., 102 Cal.App.4th 837 (Cal. App. 2 Dist. 2002).
St. Clare's Hospital, 229 NLRB 1000 (1977).
Stineman v. Fontbonne College, 664 F.2d 1082 (8th Cir. 1981).
Thompson v. Travelers Indem. Co., 789 S.W.2d 277, 278 (Tex.1990).
Townsend v. State of California, 191 Cal.App.3d 1530, 237 Cal.Rptr. 146 (1987).
Trs. of Columbia Univ. in the City of N.Y., 364 NLRB No. 90 (2016).
Univ. of Denver v. Nemeth, 257 P.2d 423 (Colo. 1953).
University of Texas at El Paso v. Moreno, 172 S.W.3d 281 (Tex. Ct. App. 2005).
Van Horn v. Indus. Accident Comm'n, 210 Cal.App.2d 457, 33 Cal.Rptr. 169 (1963).
Vanskike v. Peters, 974 F.2d 806 (7th Cir. 1992).
Waldrep v. Texas Employers Insurance Assn., 21 S.W.3d 692 (Tex. Ct. App. 2000).

STATUTES

California Education Code §§ 67450 *et seq.* (2013).
California Labor Code § 3352(k) (2017).
College Athlete Right to Organize Act, S. 1929, 117th Cong. (2021).
Fair Labor Standards Act of 1938, 29 U.S.C. §§ 201-19 (2006).
Haw. Rev. Stat. Ann. § 386-1 (2017).
Mich. Comp. Laws § 423.201(1)(e)(iii) (2014).
National Labor Relations Act, 29 U.S.C. §§ 151 *et seq.* (2012).
N.Y. Workers' Comp. § 2(4) (2017). http://www.wcb.ny.gov/content/main/coverage-requirements-wc/athletic-leagues.jsp.
Ohio Rev. Code Ann. § 3345.56 (West 2017).
Or. Rev. Stat. § 656.027(13) (2017).
Or. Rev. Stat. § 656.027(13) (2017).
Restatement (Second) of Torts § 282 (1965).

SECONDARY SOURCES

Birmingham, John F., Jr. (2015). "NLRB Calls Audible—No Union for Northwestern." *National Law Review,* August 24. http://www.natlawreview.com/article/nlrb-calls-audible-no-union-northwestern#sthash.NJqHLosb.dpuf.
Bok, Derek (1985). "Intercollegiate Athletics." In *Contemporary Issues in Higher Education,* edited by John B. Bennett and J. W. Peltason, 123–46. New York: Macmillan.
Byers, Walter, with Charles Hammer (1995). *Unsportsmanlike Conduct: Exploiting College Athletes.* Ann Arbor: University of Michigan Press.
Davis, Robert N. (1991). "The Courts and Athletic Scholarships." *North Dakota Law Review* 67, no. 2: 163–96.
DeFrancesco, Vincent (2014). "Northwestern U. Football Players Vote on Whether to Unionize." *Chronicle of Higher Education,* April 25. http://chronicle.com/blogs/ticker/northwestern-u-football-players-vote-on-whether-to-unionize/76589.
Edelman, Marc (2014). "The District Court Decision in O'Bannon v. National Collegiate Athletic Association: A Small Step Forward for College-Athlete Rights, and a Gateway for Far Grander Change." *Washington and Lee Law Review* 71: 2320–64.
Feldscher, Kyle (2014a). "Ban on Student-Athlete Unionization Heads to Governor's Desk after Passing Michigan Senate." *MLive.com,* December 16. http://www.mlive.com/lansing-news/index.ssf/2014/12/ban_on_college_student-athlete.html.

———. (2014b). "College Student-Athlete Unionization Now Illegal in Michigan." *MLive.com*, December 30. http://www.mlive.com/lansing-news/index.ssf/2014/12/college_student-athlete_unioni.html.

Gould, William B., IV, Glenn M. Wong, and Eric Weitz (2014). "Full Court Press: *Northwestern University*, a New Challenge to the NCAA." *Loyola of Los Angeles Entertainment Law Review* 35, no. 1: 1–66.

LeRoy, Michael H. (2012). "An Invisible Union for an Invisible Labor Market: College Football and the Union Substitution Effect." *Wisconsin Law Review* 2012, no. 5: 1077–136.

Libit, Daniel (2021). "NCAA's Nobel Prize-Winning Expert Witness Sounds off on Alston, NIL." *Sportico: The Business of Sports*, July 12. https://www.sportico.com/leagues/college-sports/2021/nncaa-expert-witness-economist-1234634009/.

Masteralexis, Lisa Pike (2020). "Labor Relations and Collective Bargaining in Sport." In *Sport Law: A Managerial Approach*, 4th ed., edited by Anita M. Moorman, Linda A. Sharp, and Cathryn L. Claussen. 153–194. New York: Routledge.

McCann, Michael (2015). "Breaking Down Implications of NLRB Ruling on Northwestern Players Union." *Sports Illustrated*, August 17. http://www.si.com/college-football/2015/08/17/northwestern-football-players-union-nlrb-ruling-analysis.

———. (2021). "Supreme Court Rules Unanimously against NCAA in Alston Case." *Sportico: The Business of Sports*, June 21. https://www.sportico.com/law/analysis/2021/supreme-court-rules-unanimously-against-ncaa-in-alston-case-1234632182/.

McCormick, Robert A., and Amy Christian McCormick (2006). "The Myth of the Student-Athlete: The College Athlete as Employee." *Washington Law Review* 81: 71–157.

Mitten, Matthew J., Timothy Davis, Rodney K. Smith, and N. Jeremi Duru (2013). *Sports Law and Regulation: Cases, Materials, and Problems*. 3rd ed. New York: Wolters Kluwer Law and Business.

National Collegiate Athletic Association. (2021a). LSDBi. Indianapolis, IN. https://web3.ncaa.org/lsdbi/reports/pdf/searchPdfView?id=2084&businessCode=BYLAW_SEARCH_VIEW.

———. (2021b). "1.3.1. Basic Purpose." LSDBi. https://web3.ncaa.org/lsdbi/reports/pdf/searchPdfView?id=2084&businessCode=BYLAW_SEARCH_VIEW.

National Labor Relations Board (2016). "Advice Memorandum on Whether Northwestern University's Football Handbook Rules Were Unlawfully Overbroad." September 22. https://www.nlrb.gov/guidance/memos-research/general-counsel-memos.

———. (2017). GC 17-01, "General Counsel's Report on the Statutory Rights of University Faculty and Students in the Unfair Labor Practice Context." January 31. https://www.nlrb.gov/guidance/memos-research/general-counsel-memos.

———. (2021). GC 21-08, "Statutory Rights of Players at Academic Institutions (Student-Athletes) Under the National Labor Relations Act." September 29. https://www.nlrb.gov/guidance/memos-research/general-counsel-memos.

Ross, Stephen F., Richard T. Karcher, and S. Baker Kensinger (2014). "Judicial Review of NCAA Eligibility Decisions: Evaluation of the Restitution Rule and a Call for Arbitration." *Journal of College and University Law* 40, no. 1: 79–114.

———. (1998). *Onward to Victory: The Crises that Shaped College Sports*. New York: Holt.

Symmetry Software (2017). "How Many Working Days Are in a Year?" November 13. https://www.symmetry.com/payroll-tax-insights/how-many-working-days-are-in-a-year.

US Department of Labor, Wage and Hour Division (2016). *Field Operations Handbook*.

Weiler, Paul C., Gary R. Roberts, Roger I. Abrams, and Stephen F. Ross (2011). *Sports and the Law: Text, Cases and Problems.* 4th ed. St. Paul, MN: West.

Wilkinson, Joseph (2017). "New NLRB General Counsel Rescinds Memo That Labelled Football Players as Employees." *Daily Northwestern,* December 15. https://dailynorthwestern.com/2017/12/15/lateststories/new-nlrb-general-counsel-rescinds-memo-labelled-football-players-employees/.

Yasser, Raymond L., James R. McCurdy, C. P. Goplerud, and M. A. Weston (2015). *Sports Law: Cases and Materials.* 8th ed. New Providence, NJ: LexisNexis.

Northwestern Football, Unionization Efforts, and the NLRB's Decision Not to Exercise Jurisdiction

Ellen J. Staurowsky

Just because we love the illusion of big-time college sport, that is no reason to perpetuate fraud and corruption.

—RICK TELANDER, *THE HUNDRED YARD LIE*

In January 2014 football players at Northwestern University, under the umbrella of the College Athletes Players Association (CAPA), made history by signing union cards, calling attention to the fact they believed they were employees. A month later Peter Sung Ohr, the director of the National Labor Relations Board's (NLRB) Region 13—Chicago office, agreed, signaling that Northwestern football players receiving a grant-in-aid (GIA) had the right under the National Labor Relations Act (NLRA) to collectively bargain.

In reaching his decision (Northwestern University, 2014), Ohr determined the labor performed by Northwestern football players qualified them as employees under the common-law test of employment. That test considers the relationship between employee and employer, including the nature of the work performed, compensation, evidence of the employer's control over the employee, and work conditions. Ohr found that Northwestern football players were providing a service that benefited the university and for which they were compensated. He noted that coaches and other staff members in the Northwestern athletic department exerted control over players through expectations about performance and about tasks they were to perform on a daily basis that were monitored and often recorded. He highlighted that players provided ample evidence of forty-to-sixty-hour work weeks (Northwestern University, 2014).

Rejecting Northwestern University's argument that their football work was not the primary reason players were at Northwestern and that they were first and foremost students, Ohr found that Northwestern had recruited players specifically for football. Despite the university's efforts to link the work the players performed to their educations, Orh found that while players were enrolled students at the university, their work on the football field was not a core element of the academic programs in which they were majoring (Northwestern University, 2014). In March 2014, shortly after Ohr's decision, the university appealed the decision to the full NLRB in Washington, DC.

More than a year later, in August 2015, the NLRB sidestepped the issue, declining to exercise jurisdiction and citing the potential for "instability in labor relations" due to the fact that the ruling would apply to Northwestern University as a private institution that did business primarily with public institutions. Particularly noteworthy was the assertion made by the NLRB that to deal with the case would not achieve the purposes of the NLRA (Pearce et al. 2015). In light of this ruling, two questions will be considered in this chapter: (1) Should anticipated instability in labor relations have been a deterrent to rendering a decision on behalf of the Northwestern football players? (2) Would a finding on behalf of the players have served the purpose of the NLRA?

Examining these questions requires uncovering the history of college athletes' efforts to be recognized as employees and the ongoing business practices of big-time college sport executives that reflect a tacit understanding that an employer-employee relationship exists between Power Five institutions and football and NCAA Division I men's basketball players. Initially this chapter documents the invention and strategic use of three control mechanisms: the term *student-athlete,* athletic grants-in-aid (GIAs), and the NCAA governance structure by college sport authorities. Next we will explore the history of player labor activism, including college athletes' questioning their work hours, workplace safety, type and level of compensation, and medical care and insurance coverage. Building upon this historical analysis, the chapter will next outline college sport's (e.g., Power Five) underground economy, a system that often pays big-time athletes under its own terms and conditions without being held accountable for creating an employer-employee relationship. Finally we will unpack the NLRB's decision in light of college sport history and offer some concluding thoughts.

Employees by Any Other Name: The Invention of Student-Athletes

One college athlete who envisioned a future in which Power Five football players were viewed as employees was Kain Colter, quarterback of the Northwestern University football team. Influenced initially by the experience of his uncle, Cleveland Colter, whose future as an NFL player was never realized after he suffered a knee injury while playing at the University of Southern California, Colter was aware that promises made to players by college coaches and administrators were not always kept. His uncle's injury had left him with lifelong pain and medical bills and without the benefit of a college degree that was to have been part of the deal (Staurowsky 2014b: 13–16; Nocera and Strauss 2016: 241–62).

The longer Kain Colter was in the system, the more he saw its shortcomings and came to understand the need for profound changes to protect players. By the summer of 2013, while taking a seminar course about the modern workplace, Colter saw clear parallels between his college football experiences and those of blue-collar workers in a variety of industries. His sensibilities were reinforced following a conversation with Tregg Duerson, a Northwestern graduate whose father, Dave, had played in the NFL for eleven years. In 2011 Dave Duerson had died of a self-inflicted gunshot wound. After his death it was determined that he had suffered from chronic traumatic encephalopathy, a condition associated with concussive and sub-concussive blows (Nocera and Strauss 2016: 243).

In the course of his subsequent research, Colter connected with Ramogi Huma, the executive director of the National College Players Association (NCPA) and a longtime advocate for players who had devoted his professional life to addressing injustice in the college sport system. In collaboration with the NCPA and the United Steelworkers Political Action Committee, the College Athletes' Players Association was formed, and efforts to unionize the Northwestern football team began (Banks 2014; Nocera and Strauss 2016).

On January 28, 2014, the college sport world learned Northwestern football players had engaged in a labor action during a press conference held at the Hyatt Regency in downtown Chicago. Speaking about the need for a players association similar to those that represented the interests of NBA and NFL players, Colter asserted that "just as other athletes who compete in multi-billion dollar industries have done, we must secure and maintain comprehensive protections by asserting the rights afforded to us under labor laws. . . . We recognize the need to eliminate unjust NCAA rules that create physical, academic, and financial hardships for college athletes across the nation. To remain silent while players are denied justice is to be complicit in inflicting injustice on future generations of college athletes" (quoted in Banks 2014).

The Power Five college sport establishment dismissed out of hand CAPA's efforts to access collective bargaining rights as employees. NCAA president Mark Emmert described the action as "grossly inappropriate" (Westerholm 2014). A few months later, during a hearing on unionizing college athletes, Baylor president and chancellor Kenneth Starr testified before the US House Education and Workforce Committee that Ohr's determination that Northwestern football players were employees was an "unprecedented ruling" and "in my view, misguided," emphasizing that Baylor University athletes were first and foremost students and that Baylor was "far removed from being a professional franchise" (US House Education and Workforce Committee Hearing, May 8, 2014). Starr claimed that using the NLRA as a means for players to negotiate the terms and rules they were subjected to was "exactly the wrong way to go" (ibid.).

Whether or not modern-day Power Five officials questioned the appropriateness of Northwestern football players' efforts to organize as employees under the NLRA, viewed through the lens of history, the action was actually not unprecedented or surprising. In fact the signing of union cards by Northwestern football players was predictable and logical. Today's Power Five football and Division I men's basketball players—just like their predecessors for nearly a century—are keenly aware of their economic exploitation and mistreatment. Repeatedly players have pushed back against an oppressive and coercive system.

That resistance, however, has been thwarted through the unilateral imposition of NCAA and Power Five conference rules. By design and/or impact, NCAA bylaws govern players' daily routines and activities, disallow or minimize their access to knowledgeable advocates, discourage dissent, suppress player value, prevent players from organizing, and block avenues for negotiation (Staurowsky 2014b).

Since the 1930s big-time college players have sought fair compensation, contemplated and/or engaged in work stoppages, and suffered the consequences of operating in unsafe and hazardous work environments (Karcher 2012, 2014; Oriard 2009; Staurowsky 2014b, 2014d; Tatos and Casper 2019; Tatos 2020). Players have gone on record detailing the educational compromises they made or were expected to make or were made by the institutions they attended (Burton 2017; Comeau and Grummert 2020; Gurney and Southall 2012; Southall et al. 2014; Corr et al. 2021). In the absence of long-term medical care, players have sought financial relief from injuries sustained while playing (Jacinto 2020). And among other things, they have unwittingly had their health-care rights violated by being included in concussion research without their knowledge (Tatos and Comrie 2019).

In each era college sport officials have worked tirelessly to obscure this history through the strategic execution of propaganda campaigns that cast Power Five football and Division I men's basketball players—the "talent" in mass-media televised events—as "student-athletes" whose purported reason for being on a college campus is to earn a college degree while playing their sports as an avocation or hobby (Southall and Staurowsky 2013; Staurowsky and Sack 2005). Until recent years there has been little interest in asking why the college sport industry "insists on cloaking any discussion regarding players in the term 'student-athletes'" (Staurowsky 2014c: 135).

The linguistic dishonesty in making contrived and contorted comparisons between Power Five football and Division I men's basketball players and students who participate in debate or performing arts is breathtaking. Power Five profit-athletes power a multibillion-dollar industry. These workers compete in palatial stadiums before thousands of fans and millions of viewers who watch on numerous digital media platforms. Students competing on the debate team are not referred to as "student-debaters," nor are members of a school's marching band referred to as "student-musicians" (Staurowsky 2014a: 135). The term of art *student-athlete* was developed by the NCAA in response to worker compensation claims made by injured and deceased football players and/or their families (A. C. McCormick and R. A. McCormick 2006; R. A. McCormick and A. C. McCormick 2008; Sack and Staurowsky 1998; Staurowsky and Sack 2005; *University of Denver v. Nemeth*, 1953; *Van Horn v. Industrial Accident Commission*, 1963).

In the year following his retirement from the NCAA, Walter Byers, the first full-time executive director of the NCAA, wrote about this strategy in his memoir *Unsportsmanlike Conduct: Exploiting College Athletes* (1995). Citing the "dreaded notion" that athletes might gain worker's compensation coverage, he wrote: "[We] crafted the term student-athlete, and soon it was embedded in all NCAA rules and interpretations as a *mandated* substitute for such words as players and athletes. We told college publicists to speak of 'college teams,' not football or basketball 'clubs,' a word common to the pros" (1995: 69; emphasis added). It is not surprising that Byers refers to the term being mandated. As a former journalist, he appreciated the power of messaging and understood that he could mobilize a legion of sport publicists and "sports information" professionals who were just taking up residence in college athletic departments in the 1950s and becoming fixtures of college sport promotional efforts to disseminate and embed the student-athlete concept. The media infrastructure was in place to weave a narrative that the athletes who were now being paid to play (i.e., receiving compensation in the form of athletic GIAs) were still somehow not employees but rather simply college kids playing for the fun of it (Staurowsky and Sack 2005).

Almost seventy years later, the NCAA still regularly invests in public service announcements (PSAs) to reinforce the repeated use of the term. Just three years after Northwestern football players signed union cards, the NCAA sought the services of SS&K, an advertising firm that specializes in using political strategy and creative messaging to produce a video titled "Label Me" that aired during coverage of Selection Sunday, the day when the teams that will compete in the Division I men's basketball tournament, commonly referred to as March Madness, are announced.

The video was purportedly designed to disrupt viewers' negative stereotypes of athletes from racial, ethnic, and sexual minority groups by flipping the script, "to remind the audience that the only definition of ourselves that matters is our own" (Cooper 2018). However, the so-called PSA never allows viewers to forget these athletes are first and foremost students. The athletes in the video, thinking they are conveying a message designed to challenge oppression associated with racism, sexism, and prejudice against sexual minorities, express pride in being labeled student-athletes, wholly unaware of the term's origins or meaning or that the term was—and is—designed to control them. The video is a masterful piece of propaganda, designed to deflect increased public scrutiny of Power Five college sport's exploitative nature.

The coordinated propaganda efforts (between the NCAA national office, Power Five conferences, and their media partners) bestow upon members of the college sport worker class a unique status unlike any other in American labor. Student-athletes are presented to the public—and represented in courts of law—as playing college sports not as a vocation (work) but as an avocation (leisure, hobby, something done outside of a main occupation). The term masterfully creates a netherworld where the rights of Power Five football and Division I men's basketball players are blocked from a worker status by definitional subterfuge (Staurowsky 2014b: 23).

Addressing this falsehood, Rosado Marzan (2014)—in an amicus brief supporting CAPA and the football players at Northwestern that bore the signature of nineteen law professors—wrote:

> The terms "student" and "employee" are not opposites; you can be both one and the other simultaneously. In fact, many are: it is extremely common for students to work jobs, including ones in the campus cafeteria, for example. But the difference between the student school cafeteria workers and the football player is that there are immense profits in college football, and the Employer will continue to try to convince society that these players are "student-athletes," which for some magical reason apparently means they have no statutory rights. (28)

By consistently seeking to portray profit-athletes' work as nothing more than a voluntary activity that can be abandoned on a whim or without substantial cost to the athlete, the NCAA and its members have positioned all college sport participation as a privilege rather than a right. On the rare occasions that college administrators are challenged by athletes, they simply point to the door and tell the "kids" that if they do not wish to compete under the NCAA's proscribed terms and conditions, they are free to not participate. For those who remain, there is a palpable expectation they should be grateful for the privilege and opportunity that has been granted.

In a study of public attitudes toward athletes similar to the Northwestern football players who engaged in public activism (n = 713), responses were both supportive and sharply critical. Athletes who seek change in either the sport system and/or political landscape are often viewed as arrogant, ungrateful, anti-American, and degenerate (Sappington, Keum, and Hoffman 2019). At the 2016

National Association of Athletic Compliance Convention, one session featured a panel of three college athletes, a coach, and an administrator. The theme of the session, Empowering the Student-Athlete Voice, had emerged following legal challenges such as *O'Bannon v. NCAA* (2014, 2015) and the Northwestern labor action. In that session the panelists talked about how important it was for college athletes to be taught to be grateful for what they had and that efforts were underway to engage athletes regarding how to express their gratitude. This was in response to a belief that there was an incursion of an entitlement culture that had developed in college sport.

When considered from a labor perspective, the need to educate athletes about unfair treatment and inequities in the system is vital. Such education is necessary to overcome a narrative that exploitative conditions are actually things for which athletes should be grateful. The NCAA-sponsored narrative aligns with long-standing attempts within college sport to deter unionization and, if necessary, engage in union busting, which was the case in the Northwestern University situation. Employers benefiting and profiting from exploitative business practices have historically tried to persuade the broader public that what they are doing is in the best interests of society at large while persuading workers to appreciate how well they are actually treated. Consistently workers who seek to organize for collective action are paternalistically discouraged from doing so because employers will take care of them.

As if reading from a 1921 union busting playbook, Northwestern head football coach Pat Fitzgerald was clear that he and the university's administration were going to do everything they could to prevent players from voting for a union. In an attempt to divide athletes within the athletic department, some coaches met with their teams and told them that if football unionized it would mean hardship for the rest of them. NCAA talking points, in fact, encouraged athletics administrators and coaches to talk about how the efforts of football players to organize would result in the cutting of GIAs and the loss of programs for other athletes (Solomon 2014). Fitzgerald paternalistically said that he was going to do "everything in [his] power" to educate players himself and to influence them to vote no (Zirin 2014).

The systemic power imbalance inherent in the term *student-athlete* is reinforced and fortified within the NCAA regulatory system designed to deny athletes access to their rights as workers. In the aftermath of the Northwestern football players' signing union cards, college sport administrators and apologists consistently argued that pay for play was not the answer (Solomon 2014). Simplifying the players' labor action to a sound bite ignored the fact that Northwestern football players were most concerned about workplace safety, access to better medical coverage, and the right to have a say in the rules that govern them, not compensation (Banks 2014). Clearly, having been permitted by the courts and government agencies to run its business without accountability to its college athlete labor force, the NCAA and conference officials consistently run out the clock on player challenges by occasionally tweaking the regulations that govern athlete compensation and the rules used to maintain control over the players.

Pay by Any Other Name: Athletic Grants-in-Aid

Just as the Power Five college sport labor force comprises non-worker students working in the profit sports of football and men's basketball, so too the compensation these workers receive is not pay. The NCAA regulatory scheme recasts payment for athletes' services (their labor) as grants-in-aid (more commonly known as athletic scholarships). While NCAA officials have long argued this non-pay characterization was established to create a clear line of demarcation between intercollegiate athletics and professional sports in order to prevent the exploitation of athletes by commercial entities, Byers (1995: 65) described athletic scholarships as just another payment system: "In 1956, the colleges, acting through the NCAA in the name of 'amateurism,' installed their own pay system called the athletics grant-in-aid or athletics 'scholarship.' "

Putting aside myriad statements by NCAA officials and college sport executives that paying athletes is "problematic," "would harm academics," and "will never happen" (Collins 2014; FoxSports 2013; S. Nelson 2014), the NCAA and its members are not opposed to paying athletes under the principle of amateurism. Its own definition—in bylaws 12.02.10 and 16.02.5—reveals no reservation (moral or otherwise) to pay. "Pay is the receipt of funds, awards or benefits *not permitted* by the governing legislation of the Association for participation in athletics" (NCAA 2021b). If the NCAA, its conferences, and member schools were opposed to paying athletes, it would need only to state outright that athletes may not receive payment for athletic performance. They would not trade in the currency of athletic scholarships, stipends, miscellaneous allowances, cost of attendance payments, and other benefits. They would not regulate the value and components of a grant-in-aid or athletic scholarship or so closely monitor how much money athletes receive from what the NCAA refers to as welfare funds. What the pay bylaws reveal is that college sport officials are opposed to paying anything above what they wish or might be compelled to pay for athletic talent (Smith and Hattery 2011; Staurowsky 2004).

This is not an educational or eligibility argument; this is a labor and commerce argument. The NCAA national office, conferences, and individual universities have set the compensation terms, conditions, and amounts. Because NCAA rules compel athletes to redeem the compensation for their labor in specific ways (e.g., tuition, room and board, books, other educational expenses), the NCAA effectively ensures that athletes themselves pay to support the very mythology used to suppress their value and deny their employee status.

In *O'Bannon v. the National Collegiate Athletic Association*, the Ninth Circuit Court of Appeals noted that the NCAA's assertion that its compensation rules were "merely 'eligibility rules' that do not regulate any 'commercial activity' strained credulity (Bybee 2015). Explaining that those rules were not exempt from antitrust scrutiny, modern legal definitions of commerce encompass "the transaction in which an athlete recruit exchanges his labor and NIL (names, images, and likenesses) rights for a scholarship at a Division I school because it is undeniable that both parties to that exchange anticipate economic gain from it" (ibid.: 33). The Court went on: "In other words, the substance of the compensation rules matters far more than how they are styled. And in substance, the rules clearly regulate the terms of commercial transactions between athletic recruits and their chosen schools. . . . The NCAA's argument that compensation rules are 'eligibility' restrictions, rather than substantive restrictions on the price terms of recruiting agreements, is but a sleight of hand. There is real money at issue here" (ibid: 34).

By asserting authority over how athletes can be paid, the NCAA, its conferences, and member schools engage in decision making that reflects a significant conflict of interest that serves the existing industry power structure to the detriment of college athletes. In 1956 University of Michigan athletic director Fritz Crisler reportedly observed, "We're saying that these youngsters are amateurs . . . and nobody should be permitted to professionalize them except the colleges. The colleges can pay them to play" (quoted in Byers 1995: 74). Byers further acknowledged that the NCAA's decision to formalize the athletic scholarship amounted to "forswearing old amateur principles without admitting it" (ibid.). Byers, the primary architect of the NCAA's business model, was clear-eyed about the college athlete labor market. He knew athletic programs depended on media-oriented audiences and needed college athletes to be as professional as possible in all facets except compensation. Not paying college athletes a market wage may have been unethical—especially in an educational context—but couching pay in the context of a grant-in-aid or scholarship achieved market control while protecting the NCAA and its members from workers compensation scrutiny.

Denial of Rights by Any Other Name: NCAA Bylaws as College Athlete Labor Controls

Over time the threat of revoking or non-renewing a grant-in-aid became a tool of control over the college athlete labor force. This was most vividly demonstrated at the end of the civil rights and Vietnam War eras, a time when athlete protests on college campuses were threatening the established order, requiring coaches to adjust to athlete requests and demands to be treated humanely (Underwood 1969; Demas 2011; Henderson 2013). Some coaches vigorously resisted athlete protests, characterizing athletes as uncommitted. Paternalistic coaches felt that any protests violated the spirit of an athletic scholarship, which they believed allowed them to run benign dictatorships. The NCAA responded defensively to athletes' concerns, more interested in "refuting allegations and neutralizing dissent than with actually helping to improve conditions for black athletes" (Henderson 2013: 126).

It is in that climate that college sport officials put forward proposals designed to exert greater authority over college athletes. The first of these was the "fraudulent misrepresentation rule," passed in 1967, which narrowed the terms and conditions for athletic scholarships and allowed coaches to cancel a GIA at their discretion. As Sack (2008: 70) reported, "The fraudulent misrepresentation rule allowed coaches to 'fire' athletes for insubordination and for not taking their athletic responsibilities seriously." Any athlete compelled by conscience to boycott practice as a way of expressing concern about his treatment was vulnerable to dismissal under this requirement. Indicative of the prevailing sentiment of the time, the fraudulent misrepresentation rule received overwhelming support from the NCAA membership, with 214 institutions in favor and only 13 opposed (Sack and Staurowsky 1998: 83).

Five years later in 1972 the NCAA moved away from a four-year athletic scholarship to a one-year award, a move designed to further contain and quell athlete unrest. In 1968, 130 publicized Black athlete protests on predominantly White campuses occurred, and a significant number of protests continued into the early 1970s (Edwards 1969). The new threat of being able to withhold renewal of a GIA gave coaches unparalleled power over athletes, even though their sport participation was supposed to be an avocational secondary concern to their education. Notably the college sport community's response to the athlete activism of the late 1960s and early 1970s was to attempt to silence athletes, Black and White, through the adoption of one-year GIAs (Hartmann 2008; Oriard 2009; Scott 1971; Staurowsky 2014b; Wiggins 1988).

The one-year scholarship was defended by the NCAA as an imperative component of their business model for forty years. The NCAA—notably Power Five conferences—relented in 2015 only under pressure from *O'Bannon* and *Northwestern*. Even as college sport authorities opened the door to multiyear GIAs, the award still hinged on job performance on the athletic field with the power to award or revoke left in the hands of coaches (i.e., employers). Notably athletes continue to be subject to the effects of the fraudulent misrepresentation rule.

This begrudging approach to change is a hallmark of the college sport industry's relationship with its labor force. Jack Scott, in his *The Athletic Revolution*

(1971), wrote about the NCAA's attitude toward college athlete protesters in the 1970s. He explained the NCAA and college sport officials were hostile toward athletes who spoke out and challenged the way they were treated and noted that "practices and policies that many see as evils to be remedied, the NCAA views as its greatest strength" (209).Tellingly, in the twenty-first century, the NCAA national office, Power Five conferences, and individual universities fiercely oppose the very athletes they claim to serve in the courts (both legal and public opinion) and regularly lobby against athletes' rights in the halls of Congress. Any attempts by athletes to seek fair treatment and safe work environments or negotiate the terms and conditions under which they work are met with outright hostility or dismissed out of hand.

College Athlete Unrest and the Reaction of the College Sport Industry

CAPA's efforts to organize football players at Northwestern University and advocate for better working conditions were simply a more recent iteration of a movement that started more than eighty-five years ago, during the decade when the NLRA was passed. In 1936 Howard University football players boycotted their game against Virginia Union, demanding three things: medical care for injured athletes, campus jobs, and food (McKenna 2010). Garnering support from the student body, they boycotted classes the following week, choosing instead to organize a protest march carrying signs with the message "We Want Ham and Cabbage for the Team!" (ibid.). The players, despite student support, failed to get Howard's administration to address the issue of food. Instead the administration chose to punish the players by canceling the final game of the year, a much-anticipated Thanksgiving game against Lincoln University (ibid.).

The next year, football players at Louisiana State University and the University of Pittsburgh followed suit, organizing to improve their working conditions. In what is a recurring theme, two LSU players who led the protest movement were dismissed from the team as punishment for challenging authority (Fram and Frampton 2013). At the University of Pittsburgh, a slightly different scenario unfolded. Players, with the support of their coach, Jock Sutherland, took issue with the university's profiting from the team's notoriety and performance without reasonably sharing part of the profits with team members. The dispute arose after the team won the 1936 Rose Bowl. While the university pocketed $100,000 from the game, each player was given only $7.50, totaling $250 for the entire team (Oriard 2003: 28). One report indicates that it was Sutherland himself who paid the players (Smith 2011: 79).

Influenced by regional and national labor movements, players viewed the opportunity to return to the Rose Bowl as an opportunity to negotiate. Smith (2011: 79) writes, "If the Congress of Industrial Organizations union could strike successfully during the Depression, the players figured they could do the same."

Threatening to not play, the team presented the administration with three demands—all players, not just starters, would receive funding to travel to California; pocket money per player would be set at two hundred dollars; and the team would be given a two-week vacation after the event (ibid.: 79). In the process of acceding to the player demands, the athletic director, Don Harrison, resigned and the chancellor, John Gabbert Bowman, vowed to institute reform to bring players in line (ibid.: 79).

During the 1930s and 1940s, accounts of similar confrontations between football players and their institutions were regularly covered in the *Daily Worker* (Oriard 2003: 27). It was there that readers learned that Pitt's Bowman had issued players tuition bills after limiting their compensation, a move that led Coach Sutherland to resign. Players from other teams across the country felt that their situations were also unjust. Stanford players successfully negotiated to be paid $50 each to perform in the 1940 Rose Bowl. University of Arizona players, however, were not successful, as the university administration denied their demand to be paid $175 each (ibid.: 28).

In the weeks preceding the Gator Bowl in 1945, boosters offered $100 incentives to persuade Wake Forest football players to take the field. Believing some players were worth more than the flat rate the boosters were willing to pay, the Wake players negotiated, seeking $150 for members of the starting lineup. Southall (2012: 3) noted, "The players were not uncomfortable turning their backs on amateurism and getting paid; they simply felt starters should be paid more than non-starters."

In this moment when discussions between players and their institutions about their value were commonplace, NCAA officials stepped forward to formalize the GIA arrangement (Sack and Staurowsky 1998). These negotiations were about the value of college athletes in big-time college football and how much college football players would be compensated. That was the scenario NCAA decision makers were responding to. These were not discussions about whether they should be compensated but how much institutions were willing to pay college football players.

The presence of a formalized payment arrangement would eventually begin to influence ongoing negotiations between players and their coaches. In the turbulent decades of the 1960s and 1970s, players increasingly challenged their coaches and administrations. As television coverage of games proliferated and overall revenues increased, players questioned why they were receiving nothing beyond their scholarships for their performances. In 1961 Syracuse football players refused to play in the Liberty Bowl held in Philadelphia, presenting head coach Ben Schwartzwalder with a demand that had to be met. They would play only if they were given wristwatches, a status symbol of considerable value at the time and something that they had learned other players in bowl games had been given that year (Meggysey 1971: 78). Eventually the Syracuse players prevailed—both at the negotiating table and over the Miami Hurricanes in a come-from-behind victory (Herbert 2015).

The Syracuse University program again dealt with player unrest at the end of the decade as a result of racial tensions on the team, at the university, and in the country at large. In 1970, with the assassinations of Martin Luther King, Malcolm X, and Bobby Kennedy fresh on the minds of Americans, a group of nine black players who became known (erroneously) as the Syracuse Eight boycotted spring practice in an act of solidarity following a fight that erupted on campus between a Black student and White football player (Wiggins 1988; Given and Springer 2017; Croyle 2020). The fight was reflective of simmering issues on the team that spoke to the depths of the Black players' concerns with their treatment on campus and the lack of a sincere response from the coaching staff and administration. Racial insensitivity on the part of coaches and White team members manifested in "differential treatment in medical examinations, academic advising, assignment to team positions, traveling with the squad, and recruiting and support" (Croyle 2020). A request for a Black assistant coach was disingenuously handled when a former Syracuse player, Floyd Little, was brought in for two days and represented to the players as the team's black coach (ibid.).

The Syracuse Eight dealt with the consequences of their decision to boycott spring practice throughout the following summer and fall. Suspended from their team, they faced the task of communicating with White coaches and teammates who viewed their conduct as offensive because it violated the group-think purportedly emphasized on the team. In an interview with the Associated Press in September 1970, head coach Schwartzwalder said, "We were never conscious of racism. Our white players don't feel this thing existed. They feel it is a matter of groupism versus individualism." He added, "When a group of players miss 16 days of practice, then do not want to come back except on their own terms, members of the squad feel they shouldn't be on the squad, and it wouldn't matter if they are black and white" (quoted in Croyle 2020).

Presented with a condescending and demeaning document from Syracuse's chancellor indicating that they would have to sign before being permitted to return to the team, the Syracuse Eight refused, setting in motion a chain of events that would have lifelong consequences for them. While their concerns about racism were validated in a report shared with the campus community in December 1970, based upon an investigation of the Syracuse athletic department, only two of the eight players ever played football at Syracuse again. Labeled Black troublemakers, dissidents, and militants, they were personae non grata in the sport of football, foreclosing future opportunities to play or coach professionally (Given and Springer 2017).

Within the context of the times, the Syracuse Eight were a part of a larger movement of Black athlete protests occurring around the United States. Sociologist Harry Edwards estimated that during 1968 alone there were thirty-seven Black protests (Wiggins 1988: 305). As Staurowsky (2014d) notes, "As the civil rights movement came to an end, the walk-out by Black players at Syracuse was indicative of player protests occurring at many colleges and universities around the country between 1968 and 1972."

In 1969 Coach Floyd Eaton at the University of Wyoming suspended a group of Black athletes known as the Black 14 after they sought to protest racial doctrines espoused by the Church of Jesus Christ of Latter-Day Saints in a contest against Brigham Young University. Declining to join with Wyoming's Black Student Alliance, the players had a plan to wear black armbands to express their own opposition to the church's racist policy, which at the time was that "The Negroes are not equal with other races where the receipt of certain spiritual blessings are [sic] concerned, particularly the priesthood and the temple blessings that flow therefrom" (quoted in Norman 1999: 121). Before practice the players went to talk to Eaton about possibly wearing armbands or some other form of protest. According to one of the players, Tony Gibson, the coach dismissed the players on the spot. Some of the players remember Eaton "went into a racist diatribe: telling them to go back to their fatherless inner-city homes and live off public benefits," comments the coach later denied (Lowery and Bogage 2019). In an interview in 1982, Eaton said that he expelled the players from the team for violating his policy against protesting. He elaborated further that "demonstrations have no place in athletics, not while you're on scholarship. You're trading your athletic ability for a chance to get an education. They slapped the state of Wyoming in the face" (ibid.).

In 1969 four Black players were suspended by University of Washington coach Jim Owens for what he described as a lack of commitment to him and his program (Wilma 2001). The precipitating incident was the overly harsh punishment of a Black player for a mistake in a game. Subsequent to their suspension, the four Black players, Gregg Alex, Ralph Bayard, Harvy Blanks, and Lamar Mills, asked to meet with Owens to express their concern that the player's punishment was racially motivated. He declined, choosing instead to call a meeting of the entire team. Dissatisfied with the Black players' refusal to pledge loyalty to him and the team, Owens refused to meet with them (Wilma 2001). According to Raley (2020), "Black players told how a largely Southern-oriented UW coaching staff stacked players at positions by race, denied them advancement because of skin color and regularly used racial slurs, going back to Owens' earliest days as coach."

Similar themes run through other accounts of player protests. John Pont, the head football coach at Indiana University, suspended sixteen players after they boycotted a practice, later moving to reinstate four. At Oregon State the suspension of a Black football player, Fred Milton, for violating a team ban on facial hair (Milton wore a mustache and goatee) led to a boycott of classes. Sixteen players at Iowa boycotted a spring practice; seven of them were reinstated the next academic year (Oriard 2009: 18, 30–31, 44).

Dr. Harry Edwards, a sociologist and one of the architects of the Olympic Project for Human Rights, documented the substance of the unrest in his 1969 book, *The Revolt of the Black Athlete,* with letters from Black athletes to coaches and administrators at Marquette University, Michigan State University, Oklahoma City University, Princeton University, the University of California, Berkeley, University of Kansas, University of Oklahoma, University of Texas at El Paso, and Western Michigan. Player complaints included failure to fulfill promises of athletic scholarships, failure to provide campus jobs as promised, undervaluing the talents of Black players, and showing favoritism toward White players, as well as systemic racism as evidenced in a lack of racial diversity in coaching staffs and athletic administrations, racial insensitivity in dealing with Black players, and lack of respect for Black players (18, 30, 31, 44).

While some teams were divided along racial lines, and coaches like Schwartzwalder used those divisions to alienate Black players, White players often joined Black players in solidarity regarding racial issues. Many football players both White and Black bridled against their authoritarian coaches and shared concerns about the conditions under which they worked. Training regimens employed by coaches that risked the health of players, including bans on players taking water breaks, extreme practice conditions, and sometimes brutal punishments, were fairly commonplace from the 1950s through the 1970s. The legendary Bear Bryant, in his first year as head coach of the Texas A&M football team, held a ten-day preseason training camp in 1954 with approximately one hundred players participating on the first day. Working in temperatures that surpassed 100 degrees with water withheld and food rationed, only about one third of the players survived the experience before quitting or succumbing to illness (Dent 2001). Questioning the need for inhumane coaching practices was the subject of a movement started in 1971 by Jack Scott known as the "athletic revolution," which called out coaches for imposing all manner of dictatorial controls on athletes.

Player challenges to authority reverberated throughout the college sport establishment. In August 1969 *Sports Illustrated* writer John Underwood captured many coaches' reactions in a exposé titled "The Desperate Coach." Describing player protests from the perspective of coaches, he wrote, "In the privacy of their offices, over breakfast in strange towns, wherever two or three coaches get together, they talk about The Problem."

A leading cultural historian of college football, Michael Oriard (2009), noted that coaches continued to view player concerns as matters of discipline while players believed they were questions of fairness and human rights. Confrontations between coaches and players led to some coaches' making concessions. On some campuses team rules were relaxed. Some coaches did not impose personal grooming rules (e.g., hair length, facial hair, and attire). In addition, to some degree overt racial insensitivities were addressed, and more Black assistant coaches were eventually hired.

However, given that athletes had no players association to represent their interests, several individual players paid a steep cost for challenging the status quo, as Staurowsky (2014d) notes: "For the players who boycotted, some were never permitted to return to their teams, others returned but never felt that they were welcome, and still others found it difficult to get jobs in athletics after being identified as troublemakers. Coaches, in turn, found a way to regain control over the athletes on their team."

As discussed earlier, the NCAA's 1967 fraudulent misrepresentation rule and, five years later, the reduction in an athletic scholarship from four years to one year were intended to regain control of player conduct. While a player's security was constantly in question with a one-year award, the fraudulent misrepresentation rule effectively barred player access to avenues of protest and reflected the worldview of many coaches. A refusal to play under the fraudulent misrepresentation rule became justifiable grounds for dismissal. Failure to attend practice or making only a token appearance were expressly identified as offenses that gave institutions cause to cancel or reduce an athletic scholarship (Sack and Staurowsky 1998). In 1967 a misconduct rule was also passed. Serious misconduct was defined as a refusal to "meet the normal conduct obligations required of all team members, and *defiance of the normal and necessary directives of departmental staff members*" (ibid.: 83; emphasis added). These governance actions foreclosed athletes from engaging in any civil disobedience without risking being dismissed from the team.

Modern Player Advocacy: Local to External to Social Media

These rules effectively quelled player unrest, leaving a legacy of palpable fear that retribution would be swift and lasting. It is no accident that the locus of critiques and challenges to the college sport establishment has shifted from current players to former players, investigative journalists, and college sport researchers. However, 1960s grassroots player activism did result in the development of player advocacy groups in the 1980s.

One such attempt was former Duke basketball player and Academic All-American Dick DeVenzio's *Revenue-Producing Major College $TUDENT-ATHLETE$ Newsletter,* in which he attempted to educate players about their rights and to advocate on behalf of players effectively silenced by NCAA rules. Through the College Athlete Association (CAA), DeVenzio argued for stipends and increased benefits for athletes in the revenue-producing sports of football and men's basketball. Convinced college sport administrators would never respond to players' requests for change, he attempted to convince players to strike, boycott, and engage in work slowdowns (delaying the start of games) and stoppages (refusing to play in games all together) (DeVenzio 1986). Players who shared DeVenzio's perspective and were supportive of protesting in some fashion often feared retribution from fans, teammates, coaches, administrators, and NCAA officials. The closest players came to a public demonstration at DeVenzio's urging was before a 1986 game between Oklahoma and Nebraska, when players decided to delay the start of the game by pausing and praying (DeVenzio 1986).

Another former college athlete, Allen Sack, who played football at the University of Notre Dame under Ara Parseghian and later earned a PhD in sociology, undertook a project called the Center for the Rights of Athletes in Education (CARE). Funded with a US Department of Education Fund for the Improvement of Post-Secondary Education (FIPSE) grant through an umbrella organization called Sports for the People, CARE's mission aligned with its name and sought to provide assistance and support to athletes who found themselves unjustly dismissed from their teams, stripped of their athletic scholarships, or punished in some way without benefit of due process (Sack 2008). The project was derailed when funding was withdrawn for what Sack referred to as political reasons. Explaining the reason for the defunding, FIPSE director Sven Groennings wrote that "it was our feeling, after careful monitoring, that the activities CARE was undertaking with public educational dollars were primarily advocacy and not educational. Although we recognize CARE's excellent ability to raise public awareness of abuses in college athletics, we felt that their treatment of the issues was often one-sided and confrontational" (quoted in Sack 2008: 95).

CAA and CARE advocacy dissipated in the late 1980s, and it was the mid-1990s before there was another prospect of significant player action. In 2013 Rigo Nunez, a former basketball player at the University of Massachusetts, reported that a player strike had been in the making during the 1995 postseason but had fizzled when officials and coaches learned of it. Describing the plan's possibilities, Nunez remarked, "If we had Twitter, if we had Facebook, this would definitely have had an impact on the NCAA Tournament. Player commitment to the boycott evaporated, however, amidst fear that those participating would be 'blackballed' and labeled 'troublemakers'" (Fram and Frampton 2012: 1073).

In the late 1990s a new organization led by Ramogi Huma, a former University of California, Los Angeles, football player, was established. The mission of the National College Players Association (NCPA) was and is to "provide the means for college athletes to voice their concerns and change NCAA rules" (NCPA 2013). Huma first became an athlete advocate while at UCLA when he witnessed how his former All-American teammate Donnie Edwards was treated. After Edwards accepted groceries because his GIA money ran out before the end of the month, he was deemed ineligible. A promising college career was cut short, and Edwards was subjected to public embarrassment essentially because he didn't have enough food to eat and it was against NCAA rules for anyone to buy him groceries, which was an "impermissible benefit." This situation gave Huma pause and prompted him to contemplate how college athletes could influence what was happening to them (Kaufman and Wolff 2010).

Huma has sought to address systemic inequities affecting players that the NCAA and college sport officials have been unwilling to address. The NCPA has worked to effect change on behalf of Division I football and men's basketball players in areas of medical coverage, health and safety issues, and fair compensation, sponsoring legislation in both California and Connecticut and supporting nationwide efforts to secure athlete name, image, and likeness (NIL) rights. Those laws include a requirement to disclose conditions under which an athlete may retain or lose a GIA and pay for deductibles up to five years after he has sustained an injury. Through the work of Huma and Staurowsky (2010, 2011a, 2011b, 2013), there is greater public awareness that NCAA limits on assistance belie the mythology that athletes attend college on a full or free ride. In fact up until 2015 there was a gap between what a GIA covered and the full cost of attendance.

In the fall of 2013, the NCPA supported the All Players United (APU) campaign, which amounted to a silent protest on the part of some football players at Northwestern, Georgia, Georgia Tech, and the University of North Carolina. The handwritten block letters *APU* on players' wristbands, socks, and/or shoes went unnoticed by most coaches and fans. However, some members of the media had been tipped off to the protest, while others observed the letters and asked what they stood for. Players acknowledged that they were trying to bring attention to concerns regarding health care, player safety, working conditions, and educational benefits. Some coaches and administrators appeared to be somewhat tolerant and even sympathetic to the players' right to protest. However, most programs across the country had workplace cultures that discouraged dissent and created barriers to players' stepping forward to challenge authority. Most coaches expressed concerns that the APU campaign was selfish and undermined team cohesion and coaches' authority. Several coaches questioned why players hadn't first sought their permission to take part in any such protest (Staurowsky 2014b). As Kain Colter, the leader of the APU campaign, commented, such an expectation missed the point of what the players were trying to achieve (ibid.).

While the APU campaign was underway, another college football player boycott unfolded at Grambling State. Grambling's football program was racked with instability due to coaching changes and limited financial resources, and consequently players were practicing and competing in unhealthy conditions and deteriorating facilities. They sat out two practices and a game against Jackson State in the hope of raising awareness regarding their plight (Schroeder 2013).

In March 2015 the University of Oklahoma football team organized a silent protest after a video surfaced in which two OU fraternity members participate in a White supremacist chant and use an anti-Black racial slur. Declining to go to practice, the team issued a position statement urging university leaders to examine the underlying issues of racial discrimination on the campus (Candea and Sunseri 2015).

On May 10, 2015 a player took to Twitter after his failed attempts to seek relief for his mistreatment by coaches at the University of Illinois. Simon Cvijanovic, a former football player, alleged in a series of tweets that he had been pressured by his coach, Tim Beckman, to play even though he was suffering from shoulder and knee injuries. The psychological problems Cvijanovic developed because of his treatment were the cause for his dismissal from the team. Illinois administrators initially backed Beckman, but several months later, following a call for an external investigation, the institution dismissed the coach (Sherman 2015).

In November 2015 thirty Black members of the University of Missouri football team used their platform as players to amplify concerns about the university's racialized climate and to support a student group called Concerned Students 1950 (Staurowsky 2015). A hunger strike initiated by African American student leader Jonathan Butler prompted the players to raise awareness of their campus's climate. They joined with other student leaders, faculty leaders, and members of the university community to call for the resignation of Missouri's president, Tom Wolfe. Players felt they had a moral obligation to speak, stating that the athletes of color on the Mizzou football team believed "injustice anywhere is a threat to justice everywhere." The threatened player boycott garnered national attention that resulted in President Wolfe tendering his resignation (Nadkarni and Nieves 2015; Staurowsky 2015; Yan, Pegoraro, and Watanabe 2018).

In October 2016, during a broadcast of ESPN's *College GameDay* program, one of the top men's basketball players in the country, University of Minnesota's Nigel Hayes (a named plaintiff in *Jenkins v. NCAA*), decried the mistreatment of college athletes. Citing his "awakening" after reading *The Autobiography of Malcolm X*, Hayes stated that he could no longer remain silent about the college sport system's injustice. Concurrently former UCLA quarterback Josh Rosen was vocal in his calls for systemic change (Auerbach 2016).

With the power of social media becoming ever more apparent and a growing sensibility on the part of both college and professional athletes that voices matter, college athlete protests have continued to escalate. In 2020, with the world faced with the COVID-19 pandemic and racial turmoil in the wake of the death of George Floyd, profit-athletes were in an untenable situation. Players were permitted to opt out of playing but faced pressure to play despite a lack of consistent health protocols. In this charged climate, after players threatened to boycott the season, Pac-12 commissioner Larry Scott was forced to meet with a group of eleven football players representing conference programs (Dellenger 2020). Using the hashtag #WeAreUnited, the players gave the following statement: "We believe a football season under these conditions would be reckless and put us at needless risk. The lack of regard for our health and safety is central to the systemic racial injustices imposed by NCAA sports that disproportionately exploits Black athletes physically, academically, and financially" (ibid.). This effort was joined by the #WeWanttoPlay movement, in which players from each of the Power Five schools came together to talk about conditions under which they might agree to play during the 2020 season while also working for social justice and systemic change in college sport (Hale 2020).

Reflecting the nationwide nature of player discontent, Florida State defensive tackle Marvin Wilson led his team in a June 2020 workout boycott in response to head coach Mike Norvell's claim to have spoken individually with each player about the traumatic events surrounding the murder of Floyd. In fact Norvell had not spoken with players (Bromberg 2020). At the University of Texas at Austin, football players refused to participate in recruiting and donor events until administrators agreed to a list of demands that included renaming campus buildings that bore the names of known racists and establishing an exhibition devoted to Black athletes as part of its Athletics Hall of Fame (Justin 2020).

Although moments of college-athlete resistance have at times influenced dialogue and provided fodder for the media, prior to 2021 little substantive change in the status of profit-athletes had occurred. Southall and Weiler (2014) characterized profit-athletes as migrant workers in a system that generates millions of dollars off their labor while freely distributing that revenue to others (see also Fram and Frampton 2012; Staurowsky 2004). Profit-athletes live in a state of suspension in which their lack of recognition as employees denies them basic employment rights while their rights as students are also routinely abridged.

Historically, three things have become clear. First, as employers, colleges and universities, along with their membership groups (the NCAA and conferences), have exerted considerable control over athlete workers. Following the passage of the fraudulent misrepresentation rule, misconduct rule, and one-year scholarship mandate, players' challenges were quelled and their voices effectively silenced. Over time this silencing became institutionalized. As a result players have effectively had little or no voice. Second, fear of retribution morphed over time. As television audiences grew, corporate interests became more pronounced, growing numbers of people wagered on the games, and public scrutiny became more intense, it became more difficult for players to speak out, since they lacked the protection of a players association. In 2020, even as more players publicly expressed concerns about their health, safety, and treatment, their boycott threats never came to fruition or often ended quickly. And while football players from different conferences began to engage with each other to discuss mutual interests during the pandemic, those discussions did not coalesce into a permanent infrastructure for player advocacy (Hale 2020). Third, those attempting to help athletes exert their voice or act on their own behalf had a much more difficult time, because athletes were increasingly surrounded not only by a regulatory system but also by a fortress of personnel (e.g., expanded coaching staffs, compliance officers, athletic-academic tutors) who controlled and monitored their lives.

Some scholars have argued that twenty-first-century major college football and basketball programs are akin to company towns (McCormick and McCormick 2006; Southall and Weiler 2014), in which players live, eat, take classes, travel, and spend their summers together. Players often have their social media accounts monitored by coaching staffs or athletic department personnel, are told what classes or majors to take, have their finances monitored, are required to register their cars with the athletic department, and are quizzed about their friends and associates. All the while the revenue their athletic labor produces is funneled back to their athletic departments, to be distributed as administrators see fit.

The Underground Economy

The markers of an unrecognized labor market are found throughout the college-sport industry. As the official denial of that market—coded in opposition to an actual pay-for-play system—has continued to be parroted by industry stakeholders, the market has sought a correction in the form of an underground economy that operates as an informal way to deliver, usually in modest ways, payments to players. While on the surface college sport officials offer a pretense of creating regulatory mechanisms to address this issue, the enduring nature of the underground economy speaks to the industry's investment in it. When detected, bad actors (those who offer payment and the players who accept it) are represented as immoral, unethical, or possibly criminal. The fact that the industry is controlled by individuals (athletic directors, conference commissioners) and entities (schools, conferences, corporations) that profit off of the labor of unrecognized employees is masked by the benign purpose of the enterprise, where ostensibly good actors consistently state that they take care of the kids, as if adult athletes (who could serve in the military) are children.

Given the racial composition of Power Five football and men's basketball teams (NCAA 2020), the characterization of profit-athletes as children who are incapable of handling their economic affairs and cannot be trusted with discretionary income hearkens back to attempts to justify slavery by portraying enslaved people as infantile, lazy, shiftless, untrustworthy, and in need of a highly regimented and controlled environment (Branch 2011). As Dal Lago and Katsari (2008: 211) write: "One of the essential features of the paternalistic ideal of the master-slave relationship was the implication that, within the extended household of the masters, slaves were assimilated to children." Significantly, as more money has become available to players, financial literacy modules or classes have been encouraged or mandated not as a means of empowering athletes or preparing them to invest in their futures but because of fears of what athletes will do if they are paid in actual money and permitted to spend it as they see fit. Bret Bielema, University of Illinois head football coach, expressed this paternalistic concern: "With a whole lot of money to make bad decisions, things can go sideways in a New York minute" (quoted in Carlton 2015). Former Texas Tech and current NFL Arizona Cardinals head coach Kliff Kingsbury wondered where athletes would spend their money: "Are they [the funds] going toward what we intend, which is food, housing, clothing, bettering their experience . . . and not on frivolous things?" (quoted in ibid.). Neither coach, each of whom had multimillion-dollar contracts, discussed their spending habits or what constituted a "whole lot" of money.

The Father of American Football and His Slush Fund

As early as the 1880s, college football was generating enough revenue to compensate college football players for their athletic talent. Significantly football programs had sufficient funds to pay athletes before they had full-time coaches and long before athletic directors or conference commissioners, as we understand those roles today. The competitive market for winning athletic talent led to teams relying on players who had already earned their degrees or paid ringers, athletes who could be persuaded to play for one game, or sometimes entire seasons, without attending classes (Smith 1988; Zimbalist 1999). At the advent of big-time college football, the mythology of clean amateurism, where athletes played for fun and the love of the game rather than economic enrichment, was perpetuated by none other than the "father of American football," Walter Camp. Camp, a Yale football player turned adviser and then coach, quite literally wrote the script for circumventing college sport rules. Notably he himself played beyond his undergraduate years, continuing his football career as a Yale College of Medicine postgraduate.

Camp mixed fact and fiction on a regular basis throughout his career, authoring dozens of novels about college sport targeted at young boys. His fictionalized accounts of characters bore a remarkable resemblance to some of his football players. These dime-store novels allowed Camp to promote his teams, create a brand identity for Yale (Des Jardins 2015), and make him a whole lot of money.

Camp's *Book of College Sports,* published in 1893, is a revelation. In the introduction he writes: "A gentleman never competes for money, directly or indirectly. . . . If you are enough of a man to be a good athlete, and someone asks you to use that athletic ability upon their behalf, don't take money for it, or anything that amounts to pay" (Camp 1893: 3). Camp seemed unfazed by the disconnect between his prose's moral tone and his pragmatic actions, including an estimated $100,000 "tutoring" slush fund that was used to pay players (W. Goldstein 2014; Zimbalist 1999). To put this in context, $100,000 in 1893 has a relative value of $29.9 million today.[1] Perhaps Camp reconciled the two because he knew he was writing fiction while also dealing with the stark demands of winning college football games. One of the players Camp kept on his payroll was three-time consensus All-American James Hogan, an immigrant born in County Tipperary in Ireland, who moved with his family to the US when he was five years old. Hogan played at Yale between 1901 and 1904 (College Football Hall of Fame 2022; W. Goldstein 2014). As a member of Yale's "Old Blue Line," Hogan "paid no tuition, lived in a luxurious dorm suite, had the score card franchise (with two teammates) at Yale baseball games, and enjoyed the exclusive campus cigarette franchise for the American Tobacco Co., for which he earned a commission on every box. The 'Egyptian Deities' and 'Turkish Mogul' cigarettes, on sale at Yale's famous watering hole, Mory's, were known as 'Hogan's cigarettes'" (W. Goldstein 2014).

Among the most famous college-football ringers was Fielding Yost, who after his playing career become coach and athletic director at the University of Michigan. It was under Yost's direction that the iconic stadium known as the "Big House" was built. In 1896, however, he was entrepreneurially peddling his football talents. Enrolled at West Virginia, he found his way onto a Lafayette College team that was intent on spoiling the University of Pennsylvania's thirty-six-game winning streak, a feat they accomplished by beating Penn 6–4 in a hotly contested matchup. With the mission accomplished, Yost returned to West Virginia.

During the 1920s paying college athletes was a routine practice. According to the 1929 Carnegie Report, of 112 colleges and universities studied, 84 offered "inducements" for college athletes (Griffith 1930). Of the remaining 28 institutions who did not offer inducements, 7 were Canadian institutions (Associated Press 1929). In 1930 the University of Iowa distinguished itself as the only member of the Big Ten Conference to ever be expelled, following an investigation that revealed the athletic department had two slush funds—one sanctioned by the university's president—to provide for "the upkeep of football men" (Dochterman 2020). Consistent with the times, during the university's investigation a Big Ten representative commented that Iowa was "far from the worst offender," but they just happened to have been caught (ibid.).

In the 1950s schools in several conferences were rumored to be offering improper inducements and violating recruiting rules. In his history of college football, Kurt Edward Kemper (2009: 54) noted that "by 1957, conference investigations revealed extensive violations of conference rules, including cash payments, special treatment of athletes, and academic improprieties. Once these circumstances became public knowledge, the chancellors of Washington and UCLA, two of the worst offenders, stonewalled and misled conference investigators to cover up their schools' complicity." Finger-pointing and accusations abounded, with schools found to be cheating suggesting that the only difference between them and peer institutions was that they had been caught.

In 1967 it was revealed the University of Illinois had a slush fund created from monies contributed by local businesses and boosters. Disbursements could be approved by the two head coaches and the athletic director as well as assistant and associate athletics administrators (M. Nelson 2014). When asked what the funds were used for, the head football coach at the time, Pete Elliott, said it was for "player emergencies." He described a situation where a player's wife suffered complications during childbirth and the money was used to cover those expenses. After the existence of the slush fund was exposed, Elliott was forced to resign. In 1973 he became head coach at the University of Miami (Asmussen 1999). From 1979 until 1995, he served as director of the Pro Football Hall of Fame (R. Goldstein 2013).

Paying Players: Neither Scandal nor Scheme—Merely a Reality

In the 1980s, as recounted in the 2010 documentary *Pony Excess,* Southern Methodist University paid football players to sign with the school. Culpability for these payments stretched all the way to the Texas governor's office. Governor Bill Clements is credited with making the decision in 1985 to continue the pay for play scheme (United Press International 1987). Former SMU player Eric Dickerson, who would go on to a storied NFL career, has—over the span of more than four decades—consistently maintained that while SMU did in fact pay him, all of the schools that recruited him offered financial incentives, with the highest offer being fifty thousand dollars (Dufresne 1987; Harvey 2013; Whitford and Elkind 2013).

A difference of opinion about former University of Tennessee quarterback and NFL Hall of Famer Peyton Manning between two friends who were boosters of different Southeast Conference schools resulted in the exposure of indirect player payments in the 1990s in what came to be known as the Logan Young/Albert Means scandal. Millionaire restaurateur and real estate mogul Roy Adams, a fervent Tennessee supporter, so profoundly disagreed with Alabama booster Logan Young about Manning that he cooperated with federal investigators to expose that Young paid a high school assistant coach two hundred thousand dollars to ensure that a prized recruit, Albert Means, signed with Alabama (Branston 2003; Talty 2015).

Examples of Power Five college sport's underground economy include University of Arkansas booster Ted Herrod's arranging for twenty or more football and men's basketball players to be paid between 1994–99 for part-time jobs at his Dallas trucking concern. As revealed in an NCAA investigation, players had been overpaid by more than $4,300 for work they allegedly did for the company (Yost 2010: 140). In addition, in the late 1990s Josh Luchs, a former sports agent, disclosed that he had financial dealings with college players who he was trying to sign as clients (Luchs and Dale 2013). While not all players (or family members) were comfortable being offered cash, many expected it. Some were given hundreds of dollars a month; others sought financial help to get out of debt or to help a family member (Luchs 2010).

Surreptitious pay-for-play arrangements have been widespread for many years. With a lucrative market existing and players forced to hide compensation, it is not surprising that organized crime has on occasion been rumored to be involved. One such example involved University of Iowa running back Ronnie Harmon, sports-entertainment agent Norby Walters, and Michael Franzese, a former capo in the Colombo crime family. Harmon has admitted to accepting a few thousand dollars from Walters and being paid $250 a month during his playing career at Iowa. Walters paid fifty-eight top college football players a total of $800,000 during their careers (Butler 2002). While Franzese has claimed Harmon was paid to throw the 1986 Rose Bowl, Harmon has denied doing so—though it should be noted he fumbled four times and dropped a sure touchdown pass during the Hawkeyes' 48–25 loss to UCLA (Butler 2002). Harmon played in the NFL for eleven years. He is one of only five NFL running backs to ever gain more than ten thousand all-purpose yards and have less than twenty fumbles (ibid.). After retiring from the NFL, he was a high school football coach, described as a great coach and motivator of young men.

In his book *Tainted Glory* (2012), former athletic compliance officer turned college-sport reformer David Ridpath recounts his experience in the early 2000s of discovering a bogus jobs program at Marshall University where athletes were either overpaid for their work or paid for work they never did. Ridpath became the scapegoat for the conduct of his superiors and their efforts to hide the pay scheme.

A famous case involving a high-profile player unfolded in 2010 when quarterback Cam Newton garnered an unprecedented level of social media and 24/7 sports-television coverage surrounding his recruitment by Auburn, Alabama, and several other schools. While the NCAA did not find violations of its bylaws, it was rumored that Newton's father, a former player from Mississippi State, had sought to broker Newton's talents for between $120,000 and $160,000 (Associated Press 2011).

Chris Simms, the son of NFL Hall of Famer Phil Simms, who played at the University of Texas from 2000 to 2003, admitted in 2015 that he and his teammates accepted hundred-dollar handshakes. Describing the frequency of the practice, he said, "There's $100 handshakes going on at every Division I school in the nation—college [football], basketball. . . . It's going on everywhere" (Silverstein 2015). While Simms and the legion of players he believed were paid were not punished for accepting such payments, storied University of Southern California running back Reggie Bush was compelled to return his Heisman Trophy following an investigation that revealed he and his family received more than one hundred thousand dollars from several marketing agents (Hogan 2010).

Cases involving college athletes receiving surreptitious payments for activities involving their names, images, and likenesses (NILs) have become commonplace in the twenty-first century. In 2010 Terrelle Pryor and four Ohio State teammates were suspended several games because they sold awards they had been given and received discounted services (i.e., tattoos) in violation of NCAA rules prohibiting players from monetizing their celebrity (ESPN.com News Services 2010).[2] Texas A&M quarterback and Heisman Trophy winner Johnny Manziel was suspended for a half game in 2013 for allegedly being paid for signing memorabilia (Berkes 2013). In 2014 University of Georgia running back Todd Gurley, a leading contender for the Heisman, was suspended for four games after reports he had taken more than three thousand dollars for signing autographs over a two-year period (Staples 2014). In 2013 Yahoo! Sports reported that five SEC players, Tyler Bray (Tennessee), Chad Bumpis (Mississippi State), Maurice Couch (Tennessee), Fletcher Cox (Mississippi State), and DJ Fluker (University of Alabama), were the recipients of "extra benefits" totaling more than forty-five thousand dollars (Getlin and Robinson 2013). Several agents were alleged to have worked with a former Alabama football player, Luther Davis (who served as a player "concierge"), to facilitate relationships between players, agents, and financial advisers.

In 2015 court documents unsealed in a lawsuit involving the University of North Carolina at Chapel Hill football player Robert Quinn revealed that Quinn received $13,700 to induce him to sign with an agent and financial adviser. It was also revealed that other UNC players received cash, were paid for signing memorabilia, and were guided toward particular agents (Beard 2015). *SB Nation* reporter Steven Godfrey (2014) described the passing of cash from boosters to top recruits and current players as a necessary function in big-time college sport: "This is the arrangement in high-stakes college football, though of course not every player is paid for. Providing cash and benefits is not a scandal or a scheme, merely a function. And when you start listening to the stories, you understand the function can never be stopped."

The history of under-the-table payments to profit-athletes reflects a long and consistent practice of seeking to balance players' value with compensation. Big-time college-sport's underground economy was most recently revealed in a 2017–18 FBI investigation focused on NCAA Division I men's college basketball. These consistent and increasing payments demonstrate that over decades profit-athletes have understood that their value is suppressed in the market. In addition they also show that actors throughout the system (administrators, coaches, agents, and boosters) view such payments as modest and necessary efforts at market corrections.

The Evolving and Expanding Menu of NCAA College Athlete Compensation and Benefits

In the history of college sport, there was only a brief window of time—1948 to 1951—when the NCAA attempted to effectively ban the practice of awarding scholarships on the basis of athletic performance. This attempt involved the passage of the so-called Sanity Code. Viewed as a compromise, awards under the code were to be based on financial need or superior academic performance, with the stipulation that athletic participation was not a requirement for retaining the award. The experiment did not go well. Short-lived and controversial, the code was so objectionable to many NCAA members that a power struggle ensued within the association. Some of the twenty-two schools that initially refused to comply were brought in line, but seven holdouts forced the issue to a formal discussion and the southern conferences threatened to leave the NCAA if the rule was not changed (Sack and Staurowsky 1998; McCormick and McCormick 2006). While the seven schools were deemed to have cheated, which should have resulted in NCAA expulsion, fewer than the mandatory two-thirds of members voted to expel them. This outcome was likely because some schools did not believe in the Sanity Code while others had also been cheating but had not gotten caught. Consequently the sinners escaped punishment (Byers and Hammer 1995). The introduction and subsequent abolishment of the Sanity Code and subsequent formalization of athletic GIAs represented not an embrace of amateurism but a "rearguard accommodation to professionalism" (Sack and Staurowsky 1998: 22). While credited with creating the foundation for the NCAA enforcement system, the Sanity Code also set the NCAA on a path of formalizing pay for play while attempting to ignore that athletes' being awarded GIAs for their athletic ability effectively turned them into employees. However, unlike players in the NFL or NBA, where agreements are reached through good-faith negotiations between management and players and players have access to arbitration when there is a belief that management has not acted in good faith, profit-athletes have consistently been denied employment status.

The NCAA and/or member schools such as Northwestern have consistently relied on the NCAA's principle of amateurism in defending the collegiate model of athletics. In its amicus brief supporting Northwestern University's NLRB response, the Big Ten asserted that the granting of collective bargaining rights to Northwestern football players "would plainly run afoul of the bedrock principles of amateurism on which the NCAA and the Big Ten are founded" (Rosenman, Netter, and Wolf 2014: 3). The brief noted that "wages are a mandatory subject of bargaining under the NLRA but are at the same time a major source of NCAA limitations. If Northwestern were required to compensate its scholarship football players with more than a full grant-in-aid scholarship . . . Northwestern would gain a substantial edge" (ibid.: 12). The conference went on to further assert: "Contests between a team of paid professionals and squads of student amateurs are not the picture of parity and equality that makes Big Ten football engaging, entertaining, and publicly valued" (ibid.).

The weakness in the argument, of course, beyond a broad assertion that the notion of college sport amateurism simply does not exist, is that calling something a bedrock principle suggests that it does not change, that it is unbroken and unyielding. Within the NCAA itself, there are three different principles of amateurism, one for each division. Two of those principles, in Divisions I and II, provide for compensation without sullying the meaning. Only in Division III and in Ivy League institutions that spurn the awarding of financial aid based on athletic talent does the principle of amateurism include a reference to non-payment. And even in Division III, rules governing reinstatement after an athlete has been a professional are far more liberal than those at the Division I level. The strictest implementation of rules governing payment for athletic performance are imposed on the athletes who are at the profit center of college sport, the football and basketball players (Staurowsky 2014c).

The suggestion that compensating athletes beyond a full GIA somehow threatens the mythical, universal, and sacrosanct notion of amateurism ignores the ever-expanding ways in which funds are funneled to athletes. NCAA members' opportunistic and conditional commitment to the concept of amateurism is clear in a 2008 NCAA study. The study's architect, Division I vice president David Berst, noted that members' belief in amateurism was not "steeped in any sacred absolute principle that had to be preserved" but could be "modified as views change" (Staurowsky 2014c: 47). Clearly the NCAA's defense of amateurism is not based upon a sacred belief in non-payment. Rather it is an attempt to defend the business enterprise and maintain control of players (their value, their workdays, their movement from one program to the other, and their access to educational opportunities and health care). The NCAA's definition of pay and its principle of amateurism are tools designed to control the collegiate model's labor.

When they were initially instituted in 1956, GIAs covered only tuition, room and board, and books. Subsequently there have been several public challenges to the limits on the value of a GIA. In *White v. NCAA* (2008), former NCAA Division I football and basketball players challenged the NCAA's rules governing what GIAs covered, arguing that the limits constituted a restraint of trade. While GIAs allowed athletes to receive compensation for tuition, room and board, and books, athletic scholarships had been designed so athletes did not receive the full cost of attendance (Staurowsky 2014c). The NCAA ultimately settled the case, which resulted in the creation of a $10 million fund to reimburse eligible former athletes for the gap between a GIA and the full cost of attendance. The average amount awarded to qualified members of the class in *White* was $2,500 (Hosick 2008).

In the aftermath of the *White* case, the NCAA still did not change its rules to remedy the issue of the scholarship shortfall. It took subsequent efforts to educate the public regarding the gap between cost of attendance and the value of GIAs (Huma and Staurowsky 2011a), as well as a favorable ruling on behalf of the plaintiffs in *O'Bannon v. NCAA* (2014) to convince many Division I members to begin covering full cost of attendance in the fall of 2015 (Solomon 2015). On the heels of the Northwestern football players' labor action and the *O'Bannon* ruling, in 2016 the NCAA's Board of Governors approved a one-time-only dispersal of $200 million in "special financial assistance" in response to the adoption of the new rules that allowed NCAA athletic departments to compensate (that is, pay) athletes up to the full cost of attendance (Hendrickson 2016).

Beyond GIAs and stipends that cover the full cost of attendance, NCAA officials have distributed funds to college athletes in response to market pressures. In the 1990s, following the NCAA's first $1 billion television deal, the association and its members began disbursing additional financial support to athletes for expenses associated with clothing, travel, education, and career training, as well as loss of value (in the event of injury) insurance for athletes in Division I football, men's and women's basketball, and ice hockey.

According to the NCAA, these funds—which were described as coming from benefit programs—"directly support the educational, financial, and health and safety needs of student-athletes" (NCAA 2022). In most cases the distributed funds have been quite modest in scope and have historically been underutilized.

Regarding insurance coverage, as of 2021 the NCAA lists three programs on its "NCAA 101" webpage:

- The Catastrophic Injury Insurance Program provides coverage for injuries that generate medical expenses in excess of the ninety-thousand-dollar deductible.

- A Group Basic Medical Insurance Program that offers coverage for injuries sustained while participating in intercollegiate athletics that generate expenses that fall below the ninety-thousand-dollar deductible in the Catastrophic Injury Insurance Program.
- The Exceptional Student-Athlete Disability Insurance Program allows qualified athletes with a reasonable prospect of pursuing a professional career in the sports of basketball (men's and women's), football, ice hockey, and baseball to insure against their future earnings. Through an NCAA-vetted agency, athletes may receive preapproved financing to cover the cost of these policies. (NCAA 2022)

While these programs do offer avenues for college athletes to access medical coverage, NCAA member institutions are not compelled to provide the coverage. Thus some institutions will pay athlete deductibles for injuries sustained in their sport, while other schools will not. Further, in the sports of basketball and football, NCAA bylaws 13.2.6 and 13.2.7 allow for schools to pay for medical care, including rehabilitation and physical therapy, associated with prospective athletes injured during summer activities (voluntary or required) or, in the case of basketball, during summer tryouts.

The Student Assistance Fund is an umbrella term for two funds that distribute money to Division I athletes: the Special Assistance Fund (SAF) and the Student-Athlete Opportunity Fund (SAOF). Eligibility for these funds varies by stated purpose.

- The SAF, established in 1999, originally provided support to athletes who face financial hardships and warrant support for "emergency" expenses (e.g., trips home for a funeral for athletes without means to afford travel) or "essential" expenses (e.g., a suit for a job interview) (Libit 2021).
- The SAOF, created in 2003, provides support for necessities, such as car insurance and maintenance, clothing, educational supplies, fuel, medical/dental/vision expenses, toiletries, travel home, and utility bills (Libit 2021). Disbursement is left to the discretion of individual conferences, but the NCAA has devised a list of prohibited purposes.

In 2012–13 the SAF distribution was $73.5 million (NCAA 2013). By 2021 the SAF distribution had decreased to $18.9 million, which was approximately 3 percent of NCAA distributions (NCAA 2021c). Prior to the start of each new academic year, the NCAA disburses money from the fund to conference offices. Individual conferences then distribute funds to their members on an agreed-upon basis. The 2021 SAOF disbursement was listed as $68.8 million, approximately 11 percent of the total Division I distributions (NCAA 2021c).

In addition to the limited financial, health, and educational benefits offered by the NCAA, in January 2013 the association amended its bylaws to allow Division I athletes to receive reimbursement for actual and necessary competition-related expenses (NCAA bylaws 12.02.5 and 12.02.6). According to this change, athletes who received a reimbursement of less than $301 of actual and necessary competition-related expenses retained their amateur status.

In addition to these several examples, the NCAA has long supported athletes' receiving gifts (i.e., swag) for participating in postseason tournaments and championships. This stance is wholly consistent with the NCAA's definition of pay, which restricts allowable player compensation to whatever the NCAA members decide. Thus gifts and/or awards distributed at bowl games, tournaments, and other events are consistent with the NCAA's version of amateurism. As a matter of magnitude, under Article 16.1, "Awards," athletes can receive awards and gifts totaling several thousands of dollars, depending on their class year, their sport, and the success of their teams (NCAA 2021a). When push comes to shove, the NCAA has been more than willing to increase player compensation in the face of bad publicity. For example, in 2015 the association launched a pilot program to compensate expenses (up to three thousand dollars for the semifinal round and four thousand dollars for the final round) for family members traveling to support athletes whose teams were competing in the Division I men's and women's basketball tournament (Hosick 2018). This increase came in response to numerous media reports that many players' families could not afford to attend March Madness games because teams are placed in regional brackets often far away from their campuses. In 2019 the plan was made permanent (Hosick 2019). In addition, consistent with NCAA rules, the CFP also pays for families of players to travel to CFP playoff games (ibid.).

While some NCAA athlete programs, such as the Post-graduate Scholarship Program (which provides funding for postgraduate study), disburse money to athletes in all sports in each division, other programs, such as the SAF, the SAOF, and the Exceptional Student-Athlete Disability Insurance Program, confer special status on Division I athletes, who generate the most money, inspire the most media attention, and are more likely to become professional athletes. There is a history within the NCAA of providing benefits to selected groups of athletes. Notably the SAF is not available to athletes in NCAA Divisions II or III. Similarly the Exceptional Student-Athlete Disability Insurance Program is limited to athletes who are likely to successfully pursue a professional career. As public and legal scrutiny has intensified, other avenues of sharing revenue directly or indirectly with athletes have opened.

It should be noted that college athlete pay masquerading as benefit programs has not been contained solely within the NCAA. For example, since 1959 the

National Football Foundation (NFF) has awarded postgraduate scholarships to between twelve and fourteen football players each year that are more than twice as lucrative as those awarded by the NCAA (eighteen thousand dollars for the NFF awards compared to eight thousand dollars for the NCAA awards). One recipient is awarded the William V. Campbell Trophy and receives a twenty-five-thousand-dollar postgraduate scholarship (National Football Foundation 2022).

The existence of these programs, as well as the malleable nature of GIAs to cover the full cost of attendance, shows that the NCAA's notion of amateurism does not prohibit providing monetary benefits to athletes; it merely means the NCAA wants to control and suppress any such wages.

The National Labor Relation Board's Decision in Northwestern: A Historical Perspective

What might have happened if Northwestern University football players had been found to be employees (with collective bargaining rights) by the NLRB National Board and the regional director's decision had been upheld? Would—as the National Board opined—the potential for instability in college sport labor relations really have disrupted "the symbiotic relationship among the various teams, the conferences, and the NCAA" (NLRB 2015: 4)?

Given college sport history, such a hypothetical is worth contemplating. Over time college sport has demonstrated that it is a highly adaptable, opportunistic, and flexible industry that will preserve the profitability of the enterprise and control of the players at almost any cost. As has been discussed above, in the 1990s, after signing the most lucrative television deal ever, the NCAA distributed some additional money to the players to downplay criticism from them and the public. In 2009, facing the prospect that its rules capping GIAs below the full cost of attendance would be found to violate antitrust law (see *White v. NCAA*), the NCAA settled and established a fund to compensate former players. At that time NCAA members had the opportunity to pay players by offering full cost of attendance, but—against the urging of NCAA president Myles Brand—they chose not to do so. It was only in response to *O'Bannon v. NCAA* (2014) that legislation permitting schools to offer full cost of attendance was passed, expanding player pay. Prior to that time, schools around the country had claimed they did not have the financial wherewithal to even entertain such a notion. Many members lamented that doing so would simply be too costly and that compensating some players and not others would cause internal team strife. Rebutting such arguments, Steve Berman, lead attorney for the *Alston v. NCAA* (2021) plaintiffs, noted that while Football Bowl Subdivision (FBS) schools were now offering full cost-of-attendance stipends, the defendants had not identified a single player who had been dropped or displaced as a result (Solomon 2015).

In explaining its decision not to exercise jurisdiction, the NLRB National Board wrote,

> As an additional consideration, we observe that the terms and conditions of Northwestern's players have changed markedly in recent years and that there have been calls for the NCAA to undertake further reforms that may result in additional changes to the circumstances of scholarship players. For example, the NCAA's decision to allow FBS teams to award guaranteed 4-year scholarships, as opposed to 1-year renewable scholarships, has reduced the likelihood that scholarship players who become unable to play will lose their educational funding, and possibly their educational opportunity. (NLRB 2015: 1354–55)

Oddly the board referenced only a news item reported in *USA Today,* without consideration of the lengthy and expensive court cases and unaccounted-for costs to players that led up to the change. In addition the board assumed that all such developments were in the best interests of the players.

The issue is not whether the multiyear scholarship arrangement reduces the likelihood of athletes losing their compensation. The fundamental issue is that players have no bargaining rights. For example, there is a widespread public belief that athletes will be more secure with a multiyear award. However, what is not discussed is that any such awards are no more guaranteed than any provision of the NCAA bylaws, which can be amended or deleted at the behest of NCAA members (which does not include the athletes). Second, athletes are still vulnerable to losing GIAs under the fraudulent misrepresentation and misconduct rules. And third, even with four-year awards, athlete health is still at risk, since coaches have fewer ways of culling marginal players to make way for better players.

Historically college football players have commented about the use of medical waivers by coaches in attempts to move some players to the sidelines. In 2009 three Alabama players claimed they were being persuaded to medically "waive out" even though they either did not have injuries or did not have injuries that would prevent them from playing (Karp and Everson 2010). In 2015 Ondre Pipkins, a defensive lineman at Michigan, believed the coaching staff had induced him to sign a medical scholarship form to create space on the roster for another player (Schad 2015).

As college sport authorities contemplated GIA terms between a minimum of one year and five years, there was also talk of making the consequences of player misconduct more severe. In May 2015 the SEC increased the strength of the misconduct rule by barring accused athletes from transferring within the conference. Subsequent to the NLRB's decision in Northwestern's case, other conferences reviewed similar rules. As is the case with all such rules, since players have no bargaining rights, any changes are imposed unilaterally.

In his analysis of the NLRB decision, Marc Edelman (2015) identified concerns about Northwestern's existing relationships with the Big Ten and the NCAA as a red herring. He wrote,

> The National Labor Relations Board would not deny members of the United Steelworkers the right to unionize simply because their employers, at times, may do business with state entities. . . . Similarly, Northwestern University football players should not have been denied the right to unionize simply because their "employer" scheduled games against public entities such as Ohio State University and the University of Michigan. Indeed, scheduling such games against large public colleges is entirely Northwestern's choice, and thus it should not be viewed as a factor deterring the unionization of the private college's football workforce.

Fundamentally, do Northwestern's associations with those entities provide a sufficient justification to deny athletes who have otherwise demonstrated they are employees such employee status without warning and without their knowledge? Tellingly a move on the part of state legislatures in Michigan and Ohio to pass laws barring athletes from being employees was in direct response to this case. In all these deliberations, players had no benefit of advocacy, no benefit of representation, no opportunity to weigh in, and no mechanism to protect themselves.

Conclusion

In 1935 Congress enacted the National Labor Relations Act "to protect the rights of employees and employers, to encourage collective bargaining, and to curtail certain private sector labor and management practices, which can harm the general welfare of workers, businesses and the U.S. economy" (NLRB 2022). The NLRB, on its website, notes:

> Experience has proved that protection by law of the right of employees to organize and bargain collectively safeguards commerce from injury, impairment, or interruption, and promotes the flow of commerce by removing certain recognized sources of industrial strife and unrest, by encouraging practices fundamental to the friendly adjustment of industrial disputes arising out of differences as to wages, hours, or other working conditions, and by restoring equality of bargaining power between employers and employees. (ibid.)

In light of the NLRB decision in the Northwestern case, where will profit-athletes find relief? Unfortunately the NLRB National Board justified its inaction by expressing concern for potential instability in college sport if players were granted fundamental rights afforded every American citizen. To this day the courts and the NLRB have not grappled with the overriding question of whether, when college athletes (particularly profit-athletes) sign a National Letter of Intent, do they forfeit their rights as US citizens? In exchange for their work, every profit-athlete deserves protective safeguards against injury, impairment, or interruption. Friendly adjustment of industrial disputes assumes good-faith dealing between employers and employees. As has been chronicled in this chapter—and throughout this book—the history of college sport does not reflect such good faith between college sport authorities and profit-athletes. Individual athletes usually retain limited power, and organized group action has been discouraged by NCAA members and then officially denied in the Northwestern case. Any bargaining between college sport management and labor is haphazard, often occurring via lawsuits and public exposes. The NLRB decision largely perpetuates the status quo, with no opportunity for college players to exercise their right to explore all bargaining options.

The NLRB grappled with the Northwestern case not only because it was a novel case but also because big-time college sport is a novel industry. Zimbalist (1999 6) noted that "big-time intercollegiate athletics is a unique industry. No other industry in the United States manages not to pay its principal producers a wage or salary." However, Zimbalist is wrong. Just because the NCAA says it does not pay players does not make it so. College athletes have been getting paid for their labor since college sport began. In 1915 essayist William T. Foster wrote, "Only childlike innocence or willful blindness need prevent American colleges from seeing that the rules which aim to maintain athletics on what is called an 'amateur' basis, by forbidding players to receive pay in money, are worse than useless because, while failing to prevent men from playing for pay, they breed deceit and hypocrisy" (Foster 1915: 579).

That hypocrisy is not lost on profit-athletes. In a September 21, 2015, speech at the National Press Club in Washington, DC, Big 12 commissioner Bob Bowlsby stated that when he asked a basketball player if he believed he was an employee, the player said: "My time is not my own. . . . I don't have any control over where I go, what I do, how I work out, how long I work out, what I eat, where I eat. . . . That sounds like an employee to me. . . . I'm grateful for what I'm getting, but you asked me if I feel like an employee—and I do" (quoted in Berkowitz 2015). In 2020, as the COVID-19 pandemic spread across the country, University of North Carolina men's basketball player Armando Bacot Jr. responded to a news item shared on Twitter by college basketball reporter Jon Rothstein that a president of an ACC school had been advised by medical personnel that with rising coronavirus infections on campus, classes should be held online and all students other than athletes should be sent home or moved off campus (Rothstein 2020). However, athletes would remain on campus and continue to prepare for their competitive seasons. Bacot retweeted and commented on Rothstein's (2020) tweet: "Student-athletes? Amateurism?? Or employee?" (Bacot 2020).

Just as any other workers, profit-athletes want to be heard. Like any other employees, they have the right to bargain over the terms and conditions under which they work. While this right may be inconvenient to, disagreeable to, or not in the economic interests of college sport's "owners," it is still a fundamental right. Although the full NLRB failed to protect the employment rights of Northwestern football players, the players' actions—along with the efforts of other former and current college athletes and their advocates—have led to a growing appreciation of the many ways in which profit-athletes' rights are denied.

Small but incremental change continues to occur day by day. On August 9, 2020, editors of the University of North Carolina at Chapel Hill campus news outlet the *Daily Tar Heel* announced that because of their responsibility as members of the media to be accurate in their use of language, they would no longer use the term *student-athlete,* opting instead for *college athlete, athlete, player,* or *student* depending on the context. In explaining their decision, they wrote, "To accept the term 'student athlete' is to accept the NCAA and the nation's college athletic departments' agenda that these athletes are not employees and to silence the voices of these athletes" (*Daily Tar Heel* Staff 2020). The call by the *Tar Heel* staff to alter their editorial policy prompted editors at *Sports Illustrated* to do the same (Feinstein 2020).

Notes

1. See https://www.measuringworth.com/dollarvaluetoday.
2. A discussion of the changing nature of NCAA regulations regarding college athletes monetizing their names, images and likenesses (NIL) can be found in the last chapter, "The End of the Beginning of the End?"

References

CASES

Northwestern University, Decision and Direction of Election, Case 13-RC-121359 (March 26, 2014).

O'Bannon v. NCAA (2014). 7 F.Supp.3d 955 (N. D. Cal.).

———. (2015). WL 5712106 (9th cir. 30 September 2015).

University of Denver v. Nemeth (1953). http://law.justia.com/cases/colorado/supreme-court/1953/16945.html.

Van Horn v. Industrial Accident Commission (1963). http://law.justia.com/cases/california/court-of-appeal/2d/219/457.html.

White v. National Collegiate Athletic Association. (2006, September 8). Second amended complaint for plaintiff. No. CV-06–0999 RGK (C.D. Cal. Filed September 8, 2006).

SECONDARY SOURCES

Asmussen, Bob (1999). "Darkest of Days." *Champaign (IL) News-Gazette*, March 21. http://www.news-gazette.com/.

Associated Press (1929). "Carnegie Foundation Reports Eighty-Four Colleges Support Athletes." *Cornell Sun*, October 24.

———. (2011). "Auburn Releases Cam Newton Docs." ESPN.com, November 5. http://espn.go.com/.

Auerbach, Nicole (2016). "Good for Nigel Hayes, Who Won't Sit Idly by When He Sees Injustice." *USA Today*, October 16. https://www.usatoday.com/.

Banks, Paul M. (2014). "Kain Colter Leads NU in Historic Movement towards Social Justice." *Chicago Now*, January 28. http://www.chicagonow.com/.

Bacot, Armando Jr. (2020). "Student-athletes? Amateurism?? Or employee?" Twitter, August 17, 2020. https://twitter.com/.

Beard, Aaron (2015). "Documents Details Hawkins' Payments in UNC Case." *College Football AP*, July 20. http://collegefootball.ap.org/.

Berkes, Peter (2013). "Johnny Manziel Briefly Suspended, Ending NCAA Autographs Investigation." *SB Nation*, August 28. http://www.sbnation.com/.

Berkowitz, Steve (2015). "Big 12's Bob Bowlsby Sees the Day Big-Time Athletes Refuse to Play." *USA Today*, September 21. https://eu.usatoday.com/.

Branston, John (2003). "'Tennstud' & 'Bama Booster.'" *Memphis Flyer*, November 7. https://www.memphisflyer.com/.

Bromberg, Nick (2020). "Star FSU Player 'Moving Forward' After Disputing New Coach's Claim He had Conversations with each Player Amidst George Floyd protests." Yahoo.com, June 4. https://sports.yahoo.com/.

Burton, Rick (2017). "Faculty Oversight Committee Annual Report." Syracuse University, September 1. https://www.scribd.com/document/358231143/Faculty-Oversight-Committee-Annual-Report-2017.

Butler, Dylan (2002). "Harmon Still Chased by Fix Rumor 16 Years Later." *QNS*, July 31. https://qns.com/.

Bybee, J. S. (2015). Appeal from the US District Court for the Northern District of California. O'Bannon v. National Collegiate Athletic Association. http://cdn.ca9.uscourts.gov/.

Byers, Walter, with Charles Hammer (1995). *Unsportsmanlike Conduct: Exploiting College Athletes*. Ann Arbor: University of Michigan Press.

Camp, Walter (1893). *Book of College Sports*. New York: Century. https://archive.org/stream/waltercampsbook000camprich#page/n9/mode/2up.

Candea, Ben, and Gina Sunseri (2015). "Oklahoma Football Team Stages Silent Protest over Racist Frat Video." ABC News, March 12. https://abcnews.go.com/.

Carlton, Chuck (2015). "College Football Players Are Finally Being Paid." *Dallas Morning News*, July 25. https://www.dallasnews.com/.

College Football of Fame (2022). "James Joseph Hogan." http://www.cfbhall.com/inductees (accessed August 6).

Collins, Michael (2014). "Why College Athlete Unions Will Never Happen, but the NCAA Will Never Be the Same." *Fansided*, March 31. https://fansided.com/.

Comeaux, Eddie, and Sara E. Grummert (2020). "Antiblackness in College Athletics: Facilitating High Impact Campus Engagement and Successful Career Transitions among

Black Athletes." *High Impact Practices in Intercollegiate Athletics*, special issue, edited by Ellen J. Staurowsky, Anthony Weaver, Jessica R. Braunstein, and David Shonk. *Journal of Issues in Intercollegiate Athletics*, September 15, 56–72. http://csri-jiia.org/.

Cooper, James (2018). "NCAA Launches Latest Brand PSA Focused on Inclusion." *Ad Week*, March 11. https://www.adweek.com/agencies/ncaa-launches-latest-brand-psa-focused-on-inclusion/.

Corr, Chris, E. Woodrow Eckard, Richard M. Southall, Mark S. Nagel, and Aiden Murphy, (2021). "2020–2021 Adjusted Graduation Gap Report: NCAA FBS Football." June 2. https://static1.squarespace.com/.

Croyle, Johnathan (2020). "1970: Remembering the 'Syracuse 8,' the SU Football Players Who Risked Their Playing Careers for Change." *Syracuse.com*, July 15. https://www.syracuse.com/.

Daily Tar Heel Staff (2020). "The Daily Tar Heel Will No Longer Use the Term 'Student-Athlete.'" *Daily Tar Heel*, August 9. https://www.dailytarheel.com/.

Dal Lago, Enrico, and Constantina Katsari (2008). *Slave Systems: Ancient and Modern*. New York: Cambridge University Press.

Dellenger, Ross (2020). "Pac-12 Commissioner Responds to Football Players Threatening to Boycott 2020 Season," August 3. https://www.si.com/college/2020/08/04/pac-12-responds-to-players-threatening-boycott-season.

Demas, Lane (2011). *Integrating the Gridiron: Black Civil Rights and American College Football*. New Brunswick, NJ: Rutgers University Press.

Dent, Jim (2001). *The Junction Boys: How Ten Days in Hell with Bear Bryant Forged a Championship Team*. New York: St. Martin's.

Des Jardins, Julie (2015). *Walter Camp: Football and the Modern Man*. New York: Oxford University Press.

DeVenzio, Dick (1986). *Rip-off U.: The Annual Theft and Exploitation of Major College Revenue Producing Student-Athletes*. Denver: Fool Court.

Dochterman, Scott (2020). "Slush Funds and Spite: The Story behind Iowa's Short-Lived Big Ten Ouster." *Athletic*, October 8. https://theathletic.co.uk/.

Dufresne, Chris (1987). "Dickerson Says SMU Paid Him: Claims One School Offered $50,000." *Los Angeles Times*, May 9. http://articles.latimes.com/.

Edelman, Marc (2015). "Upon Further Review: The NLRB Was Wrong to Deny Northwestern Football Players Union Status." *Forbes*, September 2. http://www.forbes.com/.

Edwards, Harry (1969). *The Revolt of the Black Athlete*. New York: Free Press.

ESPN.com News Services (2010). "Ohio State Football Players Sanctioned." ESPN.com, December 26. http://sports.espn.go.com/.

Feinstein, John (2020). "The NCAA Uses 'Student-Athlete' as a Weapon. Some College Journalists Just Stripped It Away." *Washington Post*, August 19. https://www.washingtonpost.com/.

Finkel, Ross, Trevor Martin, and Jon Paley, dirs. (2013). *Schooled: The Price of College Sports*. Makuhari Media.

Foster, William T. (1915). "An Indictment of Intercollegiate Athletics." *Atlantic Monthly*, November. http://www.unz.org/Pub/AtlanticMonthly-1915nov-00577.

FoxSports (2013). "Pay for Play? Not in Delaney's NCAA." Fox News, September 13. https://www.foxnews.com/.

Fram, Nicholas, and Thomas Frampton (2012). "A Union of Amateurs: A Legal Blueprint to Reshape Big-Time College Athletics." *Buffalo Law Review* 60: 1003–78. http://papers.ssrn.com/.

Getlin, Rand, and Charles Robinson (2013). "Documents, Text Messages Reveal Impermissible Benefits to Five SEC players." Yahoo! Sports, September 11. https://sports.yahoo.com/.

Given, Karen, and Shira Springer (2017). "Before Kaepernick, the 'Syracuse 8' Were Blackballed by Pro Football." WBUR.org, November 17. https://www.wbur.org/.

Godfrey, Steven (2014). "Meet the Bag Man: 10 Rules for Paying College Football Players." *SB Nation,* April 10. http://www.sbnation.com/.

Goldstein, Richard (2013). "Pete Elliott, Football All-American and Coach, Dies at 86." *New York Times,* January 6. https://www.nytimes.com/.

Goldstein, Warren (2014). "Walter Camp's Off-Side: A Tarnished Football Legacy." *Hartford Courant,* March 14. https://www.courant.com/.

Griffith, John L. (1930). "The Carnegie Reports." *Journal of Higher Education* 1, no. 6: 325–30. https://www.jstor.org/.

Gurney, Gerald S., and Richard M. Southall (2012). "College Sports' Bait and Switch." ESPN.com, August 9. http://espn.go.com/.

Hale, David M. (2020). "Clemson's Trevor Lawrence, Darien Rencher: We Want to Play and Bring about Change." ESPN.com, August 10. https://www.espn.com/.

Hartmann, Douglas (2008). *Race, Culture, and the Revolt of the Black Athlete.* Chicago: University of Chicago Press.

Harvey, Randy (2013). "After 34 Years, Eric Dickerson Repaid a Debt to A & M." *Houston Chronicle,* February 6. http://www.houstonchronicle.com/.

Henderson, Simon (2013). *Sidelined: How American Sports Challenged the Black Freedom Struggle.* Louisville: University of Kentucky Press.

Hendrickson, Brian (2016). "Board of Governors Approves $200 Million Distribution to DI Members." *NCAA News,* March 10. https://www.ncaa.org/.

Herbert, Geoff (2015). "Remember When . . . Syracuse Football's Comeback Win in 1961 Liberty Bowl." *Syracuse.com,* August 11. http://www.syracuse.com/.

Hosick, Michelle Brutlag (2008). "Court Initially Approves Settlement in White Case." *NCAA News,* February 5. http://ncaanewsarchive.s3.amazonaws.com/.

———. (2018). "Family Travel Program Could Become Permanent under Proposal." *NCAA News,* June 13. https://www.ncaa.org/.

———. (2019). "Council Adopts Final Four Family Travel Proposal." *NCAA News,* January 23. https://www.ncaa.org/.

Hogan, Nakia (2010). "Reggie Bush Investigation Results in Major Sanctions for Southern Cal." *The Times-Picayune,* June 11. https://www.nola.com/.

Huma, Ramogi, and Ellen J. Staurowsky (2010). "An Examination of the Financial Shortfall for Athletes on Full Scholarship at NCAA Division I Institutions—2009–2010." National College Players Association. March 26. https://www.ncpanow.org/.

———. (2011a). "The Price of Poverty: A Comparison of Big-Time College Athletes Fair Market Value, Their Current Compensation, and the U.S. Federal Poverty Line." National College Players Association. https://www.ncpanow.org/.

———. (2011b). "TV Money Windfall in Big Time College Sports: $784 Million Reasons for Reform." National College Players Association. https://www.ncpanow.org/.

———. (2013). "The $6 Billion Heist: Robbing College Athletes under the Guise of Amateurism." National College Players Association. https://www.ncpanow.org/.

Jacinto, Alexandrea (2020). "Should the NCAA Have to Pay? Long-Term Injuries in College Athletics, Improper Assumptions of Risk, and Coverage of Medical Expenses after College." *Fordham Intellectual Property, Media, and Entertainment Law Journal* 30, no. 4: 1384–1432.

Justin, Raga (2020). "UT-Austin Football Players Demand School Rename Buildings Named after Racist Figures, Donate to Black Lives Matter." *Texas Tribune,* June 12. https://www.texastribune.org/.

Karcher, Richard T. (2012). "Broadcast Rights, Unjust Enrichment, and the Student-Athlete." *Cardozo Law Review* 34, no. 1: 107–70. https://www.researchgate.net/.

———. (2014). "The Battle outside of the Courtroom: Principles of 'Amateurism' vs. Principles of Supply and Demand." *Mississippi Sports Law Review* 3, no. 1: 47–76.

Karp, Hannah, and Darren Everson (2010). "Alabama's Unhappy Castoffs." *Wall Street Journal,* September 24. http://www.wsj.com/.

Kaufman, Peter, and Eli Wolff (2010). "Playing and Protesting: Sport as a Vehicle for Social Change." *Journal of Sport and Social Issues* 34: 154–76.

Kemper, Kurt Edward (2009). *College Football and American Culture in the Cold War Era.* Champaign: University of Illinois Press.

Libit, Dan (2021). "Alston Case Turns Spotlight onto NCAA's Student Assistance Fund." *Sportico.com,* July 20. https://www.sportico.com/.

Lowery, Wesley, and Jacob Bogage (2019). "Fifty Years after the 'Black 14' Were Banished, Wyoming Football Reckons with the Past." *Washington Post,* November 30. https://www.washingtonpost.com/.

Luchs, Josh (2010). "Confessions of an Agent." *Sports Illustrated,* October 12. http://www.si.com/.

Luchs, Josh, and James Dale (2013). *Illegal Procedure: A Sports Agent Comes Clean on the Dirty Business of College Sport.* New York: Bloomsbury.

Marzan, César F. Rosado (2014). "Labor Law Professors' Brief Amici Curiae (Supporting the College Athlete Players Association)." http://www.nlrb.gov/.

McCormick, Amy Christian, and Robert A. McCormick (2008). "The Emperor's New Clothes: Lifting the NCAA's Veil of Amateurism." *San Diego Law Review* 45, 495–546. https://digital.sandiego.edu/.

McCormick, Robert A., and Amy Christian McCormick (2006). "The Myth of the Student-Athlete: The College Athlete as Employee." *Washington Law Review* 81: 71–157. http://papers.ssrn.com/.

McKenna, Dave (2010). "Athletes Don't Go to Howard University for the Food!" *Washington City Paper,* December 10. https://washingtoncitypaper.com/.

Meggyesy. Dave (1971). *Out of Their League.* New York: Coronet Communications, Inc.

Nadkarni, Rohan, and Alex Nieves (2015). "Why Missouri Football Joined a Protest against School Administration." *SI.com,* November 9. https://www.si.com/.

National Collegiate Athletic Association (2013). "2012–13 Division I Revenue Distribution Plan." http://s3.amazonaws.com/.

———. (2020). NCAA Race and Gender Demographic Database. https://www.ncaa.org/.

———. (2021a). "Awards." NCAA Legislative Services Database. https://web3.ncaa.org/.

———. (2021b). "Pay." NCAA Legislative Services Database. https://web3.ncaa.org/.

———. (2021c). "2021 Division I Revenue Distribution Plan." https://ncaaorg.s3.amazonaws.com/.

———. (2022). "NCAA 101: How We Support College Athletes." https://www.ncaa.org/ (accessed August 6).

National College Players Association (2013). "About the NCPA." National College Players Association. https://www.ncpanow.org/about-us.

National Football Foundation. (2022). "NFF® National Scholar-Athlete Awards Presented by Fidelity Investments." https://footballfoundation.org/ (accessed August 20).

National Labor Relations Board (2015). Northwestern University and College Athletes Players Association (CAPA), Petitioner. Case 13-RC-121359. *Decision on Review and Order.* https://www.nlrb.gov/.

———. (2022). National Labor Relations Act. https://www.nlrb.gov/guidance/key-reference-materials/national-labor-relations-act (accessed August 6).

Nelson, Murray (2014). "The Illinois Slush Fund Scandal of 1966–67." *Sport in American History,* October 20. http://ussporthistory.com/.

Nelson, Shellie (2014). "Northwestern Official Warns: If Players Unionize, Football Could Vaporize." WQAD ABC, March 24. https://www.wqad.com/.

Nocera, Joe, and Ben Strauss (2016). *Indentured: The Inside Story of the Rebellion against the NCAA.* New York: Portfolio/Penquin.

Norman, Keith A. (1999). "The Mark of the Curse: Lingering Racism in Mormon Doctrine?" *Dialogue: A Journal of Mormon Thought* 32, no. 1: 119–136. https://www.jstor.org/.

Oriard, Michael (2003). *King Football: Sport and Spectacle in the Golden Age of Radio and Newsreels, Movies and Magazines, the Weekly and the Daily Press.* Chapel Hill: University of North Carolina Press.

———. (2009). "College Football's Season of Discontent." *Slate,* September 3. http://www.slate.com/.

Pearce, Mark Gaston, Philip A. Miscimarra, Kent Y. Hirozawa, Harry I. Johnson, and Lauren McFerran (2015). Northwestern University and College Athletes Players Association. "Decision on Review and Order." http://www.acenet.edu/.

Raley, Dan (2020). "Legend of Sixkiller: Owens Had Detractors; Sonny Wasn't One of Them." FanNation, April 25. https://www.si.com/.

Ridpath, David (2012). *Tainted Glory: Marshall University, the NCAA, and One Man's Fight for Justice.* Bloomington, IN: IUniverse.

Rosenman, Andrew S., Brian D. Netter, Thomas P. Wolf (2014). "Brief of Amicus Curiae: The Big Ten Conference, Inc.," May 12. https://www.nlrb.gov/.

Rothstein, Jon (2020). "Source: One ACC President has been told by medical personnel that the best course moving forward is to have virtual classes with all non student athletes moving off campus." Twitter, August 17. https://twitter.com/.

Sack, Allen (2008). *Counterfeit Amateurs: An Athlete's Journey through the Sixties to The age of Academic Capitalism.* University Park: Pennsylvania State University Press.

Sack, Allen L., and Ellen J. Staurowsky (1998). *College Athletes for Hire: The Evolution and Legacy of the NCAA Amateur Myth.* Westport, CT: Praeger.

Sappington, Ryan, Brian Tael-Iyuk Keum, and Mary Ann Hoffman (2019). "'Arrogant, Ungrateful, Anti-American Degenerates': Development and Initial Validation of the

Attitudes toward Athlete Activism Questionnaire (ATAAQ)." *Psychology of Sport and Exercise* 45. https://www.sciencedirect.com/.

Schad, Joe (2015). "Ondre Pipkins, Michigan's Coach Jim Harbaugh, Staff Pressured Me to Quit." ESPN.com, June 26. http://espn.go.com/.

Schroeder, George (2013). "Grambling Players Provide Shocking Details, Reason They Ended Boycott." *USA Today*, October 21. http://www.usatoday.com/.

Scott, Jack (1971). *The Athletic Revolution.* New York: Free Press.

Sherman, Mitch (2015). "Ex-Illinois Player Blasts Tim Beckman, Says He Was Forced to Play Hurt." ESPN.com, May 11. https://www.espn.com/.

Silverstein, Adam (2015). "Chris Simms Clarifies Texas '$100 Handshake' Comments: 'It Was Cool.'" CBS Sports, June 19. https://www.cbssports.com/.

Smith, Earl, and Angela J. Hattery (2015). "The Unintended Consequences of Purposive Social Change: Conference Realignment and the Demise of the Academic Mission in US Higher Education," In *Introduction to Intercollegiate Athletics*, edited by Eddie Comeaux, 219–30. Baltimore: Johns Hopkins University Press.

Smith, Ronald A. (1988). *Sports and Freedom: The Rise of Big-Time College Athletics.* New York: Oxford University Press.

———. (2011). *Pay for Play: A History of Big-Time College Athletic Reform.* Champaign: University of Illinois Press.

Solomon, Jon (2014). "Plaintiffs Want Judge Removed in John Rock v. NCAA Scholarship Case." CBS Sports, December 12. https://www.cbssports.com/.

———. (2015). "Cost of Attendance Results: The Chase to Pay College Athletes." CBS Sports, August 15. http://www.cbssports.com/.

Southall, Richard M. (2012). "College Sport Reform: Déjà Vu All over Again and Again." In *Sports in Higher Education: Issues and Controversies*, edited by Gary Sailes, 257–98. San Diego: Cognella.

Southall, Richard M., E. Woodrow Eckard, Mark S. Nagel, Evan Keith, and Chase Blake (2014). "2013–2014 Adjusted Graduation Gap Report: NCAA Division I Basketball." March 12. https://static1.squarespace.com/.

Southall, Richard M., and Ellen J. Staurowsky (2013). "Cheering on the Collegiate Model: Creating, Disseminating, and Imbedding the NCAA's Redefinition of Amateurism." *Journal of Sport and Social Issues* 37, no. 4: 403–29.

Southall, Richard M., and Jonathan D. Weiler (2014). "NCAA D-I Athletic Departments: Twenty-First-Century Company Towns." *Journal of Issues in Intercollegiate Athletics* 7: 161–86. https://www.commerce.senate.gov/.

Staples, Andy (2014). "Man at Center of UGA's Todd Gurley Autograph Scandal Shares His Story." *SI.com*, December 2. https://www.si.com/.

Staurowsky, Ellen J. (2004). "Piercing the Veil of Amateurism: Commercialisation, Corruption, and College Sports." In *The Commercialisation of Sport*, edited by Trevor Slack, 143–63). London: Cass.

———. (2014a). "An Analysis of Northwestern University's Denial of Rights to and Recognition of College Football Labor." *Journal of Intercollegiate Sport* 7, no. 2: 134–42.

———. (2014b). "College Athletes in the Age of the Super Conference: The Case of the All Players United Campaign." *Journal of Intercollegiate Sport* 7, no. 1: 11–34.

———. (2014c). Expert witness report: O'Bannon v. NCAA.

———. (2014d). "The Significance of College Athletes Signing Union Cards." *Huffington Post,* February 1. http://www.huffingtonpost.com/.

———. (2015). "College Football Players as Employees: About This There Should Be No Debate." *Huffington Post,* January 20. http://www.huffingtonpost.com/.

Staurowsky, Ellen J., and Allen L. Sack (2005). "Reconsidering the Use of the Term Student-Athlete in Academic Research." *Journal of Sport Management* 19, no. 2: 103–16.

Talty, John (2015). "Roy Adams, Key Figure in Albert Means Investigation, Passes Away." *AL.com,* July 22. http://www.al.com/.

Tatos, Ted (2020). "Playing Games with College Athletes' Lives." *American Prospect,* May 20. https://prospect.org/.

Tatos, Ted, and Stephen Casper (2019). "Using College Athletes as Concussion Test Subjects Makes Nobody Safer." *American Prospect,* August 27. https://prospect.org/.

Tatos, Ted, and Don Comrie (2019). "Cognitive Deficits and LD/ADHD among College Football Athletes and Undisclosed Inclusion in Concussion Research." *Journal of Scientific Practice and Integrity* 1, no. 1. https://www.jospi.org/.

Underwood, John (1969). "The Desperate Coach." *Sports Illustrated,* August 25. https://vault.si.com/vault/1969/.

United Press International (1987). "Report: Texas Governor Ordered Pay for SMU Players." *South Florida Sun Sentinel,* June 20. https://www.sun-sentinel.com/.

Westerholm, Russell (2014). "NLRB Decision Ruling 'Grossly Inappropriate' to NCAA Prez Mark Emmert." *University Herald,* April 7. https://www.universityherald.com/.

Whitford, David, and Peter Elkind (2013). "SMU's Death Penalty: The Recruiting Scandal That Refuses to Die." *Fortune,* August 29. http://fortune.com/.

Wiggins, David K. (1988). "'The Future of College Athletics Is at Stake': Black Athletes and Racial Turmoil on Three Predominantly White Campuses: 1968–1972." *Journal of Sport History* 15: 304–33. http://www.jstor.org/.

Wilma, David (2001). "Huskies Coach Jim Owens Suspends Four African-American Football Players in 1969." History Link.org, November 27. https://www.historylink.org/.

Yan, Grace, Ann Pegoraro, and Nicholas Masafumi Watanabe (2018). "Student-Athletes' Organization of Activism at the University of Missouri: Resource Mobilization on Twitter." *Journal of Sport Management* 32, no. 1: 24–37.

Yost, Mark (2001). *Varsity Green: A Behind the Scenes Look at Culture and Corruption in College Sport.* Stanford, CA: Stanford University Press.

Zimbalist, Andrew (1999). *Unpaid Professionals: Commercialism and Conflict in Big-Time College Sports.* Princeton, NJ: Princeton University Press.

Zirin, Dave (2014). "Why Is Northwestern Football Coach Pat Fitzgerald Playing the Union Buster?" *Nation,* April 11. https://www.thenation.com/.

Title IX, College Athlete Employment, and the Politics of Destruction

Ellen J. Staurowsky

> I believe you should tell the story of injustices, of inequalities, of bad conditions, so that the people as a whole in this country really face the problems that people who are pushed to the point of striking know all about, but others know practically nothing about.
>
> —ELEANOR ROOSEVELT, 1931 SPEECH AT THE CIO CONVENTION

> Our needs are identical with labor's needs. Decent wages, fair working conditions, livable housing, old-age security, health and welfare measures, conditions in which families can grow, have education for their children and respect in their community.
>
> —MARTIN LUTHER KING, 1961 SPEECH AT THE AFL-CIO CONVENTION

For more than one hundred years, in team meeting rooms, courts of law, and in the court of public opinion around the country, big-time college football and basketball players have confronted their coaches, athletic directors, NCAA officials and conference commissioners about the conditions under which they work. College sport history is filled with examples of classic labor-management standoffs, with players seeking better working conditions (length of workdays, days off, and safer playing environments), benefits (health and medical coverage, educational benefits), compensation, and access to basic necessities (decent food and sufficient rest). College sport management has generally held the upper hand in those confrontations, due in large part to the regulatory system that it established to deny college athletes employment status and the means to mobilize successful challenges.

In the spring of 2014, Northwestern football players sought recognition as employees with the right to organize and collectively bargain. That effort, along with antitrust lawsuits threatening to upend long-standing caps on player value (*O'Bannon v. NCAA*, 2014; *Jenkins et al. v. NCAA*, 2014), put the NCAA and college sport officials on the defensive in ways not seen since the 1950s and 1960s. In addition to defending its long-standing practices in multiple federal courts and before the National Labor Relations Board (NLRB), the NCAA implemented a media campaign to quell future player uprisings and frame the discussion in terms favorable to the status quo.

In a concerted effort to convey the existential threat of pay for play / unionization, NCAA members—in both conference offices and college athletic departments—wrote op-eds and used their media contacts to outline the damage to the college sport enterprise should the players prevail (Hutchausen 2017; Solomon 2014a, 2014b). In addition the mega-media platforms of March Madness and Sunday morning political talk shows were leveraged by NCAA president Mark Emmert and media surrogates of the college sport enterprise to promulgate the NCAA's collegiate model messaging.

The NCAA's talking points gave the appearance of appeasement while sowing seeds of dissension and fear. The acknowledgment that those running college sport could "do better . . . in addressing some of the legitimate concerns that critics have raised" (Solomon 2014a) was tempered by rhetoric from high-profile coaches such as Clemson's Dabo Swinney that portrayed players as motivated by greed and misguided expectations: "We've got enough entitlement in this country as it is" (quoted in ibid.). The clear message was that should these profit-athletes (i.e., Power Five football and Division I men's basketball players) be certified as employees, there would be whole-scale reductions and eliminations of sports, grants-in-aid (GIA), championship opportunities, and support services (including academic support, counseling, and tutoring) for athletes in other sports. Olympic sport athletes were consistently portrayed as victims, sure targets for loss of funding and support if the NCAA were forced to treat profit-athletes as employees.[1]

The "smaller sports" (Solomon 2014a) argument was just one concern among many outlined in the NCAA talking points, but the media largely seized on the David versus Goliath analogy, with Power Five football and Division I men's basketball players cast as out-of-control and greedy behemoths. Meanwhile a primary NCAA talking point was that "the overwhelming majority of student-athletes play college sports as part of their educational experience and because they love their sport, not to be paid a salary" (Solomon 2014a).

In addition to protecting smaller sports, the NCAA portrayed itself as a defender of Title IX of the Educational Amendments of 1972, which mandates gender-equitable treatment in school settings. NCAA-approved talking points indicated that certifying profit-athletes as employees would necessitate extending the same rights to all college athletes. Since smaller sports were already losing money, the connotation was that since women's sports were already being subsidized, if athletic departments had to pay unionized profit-athletes, women's sports would simply be cut.

Mere weeks after NLRB regional director Peter Sun Ohr determined that Northwestern University football players met the definition of employees under the National Labor Relations Act (NLRA), University of Texas athletic director Steve Patterson predicted that if Power Five athletic departments were compelled to treat football players as professionals, they would simply not offer NCAA sports at all. Constrained by Title IX, Patterson predicted that only two women's sports would remain—women's basketball and rowing (Davis 2014). Interestingly, local and national media failed to address Patterson's comments. Nobody asked whether he was really suggesting that the recognition of Power Five college football and Division I men's basketball players as employees would mean the wholesale destruction of NCAA athletic departments, including at the University of Texas, which in 2014 had generated nearly $165.7 million in revenue with a $20 million surplus (Berkowitz 2014). Was he predicting that the Texas Longhorns softball team, historically one of the most successful teams in the nation and a program that garnered a national following on ESPN on its way to the NCAA Women's College World Series, would simply be eliminated? In addition no journalist asked fundamental questions regarding whether eliminating women's sports would comply with NCAA guidelines, since Division I bylaws mandate that athletic departments offer at least seven men's and seven women's sports (or six men's and eight women's).

When unpacked, Patterson's doomsday comments revealed three things. First, the head of one of the most lucrative and politically powerful athletic departments in the country was willing to trade in unsubstantiated hyperbole and scare tactics. Second, NCAA officials within the college sport industrial complex understand that the college sport industry suppresses profit-athletes' market value. If this wasn't the case, NCAA members would not have been so quick to predict that drastic changes to the collegiate model would be necessary if players were paid a negotiated wage. And third, the intentional framing of player complaints as a bid for pay for play was designed to present player concerns as being solely about money, glossing over a range of other neglected issues such as workplace safety, uneven and limited medical coverage, inadequate health care support, and lack of equal access to genuine educational benefits. Time and again the NCAA's talking points appeared verbatim in media accounts; reasoned exploration of issues was replaced with doomsday, sky-is-falling predictions.

A year earlier Big Ten commissioner Jim Delany, in a declaration filed in the US Ninth Circuit, had been asked about the potential impact of a ruling favorable to the players in *O'Bannon v. NCAA*. Delany said that an O'Bannon win would result in Big Ten athletic departments ceasing to offer athletic GIAs, with departments downsizing and adopting a Division III model. In fact, he claimed, a Division III model would be "more consistent with the Big Ten's philosophy that the educational and lifetime economic benefits associated with a university education are the appropriate quid pro quo" (Solomon 2013). In May 2014 Baylor University president Kenneth Starr, who had become the voice of presidential leadership for the Big 12 Conference, testified before the US House Education and Workforce Committee on the potential consequences of college athletes unionizing. Starr cautioned that, at a minimum, increased benefits to football players would result in "programmatic curtailments" that would upset the gender balance within athletic departments and likely violate Title IX ("Big Labor on College Campuses" 2014).

In August 2014, after Judge Claudia Wilkin ruled in favor of the plaintiffs in *O'Bannon v. NCAA* and issued an injunction requiring the NCAA to lift restrictions on GIAs to allow for payments up to the full cost of attendance, CBS reporter Jon Solomon (2014b) wrote that Title IX was assuredly triggered: "If schools don't provide new money to female athletes, someone will undoubtedly bring a Title IX claim about this issue."

This sense that paying any college athletes would inevitably trigger Title IX responses has been termed the "Title IX default position" (Staurowsky 2017) and has appeared repeatedly in both press accounts and law review articles. Theodore Ross, a writer for the *New Republic* who served as an academic adviser to athletes during his graduate studies, wrote: "The intricacies of pay systems, of who would be paid what and why, merit further deliberation. The byzantine workarounds needed to square everything with Title IX, the admirable law that requires similar provisions for male and female athletes, would have to be reckoned with" (Ross 2015). In a *University of Iowa Law Review* article, Dillon J. Besser (2016) described NCAA Olympic sports as the "forgotten party" in *O'Bannon v. NCAA*, arguing that these sports would require attention under Title IX. Matthew J. Parlow (2015: 212) discussed the "unintended consequences" of the *O'Bannon* decision: "There will almost certainly be Title IX implications and effects based on the O'Bannon decision and potential changes in the collegiate athletic system,"

United States Olympic Committee (USOC) members, including chief executive officer Scott Blackmon, have continually made references to the possibility of NCAA Olympic sports disappearing. In an April 2015 interview with Yahoo! Sports, Blackmon commented that while the prospects for college football and basketball were improving, the continued existence of Olympic sports was less secure than ever before and "men's non-revenue sports were most at risk" (Forde 2015).

During this time anti-unionization rhetoric was remarkably consistent and omnipresent. However, yet again predictions that women's and/or Olympic sports must be sacrificed if profit-athletes unionized or were paid a market wage went unexamined. Seemingly no one asked:

- Does the recognition of employment rights for profit-athletes represent a zero-sum proposition for other college athletes?
- Does Title IX really demand that if profit-athletes are compensated in a free or quasi-free market, female athletes must be compensated proportionally?
- Will support for Olympic sports actually disappear if profit-athletes receive compensation consistent with their market value?
- What if doomsday predictions about the eminent demise of the NCAA's collegiate model of athletics are based upon an amateur mythology that never was?

This chapter revisits several underlying sociohistorical assumptions regarding college athletes' employment rights. The first assumption is that all college sports are the same. The second is that all college sport programs operate under the same model. And the third is that Power Five football and Division I men's basketball are simply avocational extracurricular activities.

Acceptance of these assumptions informs and shapes many reformers' visions of the future of NCAA college sport. Under current NCAA hegemony, Title IX has become a tool that denies, rather than protects, college athletes' civil rights. Unfortunately Title IX is used by Power Five power brokers to justify and maintain current inequities inherent in the NCAA's collegiate model. Blind acceptance of these assumptions inhibits creative problem solving and forestalls the creation of a more responsive and equitable twenty-first-century model of college sport.

Flawed Assumption #1: All College Sports Are the Same

Their political and economic clout give the NCAA and Power Five athletic conferences (e.g., the SEC) singular power over the rules under which the United States' big-time college sport industry operates (Charity Navigator 2021b, 2021c). The NCAA dwarfs all other college sport entities, with more than 1,100 members and $1.1 billion in annual revenue in 2019 (Charity Navigator 2021b). The next largest national college sport governance association, the National Association of Intercollegiate Athletics (NAIA), has been reduced from a genuine competitor to the NCAA in the 1940s and 1950s to a 250-member enterprise with just $10.1 million in annual revenue in 2019 (Charity Navigator 2021a). In addition not all college sport revenue flows through the NCAA national office. The SEC, with only fourteen member universities, had $721 million in annual revenue in 2019 and distributed $624 million in television rights fees, ticket sales, and other receipts back to members (Charity Navigator 2021c).

Alternately described as a monopoly (Barro 2002), oligarchy (Koch and Leonard 1978), and a cartel (Branch 2014; Fleisher, Goff, and Tollison 1992; Kahn 2007; Koch 1973; Martin 2018; Nocera 2016; Rascher and Schwarz 2000), the NCAA represents itself as an unincorporated nonprofit association comprising colleges and universities, voting and nonvoting conferences, and affiliated groups (NCAA 2018). Soon-to-be-former NCAA president Mark Emmert periodically comments on how many people are involved in the NCAA college sport enterprise: nineteen thousand teams, nearly half a million athletes, and some four million former college athletes (*Luke Hancock v. National Collegiate Athletic Association,* 2018; Stewart 2016). However, what is often overlooked is that the NCAA's governance structure is institutional, meaning that current college athletes are not in fact members of the NCAA.

Testifying before a US Senate committee hearing on the topic of college athletics and academics in July 2014, Emmert described the NCAA as "a democratically governed membership-led association" that he serves at the pleasure of college presidents who are "the ultimate decision makers" (US Congress 2014). When committee members critiqued NCAA failures in addressing player treatment, education, health care/medical coverage, Title IX, and sexual assault issues, Emmert responded that college presidents and their representatives are responsible for the way the NCAA college sport enterprise operates and only they have the power to propose, adopt, and amend NCAA rules. He described the NCAA's deliberative process as a one-way channel, with staffers passively responding to member requests. He assured the committee that neither he nor his staffers voted on NCAA bylaws.

In response to Emmert's representation of the association and his role in it, Senator Claire McCaskill (D-Missouri) responded, "I feel sorry for you. I can't even tell whether you're in charge or whether you're a minion" (US Congress 2014). She went on to ask Emmert why—if the NCAA was, as he described, a "monetary passthrough"—does it exist (ibid.)?

Emmert omitted two pertinent facts about the NCAA in this testimony. First, the scope of the association's business interests goes beyond the bounds of the membership. As reported in its 2018, and 2019 consolidated financial audits, the association also comprises four subsidiaries, including Collegiate Sports LLC, ArbiterSports LLC, Collegiate Properties LLC, and March Madness Association LLC (Deloitte and Touche 2018, 2019), processing billions of dollars from an ever-expanding number of revenue streams tied to college sport. Second, the streamlined governance structure Emmert described in that Senate hearing omitted the NCAA national office as a standalone power structure. For the fiscal year ending August 2019, the NCAA reported spending over $44 million on day-to-day national office operations (Deloitte and Touche 2019). By way of comparison, in the same year the NCAA allocated $35 million to its largest membership group, Division III (Deloitte and Touche 2019). The amount dispersed to the 450 Division III member colleges/universities pales in comparison to the almost $9 million in compensation of just eight NCAA executives. By 2021 Emmert's base compensation was just over $2.7 million (Athletic Staff 2021), while other recent annual salaries of upper-level NCAA staff include Mark Lewis (2016), $1.7 million; Donald Remy (2019), $1.2 million; Oliver Luck (2019), $955,533; Brian Hainline (2019), $620,900; Bernard Franklin (2019), $611,570; Kathleen McNeely (2019), $577,557; and Joni Comstock (2019), $513,394 (Berkowitz 2018; Non Profit Light 2021).

In addition Emmert's assurance that the NCAA president does not vote on matters pertaining to the governance of the association was not wholly accurate. The NCAA president serves as an ex-officio member of the Board of Governors, the administrative body responsible for oversight of the entire association, which, according to bylaws 4.1.2, "employ[s] the NCAA president," who is "*permitted to vote* in the case of a tie among the voting members of the Board of Governors present and voting" (NCAA 2017: 20; emphasis added).

Depictions of the NCAA membership as being in control belies the degree to which the NCAA national office exerts influence over the business enterprise of college sport. Employees of the NCAA are not neutral parties in the organization: Emmert and his council are expected to provide "dynamic and inclusive leadership" (NCAA 2017) and set the organization's agendas, while staffers prepare briefing documents, take ideas coming out of committees and develop them into legislative proposals, interpret and enforce bylaws, and provide compliance training and oversight while being advised throughout by legal counsel. In addition to NCAA national office staff, university athletic departments have full-time staffers with expertise in the college sport industry who serve college presidents, for whom athletics are but one concern among many. College presidents often have little understanding of the inner workings of university athletic departments, with fewer than 34 percent of the presidents overseeing powerhouse college sport programs claiming any expertise in the area (Woodhouse 2015). Consequently the 514 NCAA national office staff members and associated lobbyists have both a significant stake in the overall financial health of the industry (Trahan 2014) and significant clout in establishing the rules of the game.

In a 2016 interview with the *Greater Baton Rouge Business Report,* Emmert lamented what he claimed was a biased perception of college sport, based on a portrait "painted predominantly by football and men's basketball at a relatively small number of schools, 50 or 75. . . . The world sees only a tiny fraction of that. Maybe 2% or 3% is what the world sees when they watch TV" (Stewart 2016). Emmert's narrative that our perception of college sport is biased by Power Five college football and Division I men's basketball is anchored in the assertion that the actual purpose of the NCAA is to "maintain intercollegiate athletics as an integral part of the educational program and the athlete as an integral part of the student body and, by so doing, retain a clear line of demarcation between intercollegiate athletics and professional sports" (NCAA 2017: 1).

Emmert's assertion fails to acknowledge that the NCAA national office and member conferences are the entities primarily responsible for the professionalization and commercialization of Power Five football and Division I men's basketball, which results in what he laments as a biased perception of college sport. While the NCAA claims it exists to maintain a "clear line of demarcation between intercollegiate athletics and professional sports," the association and its members have made a conscious decision that these two sports will serve as college sport's economic engine and the public face of the entire college sport industry. As codified in the NCAA's Division I philosophy statement, those few schools and the basketball and football teams that dominate media narratives are expressly privileged because they "sponsor at the highest feasible level of intercollegiate competition one or both of the traditional spectator-oriented, income-producing sports of football and basketball. In doing so, members of Division I recognize the differences in institutional objectives in support of football" (NCAA 2017: 361).

In sum it is no accident that these two big-money sports dominate the NCAA's public persona and favorably compete with their professional sport counterparts in accruing media coverage. As a consequence these sports are different than all other college sports. They serve as what Power Five college sport marketers and higher education officials refer to as the "front porch" of their institutions—marketing vehicles that generate brand awareness on a national and international scale (Bass, Schaekoetter, and Bunds 2015).

Indicative of these sports' hypercommercialism, during 2018's March Madness tournament, 142 brands ran 391 advertisements a total of 6,761 times during the tournament's broadcasts and online streaming videos (Friedman 2018). Throughout the month-long tournament, the top five advertisers' content and expenditures were

- Capitol One—188 commercial airings, $40.8 million spent;
- Buick—144 commercial airings, $38.3 million spent;
- AT&T Wireless—157 commercial airings; $31.6 million spent;
- Samsung Mobile—150 commercial airings; $31.1 million spent;
- DirecTV—145 commercial airings; $30.7 million spent. (ibid.)

In 2019 the number of brands advertising during March Madness increased to 155, a number that did not include advertising by network partners and the NCAA itself. The 2019 tournament advertising spend of $932.7 million yielded nearly 24.2 billion impressions from "363 unique ads, 5,252 airings, and 8,688 minutes of ad time" (Cassillo 2019).

Big-time (i.e., Power Five and Group of 5) college football and basketball are, more broadly, mainstays of the televised and digital sport media landscape. Of the fifty most-watched televised sporting events in the US between January and July 2016, the combined number of college football bowl and NCAA Division I men's basketball games, fourteen, was the same as NFL and NBA games combined (*Sports Illustrated* Staff 2017). In 2017 sports programming accounted for eighty-six of the top one hundred telecasts, with college football bowl games and March Madness among the most effective properties in generating viewing audiences (Nielsen Company 2018).

In what Nielsen Sports refers to as the "omnichannel" environment, in which traditional television watching is being supplemented or replaced with social media and out-of-home viewing devices, college football and men's basketball rank among the most lucrative sport properties, alongside the NFL, NBA, MLB, NHL, and the Olympics (Nielsen Company 2018). The NCAA's agreement with CBS and Turner Sports, which conveys exclusive television and other internet and multimedia rights for the Division I men's basketball championship, will yield the NCAA more than $8.8 billion over the span of sixteen years (2016–32) (Deloitte and Touche 2018). In addition, for approximately $500 million annually, ESPN holds the rights to televise selected NCAA fall, winter, and spring championships; the preseason and postseason National Invitational Tournaments; and international distribution of the NCAA men's basketball tournament under a fourteen-year contract expiring in 2024 (ibid.).

It is crucial to understand that the revenue generated from the labor of approximately 2–3 percent of college athletes—between eleven and seventeen thousand (Irick 2017; NCAA 2022)—effectively funds an entire industry. NCAA profit-athletes are the assets on which multibillion-dollar multimedia agreements are negotiated, in which the NCAA's corporate partners, many of which are Fortune 500 companies, find value. Money from those media contracts not only supports the NCAA's eighty-nine other annual championships but also pays the salaries of NCAA staffers and lobbyists. In effect the athletes fund efforts to keep them from claiming control over their working conditions.

Embedded in the NCAA's Division I philosophy statement is a further nuance that distinguishes the most elite football programs in the country, which occupy the Division I Football Bowl Subdivision (FBS), from football programs in the lower competitive tier, known as the Football Championship Subdivision (FCS). The convoluted structure speaks to the complex relationship between Power Five (Atlantic Coast Conference, Big Ten, Big 12, Pac-12, and SEC) and Group of Five (i.e., American Athletic Conference [AAC], Conference USA, Mid-America Conference [MAC], Mountain West Conference [MWC], and Sun Belt Conference) conferences and the NCAA. While the NCAA offers ninety championships each year, the association has never conducted nor officially named a football national champion at the FBS level. Not surprisingly the football powers (i.e., Power Five conferences) have long resisted any such attempt, not wanting to share the revenue from FBS football with the NCAA national office or non-FBS members (Irick 2017).

Instead CFP Administration, LLC, manages the eponymous College Football Playoff (CFP). CFP members include the top ten football playing conferences along with the University of Notre Dame, which is designated as an independent in the sport of football. CFP Administration's Board of Managers comprises eleven university presidents and chancellors and handles policy oversight, while the CFP Management Committee, comprising conference commissioners and the UND athletic director, controls day-to-day operations (College Football Playoff 2017a). The resulting championship format is designed to "increase revenue for all conferences and independent institutions" (College Football Playoff 2017b). Revenues generated from the CFP and other postseason football bowls are not shared with the NCAA.

While the general public often views the NCAA as the leader of college sport, its governance structure reveals a set of interlocking power bases that limit decision-making to a small group of individuals. The association's federated three-division configuration (Divisions I, II, and III), along with the FBS-FCS subdivision, is the result of years of negotiations between the Power Five conferences and the rest of the NCAA membership, with the NCAA national office serving in many ways as the go-between. In addition to the formation of the CFP, the most recent evidence of the increasing power of the Power Five conferences was the approval by the NCAA of legislation granting autonomy to these conferences that affords them greater latitude in conducting their business interests unencumbered by the rest of the NCAA membership (Hosick 2014).

Power Five conference autonomy capitalizes on FBS conferences' control of revenue generated from the CFP and other bowl games. Challenging the assumption that all college sports are the same requires grasping the magnitude of difference between Power Five football and Division I men's basketball and all other NCAA sports as business entities. Doing so also presents an intriguing possibility: that the interests of Power Five football and Division I men's basketball players are in conflict with the interests of female college athletes. Entertaining this idea is key to the ability to deconstruct NCAA talking points that espouse the association's traditional concept of student-athletes and contend that if Power Five football and Division I men's basketball players are granted employment status, it will mean the destruction of women's college sport.

Flawed Assumption #2: Men's and Women's College Sport Are the Same

The NCAA's imposition of college sport sameness not only fails to acknowledge the genuine market distinctions between profit college sports and loss sports, but it also elides the distinctly different models on which men's and women's college sport are built.

When the NCAA was founded in 1906, colleges and universities were largely single-sex institutions. Football became part of many schools' marketing strategies as they worked to encourage applications, boost enrollment, and help stabilize budgets (Smith 2011; Sperber 2002; Thelin 1996). For many land-grant institutions founded after the passage of the Morrill Act (1862), football games became community spectacles that bridged perceived competition between academic and community interests (Sack and Staurowsky 1998; Thelin 1996). As an anchor for school pride and brand identity, football created interstate and interregional rivalries, many of which endure to this day.

NCAA FBS rivalry football games have a storied history, with the 1887 Michigan versus Notre Dame game listed as the first FBS rivalry game (University of Notre Dame 2021) and Minnesota and Wisconsin the rivals who have met the most times (130 times since 1890) (Wisconsin Badgers 2021). Notably forty-eight FBS rivalry games have been played 100 or more times. The echoes-of-the-past marquee billings and long-standing, colorful names of the much-coveted trophies—Paul Bunyan's Axe (Wisconsin versus Minnesota), the Old Oaken Bucket (Indiana versus Purdue), the Apple Cup (Washington versus Washington State), the Little Brown Jug (Minnesota versus Michigan), the Telephone Trophy (Missouri versus Iowa State), and the Victory Bell (Nebraska versus Missouri)—speak to the cultural importance of college football. Rivalry games are "epic" confrontations: Oregon – Oregon State's Civil War and Missouri–Kansas's Border War; Texas's annual showdowns (the former Lonestar Showdown with Texas A&M and the Red River Showdown with Oklahoma); and battles such as Stanford and California's Battle for the Axe, Utah and Utah State's Battle of the Brothers, and Tennessee and Kentucky's Battle for the Barrel. Rivalries are intense—consider the annual Georgia – Georgia Tech game, which has adopted the unofficial theme "Clean, Old-Fashioned Hate"—and others are so well-known that they need no gimmicks, like Michigan and Ohio State's annual playing of "The Game."

For campus communities that would eventually become major, globally connected research institutions, football has historically served as a point of convergence for high-powered political aspirations and economic interests (Loftin and Burson 2014). College football grew up alongside emerging media technologies of the late 1800s and early 1900s, often providing compelling storylines and characters for newspapers, radio, and television. As media technologies have evolved, college sports content is now delivered through digital television networks and across multiple platforms in the twenty-first-century frontier of 24/7 sport media (Glier 2012; Huma and Staurowsky 2012; Oriard 1998, 2002, 2009; Smith 2003; Sperber 2002).

The young men engaged in the social experiment of men's college sport, football in particular, were well aware that drama, or at least the anticipation of it, needed to be part of any attention-grabbing script. These entertainer-athletes, coaches, and athletic directors knew college sport was competing for sport fans' discretionary income that could be spent on any number of entertainment products. Players knew they were a valuable commodity. Looking to satisfy the country's appetite for sports, in the late 1800s and early 1900s, several rule changes were enacted in an attempt to make games more exciting for players and spectators alike. In addition innovations to speed up the game and encourage more scoring were enacted. From alumni associations to coaches, there was a strong sense that college football needed to play to the crowd.

As a result college football history traces not only the on-field evolution of the game but also the evolution of the business of college football. Conversations about mass momentum plays, the concept of downs, the notion of a scrimmage line, techniques for blocking and tackling, and the radical idea of the forward pass were happening at the same time as consideration of how to increase ticket sales, develop effective marketing campaigns, and ensure widespread media coverage.

Amid the expansion of the college-football business enterprise, the amateur ideal of noble young men playing the game for the honor of their school and as a rite of passage emerged as a saleable narrative. College sport officials were prompted to officially discourage player subsidization, recruitment, and professional coaching while simultaneously embracing all three practices as integral to operating a successful and sustainable business model. The press of professionalism was relentless (Sack and Staurowsky 1998), with generations of college football players bound by a thread of profit seeking, from those who were paid to endorse cigarettes at Yale in the late 1890s (Goldstein 2014) to the legendary Notre Dame player George Gipp, who made money by placing bets on his own performance in the 1920s (Cavanaugh 1991); the unknown number of players who had received under-the-table payments since the game began (Godfrey 2014); and twenty-first-century five-star recruits. Big-time college football has always been "all business" (Solomon 2016).

Women's college sport, in contrast, traces its origins to the women's physical education and health movements of the late 1800s. In particular, as women sought higher education, there was public concern that this strenuous learning would take a physical toll on their bodies. Physical education offered a panacea to Victorians who thought the brainwork of college life would detract from women's duties as homemakers and mothers, couching physical exercise instead in a narrative of becoming better, more well-rounded wives and helpmates (Perry and Price 2006; Sack and Staurowsky 1998; Staurowsky 2016).

Female attractiveness and comportment were top considerations for women engaged in physical activity (Sack and Staurowsky 1998). Events such as the Fifth Annual Exhibition of Young Women in the Department of Physical Training at the University of Nebraska in 1896 offer insight into the typical curriculum and intent (Wilke 1973). Light gymnastics that included women marching in formation, twirling Indian clubs, and working out on apparatuses were interspersed with musical interludes. Graceful movement, proper posture, and the presentation of an attractive ladylike demeanor were important elements in scoring performances. Most important, "since it was considered quite improper during this era for a woman to appear in a gymnasium costume before a mixed crowd, these demonstrations were closely guarded to ensure men did not view the performance" (ibid.: 33).

While basketball made its appearance at Smith College in 1892, just a year after its invention by James Naismith, the emergent model of women's college sport also reflected public fears that too warm an embrace of sporting activities would render women unfeminine. Careful attention was paid to distinguishing women's college sport from men's and regulating it under women physical educators. Women's sporting events were never intended to be commercial enterprises. There was no thought given to event promotion to draw large crowds or sell tickets. Such events were to be extensions of the curriculum that required moderate exertion and were primarily for the participants' enjoyment. Of course, not everyone believed female students must engage only in refined and restrained forms of competition (Verbrugge 2012). In fact a motto of the professional associations governing physical education and sport for women was "A Game for Every Girl and a Girl for Every Game" (Sack and Staurowsky 1998: 59).

In many ways the development of the NCAA was the outgrowth of high-profile deaths in college football, which threatened the business interests of college football programs. Unlike men's football and basketball, which took root as businesses, women's college sport was firmly anchored in academic curriculum throughout most of the twentieth century. Three years after the passage of Title IX, in 1975, historian Ellen Gerber wrote of the period of women's college sport development between 1923 and 1936: "To date there has never been an NCAA sponsoring women's sport in the colleges. Nor has there been any other authority totally divorced from physical education specifically seeking to control college women's sport. Thus far, the physical educators have had carte blanche to control the national development and organization of collegiate sport programs" (Gerber 1975: 8).

In 1971 a governing body for women's sports was launched: the Association for Intercollegiate Athletics for Women (AIAW). Whereas the NCAA was corporate, the AIAW was linked to the National Education Association (NEA) through the Division of Girls and Women in Sport (DGWS) and its parent group, the Alliance for Health, Physical Education, and Recreation (which was a member of the NEA). As Staurowsky (2012: 586) recounts, "Proceeding from the premise that whatever model they adopted had to place the interests of female students at the core, AIAW leaders embarked on a journey to forge a new model of college sport distinct from that in place for men."

The desire to be separate from men's college sport resulted in part from women physical educators' philosophical deliberations. In a 1969 position paper outlining future AIAW guidelines, DGWS authors identified a prohibition on athletic GIAs as an ideological centerpiece for the women's college sport model. In the view of the DGWS and AIAW leaders, GIAs were antithetical to amateur educational athletics; such a financial arrangement changed the nature of the relationship between a student and the institution, rendering a student's educational interests and academic autonomy subservient to the university's sport-business interests. In addition to a "no scholarship" policy, the AIAW also limited female athletes' ability to transfer schools or travel as a team for competition outside local areas. These efforts were intended to prevent "pressurized recruiting, the possibility of exploiting athletes, and increased expenses associated with buying athletic talent" (Staurowsky 2012: 286).

In the 1972–73 *AIAW Handbook* it was noted that "recruiting practices and financial aid programs in women's athletics are often contrary to educational objectives; they impose undesirable pressures and are means of athletic control by those who offer the greatest financial inducements" (Adams and Soladay 1972: 12–13). Citing the importance of individuals' being students first and athletes second, the AIAW declared that recruiting athletes and offering athletic scholarships as compensation were disruptive to education. Privately women physical educators argued over this position, with some seeing it as arcane. Within months of Title IX's passage, these disputes became public when the AIAW's anti–athletic scholarship stance was challenged in *Kellmeyer v. National Education Association et al.* (1973).

The lead plaintiff, Fern Lee ("Peachy") Kellmeyer, was the director of physical education at Marymount College in Boca Raton, Florida (International Tennis Hall of Fame 2017; Rykoff 2011). A leading figure in the sport of tennis, Kellmeyer was the Women's Tennis Association's first full-time employee, hired in the same year she filed the lawsuit against the AIAW. Kellmeyer mobilized her teammates, as well as athletes and a coach from a neighboring school, to protest depriving female athletes of GIAs. According to the plaintiffs, the AIAW ban should be rescinded since "there is no such prohibition in any association or organization or college or university governing intercollegiate athletics for men. Virtually all males participating in intercollegiate athletics receive scholarships from their colleges or universities based upon their athletic abilities" (Kellmeyer 1973: 9–10).

Kellmeyer's lawsuit put the NEA and AIAW in a politically awkward position. Female plaintiffs challenging an athletic association that had staked its reputation on being an all-female association operated exclusively by women created a massive branding issue. Due both to the optics and the expense of litigation, AIAW leaders were encouraged by NEA legal counsel to settle quietly. This case, credited with paving the way for women's athletic GIAs, raised at least one sticky issue that would never be resolved: Did the inequitable treatment of female athletes resulting from the ban on athletic scholarships violate their rights under either or both Title IX (educational access) and Title VII (employment law)? The AIAW changed its policy without this important point being clarified.

Given the AIAW's founding philosophical position, it is also intriguing to speculate what the outcome of *Kellmeyer* might have been had it been litigated. Likely the AIAW would have argued that awarding GIAs rendered college athletes employees subject to the control of their coaches and compensated for their work. The AIAW had made it clear from the outset that its college-sport model—different than the men's—was educational.

As critical as the *Kellmeyer* case was in shaping women's college sport governance, it was the 1964–81 "wary courtship" between women college sport leaders and NCAA officials that ultimately proved to be the demise of the AIAW (Plyley 1997). NCAA record keepers note that a historic first occurred at its fifty-fourth annual convention in 1964, when Sara Staff Jernigan from Stetson University and Dr. Marquerite Clifton from the University of California at Los Angeles represented the DGWS and its Commission on Intercollegiate Athletics for Women (CIAW) in a roundtable discussion about the future of women's college sport (ibid.).

Within a year, at the request of women physical educators, the NCAA enacted a regulation preventing female athletes from participating in NCAA-sponsored championships and tournaments. In 1966, when notified the CIAW was moving forward with plans to develop an independent governing body for women's sports, the NCAA's assistant to the president, Charles Neinas, offered assurances that such efforts were not in conflict with the NCAA's interests. He wished the women well: "The NCAA limits its jurisdiction and authority to male student-athletes. In fact, Executive Regulations of this Association prohibit women from participating in National Collegiate Championship events" (quoted in Plyley 1997: 51–52).

The NCAA's behavior, however, was not consistent with such assurances. Within a year, as the AIAW was being created, the NCAA council discussed "the feasibility . . . of establishing appropriate machinery to provide for the control and supervision of women's intercollegiate athletics" (quoted in Plyley 1997: 52). When the NCAA's executive director, Walter Byers, was approached about this reversal, he denied knowing about it, saying that since no organization had yet established authority over women's college sport, the NCAA was simply studying the issue.

The AIAW's ten-year existence was marked by the struggle to control women's college sport. Title IX's 1972 passage added tension to discussions between the AIAW and the NCAA. While the AIAW developed and shared position papers with the US Department of Health, Education, and Welfare regarding the application of Title IX to athletic departments, the NCAA and major college football interests actively lobbied members of Congress in the hope of preserving the commercial viability of football and men's basketball.

Senator John Tower (R-TX) was the first to propose an amendment exempting the revenue-producing sports of football and men's basketball from Title IX's reach, but others followed suit. In 1975 alone five proposed Senate resolutions sought to preserve the commercial interests of the revenue-producing sports or exempt athletics from Title IX entirely (Women's Sports Foundation 2019). In addition the NCAA sued HEW, contesting regulations regarding the implementation of Title IX's mandate within athletic departments (*National Collegiate Athletic Association v. Joseph Califano* et al., 1980).

Behind the scenes the NCAA provided resources and support to a 1978 lawsuit filed by Grove City College, a religiously affiliated, private coeducational institution in western Pennsylvania, challenging the US Department of Education's authority under Title IX and asserting that schools that were not direct recipients of federal funding (even if they did administer federal student loan programs) should be exempt from Title IX (Sack and Staurowsky 1998). The Supreme Court agreed, significantly weakening the law by narrowing its applicability only to those programs within an institution that received federal funding. Since athletic departments received little or no direct federal funding, many schools halted or slowed initiatives to expand women's athletic programs. The passage of the Civil Rights Restoration Act four years later restored the intent of Title IX to address sex discriminatory treatment and removed barriers to educational access based on sex stereotypes (Staurowsky 2016).

During the 1970s, while AIAW membership grew from 278 to 970 institutions and the number of national championships offered to female college athletes rose from seven to forty-one, the NCAA mobilized to offer its own championships for women (Plyley 1997). In 1980 the NCAA moved to sponsor women's championships in Divisions II and III, and in 1981, at the NCAA's seventy-fifth convention, Division I voted to do the same (Hosick 2011). The debate that occurred behind closed doors was tense and heated, filled with parliamentary intrigue and palpable emotion. Dr. Christine Grant, the director of athletics for women's sports at the University of Iowa and former AIAW president, recalls of the meeting, "We were fighting for our lives. And we lost. It was a very difficult and emotional situation" (ibid.). The NCAA claimed that because the AIAW was unlikely to survive the legal vulnerabilities associated with schools operating athletic programs for men and women under two different sets of rules, it was justified in taking the reins of women's athletic championships. AIAW officials, on the other hand, viewed the NCAA's action as a blatant attempt to intrude on the progress women were making in forging their own athletic futures.

In a final attempt to fight what they saw as a hostile takeover, the AIAW filed a lawsuit against the NCAA alleging an antitrust violation. The AIAW accused the NCAA of using monopoly power amassed in running men's college sport to expand into the governance of women's college sport and claimed that the NCAA engaged in predatory pricing by maintaining its membership fee at its pre–women's championship rate, thus undermining the AIAW's ability to charge dues to its members. They also alleged that the NCAA adjusted its revenue distribution plan for teams participating in championships, creating an economic incentive for institutions to abandon AIAW membership and align their women's programs with the NCAA. Finally the AIAW alleged the NCAA used their newly sponsored women's basketball championship as a condition of its CBS television rights agreement for the broadcast of the men's tournament. In court the AIAW was unable to establish the NCAA had violated antitrust law (*Association for Intercollegiate Athletics for Women v. National Collegiate Athletic Association,* 1984).

The demise of the AIAW and the NCAA's hostile takeover of women's college sport reflected years of philosophical and policy differences between men's and women's college sport. The NCAA's Division I philosophy was primarily commercial, while the AIAW's was educational. For a variety of reasons previously outlined, the NCAA carved out a very particular space for the business enterprise of big-time football and basketball (Sack and Staurowsky 1998; Wushanley 2004). These two distinctly different models operate simultaneously within college sport. The educational model provides cover for the commercial business model, insulating it from being viewed as the profit-seeking entity it is. Allegiance to the educational model also prevents many reformers, the courts, and fans from viewing profit-athletes who work in big-time college sports as employees.

Although profit-athletes are often referred to as privileged, competing interests shape their existence. Power Five football and men's basketball players carry the weight of the business on their shoulders. In the mid-1990s Notre Dame kicker Jim Sanson missed an extra point; it cost his team both a victory and the $8.5 million payout for a Fiesta Bowl appearance (Dufresne 2000). Similarly March Madness buzzer beaters can mean tremendous increases in direct (tournament payouts) and indirect (increased exposure and donations, website hits, and applications for admission) revenues. Lucrative ticket sales, luxury-suite sales, and ever-escalating media contracts rely on the quality of player performances (ibid.), even as audiences eagerly consume the amateur narrative. However, fans (many of whom bet heavily on college games) are generally aware of the money at stake and have little tolerance for amateurish performances. Those opposed to recognizing college athletes as employees have argued that to do so would make big-time football and men's basketball minor leagues for their professional counterparts. That argument fails to take into account the fact that there is nothing minor about Power Five football and Division I men's basketball.

Educational athletic programs (the ones that don't prompt discussions about low graduation rates and whether athletes receive meaningful educations) siphon off an arbitrarily determined portion of NCAA profit sports' earnings (arbitrary in that profit-athlete labor has no say in how they are valued and where excess revenue will be directed). College sport officials justify this exploitation by claiming that the revenue from the two income-producing sports is used for educational purposes (and because of the court ruling in *O'Bannon,* athlete compensation must be tethered to education). However, the NCAA's subsidization practices are akin to local, nonprofessional city-league or recreational teams expecting the city's two professional franchises to finance their amateur championships by arbitrarily restricting professional player salaries.

Flawed Assumption #3. Big-Time College Football and Men's Basketball Are Extracurricular Activities

The case for denying profit-athletes their status as employees has been built in part on the idea that college sports are extracurricular activities. For more than sixty years, this argument has appeared in legal opinions as well as defense and amici brief in lawsuits filed by college athletes seeking employment status. As noted previously, in 2014 NLRB regional director Peter Sung Ohr found that the conditions under which Northwestern University football players worked met the common-law definition of employee (substantial control, supervision, structured work week). Northwestern and its allies drew upon the extracurricular argument to challenge the decision. Responding to Ohr's ruling that Northwestern football players were subjected to "strict and exacting" control by their bosses (coaches), the National Association of Collegiate Directors of Athletics and the Division I Athletic Directors Association countered that "it was no different than the control exercised over other students who also participate in extracurricular activities at the university" (DiPalma, Cohen, and Maxfield 2014: 10).

The Higher Education Council of the Employment Law Alliance similarly claimed Northwestern football players were engaged in "extracurricular education" (Jones et al. 2014), not employment, arguing this was not just a matter of common understanding and common usage, but a principle embedded in federal law. Connecting that argument to Title IX regulations (34 C.F.R. Section 106.31a; 106.41a), they noted that education is defined as including not only academic and research activities but also extracurricular programs such as intercollegiate athletics (ibid.).

In the majority opinion in *Berger v. NCAA* (2016), Judge Michael Kanne (Seventh Circuit Court of Appeals) agreed, holding that college athletes are not employees subject to the Fair Labor Standards Act. Kanne cited chapter 10 of the US Department of Labor's (2016) *Field Operations Handbook,* which establishes that "university or college students who participate in activities generally recognized as *extra-curricular* are generally not considered to be employees within the meaning of the [FLSA]" (9). The FOH further explains that an employer-employee relationship between a student and school does not exist when the activities, "such as dramatics, student publications, glee clubs, bands, choirs, debating teams, radio stations, intramurals and interscholastic athletics and other similar endeavors," are conducted for the primary benefit of the participants as part of educational opportunities offered by schools (Kanne 2016: 10).

Although concurring with the majority in *Berger,* Judge David Hamilton offered a cautionary note regarding the broad application of the specifics of the case. Hamilton wrote that while he was persuaded that the plaintiffs had not sufficiently demonstrated that the conditions under which they competed warranted a determination of employment, because they were not on athletic scholarships and their sports were designated as non-revenue, he was "less confident . . . that our reasoning should extend to students who receive athletic scholarships to participate in so-called revenue sports like Division I men's basketball and FBS football. In those sports, economic reality and the tradition of amateurism may not point in the same direction" (Kanne 2016: 13). Judge Hamilton's comment hints at the tangled logic behind the NCAA's conception of amateurism and college sport as an extracurricular activity. Casting Power Five football and men's basketball players as just like every other student allows the NCAA to continue to assert that student participation in intercollegiate athletics is an avocation.

In its earliest form, college athletics was conceived and operated by students (McConaghy and Woods 2005; Smith 1990). From the first intercollegiate contest, Yale versus Harvard in an 1852 rowing event sponsored by the Boston, Concord, and Montreal Railroad company, until the early part of the twentieth century, male students brought an entrepreneurial spirit to bear, creating a lasting legacy of college sport on many campuses (Wellman and Peet 1912). Notably the Yale versus Harvard rowing event was created by a Yale junior, James Whiton, who thought the idea might provide relief from the pressures of academic life while at home in New Hampshire. He planned the event while on hiatus from the third quarter of his junior year (Mendenhall 1993). Over the years the Harvard-Yale Regatta or Yale-Harvard Boat Race (aka "The Race") has been shepherded by alumni from both universities. In an ironic twist of fate, the foundation of modern-day, corporatized college sport was laid by male undergraduate students with a flair for business and a political sense of rebellion.

College sports have a long history of student agitation against paternal authority. College campuses from the post–Revolutionary War period through the mid-nineteenth century were occasionally sites of significant clashes between college authorities (whose repressive rules and harsh punishments were meant to curb youthful exuberance and social experimentation) and students. Sometimes the stakes were high. In the Rebellion of 1834, Harvard students expressed their dissatisfaction by detonating an explosive device in the chapel, lighting a recitation room on fire, beating two night watchmen, and burning the president in effigy at a gathering place called the Rebellion Tree (Ireland 2012).

Faculty included sports on the list of sinful, vain, and idle pastimes, including drinking, smoking, card playing, and dancing. Of course, many students embraced these activities as expressions of their rights to life and liberty. The activities that took place in these contested spaces on college campuses became marked as non-academic or extracurricular. In the nineteenth and early twentieth centuries, the domain of sport belonged to male college students.

During the Industrial Age, with its emphasis on efficiency and mechanization, male athletes and student managers slowly built an infrastructure that was the precursor to today's college sport enterprise. In the late 1800s, Cornell students organized independent sporting clubs, experimenting with funding models that included dues, a variety of fundraisers and/or entertainment events, and direct solicitation campaigns. Over time efforts to consolidate separate clubs required the creation of a governance structure. Each club's representative (initially one from each sport or athletic interest) to the Athletic Association carried the title "athletic director." Athletic directors scheduled events on and off campus, managed increasingly large budgets, found ways to generate revenue, negotiated land deals for the purpose of building stadiums, responded to a rising fan base, handled alumni interests, and navigated relationships with academic authorities. Soon the Athletic Association needed a full-time "graduate manager" to handle the enterprise's complex business functions. The graduate manager would evolve into a professional athletic director (Cornell University Athletics 2007).

Concerns about students controlling college athletics were never far from the minds of college presidents and faculties. Because they were not part of the curriculum, intercollegiate sport contests were likened to other kinds of "intercollegiate matches" in debate, oration, chess, and tennis (Woodward 1903). In addition to scrutiny by faculties and administrations, during the late 1800s and early 1900s, the brutal nature of college football, which was resulting in significant injuries and even deaths among players, was also drawing media criticism. However, while the takeover of student-operated college sports has most often been framed as a response to football's deaths and injuries, the genesis of the

NCAA was just as much the result of college presidents and faculties wanting to gain control of all facets of intercollegiate athletics, including revenue generation.

In 1906 the precursor to the NCAA—the International Athletic Association of the United States (IAAUS)—was formed by a group of faculty members who embraced college athletics and used the term *extracurriculum* to highlight its similarities to other forms of student activities (Smith 1990).[2] Even at this founding moment, though, the sport of football was set apart. It is notable that the proceedings from the 1907 annual meeting of the IAAUS include faculty reports about athletics on members' campuses and outline the need to take control of baseball, not football. The newly formed National Intercollegiate Football Conference, a separate organization, controlled football (Des Jardins 2015; *Harvard Crimson* 1906; Watterson 2010). While the IAAUS claimed credit for forcing a shakeup in college football's leadership, the change from the old rules committee to the new resulted "not so much in changing the rules . . . but even more in a better public sentiment" (Pierce 1907: 29).

So while faculty advocates called for college presidents and faculty to assume control of athletics, it proved nearly impossible to deny that football was truly extracurricular; the IAAUS/NCAA had little power to regulate the sport's adherence to its regulations. The organization identified a reliance on gate receipts to be the principal evil of college football and the source of its corruption. According to Hetherington (1903) and Woodward (1903), a financial model based on selling tickets to spectators inevitably led to professional, itinerate coaches; the creation of rivalries so as to have a spectacle to sell; rowdy, loyal partisan fans; a general overemphasis on winning; gambling on games; and cutthroat recruiting of high-level talent. None of these were consistent with the faculty ideal of extracurricular, nonprofessional college athletics.

The college sport environment rapidly developed in the early twentieth century. Gate receipts continued to increase. Gambling was often encouraged. Players with elite talent were aggressively recruited and compensated. Professional coaching staffs took over control of football programs. Traditional rivalries became an integral part of college sport, and rowdy fans were encouraged to take part in pre- and postgame tailgating. And critically, decade after decade, football players suffered physical injuries. They were vulnerable to abusive coaching practices and had little information about the short- and long-term consequences of violent tackles during practices and games.

The false equivalency drawn between college football and other extracurricular student activities ignored critically different underpinnings. As McKennan (2009) notes, early twentieth-century comparisons between football and debate teams began and ended with the enthusiasm of audiences and the general fanfare surrounding victories. Alluding to this superficial commonality, McKennan

(2009: 80) writes, "Policy debate—a form of speech competition in which two teams of two debate the worthiness of a particular policy action—contrasted with the brutal encounters of college football, on one hand, and the frivolity of campus society on the other." Though debate was described as an "intellectual sport," it emerged out of literary societies that encouraged students to take the material covered in their course lectures and make it their own through conversation and discussion. Coached by faculty, the college debaters of the early twentieth century became "highly skilled researchers" equipped to navigate a burgeoning flood of information found in books, manuals, and libraries (Atchison and Panetta 2009; McKennan 2009). Debaters also carved a space to express contrarian views within an accepted academic forum; if their ideas weren't welcome, the intellectual exercise, nonetheless, gained the enthusiastic support of academic leaders. By the 1930s, as the professoriate resisted pressure to sign loyalty oaths, students engaging in campus debate still benefited from a commitment to the free exchange of ideas within a free society.

In contrast football teams, with their reliance on military formations and autocratic coaching styles, chafed against ever-increasing patriarchal authority that required conformity and unquestioning compliance (Dunnavant 2005). In many ways football was perceived as an antidote to radical idealism on college campuses: a vehicle to inculcate competitive masculine values that reinforced American political and economic systems in young college males. Dissent was not a part of the picture (Austin 2015). Commissioner of the Big Ten Conference John Griffith said, "Through our athletic programs, we can help inculcate in our boys the American spirit. We can refuse to be influenced by the soft idealists" (quoted in ibid.: 67).

Such divergent histories support McKennan's (2009) contention that comparisons between college football and debate teams were superficial at best. At worst, within the context of denying college football players' employment rights, such arguments are disingenuous. Debate team members have not, over the span of nearly a century, protested their treatment by faculty advisers nor sued their universities over health care, educational benefits, or compensation. There is no national call to monitor debate team members' graduation rates, question whether they have received meaningful educations, or wonder about their primary role on campus. Also there is no concerted multibillion-dollar effort to market debate team members as "student-debaters" in order to avoid worker compensation claims.

Analogizing college students who take part in debate and other student activities with Power Five football players working in the big-time college sport industry obscures these commodified players' very legitimate grievances with universities and their corporate partners. The lifeblood of the college-sport industry is talented labor, and recruiting this talent is in and of itself big business.

Athletic departments have historically identified, recruited, and signed athletes to athletic GIAs. Today athletic directors, scouts, coaches, boosters, and the NCAA engage in state-of-the-art recruiting that makes use of sophisticated data analytics in a nationwide or even worldwide search for athletic talent (Associated Press 2017; Stancil 2014; Waldman 2017).

Other campus activities do not involve the kind of money big-time college football programs spend on a regular basis to find and sign college players. For example, all but three Power Five football recruiting budgets annually exceed $1 million (Ching 2018; Estes 2019), with the top nine annual recruiting budgets in 2017–18 all exceeding $2 million (Ching 2018). Reflecting the importance of recruiting, "during the 2018 fiscal year, public schools in the SEC averaged more than $1.3 million in football recruiting costs, compared with public schools in the Big 12 ($961,981), ACC ($938,424), Big 10 ($855,437) and Pac-12 ($708,750)" (Estes 2019). In comparison, in 2020 median spending on recruiting all other undergraduate students at four-year public institutions was $470 per student (Ruffalo Noel Levitz 2021). While recruiting budgets may fluctuate from year to year, every Power Five football program spends heavily on recruiting, understanding that "great players make great programs."

Global corporate investors, such as footwear and apparel companies Nike and Adidas, sponsor summer high school basketball showcases, many of which are broadcast on cable sport channels (Kirpalani 2016). These companies' incentive is their mutual business interest in the athlete commodity trade—the identification of profit-athlete talent that will be marketed across multiple digital and social media platforms. Much like lucrative stocks or equities, high school football and boys' basketball prospects are closely monitored by fans, recruiters,

Table 1. Top ten Power Five football recruiting budgets, 2017–18 fiscal year (Ching 2018)

RANK	PROGRAM	CONFERENCE	RECRUITING BUDGET
1	Georgia	SEC	$2,517,452.40
2	Tennessee	SEC	$2,479,672.00
3	Auburn	SEC	$2,461,960.00
4	Michigan	Big Ten	$2,365,460.40
5	Alabama	SEC	$2,314,326.00
6	Penn State	Big Ten	$2,143,474.20
7	Kentucky	SEC	$2,131,701.40
8	Nebraska	Big Ten	$2,116,756.80
9	Notre Dame	ACC	$2,069,652.20
10	Oklahoma	Big 12	$1,967,040.00

sport channels, and websites such as Rivals.com, Scout.com, and 247sports.com (Willens 2017). The best players in the country receive ratings (the better the player, the more stars), with their journeys through the recruiting process often becoming reality TV productions (24/7 Sports 2017).

The venues in which football and basketball players compete are markedly different from those for other student activities. Many college football stadiums are larger than NFL stadiums. FBS college football players routinely play (work) in front of in-person, paying crowds ranging from 60,000 to 105,000. In the 2019 football season, more than 36 million fans attended FBS football games (NCAA Staff 2019). Meanwhile the two 2021 CFP semifinal broadcasts averaged 19 million viewers (Brooks 2021). Since its inception the CFP playoffs (semifinals or championship) have been among the top cable telecasts across any network (ibid.). Advertisers pay upward of $1 million for thirty-second advertisement spots during the telecasts (Smith 2017).

Power Five college football is an advertising behemoth on par with the NFL, dwarfing other major sports properties. In 2020 ESPN, which is the dominant force in college sports, televised 282 games and generated $792.5 million in advertising revenue, more than double what ESPN's NFL package sold (Novy-Williams and Crupi 2020). Millions of fans religiously follow Power Five college football. In-game attendance and television viewership are enormous but still represent only a partial window into the business that is college football. For decades college and professional football have been the number-one betting attraction for legal gamblers in the state of Nevada (Drape 2017). Although gaming industry analysts do not distinguish between betting on college and professional football, the sport reportedly draws more than $90 billion in mostly illegal wagering per year (American Gaming Association 2016). In October 2017, for the first time, betting on college football outpaced action on NFL games by more than four hundred thousand dollars (Drape 2017).

Taken together, it is fairly easy to dispense with the pretense that profit-athletes and college debaters are both just students. That argument is useful only for those hoping to turn a blind eye to the employee-employer relationship between profit-athletes and Power Five universities (Staurowsky 2018a). The controls exerted on Power Five football and Division I men's basketball players make it clear the players are commodities. This contractual arrangement includes the GIA, the National Letter of Intent, the Student-Athlete Statement, and drug testing forms. Tellingly profit-athletes play no part in negotiating the terms under which they can lose eligibility and be penalized (National Collegiate Athletic Association 2017).

Further, player movement is constrained and regulated through transfer rules. Until 2021 players who transferred within the same NCAA division were penalized with a year-long waiting period in which they could not play—and that was assuming their coaches granted their athletic release. If such a release was not granted, the athlete had to sit out two years before competing in this supposedly extracurricular activity (NCAA Eligibility Center 2017). Even though the NCAA, in response to public pressure to allow more player movement, has rescinded some player transfer rules, coaches still retain tremendous power over players' futures.

The culture of control within Power Five college sport reveals itself in some almost laughable ways. In 2016, at the height of the US presidential race featuring Democratic candidate Hillary Clinton and Republican candidate Donald Trump, athletic compliance officers were sent a reminder regarding an NCAA staff interpretation on the endorsement of political candidates by college athletes (Condaras 2016). Originally issued in 1987, the interpretation advised that athletes could endorse political candidates if they were not paid to do so and as long as they were under no obligation to commit time to a campaign (Condaras 2016). The NCAA encouraged institutions to include in their press releases a disclaimer: "The student-athletes are acting as citizens of the state, and do not necessarily represent the views of their institutions of higher education or the NCAA" (Condaras 2016). A college or university would never think to issue such a disclaimer for all its students, but such statements are often issued by companies in regard to employee speech.

Further restrictions on players' conduct are likely violations of labor law (SI Wire 2015). In a 2016 memorandum issued by Barry J. Kearney, associate general counsel in the Division of Advice with the NLRB, certain rules in Northwestern University's football handbook were found to violate the NLRA and the rights of football players who the NLRB regional director had deemed to be statutory employees. Northwestern avoided a formal NLRB complaint by adjusting overly broad language in its social media policies as well as restrictions on information players could share about injuries and which outlets could interview players. In addition a rule regarding athletic communication had barred athletes from granting an interview with anyone not first approved by the athletic department. After Kearney's memo athletes were allowed to speak directly to the members of the media if they wished to do so. It is inconceivable that a university would have attempted to restrict a regular student's First Amendment rights.

In addition to free-speech restrictions, the time college debaters devote to debating is not manipulated through regulation to make it appear as though they only dedicate twenty hours a week to debate practice and competitions when they may in fact be required or volunteer to spend far more time than that. Such sleight of hand is achieved through NCAA bylaws that facilitate creative accounting that distills forty- or sixty-hour work weeks into tidy twenty-hour packages with one day off. The NCAA even limits the amount of competition-day time that counts toward this twenty-hour per week limit: "Competition Day. All competition and any associated athletically related activities on the day of competition shall count as three hours regardless of the actual duration of these activities" (NCAA 2021, 17.1.7.3.2). For college athletes the time spent traveling to a game, attending walk-throughs and/or meetings, warming up, playing the game, showering, taking part in postgame interviews, making more team meetings, and attending any tailgate appearances always equates to no more than three hours (NCAA 2021).

The bureaucracy necessary to execute such surveillance and control of athletes' lives is reflected in ballooning college athletic departments. Unlike debate teams, for which one faculty member may serve as a coach in addition to their regular campus duties, the whereabouts and activities of Power Five college football and basketball players are monitored nearly twenty-four hours a day, seven days a week, through athletic compliance officers, coaches, academic support personnel, sports medicine staff, and others. At the University of Georgia, for example, the football staff directory consists of sixty people (University of Georgia Athletic Association 2021), excluding class-checkers hired to go around campus to document whether football and men's basketball players are attending classes (Porter 2017). College football and basketball players, under sports footwear and apparel contracts entered into by their institutions, are often harnessed to data-tracking devices that collect player biometric data such as calories consumed, resting heart rate, and hours slept per night.

The notion that Power Five football and men's basketball players—whose public personas (names, images, and likenesses) are commodified as part of the profit-seeking multibillion college sport industry—are just like every other student simply defies logic. When college debaters take to the podium or stage, they are engaging in an exercise that connects deeply with the intellectual purpose of higher education and are empowered to use their voice to question the status quo. Profit-athletes—who ostensibly dribble, shoot, block or tackle for their university—are well aware that it is safer for them to simply shut up and play.

Conclusion

The argument that recognizing profit-athletes as employees will result in the undermining of women's sports in violation of Title IX is based on the assumption that all college sports are the same, that men's college sport and women's college sport operate under the same model, and that Power Five football and Division I men's basketball are like all other extracurricular activities. When this assumption is unmasked, NCAA hegemony falls apart.

When Title IX was passed in 1972, the all-male NCAA was undergoing a restructuring in response to the organization's growth and diversity of perspective. That reorganization resulted in the federated arrangement of Divisions I,

II, and III. In this way schools whose football teams had not had a chance to play on television were placated when the NCAA agreed to offer televised national football championships in Divisions II and III. A proposal put forward by NCAA president Stephen Horn in 1975 and derided by some as the "Robin Hood plan" would have created a fourth division. Horn's plan, which detractors called athletic "socialism," called for television revenues to be distributed across the entire membership (Koch and Leonard 1978). This rejected plan is now credited by Chuck Neinas (former commissioner of the Big Eight Conference and executive director of the College Football Association) as the inspiration for the big-time football powers to find common ground to protect their interests within the NCAA (Dunnavant 2004: 124).

In the late 1970s, as staffers at HEW set out to write the regulations and interpretations to provide guidance regarding how Title IX would apply to athletic departments, they could not have envisioned the influence ESPN and other sport channels would have on the sport media landscape nor the digital age's explosive impact on the business of big-time college football and basketball. The NCAA federation movement and the resounding defeat of the Robin Hood plan reflected the ongoing conflict within the NCAA between the proverbial haves and have-nots. The schism between the NCAA national office and big-time college football universities became publicly evident in 1977 with the formation of the College Football Association. The divide reached its zenith in 1984, when the University of Oklahoma and the University of Georgia sued the NCAA over restrictive football programming decisions that impaired the ability of big-time football schools to reap the financial benefits of negotiating individual contracts and leveraging their own brands (*NCAA v. Board of Regents* 1984). The US Supreme Court's ruling that the NCAA's television policies violated federal antitrust law allowed the College Football Association and individual schools and conferences to begin negotiating their own contracts. Over the next several years, with the growth of cable television, several conferences (e.g., the Big Ten, Pac-10, SEC, and Big East) negotiated individual game packages, with Notre Dame breaking away and signing an exclusive deal with NBC. Notably the NCAA received none of the revenue from these conference and university media rights deals.

Absent the financial support from college football, the NCAA's business model was still fiscally viable as a result of the multimillion-dollar and then billion-dollar brand known as March Madness. College football and men's basketball became sports-property fixtures for media conglomerates CBS, ESPN, FOX, and Turner, which were consolidating and expanding sports networks and multimedia platforms. Like the NFL and NBA, college conferences soon created niche digital networks that further solidified rival fan bases and increased corporate profits (Staurowsky 2018b).

The power struggles involving the competing interests of college football and Title IX compliance led to high political intrigue. Members of Congress who were aligned with big-time football schools, conferences, and the NCAA national office tried to have athletics removed from Title IX's jurisdiction. Failing this, they attempted to prevent revenue from football and basketball from being shared with other sports within athletic departments, colorfully claiming that doing so would "kill the goose that laid the golden egg" (Ware 2014: 5).

Keeping Power Five football and men's basketball programs under Title IX jurisdiction was significant, since Title IX addresses educational access. In practice, when schools determine that participating in varsity sport is educationally important, they are required to provide athletic opportunities equitably to male and female athletes commensurate with their interests and abilities (Carpenter and Acosta 2005; Staurowsky and Weight 2011; Staurowsky 2016). However, each school is afforded latitude in determining how they achieve this end.

That calculation hinges on the integrity of several assumptions: that all athletes are participating in the same type of activities, that those activities are genuinely extracurricular, and that all college sports operate under the same business and philosophical model. These assumptions ignore at least two relevant points. As recognized by the US Department of Education's Office for Civil Rights, the federal agency that oversees the enforcement of Title IX, and the federal court in *Beidiger v. Quinnipiac* (2013), a case addressing the application of Title IX to the sport of cheerleading, not all sports are the same nor need they be recognized as such under Title IX.

When considering definitional qualification under Title IX, the distinctive relationship between Power Five football and Division I men's basketball players and their institutions is too often shunted to the side. The crux of the issue involves the following questions:

- What if participation in Power Five football or NCAA Division I men's basketball team is not an avocation (implied by the definition of an extracurricular activity) but rather a vocation—akin to a job?
- What if the relationship between profit-athletes and their university is that of employees and employer?
- Would Title IX apply to a professional team sponsored by a university?
- Since professional teams are subsidized with public money as a matter of course, does Title IX apply to these entities?

Simply because a university serves as a promoter of big-time college sport entertainment does not make that entertainment nonprofessional, nor does it mean the players are not employees. Judge Hamilton's cautionary note in *Berger*—that there was something different between non-scholarship track athletes at Penn and scholarship football players competing at Penn State—was echoed by

NLRB Regional Director Ohr's finding in *Northwestern* that the "Employer never offers a scholarship to a prospective student unless they intend to provide an athletic service to the Employer" (Ohr 2014: 20). Put more bluntly: Power Five football players (including the players at Northwestern University receiving GIAs) are compensated (i.e., paid) to play football. Ohr supported this determination, noting that athletes who voluntarily opt not to play no longer retain the right to their GIA, per NCAA rules.

Critically for profit-athletes awarded GIAs, their player value is put on full public display and harvested for profit by media entities from the start of the recruiting process. The awarding of an "athletic" GIA obviously rewards athletic performance. Germane to a Title IX analysis, a GIA represents compensation for work done as a college football or basketball player rather than an untethered grant providing educational access with no outside-of-class obligations.

The rigged linkage with education is enforced through NCAA rules that strip discretionary rights from profit-athlete employees and restrict, as a matter of contract, where athletes can spend or redeem the compensation they earn. In effect the NCAA unilaterally tells athletes how they can earn their money (by playing) and spend it (on college tuition). This ought to be understood as not educational access but the sort of economic control that Southall and Weiler (2014) explicitly compare to workers in a company town. As NBA star and former Louisiana State University player Ben Simmons made quite clear in a Showtime documentary, he did not view his LSU athletic GIA as access to an education but access to a professional basketball career (Mandt 2016).

The unilaterally imposed financial arrangement of athletic GIAs should be more properly identified as a labor-control tool that obfuscates profit-athletes' employment status by forcing players to spend their earnings at the company store (the institution) and suppresses their market value by denying them access to representation and mobility. University of Michigan athletic director Fritz Crisler observed that when the NCAA adopted the athletic scholarship in 1956, the policy assigned to universities the right to exploit and exclude others from exploiting athletes' talents (Byers and Hammer 1995: 74). In 1973 US Senator Marlow Cook (R-KY) described the NCAA as a "body primarily designed to protect and defend its member institutions from the professional sports world and to make sure that collegiate sports gets its share of the sports business pie" (quoted in Koch 1973: 136).

Using Title IX as a tool to deny profit-athletes their employment rights has several logical flaws. First, Title IX regulations draw their definition of *student-athlete* directly from the NCAA manual. As a result Title IX perpetuates the propaganda campaign expressly orchestrated to avoid worker compensation claims brought by college athletes and obscures the pay-for-play system NCAA officials knew they created at the time they adopted the athletic scholarship.

Second, predictions that women's sport will be destroyed or greatly diminished if profit-athletes gain bargaining power and labor rights are about as genuine as previous NCAA officials' claims that Title IX passage would destroy college football (Staurowsky and Orleans 2014). In Title IX's almost 50 years of existence, Power Five college football and women's college sports have both grown substantially. Third, while the Power Five, Group of 5, and FCS designations may be appropriate for the business of football and men's basketball, they drive up expenses and time demands for NCAA Olympic sports. Fourth, sweeping claims that women's sports will be destroyed by profit-athletes' being recognized as employees is simply an argument of convenience, easily debunked, since women's sports have weathered major changes over the years. In a classic case of the denial of labor rights, the NCAA and college sport officials proclaim austerity and poverty even though the industry has thrived through a number of alterations. In particular Division III (the NCAA's largest membership division) has received only 3.18 percent of the NCAA revenues for more than forty years, yet it continuously fulfills its stated mission: providing opportunities for athletes to compete at a regional level. Division II, although it faces its own challenges, has thrived over the past fifty years.

A final flaw in holding up Title IX as a stop sign is that it blocks productive conversations recognizing that there is already more than one model of college sport in operation and more than one college sport market. In fact the business model of college sport should drive recognition of college athletes as employees within their respective markets. Regardless of Title IX's requirements, female athletes have a stake in the clarity that could come from such refined decision making, and many women's sports could see employee recognition too. As Southall and Nagel (2008) document, Division I women's college basketball is a commercial entity with practices that align with men's college basketball; the market the women work in is different (a multimillion-dollar market compared to a multibillion-dollar one), but the female players compete under conditions similar to those of college football and men's basketball players. That is, rather than being simply tagalong athletes whose programs are in jeopardy, Division I women's basketball players are increasingly part of an exploitative system that their male peers seek to change.

Profit-athletes share a common bond with their female counterparts: within the nation's college athletic programs, neither group has been treated with fairness and equity. College sport officials utilizing Title IX to thwart profit-athletes' attempts to organize are pursuing a political gambit to redirect attention away from the exploitation of an undervalued and unrecognized labor force by noting the unfair and unequal treatment of other athletes. Boiling down legal challenges to pay for play—as if profit-athletes' genuine labor grievances can be refashioned into a bumper sticker—pits male athletes against female athletes to the detriment of both (Staurowsky 2018a).

For profit-athletes, seeking employee recognition has never been solely about pay but also about power and dignity—issues that every American worker should understand. These individuals simply want to be free from unilaterally imposed rules. They want to be free to speak and negotiate reasonable and safe working conditions. They want their bodies to be protected by health and medical coverage when they are injured. Title IX, a civil rights law, should not be used to deny labor rights to those who rightfully deserve them.

Notes

1. For a complete list of NCAA talking points, see Solomon 2014a.
2. The IAAUS was renamed the National Collegiate Athletic Association at the fifth annual IAAUS conference.

References

CASES

Association for Intercollegiate Athletics for Women v. National Collegiate Athletic Association (1984). 735 F.2d 577; 236 U.S.App.D.C. 311, 1984–1 Trade Cases 66,007. No. 83–1342. https://openjurist.org/735/f2d/577/association-for-intercollegiate-athletics-for-women-v-national-collegiate-athletic-association.

Biediger v. Quinnipiac University, 691 F.3d 85 (2d Cir. 2012).

Jenkins v. Notional Collegiate Athletic Association (In re National Collegiate Athletic Association Athletic Grant-In-Aid Cap Antitrust Litigation), No. 14-md-2541 CW (N.D. Cal. Aug. 5, 2016).

Kellmeyer v. Nat'l Educ. Ass'n, 73-CV-21 (S.D. Fla. Jan. 4, 1973).

Luke Hancock v. National Collegiate Athletic Association. (2018). Case No: 18-CI-003982. https://interactives.courier-journal.com/pdf/UofL-basketball-Lawsuit.PDF

National Collegiate Athletic Association v. Joseph Califano et al. (1980). 622 F.2d 1382. https://law.justia.com/cases/federal/appellate-courts/F2/622/1382/65091/.

NCAA v. Board of Regents of the University of Oklahoma, et al. 468 U.S. 85 (1984).

O'Bannon v. NCAA, No. C-09–3329-CW, 2014 WL 3899815 (N.D. Cal. Aug. 8, 2014).

SECONDARY SOURCES

Adams, Martha, and Doris Soladay (1972). *AIAW Handbook of Policies and Operating Procedures 1972–1973*. Washington, DC: American Association for Health, Physical Education, and Recreation.

American Gaming Association (2016). "Football Bets to Top $90 Billion for Second Straight Season." September 7. https://americangaming.org/.

Associated Press (2017). "Numbers Game: Spreading through College Football." *USA Today*, August 5. https://www.usatoday.com/.

Atchison, Jarrod, and Edward Panetta (2009). "Intercollegiate Debate and Speech Communication: Historical Developments and Issues for the Future." In *The SAGE Handbook of*

Rhetorical Studies, edited by Andrea A. Lunsford, Kirt H. Wilson, and Rosa A. Eberly, 317–34. Thousand Oaks, CA: SAGE.

Athletic Staff (2021). "NCAA President Mark Emmet Receives Contract Extension through 2025." *Athletic*, April 28. https://theathletic.com/.

Austin, Brad (2015). *Democratic Sports: Men's and Women's College Athletics during the Great Depression*. Fayetteville: University of Arkansas Press.

Barro, Robert J. (2002). "The Best Little Monopoly in America." *Business Week*, December 9, 22.

Bass, Jordan R., Claire C. Schaepekoetter, and Kyle S. Bunds, eds. (2015). "The 'Front Porch': Examining the Increasing Interconnection of University and Athletic Department Funding." Special issue, *ASHE Higher Education Report* 41, no. 5.

Berger v. National Collegiate Athletic Association, 843 F.3d 285 (7th Cir. 2016).

Berkowitz, Steve (2014). "University of Texas Posts Record Revenues, Expenses." *USA Today*, January 30. https://www.usatoday.com/.

———. (2018). "NCAA's Mark Emmert Got a Nearly $500,000 Raise to $2.4 Million in Compensation in 2016." *USA Today*, June 21. https://www.usatoday.com/.

Besser, Dillon J. (2016). "The Forgotten Party in *O'Bannon v. National Collegiate Athletic Association*: How Non-revenue Sports Operate in a Changing Intercollegiate Landscape." *University of Iowa Law Review* 101: 2105–40. https://ilr.law.uiowa.edu/.

"Big Labor on College Campuses: Examining the Consequences of Unionizing Student Athletes." Hearing before the Committee on Education and the Workforce, US House of Representatives, 113th Cong. (2014).

Branch, Taylor (2014). "Testimony of Taylor Branch United States Senate Committee on Commerce, Science, and Transportation," July 9. https://taylorbranch.com/author/karintracy/.

Brooks, Amanda (2021). "College Football Playoff Semifinals Average Nineteen Million Viewers, ESPN's Third-Most Watched Day on Record." ESPN Press Room, January 5. https://espnpressroom.com/.

Byers, Walter, with Charles Hammer (1995). *Unsportsmanlike Conduct: Exploiting College Athletes*. Ann Arbor: University of Michigan Press.

Carpenter, Linda Jean, and R. Vivian Acosta (2005). *Title IX*. Champaign, IL: Human Kinetics.

Cassillo, John (2019). "NCAA Tournament a Slam Dunk for Brands in 2019." *TVREV*, April 12. https://tvrev.com/.

Cavanaugh, Jack (1991). "The Elusive Gipper." *Sports Illustrated*, December 30. https://www.si.com/.

Charity Navigator (2021a). National Association of Intercollegiate Athletics profile. https://www.charitynavigator.org/.

———. (2021b) National Collegiate Athletic Association profile. https://www.charitynavigator.org/.

———. (2021c). Southeastern Conference profile. https://www.charitynavigator.org/.

Ching, David (2018). "For Colleges, Spending Big on Recruiting Does Not Necessarily Translate to All-Sports Success." *Forbes*, June 5. https://www.forbes.com/.

College Football Playoff (2017a). "Governance." http://www.collegefootballplayoff.com/.

———. (2017b). "Overview." http://www.collegefootballplayoff.com/.

Condaras, Jen (2016). "Sports Psychologist Attending Practice." *Daily Compliance Item*, December 15. https://dailycomplianceitem.wordpress.com/.

Cornell University Athletics (2007). "History of Athletics at Cornell University." http://www.cornellbigred.com/.

Davis, Brian (2014). "Texas AD Steve Patterson: Northwestern Union Push Benefits Only 'Trial Lawyers.'" *Austin American-Statesman*, April 18. https://www.statesman.com/.

Deloitte and Touche (2018). "National Collegiate Athletic Association and Subsidiaries Consolidated Financial Statement as of and for the Years Ended August 31, 2017 and 2018." Indianapolis, IN: Deloitte and Touche. https://ncaaorg.s3.amazonaws.com/ncaa/finance/2017-18NCAAFin_NCAAFinancialStatement.pdf.

———. (2019). "National Collegiate Athletic Association Consolidated Financial Statement as of and for the Years Ended August 31, 2018 and 2019." Indianapolis, IN: Deloitte and Touche. https://ncaaorg.s3.amazonaws.com/ncaa/finance/2018-19NCAAFin_NCAAFinancials.pdf.

Des Jardins, Julie (2015). *Walter Camp: Football and the Modern Man*. New York: Oxford University Press.

DiPalma, D., M. C. Cohan, and H. O. Maxfield (2014). "Amicus brief by National Association of Collegiate Directors of Athletics and D1A Athletic Directors' Association". *Northwestern University v. College Athletes Players' Association*. National Labor Relations Board. Retrieved from https://www.nlrb.gov/case/13-RC-121359 (Second page, 6th brief in list).

Drape, Joe (2017). "Among Bettors, College Football Is Shoving the N.F.L. Aside." *New York Times*, November 29. https://www.nytimes.com/.

Dufresne, Chris (2000). "Making the Play Doesn't Pay Off." *Los Angeles Times*, November 23. http://articles.latimes.com/.

Dunnavant, Keith (2005). *Coach: The Life of Paul "Bear" Bryant*. New York: St. Martin's.

Estes, Gentry (2019). "The Cost of College Football Recruiting—and Winning—Is Now Through the Roof." *Louisville Courier-Journal*, August 20. https://www.courier-journal.com/.

Fleisher, Arthur A., Brian L. Goff, and Robert D. Tollison (1992). *The National Collegiate Athletic Association: A Study in Cartel Behavior*. Chicago: University of Chicago Press.

Forde, Pat (2015). "U.S. Olympic Committee 'Candidly Concerned' Non-revenue College Sports Will Be Cut." Yahoo! Sports, April 1. https://sports.yahoo.com/.

Friedman, Wayne (2018). "March Madness grows 5% in national TV ad dollars, ratings down." *MediaPost*, April 3. https://www.mediapost.com/.

Gerber, Ellen (1975). "The Controlled Development of Collegiate Sport for Women, 1923–1936." *Journal of Sport History* 2, no. 1: 1–28.

Glier, Ray (2012). *How the SEC Became Goliath: The Making of College Football's Most Dominant Conference*. New York: Simon & Schuster.

Godfrey, Steven (2014). "Meet the Bag Man: 10 Rules for Paying college football players." *SB Nation*, April 10. http://www.sbnation.com/.

Goldstein, Warren (2014). "Walter Camp's Off-Side: A Tarnished Football Legacy." *Hartford Courant*, March 14. https://www.courant.com/.

Harvard Crimson (1906). "Rules Committee Meeting." January 13. http://www.thecrimson.com/article/1906/1/13/rules-committee-meeting-pthe-old-football/.

Hetherington, C. W. (1903). "Regulation of Athletics in Missouri and Adjacent Territory." *School Review* 11, no. 5: 329–42.

Hosick, Michelle Brutlag (2011). "Equal Opportunity Knocks: National Girls and Women in Sports Day Celebrates 25 Years." NCAA.com, February 2. https://www.ncaa.com/.

———. (2014). "Steering Committee Working toward New Governance Model." NCAA.com, March 4. https://www.ncaa.org/.

Huma, Ramogi, and Ellen J. Staurowsky (2012). "Study: The $6 Billion Heist: Robbing College Athletes under the Guise of Amateurism." NCPA.org. https://www.ncpanow.org/.

Hutchausen, Amy (2017). "Pay for Play a Bad Idea for College Sports." *Albany Times Union,* November 29. http://www.timesunion.com/.

International Tennis Hall of Fame (2017). "Peachy Kellmeyer." https://www.tennisfame.com/.

Ireland, Corydon (2012). "Harvard's Long-Ago Student Risings." *Harvard Gazette,* April 19. https://news.harvard.edu/.

Irick, Erin (2017). "NCAA Sports Sponsorship and Participation Rates Report." Indianapolis: National Collegiate Athletic Association. https://ncaaorg.s3.amazonaws.com/.

Jones, P. A., Mathison, M., Reid, F. R., and Salsburey, J. (2014). "Brief of amicus curiae Higher Education Council of the Employment Law Alliance in support of employer Northwestern University. Northwestern University and College Athletes Players Association (CAPA), Petitioner." Case 13-RC-121359 Amicus Brief -8. https://www.nlrb.gov/.

Kanne, M. (2016). "Appellate opinion in Gillian Berger v. National Collegiate Athletic Association, No. 16–1558," December 5. US Court of Appeals, Seventh Circuit. http://media.ca7.uscourts.gov/.

Kahn, Lawrence M. (2007). "Markets: Cartel Behavior and Amateurism in College Sports." *Journal of Economic Perspectives* 21, no. 1: 209–26.

Kearney, Barry J. (2016). Advice memorandum to Peter Sung Ohr, Regional Director, Region 13. Subject: Northwestern University Case 13-CA-157476, September 22. Washington, DC: National Labor Relations Board. http://www.trbas.com/.

Kirpalani, Sanjay (2016). "Ten Most Important College Football Recruiting Camps to Keep Your Eye On." *Bleacher Report,* February 18. http://bleacherreport.com/.

Koch, James V. (1973). "A Troubled Cartel: The NCAA." *Law and Contemporary Problems* 38, no. 1: 135–50. https://www.jstor.org/.

Koch, James V., and Wilbert M. Leonard (1978). "The NCAA: A Socio-economic Analysis: The Development of the College Sports Cartel from Social Movement to Formal Organization." *American Journal of Economics and Sociology* 37, no. 3: 225–39. https://www.jstor.org/.

Loftin, R. Bowen, with Rusty Burson (2014). *The 100-Year Decision: Texas A&M and the SEC.* Indianapolis: Dog Ear.

Mandt, Maura, dir. (2016). *One and Done/Ben Simmons.* Produced by Showtime. http://www.sho.com/.

Martin, Nick (2018). "A College Basketball Insider Is Uniting Mid-Majors to Bust the Big Guys' NCAA Tourney 'Cartel.'" *Deadspin,* July 11. https://deadspin.com/.

McConaghy, Mary D., and Michael T. Woods (2005). "Penn Athletics in the Nineteenth Century: The Origins of Penn Athletics." https://archives.upenn.edu/.

McKennan, Claudia J. (2009). "Intercollegiate Debate: Reflecting American Culture 1900–1930." *Argumentation and Advocacy* 46, no. 2: 79–97.

Mendenhall, Thomas C. (1993). "The First Boat Race." *Yale Alumni Magazine,* March. http://archives.yalealumnimagazine.com/.

National Collegiate Athletic Association (2017). "National Office Leadership Team." NCAA.org. http://www.ncaa.org/.

———. (2018). "Composition and Sport Sponsorship of the NCAA Membership." NCAA.org. http://www.ncaa.org/.

———. (2021). "17.1.7.3.2 Competition Day." NCAA LSDBi. https://web3.ncaa.org/.

———. (2022). "Probability of Competing beyond High School." https://www.ncaa.org/ (accessed August 8).

NCAA Archives (2012). "NIT Post-season History." NCAA.org, February 16. http://www.ncaa.com/.

NCAA Eligibility Center (2017). *2017–2018 Guide for Four-Year Transfers.* Indianapolis, IN: National Collegiate Athletic Association. http://www.ncaa.org/.

NCAA Staff (2017). "Where Does the Money Go?" NCAA.org. https://www.ncaa.org/.

———. (2019). "2019 National College Football Attendance." https://www.ncaa.org/.

Nielsen Company (2018). "Nielsen Sports Year in Sports Media Report: U.S. 2017." https://www.nielsen.com/.

Nocera, Joe (2016). "One-and-Done System Gets a Documentary. Call It a Farce." *New York Times,* October 30. https://www.nytimes.com/.

Non Profit Light (2021). National Collegiate Athletic Association. https://nonprofitlight.com/.

Novy-Williams, Eben, and Anthony Crupi (2020). "ESPN's $793 Million in Ad Sales on the Line with College Football." *Sportico,* July 24. https://www.sportico.com/.

Ohr, Peter Sung (2014). "Northwestern University and College Athletes Players Association (CAPA), Petitioner," March 26. Case 13-RC-121359. https://www.nlrb.gov/.

Oriard, Michael (1998). *Reading Football: How the Popular Press Created an American Spectacle.* Chapel Hill: University of North Carolina Press.

———. (2002). "Football, Cultural History and Democracy." *Journal of Sport History* 29, no. 2: 241–49.

———. (2009). *Bowled Over: Big-Time College Football from the Sixties to the BCS Era.* Chapel Hill: University of North Carolina Press.

Parlow, Matthew J. (2015). "The Potential Unintended Consequences of the *O'Bannon* Decision." *Washington and Lee Law Review* 71, no. 4: 203–14. http://scholarlycommons.law.wlu.edu/.

Perry, Elisabeth Israels, and Jennifer Ann Price (2006). *An American Girl and Her Four Years in a Boys' College.* Ann Arbor: University of Michigan Press.

Pierce, Palmer E. (1907). "The International Athletic Association of the United States: Its Origin, Growth, and Function." *Proceedings of the Second Annual Convention of the Intercollegiate Athletic Association of the United States* 3, 85–90. December 28.

Plyley, Dale E. (1997). "The AIAW vs. the NCAA: A Struggle for Power to Govern Women's Athletics in American Institutions of Higher Education." PhD dissertation, University of Western Ontario. http://www.collectionscanada.gc.ca/.

Porter, Andrew (2017). "10 UGA Student Jobs More Fun than Georgia Football." *College Magazine,* October 3. https://www.collegemagazine.com/.

Rascher, Daniel A., and Andrew D. Schwarz (2000). "Neither Reasonable nor Necessary: 'Amateurism' in Big-Time College Sports." Special sports issue, *Antitrust Magazine,* Spring. https://papers.ssrn.com/.

Ross, Theodore (2015). "Cracking the Cartel: Don't Pay NCAA Football and Basketball Players." *New Republic*, September 1. https://newrepublic.com/.

Ruffalo Noel Levitz (2021). "2020 Cost of Recruiting an Undergraduate Student Report." https://www.ruffalonl.com/.

Rykoff, Amanda (2011). "Kellmeyer: 'Title IX Was What I Was Most Proud Of.'" ESPN.com, August 9. http://www.espn.com/espnw/features/article/6843871/title-ix-was-most-proud-of.

Sack, Allen L., and Ellen J. Staurowsky (1998). *College Athletes for Hire: The Evolution and Legacy of the NCAA Amateur Myth.* Westport, CT: Praeger.

SI Wire (2015). "Clemson Tigers Banned from Social Media During Season." *SI.com*, August 15. https://www.si.com/college-football/2015/08/15/clemson-tigers-social-media-ban.

Smith, Chris (1990). *Sports and Freedom: The Rise of Big-Time College Athletics.* New York: Oxford University Press.

———. (2003). *Play-by-Play: Radio, Television, and Big-Time College Sport.* Baltimore: Johns Hopkins University Press.

———. (2011). *Pay for Play: A History of Big-Time College Athletic Reform.* Urbana: University of Illinois Press.

———. (2017). "The Money on the Line in the College Football National Championship Game." *Forbes*, January 9. https://www.forbes.com/.

Solomon, Jon (2013). "Big Ten in Division III? Jim Delany Says It's Possible if College Players Can Share Revenue." *AL.com*, March 19. https://www.al.com/.

———. (2014a). "What NCAA Talking Points Look Like about Pay-for-Play and Unions." CBS Sports, April 13. https://www.al.com/sports/index.ssf/2014/04/what_do_ncaa_talking_points_ab.html.

———. (2014b). "If Football, Men's Basketball Players Get Paid, What about Women?" CBS Sports, June 5. https://www.cbssports.com/.

———. (2016). "'It's All Business': Jim Harbaugh and His Disappearing Michigan Recruits." CBS Sports, January 26. https://www.cbssports.com/.

Southall, Richard M., and Mark S. Nagel (2008). "A Case-Study Analysis of NCAA Division I Women's Basketball Tournament Broadcasts: Educational or Commercial Activity?" *International Journal of Sport Communication* 1, no. 4: 516–33.

Southall, Richard M., and Jonathan D. Weiler (2014). "NCAA D-I Athletic Departments: Twenty-First Century Company Towns." *Journal of Issues in Intercollegiate Athletics* 7: 161–86.

Sperber, Murray A. (2002). *Shake down the Thunder: The Creation of Notre Dame Football.* Bloomington: Indiana University Press.

Sports Illustrated Staff (2016). "The Fifty Most Watched Sporting Events in 2016." *SI.com*, July 15. https://www.si.com/.

Stancil, Benn (2014). "Ninety Years of College Football Recruiting, in One Map." *Mode Blog*, February 6. https://blog.modeanalytics.com/.

Staurowsky, Ellen J. (2012). "'A Radical Proposal': Title IX Has No Place in College Sport Pay-for-Play Discussions." *Marquette Sports Law Review* 22, no. 2: 575–95. http://scholarship.law.marquette.edu/.

———. (2016). *Women and Sport: Continuing a Journey from Liberation to Celebration.* Champaign, IL: Human Kinetics.

———. (2017). "The National Letter of Intent." In *College Athletes' Rights and Well-Being: Critical Perspectives on Policy and Practice*, 23–31. edited by Eddie Comeaux. Baltimore: Johns Hopkins University Press.

———. (2018a). "College Athletes as Employees and the Politics of Title IX." In *Sport and the Neoliberal University: Profit, Politics, and Pedagogy*, edited by Ryan King-White, 97–130. New Brunswick, NJ: Rutgers University Press.

———. (2018b). "College Scholarships and Recruiting." In *Youth Sports in America: The Most Important Issues in Youth Sports Today*, edited by Skye Arthur-Banning, 78–91. Santa Barbara, CA: ABC-Clio.

Staurowsky, Ellen J., and Jeffrey Orleans (2014). "College Sports Need a Fundamental Rethink." *US News and World Report*, April 4. https://www.usnews.com/.

Staurowsky, Ellen J., and Erianne Weight (2011). "Title IX Literacy: What Coaches Don't Know and Need to Find Out." *Journal of Intercollegiate Sport* 4, no. 2: 190–209.

Stewart, Robert (2016). "The Interview: NCAA President Mark Emmert." *The Greater Baton Rouge Business Report*, September 28. https://www.businessreport.com/.

Thelin, John R. (1996). *Games Colleges Play: Scandal and Reform in Intercollegiate Athletics*. Baltimore: Johns Hopkins University Press.

Trahan, Kevin (2014). "The 3 Big Things to Know about the SEC Network for Launch Day." *SB Nation*, August 14. http://www.sbnation.com/.

24/7 Sports (2017). 2017 Football Recruits Search. https://247sports.com/.

University of Georgia Athletic Association (2021). Staff directory. https://georgiadogs.com/.

University of Notre Dame (2021). "First Game in Notre Dame Football History." https://125.nd.edu/.

US Congress (2014). Hearing on College Athletes and Academics, US Committee on Commerce, Science, and Transportation, Washington, DC, July 9. https://www.c-span.org/.

US Department of Labor (2016). "Field Operations Handbook: Chapter 10: FLSA Coverage: Employment Relationship, Statutory Exclusions, Geographical Limits." Washington, DC, March 31. https://www.dol.gov/.

Verbrugge, Martha H. (2012). *Active Bodies: A History of Women's Physical Education in Twentieth-Century America*. New York: Oxford University Press.

Waldman, Dan (2017). "How a Northwestern Startup Plans to Revolutionize College Football Recruiting." *Daily Northwestern*, July 7. https://dailynorthwestern.com/.

Ware, Susan (2014). *Title IX: A Brief History with Documents*. Long Grove, IL: Waveland.

Watterson, John S. (2010). "Walter Camp: Gridiron Reform?" *College Football Historical Society* 23, no. 111: 1–4. http://library.la84.org/SportsLibrary/CFHSN/.

Wellman, James, and Walter B. Peet (1912). *The Story of the Harvard-Yale Race 1852–1912*. New York: Harper. https://archive.org/stream/storyofharvardyaoowell/.

Wilke, Phyllis Kay (1973). "The History of Physical Education for Women at the University of Nebraska from the Early Beginnings to 1952." PhD dissertation, University of Nebraska. http://digitalcommons.unl.edu/cgi/.

Willens, Max (2017). "Anatomy of a Media Failure: Why Scout Media Flamed Out." *Digiday*, February 14. https://digiday.com/.

Wisconsin Badgers (2022). "Football History vs University of Minnesota from Nov 15, 1890–Nov 27, 2021." https://uwbadgers.com/.

Women's Sports Foundation (2019). "History of Title IX." August 13. https://www.womenssportsfoundation.org/.

Woodhouse. Kellie (2015). “NCAA Novices: When Universities That Are Sports Powerhouses Appoint Presidents with Little Experience in Intercollegiate Athletics, New Leaders Face a Steep Learning Curve.” *Inside Higher Ed*, April 16. https://www.insidehighered.com/.

Woodward, C. M. (1903). “The New Departure in Athletic Control.” *School Review* 11, no. 5: 321–28.

Wushanley, Ying (2004). *Playing Nice and Losing: The Struggle for Control of Women's Intercollegiate Athletics, 1960–2000*. Syracuse: Syracuse University Press.

College Sport Workplace Economics

Suppressing Player Compensation to Increase Profits

Joel G. Maxcy

A frequent argument made by devotees of Power Five and Group of Five "big-time" college sports is that these universities could not afford the projected increase in labor costs if profit-athletes were to be classified as employees and compensated in accordance with their market value. Yet this fiscal excuse for not paying profit-athletes is iniquitous, and those who champion this rationale are propagating a falsehood. Since big-time college sport is a highly lucrative enterprise, restraining direct, market-based monetary compensation (i.e., pay) to the labor of its most valuable input (e.g., football) allows for the distribution of accumulated returns to other sports and various interests within athletic departments and the universities.

Currently there is no prohibition (legal or otherwise) preventing profit-athletes (or for that matter any college athletes) from being classified as employees.[1] In fact, in nearly any other context those who provide the services or products associated with a commercial enterprise are classified as employees. However, the narrative that the Division I college sport enterprise is not thriving financially is used to shield it from robust financial scrutiny. The assumption that Power Five college sport's operating costs far exceed revenues is a myth that is dispelled in this chapter.

Many people, including many college reformers, mistakenly accept the "college sport as pauper" mythology. Consequently, instead of advocating for appropriate compensation for Power Five football and NCAA Division I men's basketball players, many college sport reformers routinely offer policy solutions that do not consider profit-athletes' fundamental rights. The Knight Commission on Intercollegiate Athletics and The Drake Group are two prominent examples.[2] The concern that Power Five universities cannot afford the fiscal drag of reasonable and competitive wages for their football and basketball athletes is specious at best but is more fittingly described as corrupt. A related and equally illogical argument is the artificial redistribution problem, in which reformers claim that should profit-athletes be paid fairly, resources would be diverted from non-revenue sports or the universities' academic mission.

While Power Five universities are classified as nonprofit organizations, like some other commercial enterprises housed within a university footprint (e.g., hotels, bookstores, and hospitals), their football and men's basketball programs generate substantial revenue and often return a profit.[3]

While it is undeniable that Power Five football and men's basketball programs generate substantial revenues, several Football Bowl Subdivision (FBS) Group of 5 members and major conference men's basketball programs also produce surplus revenue.[4] Given an influx of high-value television and media contracts, that income has increased significantly since 2010. The financial returns from competing in Power Five football, and to a lesser extent Division I men's basketball, largely exceed the costs of operating those programs. Thus in a business context these programs are profitable, meaning that in isolation their revenue-less-cost equations document substantial positive financial returns.

Nonetheless, since athletic departments frequently do not follow Generally Accepted Accounting Principles (GAAP), obtaining a clear picture of individual team finances is often difficult for several reasons. First, in college sport returns are not realized by a football or basketball program independently, as would be the case for a professional sport franchise. Second, some football or men's basketball revenue may be concealed within the overall athletic department budget, which includes all other sponsored sports, most of which generate little revenue. Third, revenues can be obscured within the total university budget where financial transfers (e.g., expenses, including landscaping, custodial services, utilities, etc.) between the athletic department and the university's central fund are often ambiguous.

Considering universities' investments in varsity sport programs through the proper lens of economic objective function—that is, in the context of how such athletic programs act as a means to achieve a university's overall mission, goals, and objectives—reveals that rather than athletic programs being a fiscal drag, FBS universities' football and men's basketball programs often produce positive returns on investments. In addition it must be remembered that college athletics cannot just be measured in direct financial returns. Any calculated yield must include significant spillovers of return on objectives to overall publicity and exposure for the university, as well as the creation of significant amenity values for several constituent groups including alumni, donors, corporate partners, and students. While the deliberate suppression of compensation to the profit-athletes responsible for producing much of this value is a financially astute strategy, it is clearly remarkably exploitative and fundamentally unjust.

A subordinate argument against fairly compensating profit-athletes is that cross-subsidization from football and men's basketball to non-revenue (e.g., Olympic) sports is necessary and consistent with college sport's purported educational mission.[5] However, the argument that the survival of NCAA Olympic sports is dependent on cross subsidization from the "profit" sports is a myth.[6] Power Five universities maintain non-revenue sports for the same reasons they exist and thrive at the majority of colleges and universities whose football and basketball programs do not produce significant revenue. Universities choose to invest in intercollegiate athletics because it contributes to their mission and objectives.[7] Potential benefits from sponsored college sport include generating publicity that attracts larger student applicant pools and sport-specific donations from alumni and other stakeholders. Sponsoring Olympic sports also assists a university in meeting legal and regulatory standards including compliance with Title IX along with meeting NCAA standards for sport offerings.[8] Compensating profit-athletes equitably does not alter the rationale for sponsoring Olympic sports; the two are not mutually exclusive.

Revenue streams, along with costs that should most appropriately be attributed to the athletic department, are often confounded within full university budgets, which are separated by unit. For example, revenue from team athletic apparel sold at the college bookstore is credited on that unit's ledger, not the athletic department's. In addition, a university's budget should not be confused with that of a for-profit entity that answers to shareholders. Universities competing in Power Five and Group of 5 football and Division I men's basketball are, with rare exceptions, classified as nonprofit institutions. Their stakeholders include alumni, donors, students and their parents, faculty, administration, and, for public universities, state legislatures, taxpayers, and voters. Unlike corporate shareholders, these various constituents seek alternative and diverse returns, not simply bottom-line revenue maximization. Prestige, often represented by position in national and international rankings (e.g., those published by *US News and World Report*), is often more desirable to administrators and other constituents than simple profit goals. Arguably the positive spillovers toward increased selectivity, gifts and endowments, and recognition are all supported by the publicity and attention accorded big-time sports programs and provide a benefit to a university above and beyond an athletic department's balance sheet. If athletics helps a university improve or maintain its rank, and subsequently its enrollment, this suggests a substantial return on objectives for varsity athletics.

Athletics' Contribution to University Objectives

The prominence and commercial value of intercollegiate competitions is unique to American universities, and the argument that college sport conflicts rather than supports universities' educational objectives is nearly as old as intercollegiate athletics. The development and continued growth of college sports into a significant commercial endeavor have generated concern and controversy since the first intercollegiate competitions. A number of researchers, including Noll (1999), Fort (2010, 2015, 2016), and Getz and Siegfried (2012), have identified economic incentives for universities' ventures into athletics. While many athletic departments increasingly operate in a very businesslike fashion, Maxcy (2013) suggests the NCAA is organized and functions to maximize the economic value of college sports for its members.

Nonetheless, for a majority of US college athletic departments, expenses exceed direct revenues generated. Therefore these units (like many other departments on campus) operate in the red and require the transfer of funds from elsewhere within the university (Desrochers 2013).[9] However, to warrant these transfers, investments in support of intercollegiate athletics must generate positive economic value (i.e., spillover benefits) to other university units and departments.[10]

In addition to determining whether or not its athletic department generates direct profits, a university also evaluates the benefits derived from its sport enterprise (regardless of whether or not the enterprise is commercialized—see Mark S. Nagel's chapter "Some College Athletes Are Employees"). Many benefits may be intangible, including attempting to maximize perceived prestige in order to attract the best students and faculty as well as raise funds and build endowments through dedicated gifts and/or grants from alumni and foundations.

Two principal indirect benefits of investment in intercollegiate athletics have been widely considered in the economics literature. The first is that winning athletic programs (specifically football and men's basketball) generate additional applications from prospective students and thus a higher-quality student body drawn from a larger applicant pool. The second is that a winning intercollegiate athletic program leads to additional gifts from alumni and support from other sources. The most recent research provides convincing evidence that student applications do increase with success in intercollegiate athletics.[11] The effect of sport success on increased donations and government appropriations to a university at large remains less conclusive but more often is supported in the past two decades (e.g., Humphreys and Mondello 2007).

Interestingly most research on spillover benefits has defined athletic success in relation to a university's performance in football or men's basketball (for example, end-of-season rank in national polls, championships, football bowl game appearances, and March Madness men's basketball tournament success). This is because the national media attention of these two sports is considerable, and much of the value of intercollegiate athletics is drawn from a high-profile program's function as a public relations and marketing vehicle. In addition Pope and Pope (2009) found a strong relationship between football and men's basketball success and the quantity of student applications. They also found applications increased across a range of high- and low-quality applicants.

Consequently a university that has more athletic success can, through its process of selection, improve admissions outcomes and incoming class quality. The importance of athletics as a medium for public universities to reach potential students in a broader market is increasingly apparent. In June 2016 *US News and World Report* reported that in order to offset state budget cuts in higher education, public colleges and universities—especially state flagships—are attempting to increase out-of-state enrollment (Powell 2016).

The University of Alabama, whose football team has won six FBS national titles from 2009 to 2023, is a striking example of a university using athletic success and visibility as a marketing tool to recruit out-of-state students. Reflecting this trend, in-state residents made up only 37 percent of Alabama's 2018 senior class, compared with 73 percent of in-state first-year students in the 2004–5 school year (Koplowitz 2019). This outcome reflects a financial strategy, since in the 2019–20 academic year out-of-state tuition and fees totaled $31,050, compared with $11,580 for in-state students—a positive difference of $19,470 (University of Alabama 2020).

Funds reallocated to an athletic department are typically drawn from student fees dedicated to athletics and direct institutional support (e.g., funds drawn from tuition, endowments, state appropriations, and other university resources). Because such distributions are common, the assumption is that real or intangible benefits from intercollegiate athletics must spill over to other areas of the university, otherwise funds would not be allocated to support athletic programs.

An amicus brief filed by sport economics and sport management professors in support of Northwestern University football players' petition to the NLRB in 2014 noted several more examples of administrators' perceptions of the returns from major college sports (see Maxcy, Rascher, and Schwarz 2014). NCAA members recognize the benefits of FBS football and other successful sports programs well beyond the direct financial returns that accounting profits from these programs indicate. Historically many university executives profess a belief that NCAA sports contribute to a university's psychic and cultural development. During his tenure at Kansas State University, President Jon Wefald saw Kansas State's football team rise from the ranks of the worst in Division I to a perennial top-ten powerhouse. As he put it, "When I got here, there was a sense of futility. . . . If the old administration had stayed on here for three more years, I think football would have been dropped. We would have no marching band, and we'd be at about 12,000 students today" (quoted in Rascher and Schwarz 2015: 15). Kansas State's enrollment increased from about thirteen thousand in 1986 to twenty-three thousand by 2003, its fundraising had gone from $7 million a year to $83 million, and the economy of the city of Manhattan, Kansas, had grown exponentially (ibid.).

An increased applicant pool and higher enrollment of non-athlete students (especially out-of-state students) is an example of a benefit that does not appear as a line item on an athletic department budget. Several examples of this phenomenon—at both public and private universities—paint a consistent picture: athletic success translates into university success. Reflecting this, in 2007 a Portland State University administrator said that "because of the success of our soccer teams, we have received literally hundreds of thousands of dollars in free publicity. In addition, when the press covers sports, we are often on the first or second page of the sports section. The other local private schools barely get mentioned, or if so on the back page" (Rascher and Howell 2011: 32). Gonzaga University's president made similar comments regarding its men's basketball team's success, which was claimed to have increased applications. Interestingly, while Gonzaga had not collected any supporting data, a causal relationship was claimed: "Without trying to get too precise, because we don't have the quantitative data to support it, you'd have to say that certainly well over 50% of the application rise [is due to public relations]. And that PR is attributable in great part to basketball" (Lieber 2004). After being invited to join the Big 12 Conference in 2012, Ray Brown, dean of admissions at Texas Christian University, directly credited the success of its Horned Frogs football team for its 20 percent growth in out-of-state enrollment in 2009–15 (Powell 2016).[12]

Studies by other schools with recent athletic success support the concept of spillover effects. For example, Butler University, which reached the Division I men's basketball championship game in both 2010 and 2011, commissioned a study that found the total value of the media coverage of their basketball success over that two-year period to be in excess of $1 billion. Butler reported the number of applications for admission increased by 40 percent from the immediately preceding years, with significant increases in ticket and merchandise sales as well as donations (Imbert 2015 2011).

While returns from college sport are evident across all levels of competition, far and away the largest benefits are from Power Five football and Division I men's basketball programs, which are also profitable in and of themselves. Any argument that begins with the premise that most Power Five football programs lose money rests on a distorted picture with little relationship to the true state of the industry. Taking claims of poverty at face value without critically examining tailored analyses (by the NCAA, as well as Power Five conferences) ignores the fact that on a purely monetary basis, Power Five football programs show high profits, often exceeding millions of dollars a year. At Texas A&M, the most profitable football program in 2015–16, revenues exceeded expenses by more than $50 million (Baby 2017). By the 2017–18 season, Texas A&M's three-year average profits had increased to $94 million (Buchholz 2019). Moreover, nothing in standard NCAA analyses captures the strong positive contributions of Power Five sports to universities. In addition there is no economic justification for relying on the self-devised accounting practices of the NCAA or Power Five conferences to assess the economic health of Power Five football programs or their ability to thrive in a world in which profit-athletes would negotiate payment for their services (whether as individuals or through collective bargaining).

When economists have been able to gain access to the real numbers at a particular Power Five university, they have found that football, men's basketball, and the overall athletic department are typically much more profitable than publicly reported. The revealed preference behavior of market participants is a good indicator of the most-preferred choice among available options. The expectation is that firms that do not anticipate a reasonable probability of profits exit the market or do not enter it in the first place. According to standard industrial organization theory, an industry's profitability can be inferred from the willingness of firms to enter or exit a market (Waldman and Jensen 2019). A market in which all but a few programs (out of more than 350) are losing money does not experience the sort of entry seen in the NCAA's Division I since the 1980s when the association's television monopoly was broken. Since 1984 more than 85 Division I schools with basketball programs have entered or reentered the division, while only 15 have left. Over the same time period, 28 schools with football programs have entered or reentered FBS, while only 6 universities have reclassified their football program to a lower level. No FBS school has entirely dropped football since the University of the Pacific in 1996.[13] In that timeframe the only FBS member to drop back to FCS is the University of Idaho in 2018 (Wolverton and Bauman 2016). In 2007 the NCAA instituted a moratorium preventing further entries to DI, an indication of excess demand. Following the end of the moratorium in 2011, six then-current FCS members immediately announced a transition to FBS, and several more have entered since, bringing the current total to 130 universities (Dodd 2013).

Power Five Football and Men's Basketball as Profit Centers

Power Five college football and men's basketball are highly successful consumer products, comparable in terms of paid attendance, corporate sponsorship, and television viewership to American major league professional sports. Figure 1 shows that FBS football is indeed a profit center for university athletic departments and that those profits are concentrated in the Power Five conferences.

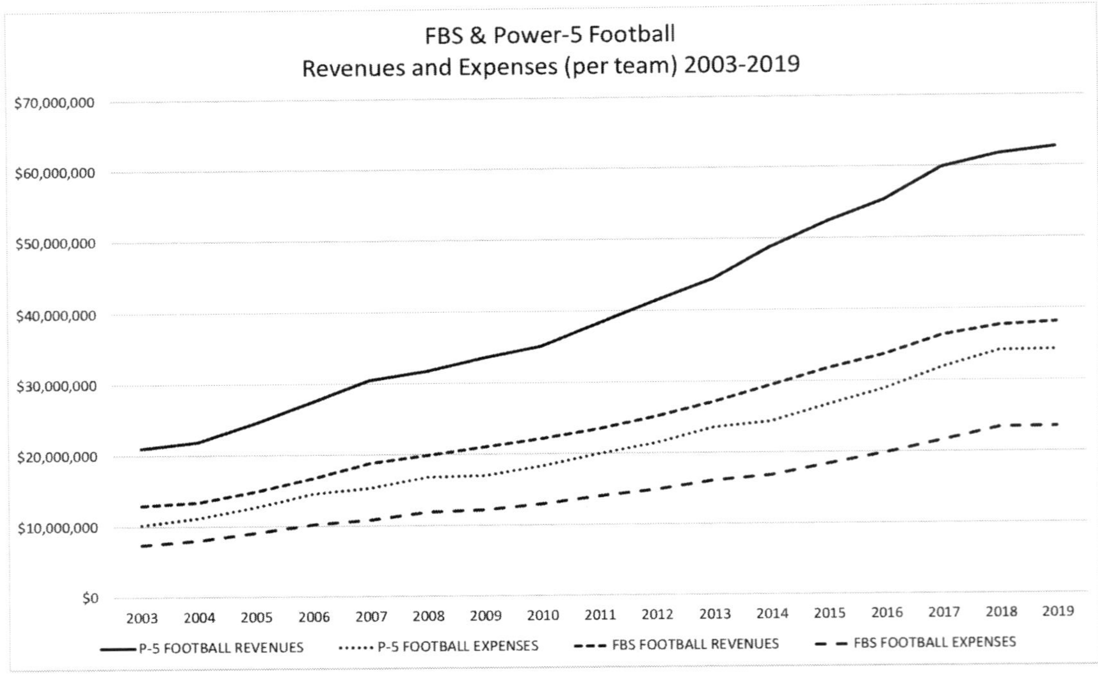

Figure 1. Football Bowl Subdivision and Power Five football revenue and expenses.

Moreover, since 2002 profits are increasing an average of 6 percent per year above the inflation rate.

College football and men's basketball collectively draw millions of in-person fans each year, and many millions more view games on television. According to ESPN, the College Football Playoff (CFP) is consistently the best "non-NFL" broadcast event, with the 2021 CFP semifinals the top cable telecasts since the 2020 CFP national championship game (Brooks 2021). In addition Division I men's basketball national championship games are consistently among the top twenty most watched sport broadcasts each year. Only the NFL's Super Bowl and playoff games and the deciding seventh games of National Basketball Association (NBA) championship finals and semifinals consistently have higher viewership (Paulsen 2016). Reflecting the robust nature of big-time college football and basketball, these sports' media rights are among the most lucrative in the entertainment industry (Cassillo 2021).

Power Five football and men's basketball spectator totals actually outpace professional sports attendance. Indicative of this, the average NFL stadium has a seating capacity of about 70,000 seats, with MetLife Stadium (where the New York Giants and New York Jets play) having the largest seating capacity at 82,500, while AT&T Stadium (where the Dallas Cowboys play) has the largest peak capacity of 100,000 spectators. By comparison twenty-five Power Five stadiums surpass the NFL average, with "crowds of 100,000-plus [having] become commonplace . . . thanks to extraordinary renovations and multimillion-dollar projects" (Chiusano 2021). Seven schools boast home stadiums that hold more than 100,000 fans, with eighteen exceeding 80,000 in seating capacity (ibid.). Many Power Five teams routinely sell out their entire home schedule. The Final Four and all regional finals of the NCAA men's basketball tournament are now held in domed football stadiums with basketball seating configurations that allow for in excess of 70,000 fans. While Division I men's basketball arenas do not dwarf NBA stadiums, they are comparable, with 6 arenas having seating capacities of greater than 20,000 (compared to 5 in the NBA) and 106 in excess of 10,000 (Fueled by Sports 2019).

In addition to ticket sales, parking, concessions, and merchandise, Power Five football annually earns hundreds of millions of dollars from lucrative media-rights deals, on average 50 percent more than Group of 5 schools. Division I men's basketball is not as lucrative, but nonetheless many programs generate substantial basketball revenue. Over the past decade, revenues in both sports have grown steadily at a rate that far outpaces inflation. Tracking this growth, the NCAA and federal government both collect detailed financial data. The federal data is compiled from annual reports from all American universities sponsoring college sports and disclosed in compliance with the Equity in Athletics Disclosure Act (EADA). Categories reported by institutions include aggregate revenue, expenses, and staffing as well as information for each sponsored men's, women's, and coed sports programs.

Despite accounting practices that obscure Power Five football's actual economic success, in their official filings to the federal government, programs consistently self-report revenues in excess of costs.[14] Table 1 reports that in 2003–18 inflation-adjusted average revenues for FBS men's football increased from more than $17 million to more than $58 million, an increase of more than 7 percent per year on average in inflation-adjusted dollars. In some years the steady growth exceeded 10 percent. At no time during the fifteen reported years did revenue or profit decline. Not surprisingly, given the nature of the NCAA's collegiate model, expenses likewise increased at a rate almost identical to revenue.

Power Five profits and growth rates are reported in Table 2 and illustrated in Figure 1.[15] Most striking is the significant gap between Power Five and Group of 5 programs, with an average Power Five football program earning nearly $60 million per year in 2017–18—nearly double the average of the full FBS group (Wolverton and Bauman 2016). In addition the growth rate in Power Five revenues, expenses, and profits is slightly higher than FBS averages (about 5 percent per year through the period). It should also be noted that by 2017–18 average Power Five profits had grown to about $35 million per school. The University of Texas led the way, earning more than $100 million in net revenues from football. Cementing the conclusion that Power Five football is in fact profitable, all but 1 of the 66 Power Five members reported revenues of at least $5 million in excess of reported costs.

Further examination of Power Five data reveals a significant and noteworthy revenue increase of more than 11 percent occurred in 2013—a surge that coincided with increased television broadcast revenue. Notably, in addition to newly negotiated broadcast rights contracts, the SEC and Pac-12 both established new and lucrative digital networks. Not surprisingly given the Power Five philosophy of spending nearly all generated revenues, the 11 percent revenue growth was nearly matched by an 11 percent increase in expenses. The increased revenue facilitated an immediately noticeable increase in head coaches' pay, which increased by almost 12 percent across the FBS in 2012–13 (Brady, Berkowitz, and Upton 2012).

While Division I men's basketball, like football, generates revenues in excess of reported expenses, it produces on average only about one-third of the revenue of FBS football. Complete major conference men's basketball profits and growth rates are reported in table 3. As can be seen, revenues are significant and growing, and by 2018 exceeded an annual average of $10 million per program. However, basketball expenses have grown at a significantly faster rate than revenues, and net revenue (profit) has increased only marginally, less than 0.25 percent per year, over the fifteen-year period. Nonetheless figure 2 clearly shows

Table 1. Football Bowl Subdivision football per-team average revenue and expenses: 2003–18

YEAR	TEAMS	REVENUE	GROWTH RATE, %	EXPENSES	GROWTH RATE, %	PROFIT	GROWTH RATE, %
2003	116	$17,335,148		$9,811,275		$7,523,872	
2004	116	$17,486,699	0.87	$10,392,707	5.93	$7,093,992	–5.71
2005	115	$19,077,365	9.10	$11,426,273	9.95	$7,651,092	7.85
2006	115	$20,759,131	8.82	$12,457,356	9.02	$8,206,737	7.26
2007	116	$22,311,104	7.48	$12,706,596	2.00	$9,604,508	17.03
2008	117	$22,659,652	1.56	$13,465,120	5.97	$9,194,532	–4.27
2009	117	$24,161,711	6.63	$13,798,717	2.48	$10,362,994	12.71
2010	117	$25,161,691	4.14	$14,595,743	5.78	$10,565,947	1.96
2011	117	$26,302,345	4.53	$15,431,117	5.72	$10,871,228	2.89
2012	122	$26,992,994	2.63	$15,812,772	2.47	$11,180,222	2.84
2013	124	$27,982,669	3.67	$16,746,252	5.90	$11,236,417	0.50
2014	124	$30,048,513	7.38	$17,087,282	2.04	$12,961,231	15.35
2015	126	$32,098,492	6.82	$18,538,233	8.49	$13,560,259	4.62
2016	124	$33,958,406	5.79	$19,977,409	7.76	$13,980,998	3.10
2017	124	$34,957,886	2.94	$20,918,441	4.71	$14,039,445	0.42
2018	125	$35,394,611	1.25	$22,002,590	5.18	$13,392,020	–4.61
2003–18			102.4		111.7		88.78
Per annum			4.91		5.56		4.13

Note. Inflation adjustments made using 2014 as base year. $ = 2014 values.

Source: EADA Database, Bureau of Labor Statistics Database.

Table 2. Power Five football per-team average revenue and expenses: 2003–18

YEAR	TEAMS	REVENUE	GROWTH RATE, %	EXPENSES	GROWTH RATE, %	PROFIT	GROWTH RATE, %
2003	65	$27,149,732		$13,215,284		$13,934,448	
2004	65	$27,303,214	0.57	$13,993,602	5.89	$13,309,612	–4.48
2005	65	$29,249,669	7.13	$15,159,995	8.34	$14,089,674	5.86
2006	65	$31,580,492	7.97	$16,755,051	10.52	$14,659,844	4.05
2007	65	$33,884,930	7.30	$17,133,512	2.26	$16,751,418	14.27
2008	65	$34,070,228	0.55	$18,151,944	5.94	$15,918,284	–4.97
2009	65	$36,072,535	5.88	$18,389,314	1.31	$17,683,221	11.09
2010	65	$37,337,350	3.51	$19,535,967	6.24	$17,801,383	0.67
2011	65	$39,020,176	4.51	$20,489,582	4.88	$18,530,595	4.10
2012	65	$40,615,318	4.09	$21,546,362	5.16	$19,068,956	2.91
2013	65	$45,295,903	11.52	$23,929,569	11.06	$21,366,334	12.05
2014	65	$48,169,119	6.34	$24,214,211	1.19	$23,954,909	12.12
2015	65	$52,280,312	8.53	$26,655,408	10.08	$25,624,905	6.97
2016	65	$55,129,764	5.45	$28,768,336	7.93	$26,361,428	2.87
2017	65	$56,963,455	3.33	$30,426,889	5.77	$26,536,567	0.66
2018	65	$58,137,643	2.06	$32,205,397	5.85	$25,932,245	–2.28
2003–18			114.1		143.7		86.1
Per annum			7.61		9.58		5.74

Note. Inflation adjustments made using 2014 as base year. $ = 2014 values.

Source: EADA Database, Bureau of Labor Statistics.

Table 3. Per-team revenue and expenses NCAA Division I men's basketball: 2002–3 to 2017–18

YEAR	TEAMS	REVENUE, M	GROWTH RATE, %	EXPENSES, M	GROWTH RATE, %	PROFIT	GROWTH RATE, %
2003	112	$6,236,506		$3,490,530		$27,45,975	
2004	111	$6,616,590	6.09	$3,770,044	8.01	$2,846,546	3.66
2005	110	$6,856,532	3.63	$4,402,728	16.78	$2,453,804	−13.80
2006	113	$6,962,163	1.54	$4,298,088	−2.38	$2,664,075	8.57
2007	113	$7,487,534	7.55	$4,684,043	8.98	$2,803,491	5.23
2008	113	$7,553,927	0.89	$4,820,267	2.91	$2,733,660	−2.49
2009	113	$8,371,719	10.83	$5,136,162	6.55	$3,235,557	18.36
2010	113	$8,555,142	2.19	$5,425,127	5.63	$3,130,015	−3.26
2011	113	$8,854,190	3.50	$5,855,138	7.93	$2,999,052	−4.18
2012	113	$9,088,343	2.64	$5,940,952	1.47	$3,147,391	4.95
2013	117	$9,061,959	−0.29	$6,248,722	5.18	$2,813,238	−10.62
2014	118	$9,162,553	1.11	$6,445,452	3.15	$2,717,102	−3.42
2015	126	$8,315,640	−0.29	$6,005,981	5.18	$2,309,659	−10.62
2016	124	$8,718,669	1.11	$6,307,867	3.15	$2,410,802	−3.42
2017	124	$9,584,605	−9.24	$6,625,749	−6.82	$2,958,856	−15.00
2018	125	$10,085,428	4.85	$6,725,525	5.03	$3,359,903	4.38
2003–18			61.72		92.68		22.36
Per annum			2.41		4.72		0.23

Note. Inflation adjustments made using 2014 as base year.

Source: EADA Database, Bureau of Labor Statistics.

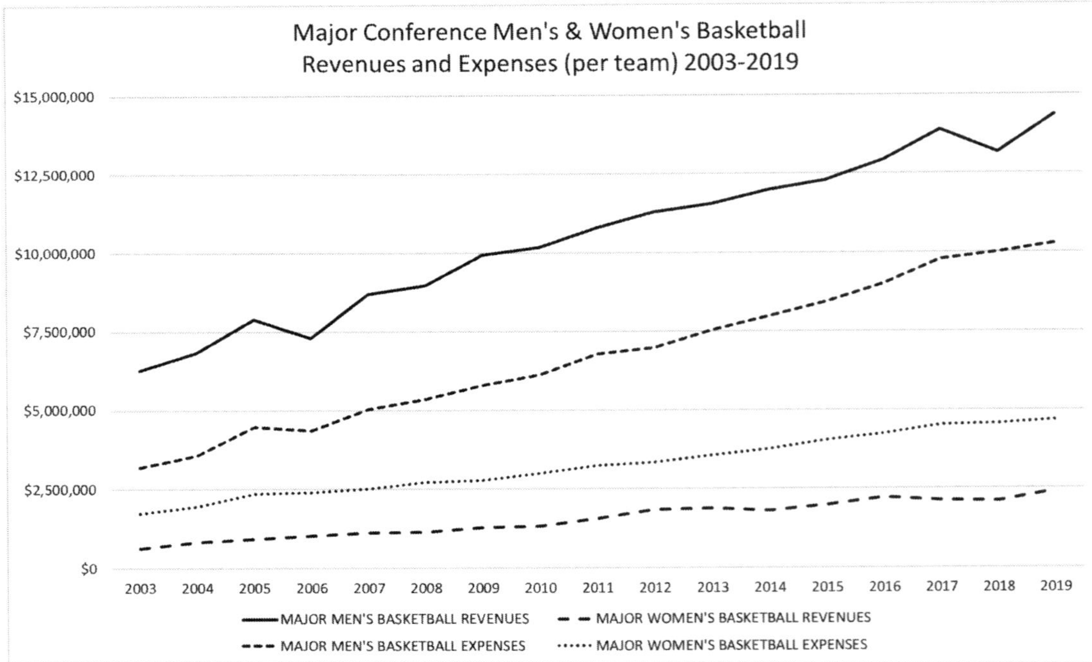

Figure 2. NCAA Major Conference Men's and Women's Basketball revenue and expenses.

that major NCAA Division I basketball programs are profit centers for athletic departments.

In contrast to the profit sports of Power Five football and men's basketball, almost all other college sports are loss centers. However, as seen in figure 2 and reported in table 4, it is apparent that average major women's basketball revenues are also considerable and growing. In fact, while total revenue is substantially less than in men's basketball, the revenue growth rate for women's basketball is actually more than double that of men's basketball and greater than Power Five conference football. However, expenses for women's basketball, though not quite as large, are comparable to those of men's basketball. As a result on average women's major conference basketball teams generate about $1 million less in annual revenue than expenses, and those inflation-adjusted losses have remained steady over the period of analysis. There are, of course, profitable women's basketball teams. Notably the Universities of Tennessee and Connecticut show positive annual net revenue throughout the period, and several other programs have periodically generated net positive revenues. However, year in and year out, the vast majority of women's basketball programs reveal an operating loss.

The comparison of Power Five football and Division I men's basketball to Division I women's basketball is not meant to single out women's basketball as an unprofitable sport but rather to show that even a sport with a significant fanbase—University of South Carolina women's basketball, for example, has led the nation in attendance (in excess of 12,000) every year since 2015–16 (NCAA 2022c)—and that generates considerable revenue and substantial media attention, when isolated as an independent business enterprise, typically operates at a loss.[16]

Even given the on-paper loss, when revenues are measured against expenses, major conference Division I universities choose to invest on average more than $1 million annually in women's basketball. Moreover, most do so without hesitation because the spillover benefits to other university objectives justify such an investment. Likewise universities invest in any number of other unprofitable sports because they also contribute to achieving the university's objectives.

Contributions to Revenue and the Correct Measure of an Athlete's Value

College players' value is at least partially determined based upon the degree to which they help fulfill an entire set of university objectives. However, since 2006, when NCAA president Myles Brand proclaimed in his state of the association address that college sport has a duty to maximize revenue (as is the case in professional sports and other industries), a fundamental measure of a college player's true economic value is the individual's contribution to revenues:

> Athletics, like the university as a whole, seeks to maximize revenues. In this respect, it has an obligation to conduct its revenue-generating activities

Table 4. Revenue and expenses per team in NCAA women's major college basketball, 2002–3 to 2017–18

YEAR	TEAMS	REVENUE	GROWTH RATE, %	EXPENSES	GROWTH RATE, %	PROFIT	GROWTH RATE, %
2003	112	$762,904		$1,934,098		–$1,171,194	–
2004	111	$952,738	24.88	$2,120,306	10.02	–$1,167,568	–0.31
2005	110	$1,098,300	15.28	$2,457,267	8.81	–$1,358,967	16.39
2006	113	$1,018,556	–7.26	$2,341,453	11.86	–$1,322,897	–2.65
2007	113	$1,218,534	19.63	$2,425,012	–1.87	–$1,206,477	–8.80
2008	113	$1,239,748	1.74	$2,531,468	7.37	–$1,291,720	7.07
2009	113	$1,407,490	13.53	$2,575,997	–5.86	–$1,168,507	–9.54
2010	113	$1,456,424	3.48	$2,743,828	5.97	–$1,287,404	10.18
2011	113	$1,633,582	12.16	$2,861,561	2.77	–$1,227,978	–4.62
2012	113	$1,835,982	12.39	$2,913,628	6.75	–$1,077,646	–12.24
2013	117	$1,823,282	–0.69	$3,005,651	3.08	–$1,182,369	9.72
2014	118	$1,776,906	–2.54	$3,103,877	10.31	–$1,326,970	12.23
2015	126	$1,818,810	–0.69	$3,084,979	3.08	–$1,266,169	9.72
2016	124	$2,007,650	–2.54	$3,242,774	10.31	–$1,235,124	12.23
2017	124	$1,862,216	2.36	$3,324,258	–3.45	–$1,462,042	–4.58
2018	125	$2,052,086	10.38	$3,354,923	3.09	–$1,302,837	–2.45
2003–18			168.98		80.61		11.24
Per annum			6.81		9.55		2.16

Note. Inflation adjustments made using 2014 as base year.

Source: EADA Database, Bureau of Labor Statistics.

> in a productive and sound business-like manner. Anything less would be incompetence at best and malfeasance at worst. . . . Commercial activity, meaning, for example, the sale of broadcast rights and logo licensing, is not only acceptable, but mandated by the business plan, provided that it is done so in a way that fully respects the underlying principles of the university. Instances in which advertising is offensive, in which it is crass or overwhelming, are incompatible with these values. But commercialism per se is not. (Brand 2006).

Brand's statement is consistent with the fact that Power Five football programs generate profitable surpluses. Excess funds are most often invested back into the football program but are also spent elsewhere in the athletic department or within the university. The success that Power Five football and men's basketball programs have at generating revenue drives expenditures to a parallel amount and rate of increase, so that profits are stagnant. Brand, in the same 2006 state of the association speech, explained the disincentive for university athletic departments to retain any profits: "Universities attempt to maximize their revenues and redistribute those resources according to their educational mission. Universities are nonprofit corporations, and as such, they do not generate profits for private owners or shareholders. But they do have an obligation to generate significant amounts of revenue to pursue their mission" (Brand 2006).[17]

By itself Brand's argument does not explain why per-unit intercollegiate athletics expenditures have far outpaced general university spending (Desrochers 2013). The fact that athletics spending mirrors substantial revenue growth suggests increased revenues drive increased spending.[18] In short, consistent with a series of reports commissioned by the NCAA, while there may not be a causal link, there is a high correlation between increases in revenue and increases in costs and expenses.[19]

In addition to reporting financial information to the federal government, athletic departments also disclose financial information to the NCAA, but in a somewhat different format. From the data submitted by its members, the NCAA reports aggregate values on its website but does not make the school-specific information public (NCAA 2022a). However, media outlets such as *USA Today* and the *Chronicle of Higher Education* have obtained records for (most) public universities through Freedom of Information Act requests and—using both NCAA and EADA sources—have compiled and publicly disseminated extensive databases of university athletic financial information.[20]

Excerpted data from the 2016 *Chronicle* report include aggregate athletic department revenue and spending totals, with no breakdown by individual sport. The database includes more detailed information regarding revenue sources than the EADA data.[21] Importantly, the report highlights three separate revenue categories, which are collectively classified as a "subsidy": (1) student fees specifically designated to athletics (including free or discounted sports event tickets); (2) direct institutional support; and (3) other government support, such as state appropriations. In this chapter's analysis, this subsidy is categorized as an investment in athletics by the university. Figure 3 presents gross investment in athletics by the Division I subdivision (i.e., Power Five, Group of 5, FCS, and Division IAAA), and figure 4 indicates the university investment as a share of total athletic revenue. Clearly Power Five athletic departments invest less (on both total and percentage bases), since they generate excess revenue. Interestingly, in an attempt to keep up with the Power Five Joneses, Group of 5 schools make the greatest absolute investment, while on average Division IAAA schools without football make the largest relative investments.[22]

There are two takeaways to note. First, Group of 5 members have entered a spending realm imposed by their Power Five peers, but their football and thus total athletic revenues are significantly lower and therefore insufficient to cover associated athletic department costs. However, as noted above, entry into this level is common, and exit is extremely rare. Second, lower division (FCS) and non-football schools spend far more money on athletics than revenue generated, and yet these schools continue to make this substantial investment.

Table 5 shows total athletic spending for FBS football over the six-year period 2010–14. The table is divided into two parts, so Power Five conferences are set apart from Group of 5 conferences. The total revenue column is inclusive of university investment, which is also shown separately. The average Power Five conference investment has held steady over the period at just under $6 million per year, while athletics revenues and expenses have both expanded considerably. Interestingly the average Power Five investment just about matches average Power Five athletic department profits each year, suggesting that on average Power Five athletic departments annually break even (spending generated revenue to meet expenses) without university support. In contrast Group of 5 data show that although athletic department revenues are growing at a comparable rate, university investment is much larger—by a factor of about three throughout the period. In fact on average Group of 5 investment constitutes more than half of total athletic department revenue, and without it the operating income for the group's athletic departments is substantially negative. Fundamentally table 5 highlights that the significantly greater revenue generated by Power Five football has historically been responsible for the subsidy-free profitability of Power Five college athletic departments.

Examining FCS and Division IAAA data (see table 6) reveals reported revenues and expenses growing well in excess of inflation. However, on average the university's investment is larger on a percentage basis than the Group of 5, up to about two-thirds of total athletic department revenue.

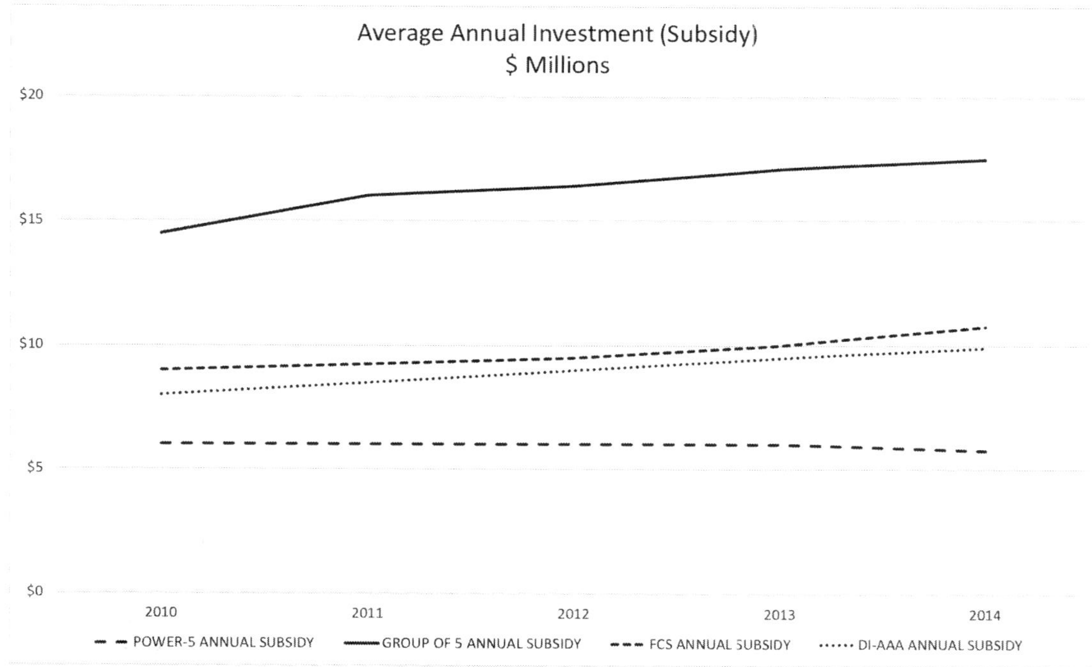

Figure 3. Average annual investment.

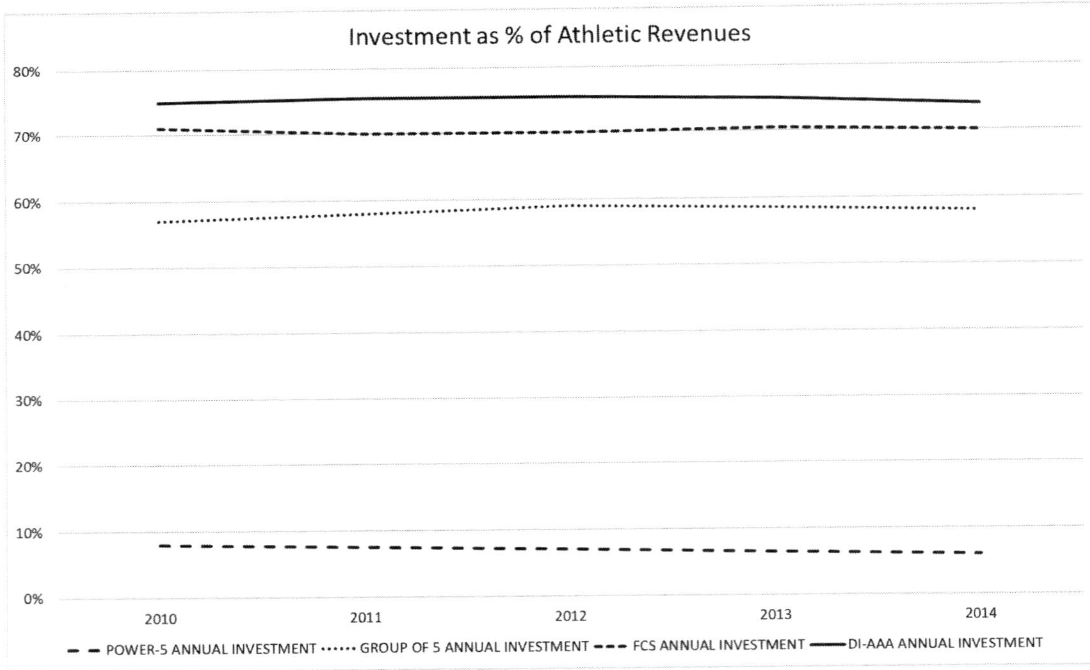

Figure 4. Annual investment as percentage of athletic revenues.

Table 5. Real revenue and expense growth: Power Five and Group of Five, 2010–14

YEAR	INSTITUTIONS	TOTAL REVENUE	GROWTH RATE, %	TOTAL EXPENSES	GROWTH RATE, %	UNIVERSITY INVESTMENT	GROWTH RATE, %
FBS POWER FIVE							
2010	51	$82.14		$76.13		$5.77	
2011	51	$83.32	1.44	$79.44	4.35	$5.84	1.11%
2012	51	$86.79	4.17	$83.65	5.30	$5.75	–1.41%
2013	50	$91.56	5.49	$87.80	4.96	$5.80	0.71%
2014	48	$97.42	6.40	$92.37	5.21	$5.64	–2.74%
Average per annum			4.65		5.33		–0.59%
FBS GROUP OF FIVE							
2010	52	$26.43	–	$26.40	–	$14.69	–
2011	52	$27.53	4.15	$27.09	2.60	$15.44	5.12%
2012	52	$28.72	4.35	$28.60	5.57	$16.44	6.51%
2013	52	$30.20	5.13	$30.09	5.21	$17.19	4.55%
2014	52	$31.16	3.18	$31.03	3.12	$17.69	2.93%
Average per annum			4.47		4.38		5.12

Note. Inflation adjustments using 2014 as base year as calculated by the *Chronicle of Higher Education*.

Source: *Chronicle of Higher Education* Database

Table 6. Real revenue and expense growth: Football Championship Subdivision and NCAA Division I non-football schools, 2010–14

YEAR	MEMBERS	TOTAL REVENUE	GROWTH RATE, %	TOTAL EXP	GROWTH RATE, %	TOTAL INVEST	GROWTH RATE, %
FCS							
2010	63	$13.00		$12.77		$9.17	
2011	64	$13.71	5.44	$13.50	5.68	$9.49	3.41
2012	65	$14.02	2.28	$13.97	3.51	$9.68	2.10
2013	65	$14.20	1.28	$14.42	3.27	$10.03	3.58
2014	64	$15.15	6.68	$15.14	4.96	$10.59	5.54
Average per annum			4.13		4.64		3.85
D-I NON FB							
2010	36	$11.30	—	$11.11	—	$8.46	—
2011	36	$11.74	3.89	$11.89	7.05	$8.87	3.89
2012	36	$11.94	1.70	$11.94	0.39	$9.05	1.70
2013	37	$12.46	4.39	$12.63	5.79	$9.41	4.39
2014	37	$13.24	6.24	$13.20	4.51	$9.82	6.24
Average per annum			4.29		4.70		4.29

Note. Inflation adjustments using 2014 as base year as calculated by *Chronicle of Higher Education*.

Source: *Chronicle of Higher Education* Database

For some observers universities investing in (i.e., subsidizing) their athletic departments is a grave concern. To these reformers big-time college sports is in the midst of an arms race, which is destructive to the sanctity of college sports and detrimental to higher education's fundamental mission.[23]

In addition to concerns of big-time college sport's corrosive effect on higher education's academic integrity, reformers contend subsidies, in the form of student fees, create unnecessary financial stress for students. An alternative interpretation is that universities—after conducting a rational cost-benefit analysis—have determined an investment in athletics is one that generates positive returns. However, in this case the payoff doesn't show on an athletic department's balance sheet but instead manifests itself to the university in other ways. The most obvious one is the promotional value of big-time sports. However, it is unlikely that revenue and expense reports on which sky-is-falling calls for reining in out-of-control sport excesses even reflect universities' true financial situations. Given that universities' accounting tends to understate revenues and overstate costs, reported spending and expenses on athletics are not authentic expenses (Maxcy, Rascher, and Schwarz 2014).

One area that masks college sport's true financial picture is significant related-party transactions (RPTs) (Maxcy, Rascher, and Schwarz 2014). In NCAA and EADA reports, athletic departments often understate revenue and overstate costs associated with RPTs. Historically, in these reports athletic department revenues are consistently undervalued in comparison to their true impact, while expenses are overvalued. As far back as 1992, researchers found that concessions revenues from athletic events were credited to university food service budgets rather than to athletics (Borland, Goff, and Pulsinelli 1992). They also found several cases of what appeared to be misappropriated charges and receivables. Common areas where accounting practices can shield a true analysis of college sport revenues and costs include field maintenance, facility and grounds upkeep, utilities, and janitorial services. Since a university's internal accounting methods are often not designed to analyze profitability on a unit-by-unit basis, such RPT-related accounting practices that do not clearly classify athletic expenses and revenues may not be purposefully dishonest but are often confusing and fail to accurately capture an athletic department's financial situation.

Excessive Spending Primarily Focused on Recruiting Athletes

Winning athletic teams help achieve identified university objectives, and acquiring high-performing players is the most important element related to winning. Financial returns associated with winning are well documented in the economics literature (e.g., Borland and MacDonald 2003; Fort 2015). Moreover returns to publicity and amenities increase (perhaps exponentially) with wins and championships. Teams with the most victories invariably go to the most lucrative bowls, which are big parties for students, alumni, and other constituents and engender significant development benefits. Power Five and Division I programs that compete in the CFP and take part in March Madness are discussed endlessly in the media. As previously mentioned, Butler University claimed $1 billion in value-in-kind publicity over two basketball seasons when its Cinderella men's basketball team made consecutive trips to the NCAA men's championship game (Woods 2015); and the University of Alabama directly credits its football national championship success to its increased ability to attract out-of-state students (Powell 2016).

Returns on sports investments (e.g., wins and championships) are, however a finite, zero-sum game. University athletic departments compete tenaciously to acquire victories and championships. Undeniably the key to wins and championships is recruiting the most-talented athletes or at least procuring better talent than one's rivals. NCAA rules eliminate a normal labor market for athletes' services. Rather than paying athletes directly, in the college sport cartel system outlays go elsewhere. Coaches with proven track records of winning and producing NFL or NBA players, as well as lavish practice facilities and competition venues, help convince sought-after players to sign with a program. Not surprisingly these are two primary areas of investment when new revenues are allocated.

Doubtless, almost every Power Five football or Division I men's basketball player is worth more than the cost of his GIA to a university. First, a GIA has no required minimum value, and yet Power Five schools rarely give partial GIAs in football or men's basketball.[24] Second, schools rarely use fewer than their full allotment of GIAs (except for frictional issues related to year-to-year roster balancing). In addition, when the NCAA Committee on Infractions chooses to punish a school for violating an NCAA bylaw, its main method is revoking GIAs.[25]

A primary symptom of rent-seeking behavior by universities is the upward spiral in coaching pay, since coaches' salaries are far beyond what they would be in a market that did not prevent direct competition for athlete services. In 2007 FBS college football coaches' pay captured 3.5 percent of a team's revenue. In comparison average NFL coaching pay represented only 1.5 percent of team revenues. Similarly for the 2008–9 season, the salaries of men's Division I basketball coaches captured 11.1 percent of revenue, while in the NBA coaches on average received only 3.2 percent of team revenue. Not only do college coaches receive a higher share of their teams' revenue, but their salaries have also increased at a much faster rate than NFL and NBA coaches. From 2007 to 2012, the average annual growth in coaches' pay in FBS college football was 9.7 percent, more than double the 4.5 percent NFL rate over the same time period (Maxcy, Rascher, and Schwarz 2014).

Coaches' compensation has also risen dramatically, because they are the recruiters who convince athletes to sign with a program. Clotfelter (2011: 121) reports that "as university athletic departments vie to recruit among the limited number of potential star players—whether with coaches or handsome facilities—spending more and more resources to sign them up makes sense if the funds are available." A coach's pay is in large part a function of his recruiting success (see, e.g., Gleeson 2013; Crabtree 2022).However, such spending above the amount that would prevail, absent restraints, is inefficient (Douglas and Miller 1974; Viscusi, Harrington, and Vernon 1997).

Likewise practice facility expenditures are inflated by rent-seeking behavior. Because providing direct economic compensation to athletes is prohibited, universities turn to a next best means of attracting valuable athletes. As Zimbalist (1999: 44) noted, facility expenditures have exploded on college campuses since the 1980s: "The cartel members found new ways to compete, and new leaks were opened. . . . The new recruiting showpieces have become mammoth training complexes, led by the University of Georgia's $12 million Heritage Hall opened in 1987. The University of Tennessee followed with its own $10 million state-of-the-art sports complex." What were viewed as outrageous capital expenditures in the 1980s are dwarfed by more recent supercharged facility spending, including the University of Oregon investing $138 million on a football training facility in 2013 and Clemson University earmarking a paltry $55 million in 2016 to upgrade its football training facility. Such palatial facilities are not simply a means of providing athletes with outstanding training complexes but send a message of how much they value present and future players: "An imported foosball table is unlikely to offer much in terms of actual, additional utility to a recruit over a domestic one, but by being able to show the recruit the program is willing to spend money to attract him, the program signals its seriousness" (Forde 2013). Like coaches' salaries, the emphasis on facilities is a consequence of agreements to cap athlete compensation.

Conclusion

The NCAA provides substantial joint-entity benefits through its maintenance of college sport's economic cartel, which creates associated market power advantages.[26] As is the case in professional sports, monopsony over the (labor) input market is of great value. However, among sports organizations worldwide, the NCAA remains unmatched in its deft preservation of its cartel power. The association's strictly enforced amateurism, undefined and malleable, allows only an in-kind exchange of athletic services for an educational product. As the association representing Division I members, the NCAA requires each university to offer an athlete no more than an agreed-upon, rigorously defined, and highly restrained level of compensation, which eliminates wage competition.

The financial returns associated with winning in Power Five college sports are considerable, and so too is the value of the most talented football and men's basketball players. Universities are therefore incentivized to vigorously compete for the services of these revenue producers. However, with profit-athlete pay strictly limited, economic rents are directed to coaches who successfully recruit top talent and lavish athletic facilities that bedazzle prospects. In addition there are great incentives to cheat—in order to circumvent the cartel's artificially capped compensation levels—by offering some players' additional compensation, which is defined by the NCAA as "improper benefits." Thus enforcing NCAA recruiting-related bylaws has become a key NCAA function, with several high-profile cases each year.

Historically the NCAA's version of amateurism has been granted great deference by courts, Congress, and state legislatures. While recent court decisions (see *O'Bannon v. NCAA*, 2014; *NCAA v. Alston*, n.d.), the Northwestern University football players' petition to the NLRB, and new state laws granting college athletes additional rights reflect a new reality in which the perception and understanding of the true nature of profit-athletes' value may be changing, the NCAA's willful entanglement of education and athletics still obfuscates the true economic realities for courts, members of Congress, and a significant portion of the public.

What needs to be remembered is that ultimately universities invest in college sports (at all levels) because considerable value is returned. While Power Five football and Division I men's basketball are explicitly profitable, all sports return some positive value to universities, or they would cease to exist. The full value of college sports is best recognized by considering how they help universities achieve identifiable objectives. As an economic cartel, the NCAA—and its collegiate model—allows universities to collectively minimize the cost of their most valuable input, athlete services. In stark contrast to other sport organizations and governing bodies, the NCAA continues to exploit profit-athletes, who should be more accurately classified as employees, through the maintenance of its amateur standards, which successfully intertwine college sports and higher education.

Notes

1. A university's nonprofit tax status does not provide an exemption from state and federal labor law and employment law. Moreover it must be understood that there is no basis to the claim that students, even when the role of providing a service is in conjunction with their education, cannot be unionized employees or considered as employees. The NLRB's August 2016 decision certifying Columbia University graduate students' collective bargaining rights is confirmation. This argument can be straightforwardly extended to college athletes as determined by Peter Sung Ohr (Regional Director – NLRB Region 13) in his initial review in 2014. Ohr found the services provided by college football players at Northwestern University, and the conditions under which those services were provided, represented an employment relationship. There is no industry where a claim of financial hardship, even when true, has denied its workers consideration as employees.

2. Both of these reform groups express concern that big-time sport detracts from the university's primary educational mission. They also point to a fiscal drag of money wasted, in their characterization, on sports that could be better spent enhancing the educational experience of non-athletes.

3. In this chapter *profit* is defined as total revenues less total expenses. For an enterprise housed within a larger nonprofit organization, the terms *net revenue* and *surplus* are less familiar but more accurate. Our purpose is to put forth the idea that revenues exceed expenses regardless of how the surplus is spent.

4. The NCAA Division I comprises three subdivisions with membership in 2020 as follows: the Football Bowl Subdivision (FBS, 130 members), the Football Championship Subdivision (FCS, 127 members), and non-football-playing institutions (100 members). Power Five and "major conference" are not official NCAA designations but recognize the most highly competitive subdivisions of Division I in football and men's basketball. The Power Five football conferences in football are the Atlantic Coast Conference, the Big Ten Conference, the Big 12 Conference, the Pac-12 Conference, and the Southeastern Conference. Notre Dame, a member of the ACC for basketball and most other sports, has no conference affiliation in football but is included with the Power Five. Big-time or major college basketball is broader in scope and consists of each of the same Power Five football conferences plus other conferences and institutions that do not sponsor FBS football. For example, the American Athletic Conference, whose membership includes traditional basketball powers Connecticut, Cincinnati, and Temple, is a major basketball conference but a member of the FBS Group of Five in football, a level down from the Power Five. The Big East Conference is now a basketball-only conference and home to 2016 and 2018 NCAA men's basketball champion Villanova University as well as Georgetown, St. John's, Marquette, and other men's basketball programs of national stature that either do not compete in football or play at the FCS level or below.

5. At some universities individual sports programs other than Power Five football and Division I men's basketball generate significant revenues: Division I women's basketball, softball, gymnastics, baseball, ice hockey, and lacrosse are the most common examples. Athletes participating in these sports sometimes face similar work environments as Power Five football and Division I men's basketball players.

6. Myles Brand, then NCAA president, put forth in a 2004 opinion that non-revenue sports and Olympic sports were synonymous (Brand 2004). He argued that continued Olympic success depends on the NCAA and that Olympic sports were fiscally unstable, citing substantial cuts of men's wrestling and gymnastics programs between 1988 and 2003. Fort and Winfree (2013) judged Brand's argument to be myth.

7. University of Michigan sports economist Rodney Fort has repeatedly argued that sports spending must be characterized as an investment consistent with university objectives and not a subsidy that competes with or detracts from a university's academic mission. See, for example, Fort and Quirk (1999) and Fort (2010, 2015).

8. The NCAA requires minimum offerings of men's and women's sports so that schools have to offer a broad-based program. Division I requires fourteen sports, seven men's and seven women's sports or six men's and eight women's; Divisions II and III require ten total sports, five each of men's and women's sports or four men's and six women's (NCAA 2022b).

9. This is not different from most units and academic departments at a university. Whether the university is subsidizing or investing in intercollegiate athletics is more a matter of semantics than procedure.

10. The economic literature supports the contention that a university's success in big-time football and men's basketball increases student applications for admissions (details follow later in this chapter). Research on the effects on donations and gifts and of direct financial support to the university is ambiguous. A school found noncompliant with Title IX could face serious financial consequences.

11. However, Robert Frank of Cornell University (commissioned by the Knight Commission on Intercollegiate Athletics) reviewed and critiqued the body of research on both claims up to 2003. He concluded there was little evidence that success in athletics improved the aptitude of the student body or increased donations beyond those directed to athletics (Frank 2004).

12. From 2005 through 2015, TCU had a win-loss record of 111–30 (a 79 percent winning percentage), with eight seasons of eleven or more victories.

13. The University of Alabama Birmingham dropped FBS football in 2015 but reinstated the program in 2017. There was considerable controversy surrounding this pronouncement with some economists even noting the decision made little economic sense (Schwarz 2014).

14. These reports do not follow Generally Accepted Accounting Principles but rather are based on self-defined NCAA accounting practices.

15. These conferences, dubbed AQ conferences for the automatic bowl-game qualification status of their conference champion, initially included the Big East Conference, which disbanded as a football conference in 2013. The Big East's exit left the Power Five conferences. Between 2012 and 2014, most football-playing Big East institutions joined a Power Five conference. These included Syracuse and Pittsburgh, which moved to the ACC in 2012, and West Virginia, which moved to the Big 12 in 2014. Texas Christian University moved from the Group of 5 Mountain West Conference to the Big 12 in 2012.

16. Division I women's basketball often garners national attention. Regular season games are televised regionally and nationally, and the Division I women's tournament is broadcast nationally by ESPN.

17. Brand's description of spending behavior is confirmed in economic analyses of higher education. Archibald and Feldman (2008) review the "cost disease" theory and revenue theory of cost. The cost disease theory is derived from an amalgamation of several of the authors' works, all listed in Archibald and Feldman's bibliography. The revenue theory of cost is put forth in Howard R. Bowen (1980).

18. Getz, Siegfried, and Zhang (1991), among others, propose that explanations of spending behavior specific to higher education are sound.

19. These NCAA-commissioned reports include Litan, Orszag, and Orszag (2003) and Orszag and Israel (2009).

20. Private universities are not included in the *Chronicle* or *USA Today* disclosures, and state law shields Pennsylvania's public universities, including Penn State, Pittsburgh, and Temple, from FOI disclosure. In addition, for no apparent reason, some other universities' information is randomly absent for some years (e.g., University of Tennessee in 2014).

21. The *Chronicle* database classifies earned revenue in detail; besides student fees and direct institutional support, they report ticket sales, broadcasting, conference and NCAA distributions, royalties, and endowments. However, they only report aggregate athletic department expenses. *USA Today* compiles a separate database of football and men's basketball coaches' salaries.

22. The Group of Five includes the American Athletic Conference, the Mid-American Conference, the Mountain West Conference, and the Sun Belt Conference. Brigham Young

University, the US Military Academy, and University of Massachusetts Amherst are independent members at the Group of Five level.

23. Fort and Winfree (2013) and Fort (2016) debunk the detrimental effects of an "arms race" from an economist's standpoint and support the position taken here that the benefits of spending on athletics exceed the costs.

24. It is possible to find a Power Five football player with a partial GIA, but this is almost always a case of a player receiving a full GIA for part of the school year rather than a partial GIA for an entire school year.

25. To the extent that GIAs are a measure of output, capping the number of GIAs and/or further lowering that cap through sanctions are clear agreements to limit output.

26. For a full discussion of the NCAA as an economic cartel, see Fleischer, Goff, and Tollison (1992).

References

CASES

National Collegiate Athletic Association v. Alston (n.d.). Oyez. Retrieved June 2, 2021, from https://www.oyez.org/.

O'Bannon v. NCAA, No. C-09–3329-CW, 2014 WL 3899815 (N.D. Cal. Aug. 8, 2014).

SECONDARY SOURCES

Archibald, Robert B., and David H. Feldman (2008). "Explaining Increases in Higher Education Costs." *Journal of Higher Education* 79, no. 3: 268–95.

Baby, Ben (2017). "A&M Athletic Department Brings in Hefty Revenue for 2015–16 Academic Year." *Dallas Morning News*, February 23. https://www.dallasnews.com/.

Borland, Jeffery, and Robert MacDonald (2003). "Demand for Sport." *Oxford Review of Economic Policy* 19, no. 4: 478–502.

Borland, Melvin V., Brian L. Goff, and Robert W. Pulsinelli (1992). "College Athletics: Financial Burden or Boon?" In *Advances in the Economics of Sport*, vol. 1, edited by Gerald W. Scully, 217–18. Greenwich, CT: JAI.

Bowen, Howard R. (1980). *The Costs of Higher Education: How Much Do Colleges and Universities Spend per Student and How Much Should They Spend?* San Francisco: Jossey-Bass.

Brady, Erik, Steve Berkowitz, and Jodi Upton (2012). "College Football Coaches Continue to See Salary Explosion." *USA Today*, November 12. http://www.usatoday.com/.

Brand, Myles (2004). "Olympic Sports Are Priceless at Colleges." College Sports Scholarships. https://www.collegesportsscholarships.com/.

———. (2006). "Brand Charts Course for Collegiate Model's Next Century." Speech delivered to the NCAA Convention, January 7. https://mylesbrand.com/.

Brooks, Amanda (2021). "College Football Playoff Semifinals Average Nineteen Million Viewers, ESPN's Third-Most Watched Day on Record." ESPN Press Room, January 5. https://espnpressroom.com/.

Buchholz, Katharina (2019). "The Richest College Football Programs." *Statista*, December 6. https://www.statista.com/.

Cassillo, John (2021). "Sports Media Rights: Current TV Deals and What's on the Horizon." *TVREV*, February 18. https://tvrev.com/.

Chiusano, Anthony (2021). "The 25 Biggest College Football Stadiums in the Country." NCAA.com, January 5. https://www.ncaa.com/.

Clotfelter, Charles T. (2011). *Big-Time Sports in American Universities.* New York: Cambridge University Press.

Crabtree, Jeremy (2022). "Elite Teams Show the Value of Recruiting." ESPN.com. http://espn.go.com/ (accessed August 8).

Desrochers, Donna M. (2013). "Academic Spending versus Athletic Spending: Who Wins?" January. Washington, DC: Delta Cost Project at American Institutes for Research. http://chronicle.com/blogs/players/files/2013/01/deltacost.pdf.

Dodd, Dennis (2013). "Sun Belt Will Grow by Four in 2013." CBS Sports, March 25. https://www.cbssports.com/college-football/.

Douglas, George W., and James C. Miller III (1974). "Quality Competition, Industry Equilibrium, and Efficiency in the Price-Constrained Airline Market." *American Economic Review* 64, no. 4: 657–69.

Fleisher, Arthur A., Brian L. Goff, and Robert D. Tollison (1992). *The National Collegiate Athletic Association: A Study in Cartel Behavior.* Chicago: University of Chicago Press.

Forde, Pat (2013). "Forde-Yard Dash: Plenty of Guilt to Go Around for Grambling's Plight." Yahoo! Sports, October 22. http://sports.yahoo.com/.

Fort, Rodney (2010). "An Economic Look at the Sustainability of FBS Athletic Departments." *Journal of Intercollegiate Sport* 3, no. 1: 3–21. https://journals.ku.edu/.

———. (2015). "College Sports Spending Decisions and the Academic Mission." In *Introduction to Intercollegiate Athletics,* edited by Eddie Comeaux, 135–46. Baltimore: Johns Hopkins University Press.

———. (2016). "Collegiate Athletics Spending." *Journal of Amateur Sports* 2: 119–40.

Fort, Rodney, and James Quirk (1999). "The College Football Industry." In *Sports Economics: Current Research,* edited by John Fizel, Elizabeth Gustafson, and Lawrence Hadley, 11–25. Westport, CT: Praeger.

Fort, Rodney, and Jason Winfree (2013). *15 Sports Myths and Why They're Wrong.* Stanford, CA: Stanford University Press.

Frank, Robert H. (2004). "Challenging the Myth: A Review of the Links among College Athletic Success, Student Quality, and Donations." Report prepared by the John S. and James L. Knight Foundation Commission on Intercollegiate Athletics. https://citeseerx.ist.psu.edu/.

Fueled by Sports (2019). "Largest College Basketball Arenas." https://www.fueledbysports.com/.

Getz, Malcolm, and John J. Siegfried (2012). "What Does Intercollegiate Athletics Do to or for Colleges and Universities?" In *The Oxford Handbook of Sports Economics,* vol. 1, edited by Leo H. Kahane and Stephen Shmanske, 349–72. New York: Oxford University Press.

Getz, Malcolm, John J. Siegfried, and Hao Zhang (1991). "Estimating Economies of Scale in Higher Education." *Economic Letters* 37, no. 2: 203–8.

Gleeson, Scott (2013). "Starting Five: The Best Recruiting College Hoops Coaches." *USA Today,* July 12. http://www.usatoday.com/.

Humphreys, Brad R., and Michael Mondello (2007). "Intercollegiate Athletic Success and Donations at NCAA Division I Institutions." *Journal of Sport Management* 21, no. 2: 265–80.

Imbert, Fred (2015). "How 'Cinderellas' Cash in on March Madness." CNBC.com, March 9. https://www.cnbc.com/.

Koplowitz, Howard (2019). "UA Is 'Extreme Case' of State Schools Recruiting Out-of-State Residents, Report Finds." *AL.com*, March 26. https://www.al.com/.

Lieber, Ron (2004). "Score! Gonzaga University Was Struggling Financially. Then It Started Winning Basketball Games." *Wall Street Journal*, March 15. http://online.wsj.com/.

Litan, Robert E., Jonathan M. Orszag, and Peter R. Orszag (2003). "The Empirical Effects of Collegiate Athletics: An Interim Report." Report prepared by Sebago Associates, August. https://ncaaorg.s3.amazonaws.com/.

Maxcy, Joel G. (2013). "Efficiency and Managerial Performance in FBS College Football: To the Employment and Succession Decisions, Which Matters More, Coaching or Recruiting?" *Journal of Sport Economics* 14, no. 4: 368–88.

Maxcy, Joel G., D. A. Rascher, and A. D. Schwarz (2014). "Brief of Amicus Curiae on Invitation by the National Labor Relations Board: Brief of Sports Economists and Professors of Sport Management." https://www.nlrb.gov/.

National Collegiate Athletic Association (2022a). "Archives of NCAA Revenues and Expenses Reports by Division." https://www.ncaa.org/ (accessed August 8).

———. (2022b). "Divisional Differences and the History of Multidivision Classification." https://www.ncaa.org/ (accessed August 8).

———. (2022c). "Women's Basketball Attendance." https://www.ncaa.org/ (accessed August 8).

Noll, Roger G. (1999). "The Business of College Sports and the High Cost of Winning." *Milken Institute Review* 28: 24–37.

Orszag, Jonathan M., and M. Israel (2009). "The Empirical Effects of Collegiate Athletics: An Update Based on 2004–2007 Data." http://fs.ncaa.org/.

Paulsen (2016). "Halftime: The 50 Most-Watched Sporting Events of 2016 (So Far)." *Sports Media Watch*, July. https://www.sportsmediawatch.com/.

Pope, Devin G., and Jaren C. Pope (2009). "The Impact of College Sports Success on the Quantity and Quality of Student Applications." *Southern Economic Journal* 75, no. 3: 750–80.

Powell, Farran (2016). "Out-of-State Enrollment Rises at State Flagship Universities." *US News and World Report*, June 13. http://www.usnews.com/.

Rascher, Daniel, and Andy Schwarz (2015). "The Incremental Benefits and Costs of Football, Bowling, and Rifle at the University of Alabama at Birmingham: A Primary and Secondary Study." April 22. http://a.espncdn.com/.

Rascher, Daniel, and Jeremy Howell (2011). "An Analysis and Assessment of Intercollegiate Athletics at the University of San Francisco." Unpublished manuscript, June 27.

Schwarz, Andy (2014). "Screw the Math: UAB Can Afford Football, So Why Is It Choosing Otherwise?" *Vice*, December 8. https://www.vice.com/.

University of Alabama (2020). "Quick Facts." https://www.ua.edu/about/quickfacts.

Viscusi, W. Kip, Joseph E. Harrington Jr., and John M. Vernon (1997). *Economics of Regulation and Antitrust*. Cambridge, MA: MIT Press.

Waldman, Don E., and Elizabeth James Jensen (2019). *Industrial Organization: Theory and Practice*. 5th ed. New York: Routledge.

Wolverton, Brad, and Dan Bauman (2016). "As Sports Spending Soars, Programs Scramble to Keep Up." *Chronicle of Higher Education*, October 9. https://www.chronicle.com/.

Woods, Bob (2015). "NCAA Tourney Run Can Bring Billions (with a 'B')." CNBC, March 10. http://www.cnbc.com/.

Zimbalist, Andrew (1999). *Unpaid Professionals: Commercialism and Conflict in Big-Time College Sports*. Princeton, NJ: Princeton University Press.

PART III

Power Five College Sport Today

The Exploitation of Power Five Profit-Athletes

Paternalism, Patriarchy, and Racialization

Richard M. Southall

As big-time college sport has become increasingly commercialized and professionalized, Power Five conferences have demanded and been granted increased autonomy within the NCAA governance structure. By the summer of 2021, NCAA president Mark Emmert had acknowledged the inevitability of this trend continuing, commenting that the time was right "to consider a decentralized and deregulated version of college sports, shifting power to conferences and campuses and reconsidering how schools are aligned" (quoted in Russo 2021). Since their inception Power Five conferences and individual athletic departments have always looked for ways to operate their college sport businesses more efficiently. Through formal governance structures, adopted policies and procedures, institutional logics that sustain college sport hegemony, and effective use of propaganda, the economic exploitation of profit-athletes has been institutionalized within Power Five college sport. However, what is often overlooked is the racialized nature of the economic exploitation of profit-athletes and the disparate negative impact this exploitation has on Black profit-athletes. Since, as Ray (2019: 26) argued, "organizations are racial structures—cognitive schemas connecting organizational rules to social and material resources," Power Five college sport not surprisingly reproduces racialization processes spanning macro-, meso-, and micro-social levels (Ray 2019). Consequently this chapter examines the historical arc of this racialized exploitation, the philosophical constructs used to justify it, and the ongoing institutionalization in NCAA and Power Five governance.

A History of Exploitation

The first step in the journey that has resulted in today's racialized exploitation of Power Five profit-athletes occurred in 1973, when the NCAA membership was grouped into three divisions. This divisional structure allowed members within each division to operate independently in a federated governance model. Five years later Division I members created two subdivisions, IA and IAA, which were rebranded in 2006 as the Football Bowl Subdivision (FBS) and the Football Championship Subdivision (FCS) based on conference affiliations and competitive structures in football. While FCS members competed in an NCAA-sponsored postseason playoff, FBS football remained associated with the traditional postseason bowl system. In response to calls by top-tier FBS football programs for increased independence in the early part of the 2000s, the FBS was eventually subdivided into what came to be known as Power Five and Group of Five conferences. While the NCAA does not formally define these designations and the precise origin of the terms is unknown, in 2014 the Power Five conferences (Atlantic Coast Conference, Big Ten Conference, Big 12 Conference, Pacific 12 Conference, and the Southeastern Conference) were granted almost complete autonomy within the NCAA governance structure.

While the NCAA Board of Directors claimed the restructuring was guided by three principles, the first principle was the real driver: "Continued revenue distributions as they currently exist" (NCAA 2014a: 6). Simply put the Power Five haves said to the NCAA have-nots, "You want our money to pay for your championships? Then stay out of our business!" As New (2014) noted, "Ultimately, the committee that recommended the governance plan and the Division I Board of Directors gave the power conferences what they wanted—continuing a historical trend in which [college] sports powers get their way because of a (not-so-veiled) threat that they will ultimately abandon the division, and maybe even the NCAA, if they don't." As one non–Power Five Division I university president said at the time, "The NCAA is letting those five conferences do whatever they want" (ibid.).

While (as of 2022) FBS universities are required (by Division I membership requirements) to sponsor at least fourteen sports, with "at least seven sports for men and seven for women (or six for men and eight for women) with two team sports for each gender" (NCAA 2022), most sponsor men's and women's teams in approximately twenty different sports (Garthwaite et al. 2020). Almost all of these sports do not financially support themselves, with 58 percent of FBS universities' revenue coming directly from football and men's basketball (ibid.). The other sports "directly account for only about 15 percent of total revenue" (ibid.: 1). Notably "the remaining 27 percent of athletic department revenue comes from other sources such as the sale of media rights" (ibid.), with football and men's basketball primarily driving the value of these contracts as well.

Separate from—but parallel to—the NCAA governance restructuring, on March 13, 2013, the FBS conferences organized a limited liability corporation, CFP Administration, LLC, to manage the administrative operations of the newly formed College Football Playoff (CFP). The LLC members are the ten FBS conferences (American Athletic, Atlantic Coast, Big Ten, Big 12, Conference USA, Mid-American, Mountain West, Pac-12, Southeastern, and Sun Belt) and the University of Notre Dame (College Football Playoff 2021). Significantly, the NCAA is nowhere to be found in the CFP governance structure: "The company's business, property and affairs are governed by the Board of Managers [eleven university presidents and chancellors]. The board develops, reviews, and approves annual budgets, policies, and operating guidelines. It also appoints and removes officers of the company. It has authority over all aspects of the company's operations" (ibid.). The CFP Management Committee, which comprises the ten FBS conference commissioners and Notre Dame's athletics director, "manages the day-to-day operations of the company. It has authority over those aspects of the company's operations that are not reserved exclusively for the board, but all of its decisions are subject to review by the board" (ibid.).

Institutionalizing Economic Exploitation

Increased governance autonomy has allowed Power Five conferences to solidify and insulate control of their football and men's basketball programs and institutionalize the economic exploitation of their profit-athletes. In a 2012 NCAA convention address, Mark Emmert justified this economic exploitation: "[The] NCAA has no reason to apologize for the fact that college football and basketball are wildly popular and generate revenue that allows the Association to benefit hundreds of thousands" (NCAA 2012). Justifying the economic exploitation of a minority population to benefit the majority is nothing new. It is almost as old as civilization itself.

As far back as Aristotle (384–322 BC), Western philosophers have used concepts of disparity of value or wrongful use to determine whether economic exchanges are fair or unfair. Aristotle posited that a "just exchange" must embody a proportional reciprocity of value (*Nicomachean Ethics* 5.5 [Aristotle 1934]). St. Thomas Aquinas (1225–1274) discussed that it was ethical to sell a product at no more than a fair market price. To sell a product for more than this price is unethical. While fairness and reciprocity are somewhat amorphous concepts, what has never been up for debate is the belief that an exchange is exploitative if a buyer or seller is forced to buy or sell a product for more or less than a mutually agreeable price (McInerny and O'Callaghan 2018).

In the eighteenth century, two prominent Western philosophers, Immanuel Kant and David Hume, viewed the exploitation of the labor value of workers (whether indentured servants, slaves, or employees) as unethical. Extending Aquinas's concept of just exchange of value from a product to a worker's labor makes sense, given that labor is in many ways the source of all economic value. Fundamentally it is well accepted in applied ethics that workers have the right to sell their labor in exchange for pay that approximates an agreed-upon value.

Kant (1724–1804) outlined two formulations of what he termed the categorical imperative in which he argued economic exploitation is unethical. The categorical imperative's first principle is that moral actions can always be universalized, while immoral or unethical actions cannot. Kant argued that exploiting another person cannot be universalized, since to do so exploiters must agree to themselves being exploited. And since agreeing to be exploited is to will harm upon oneself, which a rational being would never do, exploitation is unethical. In addition Kant's second formulation of the categorical imperative (known as the Kingdom of Ends) states that people should never be treated merely as means to an end (i.e., economic gain) but must always be treated as an end in and of themself. On a societal level, Kant declared that a desire to achieve beneficial ends for the majority does not justify harming others (e.g., economically exploiting the minority). Since people have inherent value apart from their use or labor value, economically exploiting an individual or group, even if doing so provides benefits to others, cannot be justified. Historically this "tyranny of the majority" has often resulted in the oppression of vulnerable racial or ethnic minorities (Johnson and Cureton 2021).

When college football and men's basketball were regional sports with limited national broadcast rights and coaches' salaries roughly equivalent to those of college professors, receiving an athletic grant-in-aid (GIA) in exchange for playing football or basketball was viewed as a fair exchange by college athletes, coaches, administrators, and most neutral observers. However, as college sport has morphed into a multibillion-dollar industry, the gap between a profit-athletes' market value and the value of a GIA has become harder and harder to reconcile. Faced with this ethical dilemma, many adherents to the Power Five collegiate model began to justify the exploitation of profit-athletes' by appealing to the concept of the greatest good for the greatest number, " the fundamental principle of utilitarianism that can be traced to nineteenth-century philosopher-economists Jeremy Bentham and John Stuart Mill (Brink 2018).

Utilitarian Justifications for Exploitation: "It's Not So Bad . . . We're Only Exploiting 3.5 Percent of College Athletes"

According to the most recent NCAA Demographics Database (NCAA 2021f) and Corr, Southall, and Nagel (2020), a majority of profit-athletes (most notably a high percentage of starting players) are Black. It is an economic fact that these athletes have a greater market value than the level to which NCAA bylaws allow them to be compensated. Since they are not allowed to be fairly compensated for their labor by their employer and do not control or retain the value created by their labor, they are economically exploited. Such exploitation is the result of the disparity between their labor value and compensation, measurable through calculations of surplus value. It is important to remember that this exploitation is not mitigated by these athletes' being allowed to profit from the value of their names, images, and likenesses.

Even though the current college sport business model relies on the economic exploitation of Power Five profit-athletes, NCAA and Power Five administrators have chosen to justify such exploitation by claiming college sport benefits most college students (including most athletes). This utilitarian justification for the current NCAA collegiate model can be stated in the following manner:

> (a) College sport, as a result of its attachment to higher education, has unquestioned, intrinsic, universal, and immeasurable moral/social value (e.g., goodness);
> (b) the current collegiate model maximizes this identified intrinsic value; and
> (c) the vast majority of college athletes are able to access positive consequences by their participation in intercollegiate athletics. (Southall and Karcher 2016: 213)

If unlimited and universal moral goodness is ascribed to college sport in general and if the majority of college athletes (since their market value is less than the value of their GIA compensation) economically benefit from the current system, then the economic exploitation of a relatively few profit-athletes who represent at most 3.5 percent of all college athletes is justified, since this exploitation allows the association to benefit hundreds of thousands of college athletes (NCAA 2012, 2014b). Testifying before Congress in July 2014, Emmert clearly used utilitarianism to justify the continuing and expanding exploitation of profit-athletes: "For the vast majority of those who participate in NCAA sports—more than 460,000 young men and women each year at 1,084 institutions across three divisions and in 23 different sports—the experience is exactly what it is intended to be: a meaningful extension of the educational process that provides the opportunity for students to compete fairly against other students, in an educational environment" (NCAA 2014b). Power Five college sport stakeholders (e.g., coaches, administrators, and corporate partners) are well aware that—more than anything—college sport fans love their teams and the spectacle that is big-time college sport. While nearly everyone involved in college sports knows on some level that the NCAA collegiate model economically exploits profit-athletes, they take comfort in the fact that these exploited profit-athletes make up only a small fraction of the whole. Based upon this utilitarian justification, Power Five stakeholders uniformly construct narratives that rationalize the exploitative nature of big-time college football and basketball. In 2016 Texas A&M University System chancellor John Sharp said, "Sports like football pay for themselves and generate money for virtually everyone else" (quoted in Watkins 2016). On the Power Five level, having a self-sustaining athletic department that provides athletic opportunities to all the department's Olympic sport athletes is almost impossible without the profits from a successful football program (ibid.).

As college sport continues to become more lucrative, Power Five college sport industry insiders—from conference commissioners and administrators, university presidents and trustees, athletic directors, and department staff to head coaches and their assistants—justify increasing exploitation of profit-athletes by cataloging the many good ways the generated revenue is spent. From 2006 through 2019 the revenue directly generated by Power Five athletic departments nearly doubled ($4.4 billion to $8.5 billion), with the primary source of this surge being the sale of lucrative broadcast rights of football and men's basketball (Ingraham 2020). Reflecting the industry's remarkably steady growth, by 2019 the average annual salary of football coaching staffs had more than doubled ($4.8 million to $9.8 million) from its 2006 level. In addition noncoaching administrative salaries had also doubled (ibid.). As Craig Garthwaite, lead author of a 2020 working paper published by the National Bureau of Economic Research, noted that "there's so much money . . . and the one group that really has not seen any real increase in benefits are the players who are risking their health and safety to play the sports" (quoted in ibid.). While many in college sport management are raking in the dough, almost universally these well-paid college sport professionals have expressed a strong aversion to paying profit-athletes a fair market wage for their labor. A common refrain is that allowing athletes access to the same market system of compensation that every other participant in the enterprise enjoys is untenable, immoral, and/or illegal (Schwarz 2014).

Since 2020, however, most profit-sport coaches have expressed an openness to allowing college athletes to profit from the use of their name, image, and likeness (NIL). While no coach has proposed allowing college athletes to form a union for negotiating a collective bargaining agreement or a guaranteed percentage of revenues, coaches understand that the proverbial NIL train has left the station. From a recruiting standpoint, every university must be seen as respectful of athletes' NIL. The coaches of profit sports in particular understand that in a more open (e.g., capitalistic) system, they will still make millions of dollars, so they have come out in favor of players' making as much money as they can on the open NIL market. They understand they have no choice, especially with other schools already utilizing alumni support through NIL opportunities as a recruiting pitch (Avila 2021).

However, most Power Five administrators have not come out in support of other forms of increased player compensation. If athletic department revenues are ever diverted to increased player compensation or pay, Power Five managers know that the many-layered bureaucracy that is an athletic department will be the first organizational casualty. The vice, associate, and assistant athletic directors will be the first ones who will see a pay cut or reduction in force. Consequently athletic administrators often describe generated revenue as if it were a gift to be shared with players, not a product of the players' labor: "Sharing revenue with . . . athletes is not feasible. That only works if universities are then absolved of Title IX requirements. Football revenue supports women's golf, women's tennis, women's softball, women's volleyball, women's soccer, women's track and field on this campus" (Fendrich and Pells 2021). Power Five athletic directors routinely contend that certain sports (i.e., women's sports) "would lose funding or be cut altogether if their school offered additional non-scholarship payments" (ibid.) to profit-athletes. For most Power Five universities, generating as much money as possible from their football and men's basketball programs while not equitably sharing generated revenue with players is the blueprint for a successful athletic department.

Since profit-athletes have historically lacked proportional and effective representation, it is not surprising they do not recoup the full value of what they produce.[1] Fundamentally profit-athletes are exploited since they are coerced into selling the products of their labor for less than their full value. This is the case in relation to both generated revenues and athletes' NILs, since the many guardrails in state laws and athletic department policies are designed to deter college athletes from gaining full-market access for their labor product. Several commentators (Branch 2011; Byers and Hammer 1995; Hawkins 2010; Rhoden 2014) have noted that in many ways profit-athletes resemble indentured servants or even slaves who work almost entirely for the benefit of others. (It should be noted that part of profit-athletes' labor—just like that of indentured servants—does go toward providing for their own subsistence through GIAs and cost-of-attendance stipends.)

Even though in 2021 college athletes were granted the opportunity to monetize their NILs, they are still economically exploited—systemically and organizationally excluded from fairly sharing in generated college-sport revenues. In addition, within the NCAA and conference governance structures, they have extremely limited procedural or substantive access to due process. As a result of more than a century of institutionalized exploitation, profit-athletes are marginalized within a governance structure that claims to protect them from commercial exploitation but actually does the opposite.

Not surprisingly, given their lack of institutional power, profit-athletes abdicate control, giving spontaneous consent to their exploitative status imposed by

Power Five conference commissioners, NCAA national office staff, college presidents, athletic administrators, and coaches. Institution theory labels this general direction an institutional logic, which delineates the main principles that guide the actions of members within an institutional field (e.g., Power Five college sports). This logic reflects the material practices and symbolic constructions available to institutional members (Friedland and Alford 1991). These organizing principles become a hegemonic institutional logic when informal norms, rules, or social patterns are accepted as fundamental truths, embedded in internal policies and procedures, and enforced (formally or informally) by a central authority system (Jepperson 1991). Eventually a hegemonic institutional logic forms the basis for unquestioned, taken-for-granted "facts" reflected in particular courses of action (Southall, Nagel, Amis, and Southall 2008).

Reflecting an acceptance of taken-for-granted facts within the institutional field of Power Five college sport, athletic administrators, university presidents, and other stakeholders express little to no outrage at teenage golfers and tennis players leaving school early or bypassing college altogether to go pro. Historically in the revenue sports the common refrain is to lament players leaving early, arguing that they would be better served by staying in school and taking advantage of all the opportunities afforded them by athletic departments that want to protect them from commercial exploitation. This stay-and-play hegemony, which the NCAA and its member schools claim has always been meant to protect college athletes from commercial exploitation, has long held sway within Power Five profit sports.

Hegemony has little meaning without reference to notions of domination, since a dominant group historically enjoys prestige (and subsequently dominance) because of its position and function (Gramsci 1971). Such consent may be achieved through real or perceived force or through example setting, persuasion, or coercion (Southall and Staurowsky 2013). Most notably, hegemony is rooted in—and dependent on—the hegemon's "folklore" and language (ibid.). Later in this chapter we will highlight how Power Five stakeholders utilize college-sport folklore and language to maintain hegemony and spontaneous consent to the economic exploitation of profit-athletes.

Decision science suggests Power Five stakeholders make use of heuristics (e.g., mental shortcuts) that allow them to overlook the exploitative nature of Power Five college sport and engage in motivated reasoning that confirms their assessment of amateur college sport's positive values without having to acknowledge the economic exploitation that is part and parcel of the current model. To protect and justify their in-group status, college sport fans and administrators engage in identity protection cognition that precludes admitting the current system is fundamentally exploitative. Power Five administrators not only deny that Power Five college sport is exploitative, but they also consistently hold fast to a complex, convoluted, and paternalistic code of amateurism that portrays the denial of profit-athletes' fundamental economic and employee rights as a benign and affectionate attempt to protect the "kids" from commercial exploitation (see bylaw 2.9, "The Principle of Amateurism"). Pat Forde (2011) paternalistically admonished college athletes to remember how good they have it: "Maturation, socialization, enculturation, life lessons, friendships made, spouses met, and an allegiance to a place that can last a lifetime. Find a few former college athletes in their 30s or 40s and ask them about their experience. How many say they had a lousy time?" He went on to sarcastically outline the many benefits afforded Division I men's basketball players: "[Players] know they've got a better gig as a poor, exploited, unpaid serf in college. They've got access to top-flight coaching, top-flight facilities, medical professionals, a strength and conditioning staff, maximum exposure and all the adulation they can handle. The alternative is earning more spending money in a minor league system playing games in second-rate arenas in front of nobody, with older teammates and less-proven coaches." Trapped in the collegiate model paradigm, Forde cannot imagine an alternate reality in which profit-athletes are employees (and possibly also part- or full-time students) who negotiate wage and benefits packages that could include bonuses, health insurance, and tuition remission. While this possibility is totally unacceptable, college sport apologists find it perfectly acceptable that profit-athletes must remain trapped in an amateur sport system and watch as their fellow athletes, who have little or no economic value, reap the same GIA-related benefits as do they.

For years college sport supporters have argued that profit-athletes should be thankful for low-paid college sport opportunities, seemingly ignoring the fact that the opportunities afforded Power Five Olympic-sport athletes are subsidized primarily by revenue produced by profit-athletes. In addition, while Division I men's basketball players who leave college early for professional sports opportunities are often derided as "one-and-dones," golfers who leave college early for professional golf opportunities are rarely, if ever, castigated for doing so. Olympic-sport athletes (i.e., loss-athletes) have the same access to great coaches, facilities, medical professionals as profit-athletes. However, they don't produce any appreciable revenue; they wet their beak at the college sport trough, taking advantage of a system supported by the labor of profit-athletes. In an economic sense, loss-athletes obtain disproportionate benefits from participating in college sports far exceeding their market value. The disparity of value in their economic exchange is dramatically in their favor. The athletic largesse afforded to Olympic-sport athletes might rightly be viewed as unfair: they are not exploited; they are exploiting the system to their advantage.

College-Athlete-Employee?

Different than any other college student, in the NCAA collegiate model, a profit-athlete cannot simultaneously be a university employee. Since profit-athletes cannot be employees, they cannot be paid a negotiated salary but can be compensated in other ways (Brand 2006). In this alternate reality, NCAA bylaws explicitly exclude various forms of compensation (e.g., money, funds, awards, benefits, or goods) from being referred to as pay. A cost-of-attendance check that a Power Five profit-athlete may send home to help with family expenses is not pay, since it is a form of compensation permitted by the association (NCAA 2021c). However, prior to July 2021, if college athletes received five hundred dollars for signing autographs, that constituted pay and subjected them to NCAA sanctions and possible criminal prosecution (ibid.). Magically in 2021 this previously forbidden pay became an NIL right that was embraced by everyone involved in college sport, while a negotiated salary or a percentage of generated revenues were still pay for play and banned.

Consistent with Power Five hegemony, the NCAA and its members have steadfastly refused to allow athletes access to a free market. In the new NIL market, which has been described as the Wild West, NCAA members have developed guardrails designed to control how athletes might profit from their NILs. Within the current collegiate model, highly paid coaches and administrators claim they must protect the kids under their supervision from commercial exploitation while concurrently conducting "revenue-generating activities in a productive and sound business-like manner" (Brand 2006: 7). According to this Power Five logic, revenue maximization on its input side allows an athletic department to maximize participation opportunities for all athletes on the output side (Brand 2006). Within this model "the business of college sports is not a necessary evil; rather, it is a proper part of the overall enterprise" (ibid.). The NCAA and Power Five conferences, as well as individual athletic departments, clearly want the public, Congress, and their corporate partners to believe big-time college sport is no different from Division III college sport; nothing more than an avocation inextricably linked to the pursuit of an education. They prefer to ignore the fact that a hypercommercialized institutional logic has long dominated Power Five college sport (Southall et al. 2008).

The average Power Five college sport fan never questions why Power Five football and men's basketball players cannot be paid a negotiated wage. They unquestionably accept that sponsoring Power Five football and basketball is consistent with universities' educational mission. In his role as the collegiate model's primary evangelist, the late NCAA president Myles Brand urged administrators to conduct the business of college sport in a fiscally sound manner that maximized revenue production. Since in many businesses the cost of labor is one of the largest expenses, one way to maximize Power Five revenue-producing opportunities is to declare sacrosanct the requirement that profit-athletes must remain unpaid (i.e., minimally compensated) amateurs. One of Brand's most famous hegemonic axioms justified not paying players within a multibillion-dollar enterprise because "amateur defines the participants, not the enterprise" (Brand 2006: 8).

Hegemonic Language and Folklore

The institutional field of Power Five college sport is replete with hegemonic language, folklore, and mythology. Versions of the amateur mythology are repeated at family gatherings, displayed on arena or stadium jumbotrons, and found within film and documentary plotlines. An example of such folklore is the 1940 film *Knute Rockne, All-American,* which traces the life story of football player and iconic Notre Dame coach Rockne. Rockne was an outstanding student who after graduation was initially a graduate research assistant in Notre Dame's chemistry department. However, it was soon evident to Rockne and all of Notre Dame's chemistry faculty that he had a higher calling: coaching football at Notre Dame. Rockne went on to become one of the most successful football coaches in college sport history: "No college football coach has ever had the success of Knute Rockne. In his 13 years as the leader of Notre Dame, his teams went 105–12–5, making his .881 winning percentage the highest in history. Emphasizing quickness, deception and finesse, he had five undefeated teams and won three national championships" (Carter 2022).

Rockne, a showman who seemingly stretched the truth, is universally viewed as the coach archetype, aligned in many ways with so-called muscular Christianity (McKay and McKay 2022). From the 1870s to the 1920s, the movement had a great impact in the United States and continues to have an influence in college sport to this day.

In the film Rockne is portrayed as a larger-than-life paternalistic figure who molds naive and immature children into young men of the highest moral, physical, and intellectual character. The release of the film cemented his legendary coaching status. It was also utilized as a motivational tool for US Army troops during basic-training screenings before and during World War II (Sperber 1998).

In addition to *Knute Rockne, All American,* numerous films and documentaries are part of the collegiate model's folklore. A short list of such folkloric films—some based on true stories and some fictional depictions of college sport —would include *Rudy,* "based on the true story of aspiring Notre Dame football player Daniel 'Rudy' Ruettiger, which teaches us to refuse to give up on a dream" (Beggs 2018); *Glory Road,* about the 1966 NCAA men's basketball champions Texas Western College, which was the first Division I championship team to have five Black starters; and *We Are Marshall,* the story of the 1970 plane crash that killed thirty-seven players of the Marshall University Thundering Herd football team, as well as five coaches, two athletic trainers, the athletic director, twenty-five boosters, and the flight crew of five. These films, as well as hundreds of other films and documentaries, support the perspective that college sport is a hugely important setting in which athletes learn the value of teamwork and play for the love of the game. Such NCAA hegemony portrays college sport as a setting unsullied by crass commercialization and professionalism.

The importance of supporting NCAA hegemony through the targeted use of language was not lost on longtime NCAA executive director Walter Byers. In his autobiography *Unsportsmanlike Conduct: The Exploitation of College Athletes,* Byers describes the creation of one of the most important linguistic constructions in college sport history: "We crafted the term 'student-athlete,' and soon it was embedded in all NCAA rules and interpretations as a mandated substitute for such words as players and athletes. We told college publicists to speak of 'college teams,' not football or basketball 'clubs,' a word common to the pros" (Byers and Hammer 1995: 69).

The incessant use of the word supports the narrative that profit-athletes are students first and athletes second. However, as Staurowsky and Sack (2005: 105) note, "the term student-athlete was created by the NCAA to convince workers' compensation boards, as well as the general public, that scholarship athletes are students like any others." Since its introduction into the American English lexicon in 1956, the term has become a ubiquitous part of the college sport corpus, used unconsciously and often unthinkingly to refer to all NCAA college athletes, regardless of their revenue-generating capacity.

Consistent with the use of *student-athlete,* Brand knew that it was important for the NCAA and its member universities (especially Power Five members) to successfully position profit-athletes as "amateurs in the sense of the term most often understood by the general public" (Brand 2003: 5). In addition to the use of the term of art *student-athlete,* college sport's amateur hegemony relies on historic notions of paternalism to justify the economic exploitation of profit-athletes that results in a largely ignored and institutionalized racialization within Power Five football and basketball.

Paternalistic Exploitation

The NCAA's principle of amateurism is such a vital component of the NCAA's collegiate model that NCAA member universities must unilaterally declare their commitment to the concept: "20.9.1.2 The Commitment to Amateurism. Member institutions shall conduct their athletics programs for students who choose to participate in intercollegiate athletics as a part of their educational experience and in accordance with NCAA bylaws, thus maintaining a line of demarcation between student-athletes who participate in the Collegiate Model and athletes competing in the professional model *(Adopted: 1/19/13 effective 8/1/13)*" (NCAA 2021e). Not surprisingly, the concept of amateurism is also a textbook example of paternalism, which justifies an individual, organization, or government interfering with a person's freedoms or rights against their will on the grounds the person is better off because of this interference. The unilateral paternalistic imposition of a rule, policy, or the like is also justified because the person is somehow less-than capable of fully rational thought or decision making.

Recent (2021) changes in NIL guidelines have created uncharted territory for sports agents. Within this landscape the NCAA has unilaterally implemented an agent certification process for Division I men's basketball players (NCAA 2021a). However, according to LaRose and Sawchak (2021), "Although the NCAA and many states now allow student-athletes to profit from their NIL, the rules from these bodies have generally failed to instruct sports agents on how to represent student-athletes lawfully." To muddy the proverbial waters further, most state statutes, as well as the 2021 NCAA policy, do not regulate agents but rather athletes and universities (ibid.).

In addition, while the NCAA has concluded Division I baseball and hockey players can also retain agents/advisers, the guidelines are extremely general and vague:

> **BASKETBALL**
> Rules and deadlines changed in 2016 for students exploring entering the NBA draft. The new rule allows players to withdraw from the draft as many as 10 days after the end of the NBA draft combine. Additionally, players may now declare for the draft twice—provided they withdraw before the new deadline without hiring an agent—and will be allowed to attend the draft combine and one tryout per year for each NBA team without losing college eligibility. Players are permitted to hire an advisor provided he or she does not directly market them to teams.
>
> **BASEBALL**
> High school baseball players who are drafted by a pro team are permitted to hire an agent for professional league contract negotiations, but the relationship must be severed if the student decides to enroll in college and play baseball. Those who decide to enter the MLB draft after spending three years in college—the minimum length of time required by the MLB for those who play baseball in college—are permitted to hire an advisor. The advisor may assist the student with the decision-making process but cannot act as the student's agent.
>
> **HOCKEY**
> High school hockey players who are drafted by the NHL are permitted to play hockey in college, with the NHL team that drafted them retaining

> contract rights for four years while the player attends college. Current college students eligible for the draft are also permitted to attend the NHL draft combine and hire an advisor. The advisor may assist the student with the decision-making process but cannot act as the student's agent.
>
> Students considering whether to go pro are encouraged to consult with their school's athletics compliance office and head coach. Keeping the school informed helps ensure students have the best information possible while considering their decision. (NCAA 2021b)

What is evident from the preceding NCAA policies is that the NCAA national office has unilaterally appointed itself (on behalf of its members) the arbiter of players' consideration of their professional sport opportunities. Instead of recognizing players' autonomy and agency, the NCAA and its members have exerted paternalistic control over players' postcollegiate experiences.

A famous personification of Power Five paternalism was University of Alabama head football coach Nick Saban's 2010 excoriation of sports agents for exploiting players:

> "I don't think it's anything but greed that's creating it right now on behalf of the agents," Saban said in a rant at the SEC media days. "The agents that do this — and I hate to say this, but how are they any better than a pimp?"
>
> "I have no respect for people who do that to young people. None. How would you feel if they did it to your child?" (Brackney 2010)[2]

Saban conveniently ignored that pimps control their sex workers, making a living off the labor of their prostitutes. Pimps often recruit their victims under the pretense of a paternalistic, familial, or love relationship, specifically targeting adolescents who may have escaped physical or sexual violence at home and are economically, socially, and/or sexually vulnerable. On the other hand, a sports agent is usually an athlete's or coach's legal representative, capable of providing advice regarding a variety of topics of which an athlete may have little knowledge or experience. Agents procure and negotiate employment and endorsement (NIL) contracts for an athlete or coach whom they represent. Unlike a pimp, an agent has a legal fiduciary obligation to act in the best interest of a client.

Saban and other Power Five stakeholders avoid discussing the exploitative relationship between coaches and athletic administrators and profit-athletes, which is predicated on the coaches and administrators retaining paternalistic control of the athletes. In addition, if not for the conversion of profit-athletes' athleticism into a commodity of high commercial appeal, the Power Five universities (also known as PWIs—predominately White institutions) express little if any interest in establishing a relationship with Black male students. Within the labor market for profit-athletes, PWIs benefit from the existence of a large labor pool of prospective players. Power Five football and men's basketball recruiters develop and expand this labor pool by "cultivating an image of worker success" (Stark 1991: 27). As long as a sufficient number of profit-athletes believe they will make it to the next level, it is not necessary that every player makes it to the NFL or NBA. By generating a few high-paying professional-sport jobs and heavily publicizing the associated rewards for making it to the league, Power Five PWIs can maintain a large labor pool in the presence of high levels of unemployment (Stark 1991). Displaying iconographic successes in locker rooms, meeting areas, hall of fame displays, and stadiums and arenas serves to confuse player calculations of success. A stock of past successful players at a given PWI provides evidence that may lead to greater optimism on the part of current and future-profit athletes about a successful outcome (Stark 1991).

Without offering any evidence to support their paternalistic claims, college sport advocates argue that not paying profit-athletes is actually in the athletes' best interest and prevents them from being harmed: "Colleges should not play players. Colleges cannot pay players. To do so would hurt the very athletes supposedly being helped, devaluing intercollegiate sports until they're not worth the paper that a freshman linebacker's contract is printed upon" (Plaschke 2010). Interestingly, paternalistic college-sport apologists position college sport as a valuable enterprise that will somehow be devalued by fairly compensating the players who provide the product's value. In addition it is not a coincidence that in Plaschke's narrative the player being protected is a freshman linebacker—ostensibly a child.

On an institutional level, the NCAA's principle of amateurism codifies denying profit-athletes access to a college-sport free market: "2.9 The Principle of Amateurism. Athletes shall be amateurs in an intercollegiate sport, and their participation should be motivated primarily by education and by the physical, mental, and social benefits to be derived. Student participation in intercollegiate athletics is an avocation, and student-athletes *should be protected from* exploitation by professional and commercial enterprises" (NCAA 2021e; emphasis added). Not surprisingly the NCAA paternalistically dictates players shall be amateurs while never defining what the term actually means. Two other items are noteworthy in the preceding passage. First, college athletes' participation in athletics is described as an avocation, akin to a hobby. Secondly, consistent with Power Five college-sport hegemony, profit-athletes are subtly infantilized. They need protection from exploitation from nefarious professional and commercial interests, which may include agents, gamblers, and other villains, but not the hypercommercialized college sport enterprise (Corr, Southall, and Southall 2022; Southall and Weiler 2014).

Strikingly Power Five paternalism is often normalized and celebrated by references to a football or basketball team as a family, in which the coaches (especially head coaches) are surrogate fathers or uncles who love their kids and know what is in their best interests. If Power Five football and men's basketball players are children engaged in an extracurricular hobby, it makes sense for administrators and coaches to admonish them to leave the business of college sport to the adults.

Power Five paternalism is predicated on coaches and players having reciprocal duties. Coaches are expected to provide training, playing time, and, ostensibly, emotional support in exchange for the players' performing on the field/court and following team/family rules. In addition players have an obligation to be grateful for the opportunities coaches (as representatives of the university) provide them.

The warmup shirts that many Nike-affiliated teams wore during the 2019 March Madness tournament were a concrete embodiment of a Power Five familial team hierarchy (fig. 1). While players wore shirts proclaiming their allegiance to their "family," for the most part coaches wore traditional expensive suits and ties that clearly identified them as adult authority figures.

Figure 1. 2019 Nike Family warmup shirts.

Coaches as Father Figures, Players as Kids

College sports paternalism is justified because the coaches (as surrogate fathers) are assumed to be acting in the best interest of their kids (aka players). In many cases NCAA, conference, or university athletic department administrators and coaches justify restraints on the autonomy or agency of college athletes (especially profit-athletes) by invoking a moral obligation to protect them from threats to their well-being. NCAA bylaw 20.9.1.6, "The Commitment to Student-Athlete Well-Being," codifies paternalistic exploitation, which is actually in the players' best interest: "Intercollegiate athletics programs shall be conducted in a manner designed to enhance the well-being of student-athletes who choose to participate and to prevent undue commercial or other influences that may interfere with their scholastic, athletics, or related interests" (NCAA 2021d). By this logic, preventing athletes from being paid is in their best interests, since doing so protects them from being seduced by dreams of college sport superstardom. The desire to protect profit-athletes is often proposed with the best of intentions. In 2018 Gene Demby, cohost of National Public Radio's *Code Switch,* interviewed Ekow Yankah, a professor at Yeshiva University's Cardozo School of Law (and notably a huge fan of University of Michigan sports), who—while agreeing the current collegiate model "is unfair and rife with exploitations" (Demby 2018)—had written a *New Yorker* essay titled "Why N.C.A.A. Athletes Shouldn't Be Paid." In the interview Yankah outlined a classic paternalistic argument for not paying profit-athletes: "Of course, many of these young men are under tremendous financial difficulty. I understand that a good number of them come from backgrounds which are difficult or even impoverished, and I'm well-aware that the demands of big-time college sports, but almost all college sports, are so consuming that there seems something unfair about their having to balance these two projects [education and athletics]." Yankah acknowledged that some athletes "of a certain number of sports are seen as ever more divided from the actual student body. They're seen as tangential. They're seen as not real students." He unilaterally asserted, nevertheless, that "paying college athletes is almost certainly bad for the athletes, terrible for the universities and terrible for the sports they play. Other than that, it's a great idea. There's very little reason to think that a young athlete's life will be in any substantial way better if they become, so to speak, employees of the university" (ibid.). Yankah proceeded to denigrate his employee status and reveal his limited knowledge of NCAA governance and the lack of due process protections afforded college athletes by stating that, "indeed, . . . they will then have to trade some of the minimal protections that they have as student-athletes in order to simply be employees of the university, at least in some capacity. It seems like a pretty raw deal." He ultimately retreated to a utilitarian justification for not paying profit-athletes (who he again failed to recognize and lumped in with loss-athletes): "All of this, by the way, is in exchange for what it would actually be, for the vast majority of athletes, a remarkably small amount of money on the free market" (Demby and Gutierrez 2018).

Yankah summarized his argument in a classic paternalistic proclamation in which he repeatedly infantilized the profit-athletes he claimed to want to protect:

> The point is that it's awfully hard to project which kids will be superstars. So outside of the small number of "can't-miss" prospects, most kids will actually be paid on some scale that reflects the deep uncertainty about how

> good they'll be. And if we want to see what that looks like, we don't have to use our imagination.
>
> And in particular, for the sports that are dominated by African American men, I'm deeply interested in the next generation of black doctors, black lawyers and black bankers, rather than kids who are seduced into trading that for making spending money from 18 to 22. (Demby and Gutierrez 2018)

Throughout the interview and in his *New* Yorker article, Yankah reveals his fandom and motivated reasoning as he engages in an excruciating feat of mental gymnastics to protect his revered Michigan football and men's basketball. (Here's betting he does not follow Michigan cross country or field hockey.)

In addition to infantilizing profit-athletes apologists like Yankah often argue that they cannot be paid, since they "are already paid. It's called a scholarship. In some cases, that's a salary of more than $50,000 a year" (Plaschke 2010). When the argument is challenged, an education-first imagery is invoked: "Was there nothing cooler than hearing that, on the day of the national championship basketball game last spring, some Butler University kids actually went to class? Pay the players, and it's class dismissed" (ibid.). Reflecting the paternalism of fans and defenders of the current college sport system, broadcasters frequently refer to profit-athletes as "kids" during college football telecasts. A 2020 analysis of FBS bowl-game broadcasts found that on average game announcers referred to players as "children" or "kids" six times per broadcast (Corr, Southall and Southall 2022). This infantilization of players creates a structural dynamic in which a GIA (which can include a cost-of-attendance stipend) is viewed as an allowance bestowed on a child out of the goodness of a benevolent parent figure's heart.

The Myth of the Missing Black Father

The justification of coaches' taking on the role of surrogate fathers and looking out for or protecting their "kids" has a long history. In many instances this narrative is racialized. A common refrain from White Power Five football coaches is that a majority of their Black players are poor and come from broken homes: "100% lower-class. Low-income homes, single parents, sometimes no parents, sometimes children" (as quoted in Corr, Southall, and Nagel 2020: 21). If the perception is that nearly all profit-athletes are poor, it is not a stretch to assume these players are financially illiterate. Consequently, some Power Five football programs, such as Ohio State University, have had assistant football coaches monitor players' checking accounts and spending habits (Gregory 2012). Tellingly no reports exist of Olympic sport coaches monitoring their athletes' checking accounts or spending habits.

In addition to players' socioeconomic status being a rationale for paternalistic intrusion, the mythology of the missing Black father is another justification (Levs 2020). If Black fathers are not present in Black players lives, then coaches must fill the void. "You see, in today's world you have athletes from zero stars to five stars who come from great homes and many who come from broken ones" (Kitchens 2008). In this scenario the head football coach is portrayed as the mentor and surrogate father who transforms childlike players into men: "[Coaches] have a heavier burden . . . guiding, chastising and leading these kids into becoming grown men. Ones [who] are ready for life on and off the field. Ones that have experienced the thrill of victory and the life lesson that comes with an agonizing defeat." College sports is often framed as instilling discipline in immature players, teaching kids life lessons and helping them grow into men. This infantilization denies player agency, putting coaches on a patriarchal pedestal: "Now, more than ever, we have to applaud the actions of a few grown men who have been given the daunting task of raising 85 scholarship [*sic*]—and countless others not on scholarship—kids who need to know more than when to turn their hips before being burnt deep on a post pattern" (ibid.). For many college sports fans (especially Power Five football fans) a White head coach is the default setting. Consequently college football programs are organized around their needs, reality is seen from their perspectives, their attributes are seen as most valuable and productive, and they (naturally) dominate politics and culture and often assume the role of patriarchal savior who controls and dominates his players. Johnson (1997) describes patriarchy as a male-centered, male-identified, and male-dominated social structure that promotes male privilege. It is organized around an obsession with control, through which men seek security, status, and other rewards. Profit-athlete coaches often personify this control, which they identify as their best defense against loss and humiliation. In this sense what happens among and between coaches and players is about patriarchy and paternalism.

The Racialization of College Sport Exploitation

Eventually any discussion of coaches and administrators' paternalistic exploitation of profit-athletes becomes racialized, since in the two lucrative Power Five sports—football and men's basketball—the players are overwhelmingly athletes of color while the coaches and administrators are predominately White males. Put simply, revenue from Power Five football and Division I men's basketball is transferred to coaches, administrators, and athletes in predominately White "non-revenue" or Olympic (aka "country club") sports such as golf, tennis, crew, lacrosse, volleyball, beach volleyball, and equestrian. The revenue produced by the athletic labor of profit-athletes is redistributed to these sports in order to increase athletic opportunities and help construct ever-more lavish facilities and sustain athletic opportunities for predominately White athletes.

In addition salaries of coaches and administrators have increased significantly, with the amount spent on Power Five coaching staff salaries at public colleges/universities growing from $4.8 in 2008 to $9.8 million ten years later. In addition, coaches for all other sports at Power Five schools have seen their average annual staff salary totals increase by 70 percent from 2008 to 2018, from $7.3 to $12.5 million. In this same period, not to be left out, non-coaching administrative salaries totals have increased from $12.1 to $22.3 million (Garthwaite et al. 2020).

While the overall participation rates of Black and other players of color in Power Five football and men's basketball are significant, a more telling statistic is their representation among starters, since those are the marquee players who fans primarily come to see and are subsequently the most profitable of profit-athletes. The extent to which Black players drive Power Five revenue production is reflected in the disproportionately high percentage of Black starters in Power Five football and men's basketball (see table 1).

Exploiting the revenue generated by profit-athletes has long been the goal of Power Five college sports. This focus on revenue generation and commercialization is not a recent phenomenon. College sport has always been a business. As Schwarz (2014) noted, "people who imagine a time where college sports weren't commercialized are fantasizing, because even before the NCAA existed, deep in the formative years of modern sports (the 19th century), college rowing was paying prizes larger than the median annual wage in the United States. . . . In the 1870s, the winners of an intercollegiate rowing regatta on Lake Saratoga were given silver goblets worth $500—this at a time when the average annual wage in the United States was $300."

While amateurism has been held up as a noble ideal, big-time college sport has been highly commercialized and professional from its inception. To reconcile

Table 1. 2020 Power Five football and men's basketball starters by conference

CONFERENCE	TOTAL REVENUE AVG.	FOOTBALL STARTERS, %		BASKETBALL STARTERS, %	
		BLACK	*WHITE*	*BLACK*	*WHITE*
SEC	$147,734,860	82.2	17.8	93.8	6.2
Big-Ten	$142,963,500	61.5	36.7	75.4	24.6
Big-XII	$123,566,656	72.2	26.7	90.0	10.0
ACC	$114,988,263	76.1	23.3	77.5	20.0
PAC-12	$103,221,675	58.6	31.4	74.0	22.0
Power Five	$126,494,991	70.1	27.2	82.1	16.6

this obvious disconnect, "the college-sport enterprise has been built on a series of legal fictions spun from the imaginative and strategic manufacture of language designed to create the impression that the business practices associated with the running of big-time college sport are educational and not exploitative in nature" (Southall and Staurowsky 2013: 409) As the scale of the college sport industry has increased, so has the exploitation of profit-athletes. As Mitten and Ross (2014: 848) correctly identified, "the current structure results in significant economic exploitation of elite Division I football and men's basketball players, without whose efforts these revenues would not be possible."

At every level the exploitation has been ignored or rationalized. Former NCAA president Myles Brand admonished NCAA members that since *amateur* defines the participants, not the enterprise, NCAA member universities "should not be ambivalent about doing the business of college sports. We should do it well," in order to "distribute resources to those programs incapable of generating sufficient revenues on their own" (Brand 2006: 11). For Power Five athletic departments, redistributing surplus revenues from football and men's basketball programs to support a broad range of intercollegiate sports for elite athletes that do not generate sufficient revenues to pay their costs is a socially worthy action (Schwarz 2014).

What is not mentioned is the uncomfortable reality that the vast majority of athletes in these sports that do not generate sufficient revenues to pay their costs are middle- or upper-class and White. It is no secret that other than football, basketball, and track and field, college sport—in all three divisions—is a predominately White institution. Consequently the institutionalized exploitation of profit-athletes' athletic labor is racialized. As previously discussed, more than 70 percent of Power Five football and 82 percent of men's basketball players—who almost literally fund the entire college sport industry—are Black. An examination of the NCAA's Demographics Database reveals the extent of this racialized exploitation. Of the 119 NCAA-sponsored sports across Divisions I, II, and III, 94, or 79 percent, had under 10 percent Black athlete participation in 2012–20. Excluding Power Five schools, 61 percent of sports across the three divisions (100 out of 164) have less than 5 percent Black athlete participation.

The twenty-five sports that have greater than 10 percent Black participation between 2012 and 2020 are

- Division I, II, and III football, men's basketball, and women's basketball;
- Division I and II women's bowling;
- Division I, II, and III men's indoor and outdoor track and field;
- Division I and II women's indoor and outdoor track and field;
- Division I and II women's volleyball;
- Division II men's and women's cross country.

The fact that college sport is a racialized institution does not mean that every White coach, administrator, or loss-athlete is a racist. However, it is clear that excess revenues generated from—most notably—Power Five football and men's basketball programs support what Hawkins (2010) called the "intercollegiate athletic industrial complex" that has exploited the athletic capital of (disproportionately Black) profit-athletes for decades. This revenue provides multimillion-dollar salaries for coaches, disproportionately rewards athletic administrators, and fuels a facilities arms race across campuses. In addition millions of dollars flow each year to sports that don't generate substantial revenue and hence rely on the substantial profits from Power Five football and men's basketball (as well as direct university support from student fees, etc.) to sustain them financially.

The White students playing those sports tend to come from wealthier neighborhoods than those who play football and basketball. On average Black athletes constitute nearly 60 percent of the rosters of football and man's basketball teams and just 11 percent of the rosters of all other sports. Similar racial dynamics are apparent among coaches. Football and basketball players also come from neighborhoods with higher rates of poverty and lower incomes than students in other sports. Fundamentally White athletes, coaches, and administrators often profit from Black profit-athletes' labor. While all profit-athletes, who receive no additional compensation for the considerable revenue they generate, are exploited, the extremely regressive nature of the collegiate model becomes racialized as a result of the high percentage of Black starters. This racialization is best understood as occurring on three different levels within the institution of Power Five college sports: micro, meso and macro.

Micro-level Racialization

Phillips (2011) contends racialization occurs at micro, meso and macro levels and can be both overt and covert. Micro-level or individual racialization involves actions (discrimination) that are motivated by an individual's beliefs (prejudice) about racial/ethnic minorities. Individual prejudice is often expressed within a social and cultural normative climate in which a dominant in-group (e.g., a White majority) expresses support for prejudiced attitudes, which leads to this group's positive self-image (Phillips 2011). Within Power Five college sport's institutional field, there is a complex interplay of racist attitudes and discriminatory behaviors, with individuals sometimes holding and expressing both positive and negative attitudes toward minority ethnic groups.

An example of such overt micro-level individual racialization within Power Five college sport is when University of Texas women's athletic director Chris Plonsky obliquely compared "revenue sport" athletes, a majority of whom are Black, to crack cocaine users: "I view these cases as being the result of the entitlement attitude we've created in our revenue sports. We now have threatening (student-athletes)—many of whom, based on grad rates of the 80s and 90s, sucked a whole lot off the college athletics pipe—and now want to buckle the system at the knees at the expense of today's (student-athletes)" (quoted in Trahan 2014). Plonsky's comments are indicative of a " 'new racism,' where egalitarian ideals can co-exist with an anti-Black affect" (Phillips 2011: 176). At the micro-level, attitudes toward profit-athletes are not homogenous, and individuals in positions of authority may hold both negative and positive attitudes toward profit-athletes writ large and specifically Black profit-athletes.

Meso-level Racialization

The meso-level institutional racialization found in Power Five college sport is reflected in institutional policies, practices, and procedures that result in the economic exploitation of an athletic labor force that disproportionately comprises racial/ethnic minorities. Hawkins (2010: 71) argues that in Power Five college sport meso-level racialization involves "institutionalization of cultural and social racism coupled with economic and political exploitation [of Black athletes by predominately White institutions]. . . . The dehumanization of Black athletes takes place when these institutions value Blacks more as athletes [and workers] than as students, especially when output (athletic performance) does not equal input (educational opportunities)." McCormick and McCormick (2010: 16) claim meso-level racialization is widespread, with "a matrix of NCAA rules keep[ing] these mostly African-American young men generating vast sums of money for the benefit of predominantly European Americans thereby enshrining an apartheid system in which racial minorities are held in legal servitude for the profit and entertainment of the racial majority." For McCormick and McCormick, big-time college sport is a Jim Crow system that sanctions the exploitation of Black profit-athletes for enormous commercial gain of major Power Five universities, athletic departments, and corporations.

Macro-level Racialization

Macro-level or systemic racialization reflects an underlying societal value system that normalizes both micro- and meso-level racialization. Power Five college sport is a social space replete with disparate power dynamics that result in the systemic exploitation of profit-athletes by many of America's preeminent educational institutions. It is a segment within an institutional field that Brett St. Louis (2008) refers to as "the capitalist-athletic complex" and Smith (2007) describes as "the athletic-industrial complex." Throughout Power Five college sport, there is an expectation that football and men's basketball programs will generate sufficient revenue to cover not only their expenses but also the shortfalls of all other sponsored sports. Since NCAA Division I schools are required to sponsor a minimum of fourteen teams, many Power Five athletic department have expenses that exceed a hundred million dollars annually (table 6).

The pressure to generate many millions of dollars in annual revenue to cover expenses for unprofitable sports results in Power Five schools (many of which are Carnegie Classification "R1: Doctoral Universities—Very high research activity") recruiting profit-athletes who are "often the most academically underprepared relative to other students" (Van Rheenen 2012: 551). The recruitment and "special talent admission" of academically underprepared athletes has been described by the late Gerald Gurney (Oklahoma's senior associate athletic director for academics and student life from 1993 until 2011 and OU assistant professor who taught courses on athletics in higher education, athletics academic reform and ethics in athletics from 2011 to 2021) as "the original sin of college sports" (quoted in Olson 2019). As Sonny Vaccaro famously said, "Ninety percent of the NCAA revenue is produced by 1 percent of the athletes. . . . Go to the skill positions—the stars. Ninety percent African Americans" (as quoted in Branch 2011).

The recruitment and admission of academically underprepared profit-athletes occurs against a macro-societal setting in which Black youth, especially those from poor and working-class families, are often blamed for their salient athletic identities (Kidd 2019; Steinfeldt, Reed, and Steinfeldt 2010). Simultaneously praised and villainized for their sports obsession, profit-athletes are strangers in a strange land—low-paid laborers who find themselves caught in a system that has elements of a company town, plantation, or migrant labor camp (Hawkins 2010; Southall and Weiler 2014).

While profit-athletes may be engulfed in their athletic role, PWIs also fixate on profit-athletes' athletic prowess, overlooking academic challenges and admitting a disproportionate number through a "special talent" admissions process (Espenshade, Chung, and Walling 2004; Olson 2019). Clearly many Power Five college presidents, athletic directors, coaches, and faculty view profit-athletes as valuable revenue-generating commodities. As a result of this commodified status, profit-athletes exist in a highly segregated total-institutional setting (Southall and Weiler 2014). While big-time college football and men's basketball players may walk among other athletes and students at PWIs, they exist in a racialized institutional setting with invisible but very real disparate educational effects.

The existence of profit-athletes is highly segregated. They live, work, and play their games in a physically, culturally, and socially isolated setting in which they have limited interaction with members of the campus community. While profit-athletes are promised access to a world-class education, the most successful Power Five football and men's basketball players graduate at significantly lower rates than full-time students.

Discrepancies in graduation rates at Power Five institutions raise questions about claims of unilateral academic progress of profit-athletes. Utilizing a graduation rate metric developed by Dr. E. Woodrow Eckard of the University of Colorado Denver, since 2010 the College Sport Research Institute has published a series of annual adjusted graduation gap (AGG) reports on profit-athletes as well as athletes in Division I women's basketball, softball, and baseball. The AGG reports identify gaps in NCAA and US federal graduation rates between athletes and full-time students. According to the 2020–21 AGG reports, Black profit-athletes graduate at much lower rates than full-time students in Power Five football (21.5 percent less) and in Division I men's basketball (36.4 percent less). Notably in Power Five football, White players graduate at almost the same rate as their full-time classmates (table 2).

Table 2. 2020–21 Power Five football adjusted graduation gaps (AGG) by conference

SPORT	ADJUSTED GRADUATION GAP (M)		
	COMBINED	*BLACK*	*WHITE*
Power Five Football	−17.2	−21.5	−2.1
NCAA Division I Men's Basketball	−34.7	−36.4	−28.9

Conclusion

While the value of a college education is undisputed, AGG data document that Black profit-athletes do not have equal access to educational opportunities that constitute this value. Not allowed to truly be students and denied employee protections, profit-athletes do not accrue the economic or social benefits typically associated with a postsecondary education.

In addition to being denied access to educational opportunities, profit-athletes are financially exploited. Since the dawn of big-time college sport, amateurism has been inherently exploitative. What has changed since the 1970s is the degree to which the exploitation has become racialized. In a college-sport system that is often viewed as a post-racial meritocracy, the significant and disparate negative impact of the economic exploitation on profit-athletes is often overlooked. Notably the utilitarian justification for the redistribution of the generated revenues is predicated on institutionalizing the privileged positions of White Olympic sport athletes. Power Five college sport—not surprisingly—reproduces the racialization in society at large. As today's Power Five college sport boom continues, everyone chooses to overlook the system's inherent racialization. Everyone getting rich off of the labor primarily of profit-athletes of color (70–80% of the labor force), including conference commissioners and administrators, university presidents and trustees, athletic directors and department staff, and head coaches and their assistants, ignores the blatant exploitation and ignores that the Power Five house of cards relies on a series of legal fictions and institutional propaganda.

Notes

1. Profit-athletes have limited representation on NCAA committees, boards, or councils. As of 2021 the Division I Board of Directors has a recently graduated Power Five football player listed on its roster. The expiration date of his board term is listed as May 2023. In three years, 2017–19, the player did not see game action. For the 2020 and 2021 seasons, he was not listed on his team's roster.

There are no profit-athletes on the following NCAA committees or boards: NCAA Board of Governors, Board of Governors Student-Athlete Engagement Committee, Board of Governors Committee to Promote Cultural Diversity and Equity, Committee on Competitive Safeguards and Medical Aspects of Sports, Committee on Sportsmanship and Ethical Conduct, NCAA Constitution Committee, Minority Opportunities and Interests Committee, Olympic Sports Liaison Committee, Playing Rules Oversight Panel, NCAA Division I Committee on Infractions, Division I Infractions Appeals Committee, Division I Committee on Academics, Division I Finance Committee, or the Division I Board of Directors Infractions Process Committee.

2. As of October 2021, sports agents are still regulated under the Uniform Athlete Agents Act (UAAA), a model statute that has been adopted by forty-two states, as well as the Sports Agent Responsibility and Trust Act (SPARTA), a federal statute. Both the UAAA and SPARTA prohibit NCAA athletes from entering into a representation contract with an agent. Needless to say, the current situation is in flux.

References

Aristotle. (1934). *Nicomachean Ethics.* Translated by H. Rackham. Loeb Classical Library. Cambridge, MA: Harvard University Press. http://www.perseus.tufts.edu/hopper/.

Avila, Alejandro (2021). "TCU FB coach Gary Patterson Warns Boosters to Pay Up or Watch Recruits Leave." *OutKick,* September 24. https://www.outkick.com/.

Beggs, Scott (2018). "Eleven Winning Facts about *Rudy.*" *Mental Floss,* October 22. https://www.mentalfloss.com/.

Brackney, Bryan (2010). "Nick Saban Calls Agents 'Pimps.'" *Bleacher Report,* July 22. https://bleacherreport.com/.

Branch, Taylor (2011). "The Shame of College Sports." *Atlantic,* October, 80–110. http://www.theatlantic.com/.

Brand, Myles (2003). "NCAA State of the Association Delivered as NCAA President at 2003 NCAA Convention." January 1. https://mylesbrand.com/.

———. (2006). "Brand Charts Course for Collegiate Model's Next Century." Speech delivered to the NCAA Convention, January 7. https://mylesbrand.com/.

Brink, David (2018). "Mill's Moral and Political Philosophy." In *The Stanford Encyclopedia of Philosophy,* edited by Edward N. Zalta. https://plato.stanford.edu/.

Byers, Walter, with Charles Hammer (1995). *Unsportsmanlike Conduct: Exploiting College Athletes.* Ann Arbor: University of Michigan Press.

Carter, Bob (2022). "Knute Rockne Was Notre Dame's Master Motivator." ESPN Classic. https://www.espn.com/ (accessed August 7).

College Football Playoff (2021). "CFP Governance." https://collegefootballplayoff.com/.

Corr, Chris, Richard M. Southall, and Mark S. Nagel (2020). "Southeastern Conference Recruiting and the Maintenance of Power-5 College Sport." *Journal of Issues in Intercollegiate Athletics*, 13, 252–72. http://csri-jiia.org/.

Corr, Chris, Crystal Southall, and Richard M. Southall (2022). "The Espnification of Football Bowl Subdivision College Football: The Adoption of an Integrated Marketing Communication Televisuality in Football Bowl Subdivision Bowl Game Broadcasts." *International Journal of Sport Communication*, 15, no. 2: 139–47. https://journals-humankinetics-com.eu1.proxy.openathens.net/.

Demby, Gene, and Maria Paz Gutierrez (2018). "Why Shouldn't We Pay Student-Athletes?" *The Code Switch Podcast*, March 23. https://www.npr.org/.

Espenshade, T. J., C. Y. Chung, and J. L. Walling (2004). "Admission Preferences for Minority Students, Athletes, and Legacies at Elite Universities." *Social Science Quarterly* 85, no. 5: 1422–46. doi:10.1111/j.0038–4941.2004.00284.x.

Fendrich, Howard, and Eddie Pells (2021). "In AP Survey, ADs Raise Worries about Women's College Sports." AP News, April 1. https://apnews.com/.

Forde, Pat (2011). "Myth of Exploited, Impoverished Athletes." ESPN.com, July 18. https://www.espn.com/.

Friedland, Roger, and Robert R. Alford (1991). "Bringing Society Back In: Symbols, Practices, and Institutional Contradictions." In *The New Institutionalism in Organizational Analysis*, edited by Walter W. Powell and Paul J. DiMaggio, 232–63. Chicago: University of Chicago Press.

Garthwaite, Craig, Jordan Keener, Matthew J. Notowidigdo, and Nicole F. Ozminkowski (2020). "Who Profits from Amateurism? Rent-Sharing in Modern College Sports." Working Paper 27734. National Bureau of Economic Research, working paper 27734. https://www.nber.org/papers/w27734.

Gramsci, Antonio (1971). *Selections from the Prison Notebooks*. Edited and translated by Quentin Hoare and Geoffrey N. Smith. New York: International.

Gregory, Sean (2012). "Why Is Ohio State Football Monitoring Player Checking Accounts?" *Keeping Score*, December 13. https://keepingscore.blogs.time.com/.

Hawkins, Billy (2010). *The New Plantation: Black Athletes, College Sports, and Predominantly White NCAA Institutions*. New York: Palgrave Macmillan.

Ingraham, Christopher (2020). "NCAA Rules Allow White Students and Coaches to Profit off Labor of Black Ones, Study Finds." *Washington Post*, September 7. https://www.washingtonpost.com/.

Jepperson, Ronald L. (1991). "Institutions, institutional effects, and institutionalism." In *The New Institutionalism in Organizational Analysis*, edited by Walter W. Powell and Paul J. DiMaggio, 143–63. Chicago: University of Chicago Press.

Johnson, Allan G. (1997). *The Gender Knot: Unraveling Our Patriarchal Legacy*. Philadelphia: Temple University Press.

Johnson, Robert, and Adam Cureton (2021). "Kant's Moral Philosophy." In *The Stanford Encyclopedia of Philosophy*, edited by Edward N. Zalta. https://plato.stanford.edu/archives/.

Kidd, Victor Dion (2019). " 'WE NEED DAWGS!': Narrative Construction of Athletic Identity among Black High School Football Players." PhD dissertation, University of South Carolina.

Kitchens, Kit (2008). "College Football: The Coach as Father Figure." *Bleacher Report*, July 15. https://bleacherreport.com/.

LaRose, Brandon, and Matthew W. Sawchak (2021, August 2). "Not so Alike: Current Impact of NIL Administration on the Regulation of Sports Agents." Robinson Bradshaw, August 2. https://www.robinsonbradshaw.com/.

Levs, Josh (2020). "They're Dragging out the 'Absent Black Fathers' Myth Again. Can We Give It a Rest?" *Newsweek,* June 5. https://www.newsweek.com/.

McCormick, Robert A., and Amy Christian McCormick (2010). "Major College Sports: A Modern Apartheid." *Texas Review of Entertainment and Sports Law* 12, no. 1: 13–51.

McInerny, Ralph, and John O'Callaghan (2018). "Saint Thomas Aquinas." In *The Stanford Encyclopedia of Philosophy,* edited by Edward N. Zalta. https://plato.stanford.edu/.

McKay, Brett, and Kate McKay (2022). "When Christianity Was Muscular." *The Art of Manliness.* https://www.artofmanliness.com/ (accessed August 8).

Mitten, Matthew J., and Stephen F. Ross (2014). "A Regulatory Solution to Better Promote the Educational Values and Economic Sustainability of Intercollegiate Athletics." *Oregon Law Review* 92, no. 4: 837–77.

National Collegiate Athletic Association (2012). "Emmert Cheers on the Collegiate Model." NCAA.org, January 12. http://ncaanewsarchive.s3.amazonaws.com/.

———. (2014a). "Division I Steering Committee on Governance: Draft Governance Model." https://sports.cbsimg.net/.

———. (2014b). "NCAA President's Testimony on Value of College Model." NCAA.org, July 9. https://www.ncaa.org/.

———. (2021a). "Agent Certification." NCAA.org. https://www.ncaa.org/.

———. (2021b). "Deciding Whether to Go Pro." NCAA.org. https://www.ncaa.org/.

———. (2021c). "Pay." LSDBi. https://web3.ncaa.org/lsdbi/search/bylawView?id=103593#result.

———. (2021d). "The Commitment to Student-Athlete Well-Being." LSDBi. https://web3.ncaa.org/.

———. (2021e). "The Principle of Amateurism." LSDBi. https://web3.ncaa.org/.

———. (2021f). NCAA Demographics Database. https://www.ncaa.org/.

———. (2022). "Divisional Differences and the History of Multidivision Classification." https://www.ncaa.org/.

New, Jake (2014). "Autonomy Gained." *Inside Higher Ed,* August 8. https://www.insidehighered.com/.

Olson, Eric (2019). "Special Admissions Called 'Original Sin' of College Sports." AP News, March 16. https://apnews.com/.

Phillips, Coretta (2011). "Institutional Racism and Ethnic Inequalities: An Expanded Multilevel Framework." *Journal of Social Policy* 40, no. 1: 173–92.

Plaschke, Bill (2010). "Paying College Players Is an Inherently Bad Idea." *Los Angeles Times,* November 18. https://www.latimes.com/.

Rhoden, William C. (2014). "A Victory for Athletes as University Employees." *New York Times,* March 26. https://www.nytimes.com/.

Russo, Ralph D. (2021). "NCAA's Mark Emmert: It Is Time to Decentralize College Sports." *Los Angeles Times,* July 15. https://www.latimes.com/.

Schwarz, Andy (2014). "How Not to Reform the NCAA." *Deadspin,* August 1. https://deadspin.com/.

Smith, Earl (2007). *Race, Sport, and the American Dream.* Durham, NC: Carolina Academic Press.

Southall, Richard M., Mark S. Nagel, John Amis, and Crystal Southall (2008). "A Method to March Madness?: Institutional Logics and the 2006 National Collegiate Athletic Association Division I Men's Basketball Tournament." *Journal of Sport Management*, 22, no. 6: 677–700. https://doi.org/10.1123/jsm.22.6.677.

Southall, Richard M., and Ellen J. Staurowsky (2013). "Cheering on the Collegiate Model: Creating, Disseminating, and Imbedding the NCAA's Redefinition of Amateurism." *Journal of Sport and Social Issues*, 37, no. 4: 403–29. https://doi.org/10.1177/0193723513498606.

Southall, Richard M., and Jonathan D. Weiler (2014). "NCAA D-I Athletic Departments: Twenty-First-Century Company Towns." *Journal of Issues in Intercollegiate Athletics* 7: 161–86. http://csri-jiia.org/.

Southall, Richard M., and Richard T. Karcher (2016). "Distributive Injustice: An Ethical Analysis of the NCAA's 'Collegiate Model of Athletics' and its Jurisprudence." *International Sports Law Journal*, 15, no. 3: 210–25. https://doi.org/10.1007/s40318-015-0084-6.

Sperber, Murray A. (1998). *Onward to Victory: The Crises That Shaped College Sports.* New York: Holt.

St. Louis, Brett (2009). "Post-Marxism, Black Marxism and the Politics of Sport." In *Marxism, Cultural Studies and Sport,* edited by Ben Carrington and Ian McDonald, 109–30. New York: Routledge.

Stark, Oded (1991). *The Migration of Labor.* Cambridge, MA: Blackwell.

Staurowsky, Ellen J., and Allen L. Sack (2005). "Reconsidering the Use of the Term Student-Athlete in Academic Research." *Journal of Sport Management* 19, no. 2: 103–16.

Steinfeldt, Jesse A., Courtney Reed, and M. Clint Steinfeldt (2010). "Racial and Athletic Identity of African American Football Players at Historically Black Colleges and Universities and Predominantly White Institutions." *Journal of Black Psychology* 36, no. 1: 3–24.

Trahan, Kevin (2014). "Texas Women's AD Says Athletes Who Want a Cut Are 'Entitled.'" *SB Nation,* June 17. https://www.sbnation.com/.

Van Rheenen, Derek (2013). "Exploitation in College Sports: Race, Revenue, and Educational Reward." *International Review for the Sociology of Sport* 48, no. 5: 550–71.

Watkins, Matthew (2016). "Football Revenue Helps Other Sports in Colleges." *El Paso Times,* September 20. https://eu.elpasotimes.com/.

The End of the Beginning of the End?

Richard M. Southall
and Mark S. Nagel

> Now this is not the end. It is not even the beginning of the end. But it is, perhaps, the end of the beginning.
>
> —WINSTON CHURCHILL

In 2014, as part of its "State of College Athletics Forum," the Big 12 Conference sponsored a panel discussion titled "Are Student-Athletes Employees?" Panelists included journalists, athletics officials, and former professional basketball players. Not surprisingly, given the panelists' backgrounds, no one was in favor of a system in which any players in any sports were paid to play. When asked by moderator Jimmy Roberts whether college athletes should be paid, Christine Brennan, a *USA Today* sports columnist and commentator for ESPN, ABC, and Fox Sports, bluntly responded, "Absolutely not! They are in many ways receiving a lot of benefits now, with a college scholarship . . . $100,000 a year . . . in terms of coaching, exposure, training, all the things and [*sic*] receiving a first-class education at the finest educational institutions on earth (Big 12 Conference 2014).

While none of the panelists espoused the radical notion that college athletes should be paid employees, several discussed the need to address economic inequities in college sport. Tom McMillen, former member of Congress (D-MD) and the future president and CEO of LEAD1 Association,[1] proposed creating "equities across the board for every athlete where they get a basic stipend that allows them to have a life" (Big 12 Conference 2014). Despite some support for permitting athletes greater compensation, the consensus of the panelists was that radical industry reform was unnecessary. Strikingly none of the panelists mentioned that profit-athletes' expectations or experiences were in any way different from those of other college sport athletes.

Every panelist defended the current collegiate model and characterized paying profit-athletes as unfair to all other hardworking college athletes, antithetical to broad-based intercollegiate athletic programs, detrimental to the US Olympic movement, or a clear violation of Title IX. Texas women's athletic director Chris Plonsky contended that college athletes were entitled to a full cost-of-attendance GIA but not "remuneration or pay for play," noting that collegiate athletics is a "volunteer type of situation. No one is twisting your arm to embark upon what today NCAA Division I athletics requires" (Big 12 Conference 2014). Plonsky's opposition to paying profit-athletes was consistent with a 2013 statement in a federal court filing (*O'Bannon v. NCAA*) in which the University of Texas Exec. Sr. Associate AD/Chief of Staff attested that the school "has no interest in a model that would force us to professionalize two sports to the detriment of the balance of the athletics department's sports, fitness and educational programs" (quoted in Berkowitz 2013). During the 2014 panel, Plonsky refrained from repeating her earlier attacks on profit-athletes who desire access to fundamental individual rights. In 2012 correspondence unsealed in *O'Bannon v. NCAA*, Plonsky had ridiculed O'Bannon plaintiffs as selfish and entitled: "I view these cases as being the result of the entitlement attitude we've created in our revenue sports. We now have threatening (student-athletes)—many of whom, based on grad rates of the 80s and 90s, sucked a whole lot off the college athletics pipe—and now want to buckle the system at the knees at the expense of today's (student-athletes)" (quoted in Solomon 2012). While most other commentators do not openly mock or attack big-time college football and basketball players, Plonsky is certainly not the only college sport stakeholder who has gone on record opposing pay for play.

In 2015 Clemson's head football coach, Dabo Swinney, said he would quit coaching if his players were paid: "As far as paying players, professionalizing college athletics, that's where you lose me. . . . I'll go do something else because there's enough entitlement in this world as there is" (quoted in Watson 2015). In an extended commentary on big-time college sport, John Oliver, host of HBO's *Last Week Tonight with John Oliver,* noted Swinney's hypocrisy and entitlement: "The larger point is, Swinney has trademarked his name for use on shirts because he's allowed to do that. The NCAA manual explicitly states coaches are free to pursue endorsements or consultation contracts and players are acutely aware of this discrepancy" (quoted in Watson 2015). In fairness to Swinney, he is not the only college coach or administrator who has claimed that college sport reforms were misguided and—if implemented—would cause them to seek alternative employment. In 2019 Swinney and Clemson agreed to a ten-year contract extension worth $93 million in salary, endorsement deals, and radio and television show contracts (Bromberg 2019). Interestingly, at the time of Dabo's extension, a number of college sport reforms that would provide increased commercial opportunities for college players were being openly discussed, but no one asked, and Swinney did not bother to indicate, whether he planned to terminate his contract if college players were paid for their name, image, and likeness (NIL).

The rejection by industry insiders of radical reform efforts follows a familiar pattern: they decry proposed reforms as potentially ending college sport as we know it but then conveniently ignore that the sky didn't fall when the reforms are enacted. In 2013, when NIL rights were a central focus of *O'Bannon v. NCAA* (2015), Big Ten Conference commissioner Jim Delany asserted—and in subsequent interviews reaffirmed—that conference members would likely stop competing at the Division I level if players were permitted to share in a greater portion of overall generated revenues. He indicated that in such a world of higher compensation for athletes, a Division III model would "be more consistent with The Big Ten's philosophy that the educational and lifetime economic benefits associated with a university education are the appropriate quid pro quo for its student athletes" (Solomon 2013). Years later, as Delany was interviewed about his retirement in 2020, he indicated that more open NIL rules for college players were going to be enacted because it was an issue that united "civil libertarians, economic people and also social justice people who feel this is an unfair state of affairs." He continued: "That's going to get resolved. There's a lot of people who think this is going to happen quickly. It almost has to, doesn't it, given the constraints of states adopting their own name, image and likeness laws?" (Dodd 2020). Tellingly, during the interview Delany focused more on the Big Ten's success in basketball and football, the expansion of the College Football Playoff, the future of the Rose Bowl, and his longing for a past when freshman were ineligible than on college athlete's rights.

For those paying close attention, fifty years of reforms have repeatedly caused big-time college sport officials to cry wolf, only for such reforms to be enacted and big-time college sport to abandon yet another exploitative practice. At the time of this writing, the term "pay for play" (which is coded language for employment status and revenue sharing) remains the proverbial line in the sand as NIL (including athletes entering into individual NIL contracts, and athletes being paid by third-party collectives for charitable activities and/or other appearances) has quickly become an accepted Power Five industry best practice. While amateurism has been extinct since at least 1956, the NCAA clings to its collegiate model, which continues to represent "a clear line of demarcation between intercollegiate athletics and professional sports" (bylaw 1.3.1). Clinging to an amateurism that frankly never was, highly commercialized and professionalized Power Five football and basketball coaches and administrators publicly express allegiance to a collegiate model that barely resembles what Myles Brand outlined in his 2006 state of the association address. The US Supreme Court case *NCAA v. Alston* (2021) revealed how the Court's view of the NCAA has changed since *NCAA v. Board of Regents* (1984) and established a path forward to fix a corrupt system that has for decades exploited thousands of profit-athletes.

NCAA v. Alston (2021)

Calls for college sport reform have become as much a part of Power Five college sport as National Signing Day, March Madness, and the College Football Playoff. However, for the most part such reform efforts have been ineffectual at best at addressing the college sport industry's core employment problem. In addition to most reformers and NCAA members clinging to a revered tradition of amateurism, historically the US legal system has frequently unilaterally accepted the NCAA's undefined amateurism (Corr et al. 2022). While in *NCAA v. Board of Regents* the Supreme Court found that the NCAA cartel had violated the Sherman Act, the Court still commented that the NCAA "plays a critical role in the maintenance of a revered tradition of amateurism in college sports" (20). Consequently the Court suggested the NCAA "needs ample latitude to play that role" (ibid.).

Many college sport administrators and NCAA supporters have cited the Court's dicta as persuasive authority justifying the NCAA's imposing restrictions on college athlete compensation to maintain its amateurism. However, while this comment seemingly protected the NCAA's business model, Myles Brand presciently recognized the need for a better-understood definition of amateurism.[2] Brand hoped his rebranded collegiate model of athletics would accomplish this goal: "Critical for the future of intercollegiate athletics will likely be a better understood definition of amateurism that isolates the principle to the way in which student-athletes are viewed without imposing its avocational nature on revenue-producing opportunities" (NCAA 2010).[3] For Brand, a crucial subtlety of his reformulated collegiate model was that *amateurism* defines the participants, not the enterprise:

> Commercial activity, meaning, for example, the sale of broadcast rights and logo licensing, is not only acceptable, but mandated by the business plan, provided that it is done so in a way that fully respects the underlying principles of the university. Instances in which advertising is offensive, in which it is crass or overwhelming, are incompatible with these values. But commercialism per se is not. It depends entirely on how the commercial activity is conducted. (Brand 2006: 11)

In addition, for college athletes to be protected from commercial exploitation, they must remain amateurs:

> The fundamental reason we do not pay student-athletes to play is because they are students. This commitment is captured in the first principle of the collegiate model. The participants in intercollegiate athletics are students.

> They are not, in their roles as athletes, employees of the university. They are students who participate in athletics as part of their educational experience. This is the heart of the enterprise. (ibid. 5)

This subtle and nuanced view of all college athletes as amateurs who are students first normalizes that an employer–employee relationship cannot exist in big-time US college sport. However, within the confines of the collegiate model, "the business of college sports is not a necessary evil; rather, it is a proper part of the overall enterprise" (ibid.: 10). For Brand thinking that commercialism is incompatible with amateurism is "nonsense! This type of thinking is both a misinterpretation and a misapplication of amateurism. 'Amateur' defines the participants, not the enterprise" (ibid.: 11).

Brand's greatest fear, that his collegiate model would not prevent the courts from "misinterpreting" amateurism, came to pass in *O'Bannon v. NCAA* (2015), six years after his death. Both the district and circuit courts displayed a deep skepticism of the NCAA's explanation and justification for its amorphous concept of amateurism.

Following the decision in *O'Bannon* that dealt with NIL rights, former college athletes, led by former West Virginia football player Shawne Alston, argued that the entire NCAA system that capped a player's education-related compensation was an illegal restraint of trade (*NCAA v. Alston,* 2021). The NCAA repeated its "world will end" mantra, both in court and in a public relations campaign designed to win the hearts and minds of not only court officials but also the public. At each level of litigation, the NCAA claimed to anyone who would listen that college sport fans would reject players receiving financial benefits that exceeded the NCAA's defined GIA limits (which had changed numerous times since 1956). As the NCAA lost at the district and appellate court levels, it became desperate to avoid a monumental Supreme Court loss. Arguing before the Court, NCAA attorney Seth Waxman claimed that the cost of labor helped define and differentiate college sport from professional sport and was a critical component of the industry's collegiate model (Wetzel 2021).

Although the NCAA vehemently argued its position, the Supreme Court was not swayed. Any legal deference to amateurism had been seemingly replaced by outright hostility to not only historical notions of amateurism but also Brand's reformulated collegiate model.

A passage from *NCAA v. Alston* reveals how much the NCAA's standing with the Court had diminished since *NCAA v. Board of Regents:*

> The NCAA next contends that the Court's decision in Board of Regents expressly approved the NCAA's limits on student-athlete compensation. That is incorrect. The Court in Board of Regents did not analyze the lawfulness of the NCAA's restrictions on student-athlete compensation. Rather,

> that case involved an antitrust challenge to the NCAA's restraints on televising games—an antitrust challenge the Court sustained. Along the way, the Court commented on the NCAA's critical role in maintaining the revered tradition of amateurism in college sports as one "entirely consistent with the goals of the Sherman Act." Id., at 120. But that sort of passing comment on an issue not presented is not binding, nor is it dispositive here. Pp. 19–21. (3)

Writing for the Court's 9–0 majority, Justice Neil Gorsuch described the NCAA as a "massive business," one in which "those who run this enterprise profit in a different way than the student-athletes whose activities they oversee" (7). Emphasizing the disparities between the amateur athletes and the overseers, Gorsuch made note of the NCAA president's $4 million annual salary, the multimillion-dollar salaries of Power Five conference commissioners, and annual salaries for Power Five football coaches that sometimes approach $11 million.

Though during questioning a few justices expressed begrudging support for at least some elements of Brand's collegiate model, overall all nine justices sided against the NCAA's position. Justice Brett Kavanaugh, in a concurring opinion that contained a "series of blistering attacks on the longstanding NCAA model" (Myerberg 2021), described the Court's decision as "an important and necessary course correction." Kavanaugh eviscerated Brand's college-sport enterprise:

> Nowhere else in America can businesses get away with agreeing not to pay their workers a fair market rate on the theory that their product is defined by not paying their workers a fair market rate. . . . And under ordinary principles of antitrust law, it is not evident why college sports should be any different.
>
> The NCAA is not above the law. (quoted in ibid.)

In language that illustrated how far in the past *Board of Regents* really was, Kavanaugh concluded: "The N.C.A.A. couches its arguments for not paying student-athletes in innocuous labels. . . . But the labels cannot disguise the reality: The N.C.A.A.'s business model would be flatly illegal in almost any other industry in America" (Concurring opinion, *NCAA v. Alston,* 2021: 3). "Price-fixing labor is price-fixing labor," Kavanaugh wrote. "And price-fixing labor is ordinarily a textbook antitrust problem because it extinguishes the free market in which individuals can otherwise obtain fair compensation for their work" (ibid.).

It is evident the NCAA can no longer simply justify exploitation of profit-athletes as a necessary component of the long-standing tradition of college sport. The Court admonished the NCAA that unilaterally invoking bylaw 12.02.3 does not allow the NCAA to avoid an antitrust challenge: "A party cannot declare a restraint 'immune from §1 scrutiny' by relabeling it a product feature" (3).[4] In addition, in an aside that suggested the NCAA's rebranding of *amateurism* as the "collegiate model of athletics" had not served its intended purpose, the Court noted, "the district court found that the NCAA had not adopted any consistent definition [of amateurism]" (29–30).

While *NCAA v. Alston* clearly demonstrates the Court will no longer passively endorse the NCAA's collegiate model, the decision's narrow scope has not unilaterally changed college sport as we know it. While the plaintiff Alston initially sought a broad, blanket determination that NCAA restrictions on compensation violate the Sherman Act, the ruling simply upholds the trial court's injunction that allows athletic departments to provide additional educational benefits, including such things as academic awards, computers, musical instruments, tutoring, postgraduate scholarships, and internships. However, it is not insignificant that the Supreme Court did conclude the defendants, the NCAA and member universities, did violate the Sherman Act and were engaged in an illegal price-fixing arrangement to limit college-athlete compensation in the form of academic-related benefits.

NIL: Approved Compensation but Still NOT Pay

Since the 1956 adoption of the athletic grant-in-aid, NCAA Division I universities have compensated college athletes for their services while denying that a GIA is pay for play. While bylaws regarding the GIA system have been amended, fundamentally the GIA system restricts how athletes are compensated, since much of the value of a GIA—in the form of a tuition remission—is as a type of scrip, which universities use to substitute value-in-kind for legal tender, thus obscuring the nominal value of a GIA. In keeping with historic scrip-system accounting practices, value-added proponents calculate a GIA's value on a retail instead of an actual expenditure basis. Consequently the NCAA GIA scrip system forecloses profit-athletes from participating in the cash-based market economy in which college coaches, athletic administrators, and corporate stakeholders are free to negotiate the terms of their employment (Brand 2006; McCormick and McCormick 2006). Finally, as Southall and Weiler (2014) noted, a GIA's nonfungible nature is exacerbated by variables (e.g., clustering, practice, and competition scheduling conflicts) that restrict profit-athletes' access to the education promised.

A personification of the cash-starved nature of the GIA system was University of Connecticut's Shabazz Napier, who in 2014—after leading his team to a victory during the NCAA's March Madness basketball tournament—told reporters he sometimes went to bed hungry because he couldn't afford food, despite UConn's GIA guidelines including provisions for meal plans.[5] As would be expected, after the enormous embarrassment and negative publicity generated by Napier's comments, the GIA system was quickly amended to allow athletes greater access to food. As profit-athletes have continued to generate billions of dollars in revenue, athletic administrators (most notably at the Power Five level) have granted—almost begrudgingly—additional permitted compensation, including cost-of-attendance stipends and varying benefits programs. While the GIA system continues to be a tightly regulated, primarily scrip-based system in which college athletes have limited access to cash-based compensation, what has been described as a sea change in college sport took place on June 30, 2021, when college athletes were allowed by the NCAA to commercially exploit their NIL (Marino 2021). What was seemingly lost in the NIL metaverse was that this newly granted opportunity was a fundamental right that the NCAA had inappropriately denied for decades.

In 2014, during the O'Bannon trial, NCAA president Mark Emmert testified that college athletes could receive a cost-of-attendance stipend, which had earlier in 2014 morphed from a prohibited form of "pay" to an approved "benefit" associated with a "Full Grant-in-Aid."[6] (Notably cost-of-attendance stipends had been rejected by the majority of the NCAA membership but mandated by the Power Five conferences—an example of how autonomy conferences act on their own.) However, Emmert contended that college athletes endorsing commercial products or services was a bridge too far:

> Emmert said officials at several member schools have told him that if athletes were to start getting paid beyond the cost of attendance, institutions would ditch Division I sports and opt for Division II or III, in which coach's salaries, stadiums, hype and scholarships are much smaller.
>
> "Do the members want the sports to remain amateur?" an NCAA lawyer asked.
>
> "Yes," Emmert replied.
>
> "If the rules were changed to permit student athletes to be paid for (names, images, and likenesses), would that change what college sports is all about?"
>
> "Yes, it would." (Ganim 2014).

"Citing the organization's century-old history," Emmert seemed to argue that the NCAA was wedded to a "no-budge, no-compromise position on the issue of pay-for-play," journalist Sara Ganim reported, which included prohibitions against college athletes monetizing their NILs. Emmert made "no concessions to the argument of hypocrisy in college sports—the idea that everyone else involved makes money, except the athletes—Emmert did concede that the commercialization of college sports is overwhelming the amateurism. He said the use of athletes' names, images and likenesses is 'one of the most debated topics in NCAA history.'" One of O'Bannon's lawyers, Bill Isaacson, displayed picture after picture of athletes with corporate logos and asked, "Putting athletes in front of logos, that's all fine under NCAA rules?"

> "It's not something I'm personally comfortable with," Emmert responded. ". . . It's certainly not where I would prefer the rules be drawn."
>
> Responding to questions from U.S. District Judge Claudia Wilken about commercial exploitation, Emmert said the schools have chosen to define it to mean that college athletes should not be acting as "pitchmen" for products. (Ganim 2014)

At the time it seemed amateurism's bright line was that commercial endorsements are pay for play and therefore prohibited by bylaw 12.02.3.

In 2014 the NCAA argued vehemently (paying millions of dollars in attorney's fees to do so) that allowing players to commercially exploit their NIL would destroy college sport. By 2021, under increasing legislative and public pressure, the NCAA and all three member divisions adopted interim measures that, for the first time, allowed college athletes the ability to monetize and financially benefit from their NIL without being subject to an NCAA infraction penalty. Though many pundits reported extensively on the NIL policy change, few noted that for decades the NCAA (which is a voluntary, private association and not a state actor) had denied college athletes the ability to control their NIL, a fundamental right of every person. Instead of criticizing the NCAA for decades of exploitation, most media outlets simply reproduced elements of NCAA press releases.

> The policy provides the following guidance to college athletes, recruits, their families, and member schools:
>
> - Individuals can engage in NIL activities that are consistent with the law of the state where the school is located. Colleges and universities may be a resource for state law questions.
> - College athletes who attend a school in a state without an NIL law can engage in this type of activity without violating NCAA rules related to name, image and likeness.
> - Individuals can use a professional services provider for NIL activities.
> - Student-athletes should report NIL activities consistent with state law or school and conference requirements to their school. (Hosick 2021)

Interestingly, while the policy changes clearly allowed college athletes access to previously denied compensation (i.e., pay), according to the NCAA the collegiate model was still intact. "While opening name, image and likeness opportunities . . . , the policy in all three divisions preserves the commitment to avoid pay-for-play and improper inducements tied to choosing to attend a particular school. Those rules remain in effect" (ibid.). In a remarkable attempt at institutional propaganda, Division II Presidents' Council chair Sandra Jordan (chancellor at the University of South Carolina Aiken) proclaimed, "The new policy preserves the fact college sports are not pay-for-play" (ibid.). Technically Jordan was correct that NIL is not pay for play, since in a linguistic sleight of hand, according to NCAA bylaws college athletes can never be paid, since any form of approved funds, awards, or benefits cannot by definition be pay (as covered in bylaw 12.02.3).

Insisting that NIL is not pay for play, the NCAA and athletic department administrators deployed Adamson's (1980) "armor of coercion," claiming victory in the face of retreat and continuing to proclaim that they would never pay college athletes. Eager to accept this latest version of the NCAA's mythological amateur ideology, college athletes, boosters, members of the media, and the public breathed a sigh of relief that college sport was safe: the "kids" were now being treated fairly. With a wink and a nod, these propagandists maintained and reinforced the continuing fiction that college athletes had never been and still weren't being paid.

Overlooked in most NIL discussions was that prior to the NCAA's implementation of its 2021 NIL policy, the NCAA Board of Governors had appointed a "Federal and State Legislation Working Group" to explore possible responses to proposed state and federal NIL legislation. On April 17, 2020, the working group submitted a twenty-page report offering several recommendations. The Board of Governors was encouraged to

> stress to the divisions that any modernization of their NIL bylaws must be accompanied by guardrails sufficient to ensure that:
>
> a. Any compensation received by student-athletes for NIL activities represents a genuine payment for use of their NIL, and is not simply a disguised form of pay for athletics participation;
> b. Schools and conferences play no role in a student-athlete's NIL activities;
> c. Student-athletes are not being compensated for uses of their NIL in situations in which they have no legal right to demand such compensation;
> d. Schools or boosters are not using NIL opportunities as a recruiting inducement;
> e. The role of third parties in student-athlete NIL activities is regulated; and
> f. Modernization of NIL rules does not interfere with NCAA members' efforts in the areas of diversity, inclusion or gender equity. (NCAA 2020: 1–2)

The working group also recommended the board develop a timeline so that each division could fully develop legislative proposals no later than October 31,

2020; vote on proposals no later than January 31, 2021; and implement approved proposals by the 2021–22 academic year. However, after *NCAA v. Alston,* the proposed legislation was never drafted or voted on, since doing so might expose the NCAA to future antitrust lawsuits, and perhaps more important, any proposal was likely not going to pass.

Tellingly none of the recommendations from the working group appear in the NCAA "guidance" or updated interim NIL policy.

1. NCAA Bylaws, including prohibitions on pay-for-play and improper recruiting inducements, remain in effect, subject to the following:
   - For institutions in states without NIL laws or executive actions or with NIL laws or executive actions that have not yet taken effect, if an individual elects to engage in an NIL activity, the individual's eligibility for intercollegiate athletics will not be impacted by application of Bylaw 12 (Amateurism and Athletics Eligibility).
   - For institutions in states with NIL laws or executive actions with the force of law in effect, if an individual or member institution elects to engage in an NIL activity that is protected by law or executive order, the individual's eligibility for and/or the membership institution's full participation in NCAA athletics will not be impacted by application of NCAA Bylaws unless the state law is invalidated or rendered unenforceable by operation of law.
   - Use of a professional services provider is also permissible for NIL activities, except as otherwise provided by a state law or executive action with the force of law that has not been invalidated or rendered unenforceable by operation of law.
2. The NCAA will continue its normal regulatory operations but will not monitor for compliance with state law.
3. Individuals should report NIL activities consistent with state law and/or institutional requirements. (NCAA 2022a)

Despite a fierce, decades-long rejection of college athletes' having the right to monetize their NIL, in the summer of 2021 the NCAA national office and members in all divisions quickly embraced this once-prohibited payment method. What was—as recently as 2019—viewed as "exploitation by professional and commercial enterprises" from which college athletes must be protected (See bylaw 2.9, "The Principle of Amateurism") was suddenly trumpeted by coaches as the newest iteration of approved compensation and indicative of their commitment to doing what was in their players' best interest. Within days of their being permitted, reports circulated on social and traditional media that some college athletes had not only been approached but had signed deals with sponsors. Three weeks into the NIL era, at the Texas High School Coaches Association's annual convention, University of Alabama head football coach Nick Saban revealed that the Crimson Tide's sophomore quarterback, Bryce Young, was "already raking in nearly $1 million in deals under the new name, image and likeness (NIL) policy" (Athletic Staff 2021). Media accounts of Young's NIL windfall, characterized as "ungodly numbers" of "almost seven figures" (Dedaj 2021), intimated the college-sport industry was poised for a significant change to its business model. For some Saban's comments confirmed their worst fears; the dreaded NIL free market had suddenly been unleashed on college sports.

Given the past structure of college sports, where sponsors could only access the market via the NCAA or its members, some college sport administrators were concerned that a significant number of sponsors might substantially decrease or even eliminate their direct support of college sport teams, venues, and events in favor of NIL deals with college athletes. An expressed fear was that non-revenue teams might no longer be able to operate, the result of a domino effect of shifting college sport revenues and expenses. In addition no one had determined how college sport administrators could "support" college athletes' NIL rights while still monitoring these deals to make sure they adhered to a vague NCAA policy or state NIL laws. An immediate concern among NCAA leadership was the potential need to change newly implemented NIL policies:

> Emmert indicated that the NCAA may continue to tinker with its stopgap NIL solution. "As we see the experience playing out in the various states," he said, "we're going to have all the member (schools) continue to track on what's working and what's not working and make adjustments as we need, and as the legal landscape allows, to provide greater clarity and better guardrails around what fits and what doesn't fit and what supports a collegiate model of sport." . . .
>
> Said Emmert: "States have to know that" the NCAA, for now, has "broad boundaries" and "inside that, there's a lot of latitude. And we've been trying very hard to make sure everybody understands there's latitude there. Most all of the schools are fine with behaviors that are in between (pay for play and recruiting inducements). But (prohibitions on) those two things have got to remain the bedrock of what it means to be a collegiate athlete." (Berkowitz 2021)

As the 2021–22 academic year began, media reports indicated many prominent college athletes were engaging in permitted NIL activities. However, despite the fanfare the new NIL rules generated, the widespread proliferation of significant college athlete NIL deals did not immediately materialize. Despite the increase in NIL entrepreneurship activity, it was reported that "much less than half of all NCAA athletes appear to have made any NIL deal at all" (Kirshner 2021a). In addition most college athletes who had made deals often received minuscule renumeration. "Over the first four months of NIL, according to Opendorse, the average Division I athlete who made at least one deal earned $686 before taxes. In Divisions II and III, it was $68 and $35 per athlete" (Kirshner 2021b). By January 2022 Opendorse reported the average Division I compensation had increase to $1,036, while Division II pay had decreased to $58, and Division III ticked up to $40 per deal. The market's initial fluidity was reflected in the fact that earlier reports put the median endorsement-related transaction at less than $63 (Barnett 2021). In addition to mostly minuscule compensation, most early NIL deals appeared to be focused on value in kind (VIK) product exchanges rather than significant cash deals. Though an undetermined number of VIK deals involved significant products (e.g., automobiles and trucks), the majority involved products of much lesser value. Regardless of the overall value of the NIL market, the dominant narrative was, college kids now had the right to get part-time gig jobs, which rewarded entrepreneurial college athletes or those who for a variety of reasons had a greater market value. As Alabama's Saban noted, in many ways the new NIL collegiate model reflected professional sport:

> "You have to understand that everybody has a different amount of opportunity, relative to what's going to happen here," Saban said. "Everything in college football, everything in high school football has always been equal for everyone. It's not gonna be that way anymore."
>
> "Aaron Rodgers makes $24 million a year and probably makes several million dollars in endorsements because he's the quarterback," he added. "The right guard probably makes a million dollars a year, and he doesn't get any money for endorsements. The same thing is going to happen to our team." (Athletic Staff 2021)

The overriding sentiment was that while some college athletes would undoubtedly strike it rich, every college athlete at least had an opportunity to get some much-deserved non-pay spending money.

NIL Collectives: Above-the-Table Payments by Boosters

After an initial 3–4 months during which the nascent NIL gig economy failed to generate across-the-board lucrative NIL activities, in late January 2022 Dennis Dodd reported on a new development in the NIL industry, the emergence of "collectives" that had quickly become major influencers in the monetization of athletes' NIL rights. These standalone, third-party boutique businesses were established to create financial opportunities for athletes. Through a collective, "boosters can accomplish—above board—what was previously a major NCAA violation" (Dodd 2022a): funneling cash and other forms of compensation to athletes.

What became increasingly clear was that the burgeoning collective market showed no signs of slowing down. Within weeks of the establishment of the first collective, the Business of College Sport website had developed a list of twenty-seven NIL collectives as well as six university-specific marketing and talent agencies (Dodd 2022a).

Examples of such collectives included the Gator Collective, which, according to the collective's website, "provides [University of Florida] fans with exclusive access to, and experiences with, their favorite athletes while allowing the athletes to earn compensation for their name, image, and likeness. At the heart of it, The Gator Collective unites fans with athletes" (Gator Collective 2022). As of January 2022 there were twenty-three "Gator Collective Athletes" from football (seventeen), women's gymnastics (three), women's soccer (two), and men's basketball (one).

For $5.99 to $999.99 per month, "Gators fans get exclusive autographs, interviews and even personal appearances" (Dodd 2022a). While the fan subscription fees are the public face of Gator Collective, its website claims the collective is much more than just a marketplace:

> The Gator Collective is not simply a broker for NIL deals. The Gator Collective provides the tools and resources to allow the student-athletes to succeed in this new business world. This includes connecting the student-athletes with professionals in various industries to assist them with public relations, marketing, finance, tax, and community service. We've all heard the phrase, "Gators help Gators," and The Gator Collective is a clear example of that playing out. (Gator Collective 2022)

Horns with Heart claims that it "was founded with the goal of using the Name, Image, and Likeness of University of Texas student-athletes to help promote worthy charitable causes and make positive contributions to our local communities" (Horns with Heart 2022b). One way the collective seeks to accomplishes this mission is through the establishment of an eight-hundred-thousand-dollar sponsorship beginning in 2022. A December 6, 2021, press release heralded the program: "Horns with Heart, a new non-profit entity, has announced their 2022 sponsorship to extend an offer to every University of Texas offensive lineman totaling $50,000.00 in annual financing per player. The program, dubbed The Pancake Factory, will be the first of its kind to support a football position group to participate in charitable endeavors that impact both the University of Texas as well as the community at large" (Horns with Heart 2022a).

Illini Guardians, a collective associated with the University of Illinois athletic department, lays out its mission and working model in typical midwestern fashion:

> **MISSION**
>
> The Illini Guardians is comprised of dedicated supporters of the University of Illinois Fighting Illini athletics, committed to fostering powerful and positive relationships between the student-athletes and the University of Illinois business community by harnessing the opportunities created by Illinois' Name, Image and Likeness legislation, known as the *Student-Athlete Endorsement Rights Act.*
>
> How does this work?
>
> The dollars raised by Illini Guardians are pooled to create carefully vetted NIL contracts with the student athletes. As among the highest profile students at the university, Illinois student-athletes are indeed ambassadors to reflect on their experiences and connect with outside organizations. For example, Illini Guardians enter approved NIL contracts with the students to make appearances at schools and youth organizations both in their home communities and throughout Illinois. Through the outstanding professional networks that run through Illini Guardians, we help match NIL opportunities between the student-athletes and interested businesses. The Illini Guardians are positioned to ensure that such NIL contracts do not interfere with the students' academic or athletic obligations, and that transparency and accountability are maintained. We need your help to fuel the NIL opportunities that will allow Illinois athletics to compete and thrive!
>
> Who are we?
>
> The Illini Guardians are volunteers. We are alumni. We are leaders. We come to this effort with decades of professional success in the fields of law, banking, business, and other areas. We are motivated only by the desire to create a pillar of strength for the Illini student-athletes that allows (1) Illini programs to remain at the very pinnacle of their sports, (2) while elevating the profile of the programs and deepening the ties with the business and alumni communities, (3) and working toward opportunities that allow young people to give back to their communities, to financially benefit from their skills, talents and unending work ethic, and to position them for opportunity and success that will stretch far into their own alumni years. (Illini Guardians 2022)

The collective Valiant MGMT, associated with the University of Michigan, says its mission is "To represent University of Michigan college athletes in name, image and likeness ('NIL') opportunities which are consistent with the university's high standards for ethics and compliance. To maximize the individual earnings for our athletes in opportunities which are consistent with their personal brand while providing an experience optimized for the student-athlete" (Valiant Management 2022). As of August 24, 2022, on its website Valiant MGMT claims to have secured nearly one million dollars in NIL deals for University of Michigan athletes through

- group licensing apparel deals with the football, basketball, and hockey teams;
- signing events at the MDen [The official merchandise retailer of Michigan Athletics. There are six locations.];
- marketing partnerships with local and national brands;
- licensed NFTs;
- media appearances;
- signed memorabilia;
- podcast appearances;
- private training sessions. (Valiant Management 2022)

In September 2021 several prominent University of Oregon alumni and donors, including Nike cofounder Phil Knight and Rosemary St. Clair, a former Nike vice president and general manager of Nike Women, founded Division Street, Inc., one of the first collectives, before the term was widely used. According to Kristi Dosh (2021), Division Street, Inc., was committed to helping college athletes "figure out how to monetize their brands." St. Clair spoke of how helpful the decades of experience of the principals involved would be to college athletes: "Our team has spent decades building the brands of the world's best athletes, and we will use that experience to elevate NIL opportunities by bringing in leading expertise across brand, marketing, sponsorship, digital and creative to support all Oregon student-athletes, inclusive of every sport and across gender" (quoted in Dosh 2021).

The Reality of NIL

It is important to remember that NIL does not provide profit-athletes access to shared revenues from ticket sales, media rights, sponsorship, merchandise sales, or many of the other facets of the multibillion-dollar college sport industry. While athlete-initiated endorsement deals have, for the most part, not been extremely lucrative, collectives seem poised to—once again—separate NIL contenders from pretenders, with boosters, fans, and coaches working to shape the NIL market into one that recognizes the market values of profit-athletes. Collective members appear willing to sign less lucrative NIL deals with a few loss-athletes to provide adequate pay for play for previously woefully underpaid profit-athletes. Some observers have taken a pragmatic view of collectives and booster involvement (which has always been omnipresent in big-time college sport), recognizing that if boosters have money and want to spend it as if they are part owners of their favorite athletic department, what is the real harm?

While many NIL doomsayers lamented that NIL locker rooms would be rife with conflict, full of players jealous of celebrity teammates, such discord has largely not materialized. Some teams have better team chemistry than others, but that has always been the case. College athletes, just as other workers in gig and traditional jobs, have adjusted to a hierarchy of pay. The right guard at Alabama still blocked for Bryce Young during the 2021 football season. The point guard at Duke still passed the ball to the Blue Devils' latest star player, Paolo Banchero, in the 2021–22 college basketball season. Some players achieved celebrity status on Tik Tok or Instagram, some received meals at a local restaurant. What didn't noticeably change was college fans' avidity.

When the Duke University men's basketball team traveled the seven miles to the University of North Carolina at Chapel Hill Dean Smith Center for head coach Mike Krzyzewski's last game at the "Dean Dome," a sellout crowd of 21,750 fans jammed the arena. For the 2022 College Football Playoff (CFP) championship, more than 68,000 fans packed Lucas Oil Stadium and more than 22 million tuned in to ESPN's broadcast (Saul 2022). Instead of amateur college sport imploding, "the customs that most college sports fans hold most dear—the camaraderie of game day, the tailgating, the atmosphere of a stadium packed with nearly 100,000 fans and the pride of cheering for a university team" (Ganim 2014)—have not disappeared.

While profit-athletes have signed more—and more lucrative—NIL deals overall, they have not magically gained economic, political, or social freedom. They still exist in a total-institution setting (Goffman 1961), in which their daily existence is tightly controlled. While free to seek NIL deals, profit-athletes still eat, train, and study in isolation from the rest of the student body (Southall and Weiler 2014). Athletes' daily grind takes place within segregated training and rehabilitation facilities, academic-support centers, and feeding stations and dining facilities closed off from their fellow students.

Even though college athletes are now free to sign endorsement deals, collect appearance fees, and be paid for signing autographs (activities seemingly inconsistent with bylaw 2.9), these commercial opportunities are most often not called what they are—part and parcel of the business of college sport—but are lumped under a generic acronym NIL, a term that seems to obfuscate that in the real world beyond NCAA bylaws, college athletes are now paid to endorse commercial products and services. While NCAA members swear allegiance to an amateurism that never was, the business of college sport continues apace with vague guardrails intended to ensure continued exploitation of profit-athletes.

It seems clear the developing NIL landscape will mirror the existing college sport terrain. Most (but not all) of the best NIL opportunities will flow to Power Five profit-athletes, because they are the college athletes with the greatest market value. There will be NIL outliers, athletes who will develop a fairly lucrative market niche, within which they will monetize endorsement opportunities. The development of collectives will replicate the bifurcation of college sport, in which the haves (Power Five football and men's basketball programs) and have-nots will sort themselves into an NIL hierarchy as programs determine ways to not pay players, while making sure to adequately compensate their Gators, Longhorns, Wolverines, or Buckeyes.

The first few months after college athletes flooded the endorsement marketplace were not that much different from the previous one hundred plus years of big-time college sport. In many ways NIL monetization has been a breath of fresh economic air. In addition—and not surprisingly—fights have not broken out in locker rooms among players jealous of each other's NIL deals. Few if any fans turned off the College Football Playoff games because impure professional players were scoring touchdowns and making tackles. There have been heartwarming stories of college athletes contributing some or all their new NIL compensation to charities. Significant money flowed to select players whose market value exceeded their GIA, but this time much of the payments were aboveboard rather than under the table. In 2021–22 nobody batted an eye when a college athlete drove a new sports car on campus. In the NIL era, college athletes need no longer feel guilty for being paid. In fact, in an interesting way, they can feel proud of their accomplishment. They earned it.

NCAA Transfer Portal

Historically Division I college athletes have not transferred from school to school. In fact their transfer rates from 2004 to 2019—approximately 16 percent for men and 10 percent for women (NCAA 2022b)—were much lower than those for college students generally (37 percent [Brinks 2021]). Proportionally college coaches have changed jobs more frequently than college athletes have transferred (Kirshner 2019). Given the NCAA's repeated claim that college athletes are just normal students, the number of transfers is interesting to note in the context of evolving NCAA rules.

In the 1960s and early 1970s, strict eligibility standards for NCAA and junior college transfers were largely opposed by football and basketball coaches. Since 1961 a policy requiring a year in residence had been in place. In addition an NCAA athlete transferring from another Division I school needed a 1.6 GPA to be eligible. Transfers from junior colleges needed two years of credit hours at their school and a 1.6 average or one year and a 3.0 GPA (Kirshner 2019). In 1993 a new transfer exception bylaw precipitated a heated and protracted battle between Division IA (i.e., FBS) and Division IAA (i.e., FCS). The policy allowed FBS players to transfer down to FCS without having to sit out a year; however, FCS players transferring up still had to sit out a year (ibid.). Notably these policy changes did not apply to transfers in FBS basketball, baseball, and men's ice hockey (ibid.). In most cases a potential transfer had to seek the release from their current institution. Without such a release, the sit-out penalty could be two years. In 2011 Division I graduate students who had a year of eligibility remaining were allowed to transfer without the normal penalty year. "Schools were so incensed that they used an option to override the vote, something that had only happened once before" (ibid.). Current NFL Denver Broncos quarterback Russell Wilson famously "grad-transferred" from North Carolina State to Wisconsin, beginning a trend that continues to this day.

Prior to 2018 only profit-athletes were required to get permission from their current school to contact another school and receive a GIA offer. This rule was designed to discourage coaches from recruiting players from competing Division I schools. The rule served its purpose, with only 577 Division I men's basketball players transferring in 2012 (Verbal Commits 2022).

In 2018 Division I profit-athletes were given the ability to transfer and receive a GIA without having to ask their current school for permission. This new "notification of transfer" model allowed athletes to simply inform their current school that they wished to transfer and required the current school to enter the athlete's name into a "transfer portal" within two business days. Once in the database, other coaches were free to contact those athletes without concern for violating NCAA tampering rules (Hosick 2018). In the portal's first year of existence, more than fifteen thousand athletes from all sports entered their names in the database (Golembeski 2021). However, it wasn't until the NCAA's new transfer rule (which said any athlete could transfer one time from one Division I school to another without penalty during their four years of eligibility) took effect on April 28, 2021—followed by the NCAA's interim NIL policy (effective July 1, 2021)—that the full impact of the transfer portal became apparent.

Division I men's basketball is illustrative of the new college-sport transfer market. According to the website Verbal Commits, transfer activity has gone from 883 in 2018 to 987 in 2019, 1,013 in 2020, and 1,730 in 2021. More than one quarter of all players on Division I rosters in the 2020–21 season played for different teams in the 2021–22 season (Verbal Commits 2022). Though athletes in college basketball and football have always wanted to better position themselves for playing time and an opportunity to later pursue a professional career, the loosening of transfer rules and the creation of the transfer portal has ushered in a more open age of college sport free agency, in which college athletes (especially Power Five football and men's basketball players) can change teams one time without restriction. The effect has been an off-season "warm-stove league" in which coaches recruit high school athletes, re-recruit their own players, and monitor the portal, looking for immediate help in addressing a weak area of their program. Now, just like coaches who are under an employment contract (as with Brian Kelly's move from Notre Dame to Louisiana State University or Lincoln Riley's from Oklahoma to Southern Cal), players can change schools—a form of free agency that is in many ways more flexible than that found in professional sports. Since players have not signed an employment contract and are not paid to play, they can simply choose to transfer from one school and enroll at another, accepting the latter school's proffered GIA.

By Christmas 2021 the transfer portal had clearly become college sport's version of eBay. As Ross Dellenger (2022) reported,

> On Christmas Eve, Wyoming coach Craig Bohl posted a message on Twitter that many found flatly bizarre.
>
> In the tweet, Bohl revealed that his program needed a quarterback—for starters, an unusual approach—and that he planned to acquire that quarterback through the transfer portal or a junior college. It was a loud and public cry to the dozens of quarterbacks in the portal.

Between December 2021 and January 2022, more than three thousand college football players from Divisions I, II, and III entered the transfer portal (Dellenger 2022). In only four short years, an innocuous transfer database has morphed into an integral part of a college sport fan's lexicon. The portal even appeared as an actual "portal" in a Dr. Pepper "Fansville" commercial, into which Clemson quarterback DJ Uiagalelei, who had signed an NIL endorsement deal with Dr. Pepper, disappeared. Notably, as of this writing, Clemson has not yet given its athletes the right to use the athletic department's paw logo in their endorsement activities.

The combination of the transfer portal database and the one-time transfer rule have resulted in a recruiting calendar that looks an awful lot like NFL off-season free agency. Recognizing the 24/7/365 nature of college football recruiting, in January 2022 South Carolina Gamecocks head coach Shane Beamer "smirked as he opened a news conference Friday mentioning the work South Carolina football has been doing in the NCAA transfer portal. . . . 'We've been hard at work at that. . . . We are still not slowing down on that, and we never will. Been busy recruiting for the class of 2022, 2023 and beyond' " (Stone 2022). Beamer acknowledged that what used to be a quiet time of the year (first week in January) had become a time when he was working the phones while he was on a new year's beach vacation: 'With the transfer portal, it's kind of wide open, do whatever you need to do, Beamer said. Last week would have normally been a slow week, relatively speaking, but it wasn't because all we were doing last week was visiting with potential transfers' (quoted in ibid.). The transfer portal has accelerated the professionalization of college sport. According to Beamer, recruiting has become "a 24/7 cycle. . . . The recruiting never ends. You're constantly texting and talking to guys, even when you can't be on the road recruiting. . . . You never really turn that off" (quoted in ibid.).

The Power Two: Professional Sport Without Player Compensation

As Power Five college sport prepared for the 2022 fall sports season, the Big Ten Conference sent shockwaves through the Power Five landscape with the announcement that UCLA and USC—both powerhouse Los Angeles Power Five programs—had been invited to join the Big Ten. Despite both schools being on the Pacific Coast, and having been members of one or more iterations of a "Pacific Coast" conference (i.e., PCC, Pac-8, Pac-10, & Pac-12) for nearly a century, the two schools agreed to join a conference whose nearest member—the University of Nebraska—is roughly 1,500 miles from Los Angeles, and its three farthest members—Penn State University, the University of Maryland, and Rutgers University—are more distant from Los Angeles than the University of Hawaii (Maisel 2022). Both schools decided to leave the Pac 12 without notifying any of their longstanding conference brethren (including the University of California at Berkeley which had long worked closely with UCLA as the two preeminent campuses of the University of California system). The primary justification for leaving for the Big Ten was that the move would provide a financial windfall. For UCLA, the move meant that over $100 million in athletic department debt could be more quickly paid off and Olympic (e.g., loss) sports that might have been cut could be saved (Gentrup 2022). The addition of the two powerhouse football brands would also better position the Big Ten to compete with the SEC.

In many fundamental ways, the addition of UCLA and USC was a logical response to the SEC's earlier expansion salvo, when it added two national big-time football brands—the University of Texas and University of Oklahoma—in 2021 (Galatzan 2021). Shortly after the UCLA-USC/Big Ten announcement, the conference announced a new media rights deal that beginning in 2023 will pay the Big Ten $7 to $8 billion over seven years (Connon 2022). Eventually the Big Ten will distribute $80 million-$100 million per year to each member. This is significantly greater than the per-member conference distribution of $54.3 million during the most recent fiscal year (2019–20) not impacted by the coronavirus pandemic (ibid.).

Not surprisingly there was little-to-no discussion of any negative educational impacts of the new conference membership, no mention of scheduling or travel difficulties—particularly for loss-athletes who would now need to travel coast-to-coast on a regular basis—or worries about any adverse effects on athlete well-being. However, the Big Ten's media deal was heralded as yet another indication the conference was intent on becoming the most powerful player in a big-time college sport environment rapidly evolving into a Power Two "haves and have-nots" model, with the Big Ten and SEC feasting on billions of media-rights' dollars, while everyone else settled for media scraps. Kevin Warren, who prior to becoming Big Ten Commissioner was a prominent front office executive with the NFL's Minnesota Vikings, was quick to note that the addition of UCLA and USC and the conference's new media deal would not only be an immediate financial windfall but would also dramatically affect the Big Ten's brand positioning moving forward. The media megadeal with CBS, Fox, FS1, NBC, NBC Universal (Peacock) and the Big Ten Network substantially increased the conference's reach throughout the digital landscape. Starting July 1, 2023, college sport consumers would have non-stop Big 10 football action on linear television from noon Eastern Time until well into the evening. As Kevin Warren noted, "The Big Ten will be a dominant force from a media standpoint on Saturday" (Dodd 2022b). The deal was modeled after the NFL media rights package (with which Kevin Warren was intimately familiar from his time in the NFL) that allows NFL fans to enjoy Sunday professional football action in the morning (West coast), afternoon and evening on a variety of digital outlets. Consequently, Big Ten games will not only be broadcast by a variety of networks but those networks will also create pre- and post-game content and market the Big Ten product throughout the regular and post-season, as well as the offseason. This positioned the Big Ten to be top-of-the-mind for consumers every week of the year, even when the profit sports of football and basketball are not in season.

Notably, almost totally absent in the news cycle about the billion dollar a year deal was a discussion of profit-athlete employment opportunities or revenue sharing. Even though Warren indicated that the new conference membership and new media deals would, ". . . help our student-athletes in their continued pursuit of name, image and likeness opportunities, because now you're going to be on linear TV from morning to night on Saturday with three massive organizations" (WQRT 2022), there was no dialogue regarding Big Ten football and men's basketball players being treated or compensated as employees. Instead, the revenue from the labor of the conference's profit-athletes would be transferred to Big Ten athletic departments in order to enhance opportunities for Big Ten loss-athletes. Warren noted, "These new deals will continually provide stability for our athletic departments to service our students in a highly productive manner, allowing them to get a world-class education but be treated in a manner that they rightfully deserve" (WQRT 2022). Interestingly, it was not known if Warren's statement about athletes was referring to profit-athletes, loss-athletes or both. However, given the need to exploit new revenue streams to fund the college sport enterprise and retain as many current non-revenue, loss-sports as possible, it is likely Warren was surreptitiously acknowledging the need to exploit unpaid profit-athletes to maintain the high salaries of administrators and allow loss-athletes to be treated in the manner to which they had become accustomed.

Once Again: Are Profit-Athletes Employees?

The move toward big-time college football and basketball players' having greater freedom to seek endorsements and potentially pursue a new playing situation once during their career has spurred additional talks concerning profit-athletes' on-campus educational and commercial roles. While many NCAA officials, coaches, and college sport administrators want to maintain the status quo with profit-athletes denied full labor rights, as of September 2022 two pending developments seem destined to answer one of this book's fundamental questions: Are profit-athletes employees? The first is *Johnson v. NCAA* (2021), a proposed class-action lawsuit filed in the US District Court for the Eastern District of Pennsylvania. The second is a memo from the National Labor Relations Board's (NLRB) General Counsel and subsequent Unfair Labor Practice (ULP) complaints filed by the National College Players Association (NCPA) and the College Basketball Players Association (CBPA). One or both may definitively clarify profit-athletes' employment status.

Johnson v. NCAA

In *Johnson v. NCAA,* the plaintiffs (a group of college athletes) assert that they are employees under the Fair Labor Standards Act. According to the US Department of Labor (2022), "The Fair Labor Standards Act (FLSA) establishes minimum wage, overtime pay, recordkeeping, and youth employment standards affecting employees in the private sector and in Federal, State, and local governments." The athletes contend they should therefore be paid at least minimum wage and overtime pay for the time they spend engaged in athletic activities.

In denying the defendants' motion to dismiss, the district court applied the intern test from *Glatt v. Fox Searchlight Pictures, Inc.* (2015), which examines the primary beneficiary of a labor relationship between intern and employee and found that the NCAA and member universities exercise significant control over college athletes. Through bylaws that address "recruitment, eligibility, hours of participation, duration of eligibility and discipline" (*Johnson v. NCAA,* 2021: 3), NCAA athletes are supervised by coaches and staff members who "impose discipline, including suspension and dismissal from a team, in instances of specified misconduct" (5). The judge admonished the defendants that they were engaging in circular reasoning in arguing "they should not be required to pay Plaintiffs a minimum wage under the FLSA because Plaintiffs are amateurs and that Plaintiffs are amateurs the ASD [Attended Schools Defendants] and the other NCAA member schools have a long history of not paying" (11). Strikingly the court concluded that the plaintiffs' participation in college sport "does not provide them with significant educational benefits"; thus, "balancing all of these [*Glatt*] factors," the Court concluded that "the Complaint plausibly alleges that Plaintiffs are employees of the ASD" (29).

As of September 2022, *Johnson v. NCAA* had not gone to trial. While the case received much less press than the NLRB General Counsel's memorandum on the subject (GC 21-08), it was viewed by many sport law experts as an extremely important case that—if it went to trial—stood a very likely chance of resulting in a significant change to the big-time college sport landscape.

NLRB General Counsel Memorandum GC 21-08

On September 29, 2021, Jennifer A. Abruzzo, NLRB general counsel (GC), sent a memorandum (GC 21–08) to all NLRB regional directors, officers in charge, and resident officers addressing the statutory rights of certain college athletes under the NLRA. With the issuance of the GC 21-08 memo, Abruzzo reinstated a previous memo (GC 17-01), that had been rescinded by GC 18-02. (We have discussed Northwestern University and the potential NLRB involvement at private institutions at length in Richard T. Karcher's chapter, "The Legal Status of College Athletes as Employees under Workers' Compensation and Labor Laws," and Ellen J. Staurowsky's chapter "Northwestern Football, Unionization Efforts, and the NLRB's Decision Not to Exercise Jurisdiction."). In GC 17-01 Abruzzo had set forth "that certain Players at Academic Institutions are employees under the Act and are entitled to be protected from retaliation when exercising their Section 7 rights" (NLRB 2021a: 2). GC 21-08 detailed the general counsel's position that "developments in the case law and [NCAA] rules related to Players at Academic Institutions, and contemporaneous societal shifts, including a dramatic increase in collective action among Players at Academic Institutions, . . . reinforce my position that [certain Players at Academic Institutions] are protected by the Act" (ibid.). Abruzzo wrote that under the NLRA, "scholarship football players at Division I FBS private colleges and universities, and other similarly situated Players at Academic Institutions, are employees under the NLRA. Indeed, Players at Academic Institutions perform services for their colleges and the NCAA, in return for compensation, and subject to their control" (3).

In language that echoed the judge in *Johnson v. NCAA*, the general counsel reiterated that evidence presented in *Northwestern University* and outlined in GC 17-01 supported a finding that FBS football players receiving a GIA are employees under the NLRA, since

- the athletes play football (perform a service) for the university and the NCAA, which has an immeasurable positive impact;
- football players receive significant compensation (a Northwestern University football GIA is valued at $76,000 per year);

- the NCAA controls players terms and conditions of employment (e.g., number of practices, competition hours, eligibility, limits on compensation, gifts, and benefits) through a "Compliance Assistance Program";
- the university controls the manner and means of the players' work on the field and various facets of the players' daily lives to ensure compliance with NCAA rules. (3–4)

Abruzzo stated unequivocally that Northwestern University scholarship football players (i.e., profit-athletes) "clearly satisfy the broad Section 2(3) definition of employee and the common-law test [and] . . . should be protected by Section 7 when they act concertedly to speak out about their terms and conditions of employment, or to self-organize" (4).

In addition, in a stunning repudiation of Walter Byers and the NCAA's student-athlete, the general counsel opined that since

> Players at Academic Institutions are employees under the Act, misclassifying them as 'student-athletes,' and leading them to believe that they are not entitled to the Act's protection, has a chilling effect on Section 7 activity. Therefore, in appropriate cases, I will pursue an independent violation of Section 8(a)(1) of the Act where an employer misclassifies Players at Academic Institutions as student-athletes. Accordingly, cases involving the misclassification of Players at Academic Institutions should be submitted to Advice. (4)

Throughout the memo well-known NCAA talking points (e.g., the immense value of a free education, the bylaws regarding amateurism, the vaunted compliance program, and enormous governance structure) were deconstructed and exposed as nothing more than institutional propaganda designed to protect an exploitative business model and convince profit-athletes that exercising their employment rights would either be futile or result in "adverse employer action" such as NCAA sanctions or loss of GIAs (4).

As if channeling Walter Byers's confession in his 1995 memoir *Unsportsmanlike Conduct: Exploiting College Athletes,* the general counsel accused the NCAA of intentionally misclassifying college athletes as student-athletes to avoid having to provide protections and benefits under employment laws (4). In a backhanded aside to the NCAA's newly instituted NIL interim policy, Abruzzo denounced the association as a gig employer who sought to misclassify entrepreneurial profit-athletes as independent contractors to discourage them from acting "concertedly to speak out about their terms and conditions of employment, or to self-organize" (4).

In many ways GC 21-08 reflects how much the landscape of big-time college sport—including traditional notions of amateurism—has changed in the past few years. College players in all sports are "engaging in collective action at unprecedented levels" (7). Abruzzo noted that college athletes were drawing attention not only to "social justice issues following the murder of George Floyd" but also to health and safety issues "in the face of the Covid-19 pandemic" (7). According to Abruzzo, instances in which players across the country were banding together, speaking out against racism on their campuses, demanding change and threatening to withhold their services in response to coaches' actions, and openly supporting the Black Lives Matter movement all directly concern "terms and conditions of employment and [are] protected concerted activity" (7).

While the memo in and of itself is clearly a proverbial shot across the NCAA's collegiate-model bow, as Edelman (2021) noted, perhaps the most important statement in the memo was found "in the memo's final footnote—one that gave new life to the possibility that either the NCAA or a college sports athletic conference may constitute a 'joint employer' of certain college athletes." Abruzzo concluded that "it may be appropriate for the Board to assert jurisdiction over the NCAA and an athletic conference, and to find joint employer status with certain member institutions, even if some of the member schools are state institutions. . . . *Therefore, I will consider pursuing charges against an athletic conference or association even if some member schools are state institutions*" (NLRB 2021b: 9; emphasis added). With GC 21-08 Abruzzo is not only attacking the core of the NCAA's long-standing collegiate model but also indicating that state colleges and universities, which would traditionally be viewed as immune from NLRB scrutiny in these types of situations (given state laws and jurisdictions), will be in the NLRB's crosshairs in future deliberations regarding profit-athletes' employment status. The significance of this shift cannot be overstated.

NCPA and CBPA: Unfair Labor Practice (ULP) Charges

NLRB regulations provide that "any person may file a charge alleging that someone has engaged in an unfair labor practice" (Jackson Lewis 2021). Since the NLRB general counsel is precluded from searching for possible violations, the filing of an Unfair Labor Practice (ULP) charge gives the general counsel notice "that a possible violation of the NLRA may have occurred and should be investigated" (ibid.). After the publication of GC 21-08, on November 10, 2021, Michael Hsu, former University of Minnesota regent and cofounder of a nascent college basketball player advocacy group the College Basketball Players Association (CBPA), filed a ULP charge (case no. 25-CA-286101) with Region 25 of the NLRB (Indianapolis, IN) accusing the NCAA of violating Sec. 8(a)(1) of the NLRA "by classifying college athletes as student-athletes" (NLRB 2021b).

In addition to the CBPA's ULP charge, on February 8, 2022, the National College Players Association (NCPA)—a long-established college athlete advocacy organization—also "filed unfair labor practice charges against the NCAA,

Pac-12 Conference, UCLA and USC, claiming . . . the schools and organizations [had] unlawfully violated the employee rights of college football and basketball players under the [NLRA]" (McCann and Libit 2022). Justifying its filing of the ULP charge, the NCPA wrote, "Within the past 6 months, the employers have interfered with, restrained, and coerced its employees . . . by repeatedly misclassifying employees as 'student-athlete' non-employees" (McCann and Libit 2022). Expanding the CBPA ULP filing, the NCPA highlighted "various rules and restrictions on athletes, such as those dealing with social media or third-party communications" (ibid.), that impede profit-athletes' employee rights.

NCPA executive director Ramogi Huma proclaimed "athletes deserve every right afforded to them under labor laws—just like other hard working (sic) Americans. . . . College athlete employee status will be key, in part, because employees get paid" (McCann and Libit 2022).[7] In his statement Huma discussed the NCPA's strategy of only including profit-athletes in its filing, highlighting the fact that GC 21-08 specifically referenced Northwestern University football players' unsuccessful unionization efforts: "We're not against other athletes pursuing employee status, [but] FBS football and Division I basketball players are all similar in that they are the only college athletes that are paid full scholarships and receive less than their fair market value" (*Daily Mining Gazette* 2022). Huma contended that profit-athletes' receiving fair compensation is a matter of economic and social justice, since Black athletes are the majority of Power Five football and men's basketball players and at the same time "face a disparate impact from NCAA sports' illegal compensation prohibition" (ibid.).

The NCPA charge seems specifically designed to test the joint employer argument that stipulates an employee of a primary employer (i.e., UCLA and/or Southern Cal) may be employed by a secondary employer (i.e., the NCAA and/or Pac-12) "if that entity holds certain sway over the employee's terms and conditions" (McCann and Libit 2022). It is notable that to date the joint employer argument has not been used successfully in college sport litigation (see *Dawson v. NCAA,* 2019, and *Berger v. NCAA,* 2016), which is what *Johnson v. NCAA* and the NLRB ULP charges seek to achieve.

With these two filings, Abruzzo can now attempt to use her prosecutorial authority to have an administrative law judge decide that certain college athletes (i.e., profit-athletes) must be reclassified as college or university employees pursuant to the NLRA. In her memorandum Abruzzo asserted that the mere reference by schools to college athletes as anything other than employees is a misclassification of their status and a violation of Sec. 8(a)(1).

While Abruzzo's memo does not have the force of law and a general counsel does not have a vote on board decisions, the counsel is an influential advocate for a legal theory embedded in a memorandum. Abruzzo—who will oversee the investigation of the NCPA and CBPA charges—has publicly stated her confidence that the NLRB board will concur with her memorandum's legal position. In addition she solicited a ULP charge, specifically appealing to "athletes or their representatives" to file a charge to "jumpstart the process" (Libit and McCann 2021) of investigating the NCAA's collegiate model.

Since the NCPA and CBPA charges were invited by the NLRB general counsel in GC 21-08, have general counsel support, and seek to change NLRB law, they will likely be referred to the NLRB's Division of Advice in Washington DC, which will most likely direct the regional directors to issue a formal charge against the NCAA and schedule a formal hearing in Indianapolis. An NLRB trial before an administrative law judge could begin shortly thereafter.

While, as of this writing, the ultimate results of *Johnson v. NCAA* and the NLRB investigations are as yet unknown, what is clearly evident is that government officials continue to be more and more engaged with the issue of profit-athletes' employment rights and are increasingly questioning NCAA hegemony and its use of language as an institutional propaganda technique. Many legislators and a significant segment of the public are no longer willing to sit idly by while the NCAA waxes poetic about an amateurism that never was.

The Beginning of the End

So where do we go from here? Do we double down on utilitarian arguments that justify economically exploiting profit-athletes—the majority of whom are athletes of color—to generate the revenue necessary to support athletic opportunities for most college athletes, who (perhaps not coincidentally) happen to be overwhelmingly White and from the middle or upper class? Do we retreat to a pre-1956 version of amateurism in which even more White, upper-class Olympic sport athletes will populate college sport's fields, courts, pools, and tracks? Do we simply choose to ignore college sport's exploitative nature and consume more and more of it, gorging ourselves on March Madness, the College Football Playoff, and the other eighty-eight collegiate national championships? Or do we commit to a long-term paradigm shift that leads to meaningful systemic change, looking to the legal system, elected state legislators, members of Congress, activist scholars, and committed advocates to eventually rescue college sport from itself?

As activist scholars who have researched college sport for decades, we are not optimistic that such change is at hand. However, we do believe a best first step is truth telling, which includes recognizing that amateurism has been and will always remain a fiction. The NCAA collegiate or college sport model is—and always will be unless significantly altered—an immoral mythology designed to forestall college athletes from exercising fundamental human rights.

However, we were recently heartened to hear some candid truth telling from Power Five power brokers. Much like Walter Byers detailed only after he retired the legal and moral fallacies of the NCAA system he helped create and mold, former Big 10 commissioner Jim Delany indicated that the industry was rapidly moving toward much greater big-time college athlete rights (Dodd 2020). It should be noted Delany's most recent comments regarding the future of college sport (which were in stark contrast to his continual "sky is falling" rhetoric during his thirty-plus years as a major power broker in the college sport industry) were made from the safe harbor of retirement after a long, successful, and lucrative career. More important, in an interview with AthleticDirectorU's Matt Brown, University of North Carolina at Chapel Hill athletic director Bubba Cunningham (who has more than twenty-five years in athletic administration and more than a decade in his position at UNC) candidly admitted that college sport's current economic model must change: "What we have been building for thirty years is an economic model that generates a lot of money based on a small number of sports. In our case—in most cases—it's football and basketball. . . . As we continue to generate more and more money in football and basketball in particular that money now seems as though it should go to football and basketball" (AthleticDirectorU 2021). Cunningham touched on the need to explore alternative funding models for Olympic sports, noting that universities need to embrace and cultivate philanthropic opportunities for them: "If we want a great Olympic program in the United States, we need somebody to sponsor Olympic sports. Maybe it's the [individual sport's] national governing body, perhaps it's the NCAA. All I know is it's not going to be what it was ten years ago, fifteen years ago. So, the economic model has to change" (ibid.). Cunningham noted that as the college sport NIL market evolves and comes to resemble a more professional model, the marketplace will skew toward men's programs and specifically toward football and men's basketball. He admitted that while he is not used to this more "professional model," in which all sports and all athletes do not share equally in generated revenue such as NIL, jersey sales, and merchandise, "we do have to consider if this is the new economic model and how does it work" (ibid.). He further stated,

> The money will start to funnel toward the most popular teams, as it has in our media rights and ticket sales, and when that happens, then it's going to create some challenges for the teams that don't generate the money. That's why that economic model needs to change. And so maybe it's camps, maybe it's youth [sports], maybe it's the families that are going to have to support those teams at the collegiate level? They are doing it now at the youth sport level, the high school level, at the AAU level but not at the collegiate level, but I think that is going to have to change as we go forward. (ibid.)

In a frank assessment that was seemingly informed by *NCAA v. Alston* and *Johnson v. NCAA*, the changing NIL landscape, the NLRB general counsel memo, and a forthcoming ruling on the NCPA and CBPA ULP charges, Cunningham conceded that holding on to an outdated amateur mythology may no longer be a viable option:

> The thing we need to talk about is "What is the relationship between the student and the university?" Traditionally it has been a scholarship and you're a student and the university is the place where you get your education through your scholarship. The courts and the NCAA and particularly the Supreme Court and the National Labor Relations Board are suggesting that might not be the appropriate relationship going forward. There might be an employee-employer relationship between the student and the university, and I think within the next two to three years we'll have to sort through that and figure out what does that look like. Does it make sense to modify where we are today. . . ? If we have to change the economic model and that's part of tweaking the model, then we have to take a look at it. Maybe we're in a collective bargaining position within the next couple of years. Maybe the football group is different than the basketball group, which is different than the Olympic sport group. I think we have to consider all of that. Because, if we think we're going to continue on five years from now like it looked like five years ago, that's just not the case. We're seeing that in every lawsuit. (ibid.)

Ever the pragmatist, Cunningham conceded the college sport industry must be open to a new structure. Perhaps his statements should be viewed as a direct rebuff to the well-worn NCAA tagline that justifies exploiting profit-athletes, since most of the more than 460,000 NCAA college athletes go pro in something other than sports.

The End of College Sport as We Know It

Without a doubt college sport has been "backed into a corner surrounded by barbed wire" (Dodd 2022). The many changes taking place across the college sport landscape have seemingly transported the industry to a place and time sixty-six years in the making. Regardless of what any NCAA bylaw says, since 1956 college athletes have been getting paid to play. Hiding behind institutional doublespeak of approved benefits, cost-of-attendance stipends, or NIL collectives is no longer an option. At the very least, there must be a new environment in which profit-athletes can openly negotiate their wages and working conditions. For this to occur, athletes (and their representatives) must have the right to bargain freely with their employers, potentially unionize, and negotiate a collective bargaining agreement with management (e.g., NCAA, Power Five conferences, and athletic departments). Individual labor contracts or a potential collective bargaining agreement must address compensation and working conditions within (at a minimum) Power Five football and Division I basketball. While profit-athletes are closer than ever to achieving this reality, college sport cannot truly claim to be an ethical activity until they can claim fundamental employment rights available to all other workers.

Some college sport power brokers lament these dramatic changes. Pat Kilkenney, former Oregon alumnus and athletic director, waxed nostalgic for the more exploitative good old days, in which players had less power. "It's too bad the NCAA didn't control the narrative . . . The smarmy nature of what's going on. These kids are in power. It's taking away the charm of the business" (quoted in Dodd 2022a). Though people of Kilkenney's ilk are resistant to the future we envision, most fans do not seem to mind if profit-athletes are paid for their athletic exploits. Most recently college sport fans were unaware of—or largely ignored—University of Texas swimmer Joseph Schooling's receiving a US$740,000 bonus from his native country of Singapore for defeating Michael Phelps and winning a gold medal in the 2016 Rio Olympics (Solomon 2018). They also paid little attention to United States wrestler Kyle Snyder's receiving a $250,000 payment from the US Olympic Committee for winning the 97-kilogram freestyle competition at the same 2016 Summer Olympics.[8]

Big-time college basketball and FBS football coaches—as well as NBA and NFL coaches—are largely supportive of players being more equitably compensated. Such statements of support from coaches are undoubtedly made to mollify players (both collegiate and professional). The acceptance of college athletes having access to NIL opportunities is widespread, with two polls, in 2019 and 2021, finding 60 percent or more of college sport fans supporting athletes' getting a fair share of the enormous big-time college sport pie through NIL deals, with only 20 percent opposing such compensation (Ellis and Ferlazzo 2021; Ricciardelli 2019; Valbrun 2021). However, the effectiveness of the college sport industry's messaging of no pay for play is still apparent, with a 2021 Bucknell poll finding 26 percent of respondents supporting paying college athletes directly from university funds, 29 percent having no opinion, and 45 percent opposing pay for play (Ellis and Ferlazzo 2021; Valbrun 2021). Interestingly, in an intellectual sleight of hand, 33 percent of respondents were okay with boosters (e.g., collectives) paying college athletes (Ellis and Ferlazzo 2021). Strikingly, in the same 2021 poll, 36 percent of respondents supported athletes forming a labor union (37 percent had no opinion), while only 20 percent opposed unionization. What these and other polls reveal is that if respondents are educated about the realities of college sport, they are particularly inclined to support college athletes having employment status and getting paid. These realities include

- Restrictions on college athlete compensation hurt low-income athletes.

- College athletes put their bodies on the line and take substantial risks that could result in career-ending injuries, yet they are denied opportunities to financially benefit from sports.
- The time commitment to their sport makes it difficult to find a job elsewhere.
- Everyone associated with college sports is making money except the players. (Fans for Fair Play 2021)

To those of us who know the history of NCAA institutional propaganda, the deliciously ironic scenario of the snake eating its tail is a real possibility. It seems probable that a significant factor contributing to the end of big-time college sport as we know it just might involve Walter Byers's infamous term-of-art *student-athlete*. With the NLRB poised to "pursue an independent violation of Section 8(a)(1) of the Act where an employer misclassifies Players at Academic Institutions as student-athletes" (NLRB 2021a: 4), the very term created, embedded, and disseminated to protect the NCAA collegiate model from employment law and workers' compensation scrutiny just might be the proverbial straw that breaks the model's back.

Notes

1. According to its website, the LEAD1 Association is "the membership association that represents the 130 NCAA Division I Football Bowl Subdivision ('FBS') athletic directors and their departments" (LEAD1 Association 2022).

2. Perhaps not coincidentally, there is no definition of amateurism in NCAA bylaws. The nearest is 2.9, "The Principle of Amateurism," which states: "Student-athletes shall be amateurs in an intercollegiate sport, and their participation should be motivated primarily by education and by the physical, mental and social benefits to be derived. Student participation in intercollegiate athletics is an avocation, and student-athletes should be protected from exploitation by professional and commercial enterprises."

3. After a link to the NCAA's President's Briefing Documents was published March 30, 2012, in the *New York Times* (Nocera 2012), the NCAA deactivated all associated URLs. Currently, an "Entry Page for fs.ncaa.org This page contains no content" message appears. The NCAA does not deny the existence of the documents.

4. See NCAA bylaw 12.02.3, "Pay": "*Pay* is the receipt of funds, awards or benefits not permitted by the governing legislation of the Association for participation in athletics."

5. At the time UConn's athlete handbook's provisions for dining were that athletes could eat in any residence hall between 7:00 AM and 7:15 PM.

6. Bylaw 15.02.2, "Cost of Attendance": "The 'cost of attendance' is an amount calculated by an institutional financial aid office, using federal regulations, that includes the total cost of tuition and fees, room and board, books and supplies, transportation, and other expenses related to attendance at the institution. (Adopted: 1/11/94)." Bylaw 15.02.6, "Full Grant-in-Aid": A full grant-in-aid is financial aid that consists of tuition and fees, room and board, books and other expenses related to attendance at the institution up to the cost of attendance established pursuant to Bylaws 15.02.2 and 15.02.2.1."

7. Huma, who was instrumental in passage of California's first-in-the-nation college athlete NIL law, was previously behind the collective bargaining effort, in 2013, of six Northwestern football players, whose union bid won support from the NLRB's regional office in Chicago before being unanimously rejected by the national board (McCann and Libit 2022).

8. It should be noted both awards were permitted under current "no pay for play" NCAA rules. See Berkowitz (2016).

References

CASES

Berger v. NCAA-843 F.3d 285 (7th Cir. 2016).
Dawson v. NCAA No. 17–15973 (9th Cir. 2019).
Johnson v. NCAA, Civil Action 19–5230 (E.D. Pa. Aug. 25, 2021)
NCAA v. Board of Regents, 468 U.S. 85 (1984).
NCAA v. Alston, 141 U.S. 2141 (2021).
O'Bannon v. NCAA-802 F.3d 1049 (9th Cir. 2015).

SECONDARY SOURCES

Adamson, Walter L. (1980). *Hegemony and Revolution: A Study of Antonio Gramsci's Political and Cultural Theory.* Berkeley: University of California Press.

AthleticDirectorU (2022). "Navigating Change: North Carolina's Cunningham." https://athleticdirectoru.com/.

Athletic Staff (2021). "Nick Saban: Alabama's Bryce Young Earning Near 'Seven Figures' in NIL Deals." *Athletic,* July 20. Theathletic.com. https://theathletic.com.

Barnett, Zach (2021). "NIL Data: Median Transaction Goes for Less than $63." *Football Scoop,* November 15. https://footballscoop.com/.

Berkowitz, Steve (2013). "NCAA Legal Filing Reveals Fears of College Sports Officials." *USA Today,* March 15. https://www.usatoday.com/.

———. (2016). "Ohio State's Kyle Snyder Due $250,000 Bonus after Wrestling Gold in Rio." *USA Today,* August 21. https://www.usatoday.com/.

———. (2021). "NCAA President Mark Emmert Still 'Hopeful and Optimistic' Congress Will Pass NIL Bill." *USA Today,* July 2. https://www.usatoday.com/.

Big 12 Conference (2014). "Are Student-Athletes Employees?" Panel discussion at "The State of College Athletics Forum." October 21. https://www.c-span.org/.

Brand, Myles (2006). "Brand Charts Course for Collegiate Model's Next Century." Speech delivered to the NCAA Convention, January 7. https://mylesbrand.com/.

Brinks, Melissa (2021). "College Transfer Acceptance Rates: Which Schools Accept the Most Students?" PrepScholar, October 23. https://blog.prepscholar.com/.

Bromberg, Nick (2019). "Clemson and Dabo Swinney Agree to College Football's Biggest Contract: 10 Years, $93M." Yahoo! Sports, April 26. https://www.yahoo.com/.

Byers, Walter, with Charles Hammer (1995). *Unsportsmanlike Conduct: Exploiting College Athletes.* Ann Arbor: University of Michigan Press.

Connon, Sam (2022). "Big Ten Signs $7 Billion Media Deal, UCLA Included Amid Roadblocks." Si.com, August 18. https://www.si.com/.

Corr, Chris, Michael S. Carroll, Richard M. Southall, and Caroline Jenkins (2022). "Identity Protective Cognition and Judicial Decisions Involving the NCAA." Paper presented at the annual meeting of the Sport and Recreation Law Association, Atlanta, GA, February 24. https://www.srlaconference.com/.

Daily Mining Gazette (2022). "College Athlete Group Files Complaint, Seeks Employee Status." February 9. https://www.mininggazette.com/.

Dedaj, Paulina (2021). "Nick Saban Says Alabama Quarterback Bryce Young Already Earning Nearly $1 Million in Endorsement Deals." Fox Business, July 21. https://www.foxbusiness.com/.

Dellenger, Ross (2022). "Used to the Coaching Carousel? Meet the QB Shuffle." *SI.com,* January 3. https://www.si.com/.

Dodd, Dennis (2020). "Exiting Big Ten Commish Jim Delany on His 30-Year Tenure and the Future of College Sports." CBS Sports, January 2. https://www.cbssports.com/.

———. (2022a). "Inside the World of 'Collectives' Using Name, Image and Likeness to Pay College Athletes, Influence Programs." CBS Sports, January 26. https://www.cbssports.com/.

———. (2022b). "Big Ten Reaches Seven-year Media Rights Deal with CBS, Fox and NBC for Football, Basketball through 2029–30." Cbssports.com, August 18. https://www.cbssports.com/.

Dosh, Kristi (2021). "Oregon-Focused NIL Company Division Street Joins Forces with Opendorse." *Forbes,* November 18. https://www.forbes.com/.

Edelman, Marc (2021). "The Future of College Athlete Players Unions Lies in an NLRB Memo Footnote." *Forbes,* October 4. https://www.forbes.com/.

Ellis, Chris, and Mike Ferlazzo (2021). "Bucknell Poll Finds Mixed Support for College Student-Athlete Compensation." For the Media, June 23. https://forthemedia.blogs.bucknell.edu/.

Fans for Fair Play (2021). "New Poll Shows Majority of Americans Support Compensating NCAA Athletes." Fox Sports Radio, May 18. https://foxsportsradio.iheart.com/.

Galatzan, Matt (2021). "SEC Officially Add Texas and Oklahoma by Unanimous Vote." Si.com, July 29. https://www.si.com/.

Ganim, Sara (2014). "Paying College Athletes Would Hurt Traditions, NCAA Chief Emmert Testifies." CNN, June 19. https://www.cnn.com/.

Gator Collective (2022). "Our Athletes." https://gatorcollective.com/.

Gentrup, Abigail (2022). "UCLA Move to Big Ten Might Save Sports from Being Cut." Front Office Sports, July 6. https://frontofficesports.com/.

Goffman, Erving (1961). *Asylums: Essays on the Social Situation of Mental Patients and Other Inmates.* New York: Doubleday.

Golembeski, Dean (2021). "Here's How the NCAA Transfer Portal Changed College Athletics in 2021." Best Colleges, December 22. https://www.bestcolleges.com/.

Horns with Heart (2022a). "Horns with Heart Announces $800,000 Sponsorship for Texas Longhorn Offensive Line Beginning in 2022." https://hornswithheart.org/press-release.html.

———. (2022b). "Our Mission." https://hornswithheart.org/#real-mission.

Hosick, Michelle Brutlag (2018). "New Transfer Rule Eliminates Permission-to-Contact Process." NCAA.org, June 13. https://www.ncaa.org/.

———. (2021). "NCAA Adopts Interim Name, Image and Likeness Policy." NCAA.org, June 30. https://www.ncaa.org/.

Illini Guardians (2022). "What Is Illini Guardians?" https://illiniguardians.com/.

Jackson Lewis, P.C. (2021). "First NLRB Charge Filed Alleging Student-Athletes are Employees since NLRB General Counsel's Memorandum." *JDSupra.com*, November 16. https://www.jdsupra.com/.

Kirshner, Alex (2019). "Yelling about Transfers Is More than a Century-Old College Football Tradition." Banner Society, September 24. https://www.bannersociety.com/.

———. (2021a). "How College Athletes Are Making 'Massive Decisions' in the NIL Era." Global Sport Matters, December 7. https://globalsportmatters.com/.

———. (2021b). "How Some Very Busy College Athletes Have Profited in the Name, Image, and Likeness Era's First Season." *Slate*, December 28. https://slate.com/.

LEAD1 Association (2022). "Who We Are." https://lead1association.com/whoweare/.

Libit, Daniel, and Michael McCann (2021). "Unfair Labor Charge Against NCAA May Offer NLRB a New Test Case." *Yahoo! Sports*, November 16. https://www.yahoo.com/.

Maisel, Ivan (2022). "UCLA and USC to the Big Ten? Simply More Proof that Money Wins Out." On3+, June 30. https://www.on3.com/.

Marino, Gregory A. (2021). "The NCAA Declares Independence from NIL Restrictions." Foley and Lardner, LLP, August 20. https://www.foley.com/.

McCann, Michael, and Daniel Libit (2022). "NCAA, PAC-12 accused of athlete labor violations in new filing." *Sportico*, February 8. https://www.sportico.com/.

McCormick, Robert A., and Amy Christian McCormick (2006). "The Myth of the Student-Athlete: The College Athlete as Employee." *Washington Law Review* 81: 71–157.

Myerberg, Paul (2021). "Supreme Court Justice Brett Kavanaugh Rips NCAA in Antitrust Ruling, Says It 'Is Not Above the Law.'" *USA Today*, June 21. https://www.usatoday.com/.

National Collegiate Athletic Association (2010). "Amateurism." NCAA President's Briefing Documents. Indianapolis, IN: Author. http://fs.ncaa.org/.

———. (2020). "NCAA Board of Governors Federal and State Legislation Working Group Final Report and Recommendations: April 17, 2020." https://ncaaorg.s3.amazonaws.com/committees/ncaa/wrkgrps/fslwg/Apr2020FSLWG_Report.pdf.

———. (2022a). "Interim NIL policy." http://ncaaorg.s3.amazonaws.com/ncaa/NIL/NIL_InterimPolicy.pdf.

———. (2022b). "Transfers in Division I." NCAA.org. https://www.ncaa.org/sports/2017/8/3/transfers-in-division-i.aspx.

National Labor Relations Board (2021a). Office of the General Counsel: Memorandum GC 21-08, September 29. https://apps.nlrb.gov/.

———. (2021b). Charge Against Employer: The National Collegiate Athletic Association, November 10. Charge 25-CA-286101.

Nocera, Joe (2012). "Orwell and March Madness." *New York Times*, March 30. https://www.nytimes.com/.

Ricciardelli, Michael (2019). "American Public Supports College Athletes Receiving Endorsement Money for 'Image and Likeness,' as Approved in California This Week." *Seton Hall Sports Poll*, October 3. http://blogs.shu.edu/.

Saul, Derek (2022). "Viewership for College Football Playoff Championship up from Record Low 2021—but Still Below NFL's Ratings." *Forbes*, January 11. https://www.forbes.com/.

Solomon, Jon (2012). "EA Sports and Collegiate Licensing Co. Used Real NCAA Players in Video Games, E-Mails Suggest." *AL.com*, September 19. https://www.al.com/.

———. (2013). "Big Ten in Division III? Jim Delany Says It's Possible If College Players Can Share Revenue." *AL.com,* March 19. https://www.al.com/.

———. (2018). "The History behind the Debate Over Paying NCAA Athletes." Aspen Institute, April 23. https://www.aspeninstitute.org/.

Southall, Richard M., and Jonathan D. Weiler (2014). "NCAA D-I Athletic Departments: Twenty-First=Century Company Towns." *Journal of Issues in Intercollegiate Athletics* 7: 161–86.

Stone, Augusta (2022). "Why Gamecocks Coach Shane Beamer Says He Will 'Never' Slowdown in Transfer Portal." *Columbia (SC) State,* January 24. https://www.thestate.com/.

US Department of Labor (2022). Wages and the Fair Labor Standards Act. https://www.dol.gov/agencies/whd/flsa.

Valbrun, Marjorie (2021). "Poll Finds Mixed Public Support for Paying College Athletes." *Inside Higher Ed,* June 25. https://www.insidehighered.com/.

Valiant Management. (2022). https://valiantuofm.com/pages/about.

Verbal Commits (2022). "2022 D1 Basketball Transfers." https://www.verbalcommits.com/.

Watson, Graham (2015). "Comedian John Oliver Calls Out Clemson's Dabo Swinney's during NCAA Rant." Yahoo! Sports, March 16. https://sports.yahoo.com/.

Wetzel, Dan (2021). "NCAA's Sky-Is-Falling NIL Rhetoric Looks All the More Ridiculous Now." Yahoo! Sports, September 21. https://sports.yahoo.com/.

WQKT (2022). "Big Ten Signs Media Deal with Fox, CBS and NBC." Wqkt.com, August 18. https://wqkt.com/.

CONTRIBUTORS

Richard T. Karcher, associate professor, Eastern Michigan University, is the author of *Sports Ethics for Sports Management Professionals* (2nd ed.).

Joel G. Maxcy is professor, Drexel University.

Mark S. Nagel, professor, University of South Carolina, is the author of *Financial Management in the Sport Industry* (multiple editions); *Developing Successful Sport Marketing Plans* (5th ed.); *Developing Successful Sport Sponsorship Plans* (5th ed.); *Sport Facility Management: Organizing Events and Mitigating Risks* (multiple editions); and *Introduction to Sport Management: Theory and Practice* (multiple editions).

Richard M. Southall, professor, University of South Carolina, is the author of *Sport Facility Management: Organizing Events and Mitigating Risks* (multiple editions) and *Introduction to Sport Management: Theory and Practice* (multiple editions).

Ellen J. Staurowsky, professor, Ithaca College, is the author of *College Athletes for Hire: The Evolution and Legacy of the NCAA's Amateur Myth, Women and Sport: A Continuing Journey from Liberation to Celebration* and *Diversity, Equity, and Inclusion in Sport.*

INDEX

#WeWanttoPlay movement, 165

Abrams, M. H., 87
Abruzzo, Jennifer A., 313, 314, 315, 316
academic capitalism, 11, 21, 71, 88
ACC Network, 77
Adams, Roy, 169
Adidas, 7, 17–18, 20, 21, 211
advertising revenue, 1, 2, 3, 5–6, 150, 196, 212, 243, 293
Aer Lingus College Football Classic, 2
Alex, Gregg, 159
All Players United Movement (APU), 31, 163
All-America Football Conference, 47, 48
Alston v. NCAA (2021), 177
Alston, Walter, 55
amateurism: 1, 38, 61, 92, 140, 157, 167, 269, 285; as classist structure, 23–24, 33; and LEAD1 Association, 30–32; as myth, 10, 11, 20, 27, 33, 87, 317; and NCAA, 19, 22–24, 26–33, 71–72, 79–80, 95–97, 153, 172–74, 176–77, 207, 251–52, 272–73, 275, 280, 292, 293–98, 300, 306, 314–15, 317, 321n2; *see also* National Collegiate Athletic Association (NCAA): amateurism
American Association (baseball), 40
American Athletic Conference, 5, 197, 253n4, 254–55n22
American Baseball Guild, 48
American Basketball Association, 48
American Football League (AFL), 48, 49
American Gaming Association, 3–4, 212
American League (AL), 45
antitrust laws: 38, 44, 46–47, 93; see also *Federal Baseball Club v. National League* (1922); *Flood v. Kuhn* (1972); *Gardella v. Chandler* (1948); *Mackey v. NFL* (1976); *Radovich v. National Football League* (1957); *Robertson v. National Basketball Association* (1976); *Toolson v. New York Yankees* (1953); *United States v. International Boxing Club* (1955)
Aspire Group, 2
Association for Intercollegiate Athletics for Women (AIAW), 201, 205–11
athlete unionization, 152, 153, 156, 179, 190–93, 252n1, 266, 316, 319, 320, 322n7
Atlanta Braves, 55
Atlantic Coast Conference (ACC): 76, 78–79, 80, 82n3, 64, 104, 180, 211, 253n4, 254n15, 280; *see also* ACC Network
Auburn University, 18–19, 78, 92, 170, 211

Baer, George, 52
Baltimore Terrapins, 45
Barcot, Armando, Jr., 180, 181
Barkley, Charles, 42, 59
Bavasi, Buzzie, 52–53, 62
Bavasi, Peter, 62
Bayard, Ralph, 159
beach volleyball, 72, 279
Beamer, Shane, 309, 310
Beckman, Tim, 164
Beebe, Dan, 63
Benedict, Jeff, 8
Berger v. NCAA (2016), 140
Berman, Steve, 177
Berst, David, 30, 173

Bielema, Bret, 167
Big 12 Conference, 62, 76, 78–80, 82n3, 192, 197, 211, 232, 253n4, 254n15, 262, 263
Big 12 Digital Network, 77
Big Ten Conference: 30, 57, 76, 78–79, 80, 82n3, 168, 197, 210, 211, 215, 253n4, 262, 263, 310; player compensation concerns, 60–61, 191–92, 292, 311; player bargaining concerns, 126, 132, 137, 141, 173, 179
Big Ten Network, 4, 77
Bilas, Jay, 22, 33, 64
Bird, Larry, 58, 59
Bisher, Furman, 43
Black basketball players: 32, 33; *see also* National Basketball Association (NBA): Black players
Black players: 102, 161, 284, 285; activism, 155, 158–60, 164, 315; exploitation, 32, 33, 82n2, 165, 271–72, 280, 281–83, 316; racist experiences, 164, 165, 274, 278–79, 282–83
blackballing, 46, 162
Blanks, Harvy, 159
Boinski, Kaz, 10
Bok, Derek, 118
Bonds, Barry, 59
bonuses, 7, 29, 269, 320
Boros, Steve, 41
Bowen, Brian, II ("Tugs"), 17, 18
Bowen, Brian, Sr., 17, 18
Bowlsby, Bob, 180
Bowman, John Gabbert, 157
Brand, Myles, 27, 28, 48, 99, 101, 106n3, 253n6, 272, 292–95; collegiate athletic revenues, 241–43, 254n17, 270–71, 281, 293–94; player grants-in-aid, 177, 270
Bray, Tyler, 171
Brewer, Ryan, 8
Brigham Young University, 5, 159, 254–55n22
broadcasting/livestreaming: 205, 211, 212, 235, 254n16, 264, 278, 311; March Madness, 196; Power Five football/men's basketball, 7, 77; revenues, 5, 7, 99, 236, 243, 254n21, 266, 293
Brotherhood (baseball players' union), 40
Brown University, 131
Bryant, Bear, 160
Buffalo Bills, 8
Bumpis, Chad, 171
Burke, Mike, 31
Bush, George W., 31
Bush, Reggie, 171
business intelligence, 2
Butler, Jonathan, 164
Byers, Walter: 20, 21, 203–4, 317–18; NCAA bureaucracy, 20, 89; player exploitation, 21, 31, 100, 153, 154; student-athlete branding, 94–95, 96, 121–22, 150, 272, 314, 321

California's SB 206, 62
Camp, Walter, 167–68
Cannon, "Judge" Robert, 50
Center for the Rights of Athletes in Education (CARE), 162
Chandler, A. B. "Happy," 43, 46
Chicago Cubs, 46
Cincinnati Red Stockings, 37, 39
classism, 38
Clements, Bill, 169
Clemson University, 78, 81, 190, 251, 291, 309
collective bargaining rights, 22, 49, 54, 57, 59, 114, 125–31, 135–37, 141, 148, 149, 150, 179, 233, 252n1, 266, 319, 322n7
College Athlete Association (CAA), 161, 162
College Athlete Right to Organize Act (CORA), 138, 139
College Football Playoff (CFP), 3, 5, 6, 61, 80, 89, 119, 176, 198, 212, 235, 250, 263, 306
College GameDay (ESPN), 3, 164
College Sports Congressional Gala, 31
Collegiate Athletes Coalition, 51
Collegiate Consulting, 2
Colorado Rockies, 29, 30
Colter, Kain, 56–57, 147–48, 163
Columbia University, 131
commercialism, 1, 25, 40, 70, 72, 96, 98, 99, 196, 243, 272, 293–94

Concerned Students (University of Missouri), 164
Conference USA, 5, 197, 263
corporate hospitality, 2
corporate sponsorships, 2–3, 69, 233, 303, 305
Cotton Bowl, 5
Couch, Maurice, 171
Cousy, Bob, 49
Cox, Fletcher, 171
cricket, 38, 76
Cvijanovic, Simon, 164

Dal Lago, Enrico, 167
data analytics, 2, 211
Davis, Luther, 171
De La Haye, Donald, 30
Delany, Jim, 4, 21, 60–61, 191–92, 292, 318
Detroit Lions, 46
Detroit Red Wings, 50
DeVenzio, Dick, 161, 162
Dickerson, Eric, 169
Disney Institute, 2
Division 1AA schools, 69, 308
Division 1-AAA schools, 69, 244
Division I athletics: 73, 80, 81, 82n1; budgets, 68, 69, 82, 208, 211, 228, 229, 232; donor contributions/endowments, 73, 88, 165, 229, 305; institutional support, 72, 231, 244, 254n21; media rights, 1, 2, 4, 6, 73, 75, 197, 215, 235, 263, 305, 310–11, 318; student fees, 73, 231, 244, 249, 254n21, 282
Division I men's basketball, 2, 3, 9, 20, 70, 89, 96, 97, 98, 285, 308; employer/employee relationship, 147, 151, 190–91, 193, 195–96, 206, 216, 227; finances/revenues, 114–15, 119, 197, 198, 207, 228, 229, 232, 235–36, 239, 250, 252, 253n5, 279; player exploitation, 149, 190, 195–96, 206, 212, 214, 250, 269, 273, 308; *see also* March Madness
Division I Olympic sports, 70, 71, 72, 73, 97
Division I women's basketball, 70, 71, 218, 241, 253n5, 254n16, 285
Division II sports, 1, 29, 70, 71, 218, 281, 297, 299, 302
Division III sports, 61, 70, 71, 72, , 73, 75, 173, 192, 195, 270, 292, 302
Drake Group, 91, 228
Drysdale, Don, 52, 53
Duke University, 64, 98, 161, 306

Eagleson, Alan, 50
Eaton, Floyd, 159
e-commerce, 2, 160
Edelman, Marc, 179
Education Amendment Act (1972), 136; *see also* Title VII; Title IX
Edwards, Donnie, 51, 163
Edwards, Harry, 159, 160
Electronic Arts (EA) Sports, 7, 60
Elliott, Pete, 169
Elmore, Len, 41, 42
Emmert, Mark: athlete bargaining rights, 62, 148, 301; athlete exploitation, 263, 265, 297; Commission on College Basketball, 17, 32–33; student-athlete model, 87–88, 93, 96–97, 98–100, 190, 194–96, 297–98
Erving, Julius, 58
ESPN: 4, 212, 215, 290; *College GameDay Built by the Home Depot*, 3, 164; television/live-streaming rights, 4, 77, 191, 197, 254n16, 306; *see also* College Football Playoff (CFP); March Madness

FBS football programs: 253n4, 254n13; expenses/spending, 244; member market values, 8, 69, 73, 87, 88, 97–98, 212, 233; revenues, 198, 231, 233, 236; structure of, 136–37, 138, 262; student-athlete model, 207, 313, 316
Federal Baseball Club v. National League (1922), 45, 54
Federal League, 45
fencing, 72
field hockey, 72, 278
Finley, Charlie, 43, 56
Flood v. Kuhn (1972), 53, 54
Flood, Curt, 53, 54

Fluker, DJ, 171
Football Bowl Subdivision, 2, 26, 69, 71, 72, 73, 87, 88, 97, 126, 177, 197, 228, 234, 237, 253n4, 262, 321n1
Football Championship Subdivision, 5, 69, 70, 71, 73, 197, 248, 253n4, 262
football stadiums, 24, 76, 80, 97, 98, 150, 168, 208, 212, 235, 275, 297, 306
Forde, Pat, 269
Foster, William T., 180
Franzese, Michael, 170
fundraising, 2, 208, 232

Gallagher, Jim, 46
gambling: 5, 38; *see also* Professional and Amateur Sports Act (PASPA, 1992)
gaming industry, 81, 212
Gardella v. Chandler (1948), 46, 47
Gardella, Danny, 46
Garthwaite, Craig, 8, 266
Gator Bowl, 157
Georgia Tech University, 2, 163, 199
Gibson, Tony, 159
Godfrey, Steven, 171
golf, 72, 88, 267, 268, 269, 279
Grambling State University, 163, 164
Grant, Chet, 9, 10
Grant, Christine, 204
Greenburg, George, 10
Gretzky, Wayne, 59
Groennings, Sven, 162
Group of Five conferences, 5, 6, 70, 73, 75, 197, 227, 247, 253n4, 254–55n22, 262
Gruber, John, 10
Gurley, Todd, 171

Hancock, Bill, 5
Harmon, Ronnie, 170
Harrison, Don, 157
Harvard University, 71, 118, 207–8
Harvey, Doug, 50
Hayes, Nigel, 164
Hedlund, David P., 2
Heisman Trophy, 7, 171
Herrod, Ted, 170
horse racing, 38
Howard University, 156
Howe, Gordie, 50
Hulbert, William, 39
Huma, Ramogi, 51, 52, 56, 148, 162–63, 316, 322n7
Hume, David, 264
Hunter, Jim "Catfish," 43

ice hockey, 72, 174, 175, 253n5, 308
Indiana University, 7, 77, 78, 159–60, 199
Ingersoll, Mike, 23
Intercollegiate Athletic Association of the United States (IAAUS): 40, 209, 219n2; *see also* National Collegiate Athletic Association (NCAA)
International Olympic Committee (IOC), 61
Irish Americans Events Limited, 2
Ivy League sports, 70, 71

Jackson, Bo, 59
Johnson v. NCAA (2021), 312–13, 316, 317, 318
Johnson, "Magic," 58, 59–60
Johnson, Allan G., 279
Johnson, Ban, 45
Jones Concessions LLP, 2
Jones, Cardale, 91
Jones, Jerry, 2
Jordan, Michael, 58, 59,
Jordan, Sandra, 299

Kant, Immanuel, 264
Katsari, Constantina, 167
Kearney, Barry J., 213
Keller, Kevin Lane, 89
Kemper, Kurt Edward, 169
Kennedy, Bobby, 158
Kennedy, J. Walter, 49
Keteyian, Armen, 8
Kim, Joon K., 17, 32
King, Lilly, 29
King, Martin Luther, Jr., 158
Kingsbury, Kliff, 167
Knickerbocker Club (New York), 38
Knight Commission on Intercollegiate Athletics (KCIA), 30, 33, 91, 92, 95, 227–28, 254

Koufax, Sandy, 52, 53
Kubarakis, Anastasios, 29
Kuhn, Bowie, 53, 55, 56, 60
Kuhn, Thomas S., 90, 105
Kunda, Ziva, 86

labor litigation/organizing: 44, 48–59, 147; see also American Baseball Guild; antitrust laws; Cousy, Bob; Eagleson, Alan; Harvey, Doug; Lindsay, Ted; Murphy, Robert; National Football League Players Association (NFLPA); NBA Players Association (NBAPA); National Hockey League Players Association (NHLPA); *O'Bannon v. NCAA* (2014, 2015); *Oliver v. NCAA* (2009); *White, et al. v. National Collegiate Athletic Association* (2008)
lacrosse, 88, 253, 279
Lango, Luke, 6
Lanier, Max, 46
LEAD1 Association, 30–32, 290, 321n1
Learfield, 2, 7
Ledecky, Katie, 29
Legends, 2
Lehmann, David R., 89
Lemieux, Mario, 59
Leslie, Larry L., 88
Liberty Bowl, 157
licensing services/revenues, 6–7, 42, 57, 59, 127, 243, 293, 305
Lindsay, Ted, 50
Lisa, Andrew, 5
Little, Floyd, 158
Logan Young/Albert Means scandal, 169
Los Angeles Dodgers, 52, 55
Los Angeles Dons, 46
loss-athletes/loss-sports, 1, 44, 82n2, 92, 95, 198, 269, 277, 282, 305, 310–12
Louisiana State University (LSU), 156
Luchs, Josh, 170
Lyle, Sparky, 55

Mackey v. NFL (1976), 54
Mackey, John, 54, 56
Maglie, Sal, 46
Major League Baseball (MLB): 37, 41, 48, 197, 273; advertising revenue, 2, 3; free agents/free agency, 53, 54–56; labor relations, 45–47, 50–51, 62, 126; owners, 41, 43, 45, 58; player movement, 42, 45; player salaries, 42–43, 45, 51, 63; player strikes, 58–59; reserve clause, 41, 42, 45, 48, 54, 55; *see also* American League (AL); Federal League; National League (NL); MBL Network
Major League Baseball Players Association (MLBPA), 41, 51, 54, 56
Malcolm X, 158
Manley, Dexter, 100
Manning, Peyton, 169
Manuel, Simone, 29, 317
Manziel, Johnny, 42, 171
March Madness: 6, 81, 83n8, 89, 119, 190, 215, 231, 250, 276, 293, 296; advertising revenue/spending, 3, 81, 196s; brackets, ix, 150, 176; revenue, 80, 81, 12n2, 194, 197, 205; ticket sales, 81, 176
marketing deal, for universities, 7, 61, 88, 199, 231, 303, 305
Marshall University, 170
MBL Network, 4
McGery, William R., 63
McMillen, Tom, 30, 31, 290
McNally, Dave, 40, 55
Means, Albert, 169
media partnerships, 3, 6, 92, 151
Merrilees, Bill, 90
Messersmith, Andy, 40, 55
Mexican League, 46
Michel, Rashan, 19
Mid-American Conference, 5, 254–55n22, 263
Miller, Bill, 3
Miller, Dale, 90
Miller, Marvin, 41, 50–51, 52, 53, 54, 62–63
Milton, Fred, 160
Minor League Baseball, 71
Montana, Joe, 59
Montreal Canadiens, 50
Montreal Expos, 55

Mountain West Conference, 5, 197, 254n15, 254–55n22, 263
Murphy, Chris, 138
Murphy, Robert, 48
Murphy, Ryan, 29
Muzellec, Laurent, 90

names, images, and likenesses (NIL): 7, 60–62, 93, 98, 127, 154, 163, 171, 266–67, 270, 273–74, 291–92, 294, 296–309, 314, 318–20, 322n7
National (Baseball) League (NL), 39, 45
National Association of Base Ball Players (NABBP), 38, 39
National Basketball Association (NBA): 2, 22, 33, 37, 42, 49, 57, 60, 81, 197, 215; advertising revenues, 2, 3; Championship, 5, 235; coaches, 250, 320; draft system, 6, 48, 273; labor activism, 49, 52, 54, 59, 148, 172; licensing deals, 57, 59; player salaries, 42, 48, 54, 57–58, 59; playoffs, 3, 235; reserve clause, 42, 47, 48; *see also* NBA Players Association (NBAPA); NBA TV
National College Players Association (NCPA), 52, 148, 162, 163, 312, 315
National Collegiate Athletic Association: 11, 12, 37; academics, 72, 100–101, 153; amateurism mythology, 71, 72, 79, 87, 88, 90, 92, 93, 95–98, 147, 173, 177, 181, 207, 251, 252, 269, 272–73, 275, 280, 285, 292–96, 297–98, 300, 306, 314, 317, 321n2; antitrust lawsuits, 126–27, 137, 139–40, 177, 295, 300; athlete activism, 99, 147, 151, 155, 161–62; athlete exploitation, 20–21, 22, 70, 87, 95, 99, 104, 154–56, 165–67, 202, 206, 217–18, 229, 252, 261, 263–65, 267–70, 272, 274–83, 285, 292, 293, 295, 297–98, 300, 306, 311, 314, 317, 319–20, 321n2; branding/rebranding, 4, 88–92, 93, 94–100, 104, 106n1,2, 196, 215, 262, 293, 296; health insurance programs, 28, 57, 99, 116, 147, 174–75, 176, 269; collegiate athletics model, 65, 70, 82n4, 87–88, 89, 97, 98, 104–105, 150, 190, 191, 193, 236, 252, 264, 265, 269–72, 277, 282, 290–98, 301, 302, 315, 317, 321; commercialization of, 40, 64, 70, 72, 96, 98, 196, 243, 261, 270, 272, 275, 280, 293–94, 297; Commission on College Basketball, 17, 33; corporatization, 71, 72; Federal Bureau of Investigation probe, 17–18, 172; formation/structure of, 11, 25, 28, 33, 40, 63, 68, 70, 88, 106n1, 147, 154, 194, 198, 261–62, 267, 281, 301, 314; graduation success rates (GSR), 101, 102, 103–104; grants-n-aid (GIAs), 9, 20, 24–25, 28, 40, 41–42, 43–44, 47–48, 57, 113–14, 120, 121, 147, 153–54, 157, 174, 178, 190–92, 202–3, 211, 212, 217, 250, 255n24,25, 264, 265, 267, 269, 296–97, 308, 313–14; group licensing deals, 6, 42; marketing, 1–2, 5, 37, 38, 60, 88, 90, 92, 94, 104, 196, 200; media partners/rights, 1, 92, 99, 197, 215; monopoly power, 47, 194, 205, 233; pay-to-play culture, 17, 168–71; player transfer policies, 18, 40, 178, 202, 212–13, 307–10; Principle of Amateurism, 19, 72, 79–80, 275, 321n2; race issues, 70, 158, 159, 160, 164–65; Sanity Code, 172, 173; slush funds, 24, 167–72; Special Assistance Fund (SAF), 175, 176; sports-as-extracurricular activity model, 8, 60, 86, 95, 121–22, 141, 151, 193, 206–9, 213, 214, 216, 276; Student-Athlete Opportunity Fund (SAOF), 28, 175, 176; workers' compensation, 11, 94, 113–17, 119–24, 139, 142, 150, 272, 321
National Collegiate Athletic Association: athlete activism, 147, 151, 155, 161–62
National Football Foundation (NFF), 3
National Football League (NFL), 2, 3, 4, 6, 22, 37; coaches, 8–9; draft system, 48; free agents/free agency, 54, 60; grievance arbitration, 49; medical care, 49; owners, 58; pension plans, 49; player movement, 42, 47; player salaries, 42, 48, 49; reserve clause, 42, 47, 48
National Football League Players Association (NFLPA), 49, 52

National Hockey League (NHL): 37; draft system, 48; free agents/free agency, 60; pension plans, 50; player movement, 42; player salaries, 42, 48, 50, 59; player strikes, 58–59; reserve clause, 42, 47, 48; revenues, 59
National Hockey League Players Association (NHLPA), 50, 52
National Invitation Tournament (NIT), 47
National Labor Relations Act (1935), 51, 179
National Labor Relations Board (NLRB): 179–80, 190, 312, 313; Brown University decision, 128, 129, 130, 131, 132, 136; Columbia University decision, 131, 132, 139, 252n1; jurisdictional issues, 11–12, 57, 138, 147, 178; New York University decision, 128, 130, 138; and Northwestern University decision, 57, 132–33, 135–39, 141, 147, 173, 177–81, 191, 206, 213, 217, 231, 252, 322n7; and student athletes/student workers, 127–28, 129–30, 131, 132, 139, 315, 321; unfair labor practices, 315–16, 317; unions, 125, 126, 132–33
Naylor, Michael E., 2
NBA Championship, 5
NBA Players Association (NBAPA), 49, 52, 54
NBA TV, 4
NCAA Division I Men's Basketball Tournament, 5–6
NCAA v. Alston (2021), 105, 119
NCAA v. Board of Regents (1984), 69
NCAA v. Tarkanian (1988), 32
NCCA Football Championship Subdivision (FCS), 5
New York Rangers, 50
New York Yankees, 46
Newsome, Gavin, 62
Newton, Cam, 170
Nike, 7, 18
NLRB v. Town & Country Electric (1995), 130
Norris, James, 46
North American Soccer League v. NLRB (1980), 126
Northwestern University, 12, 31, 81, 139, 177–80
Norvell, Mike, 165
Nunez, Rigo, 162
Nyad, Diana, 100

O'Bannon v. NCAA (2014), 7, 26, 29, 47, 60, 61–62, 79, 93, 152, 174, 177
O'Bannon, Ed, 60, 61
Oakland A's, 56
Ohio State University, 7, 8, 98, 171, 179
Ohr, Peter Sung, 57, 132, 133, 146–47, 148, 191, 206, 217, 252n1
Oklahoma State University, 8, 92, 100
Oliver v. NCAA (2009), 47
Oliver, Andy, 47
Olympics, 5, 29, 61, 73
Olympic-sport athletes, 97, 98
Oregon State University, 160
Oriard, Michael, 160
Owen, Mickey, 46
Owens, Jim, 159

Pac-12 Conference, 62, 80, 82n3
Pac-12 Network, 77
Painter, Richard, 31
Parseghian, Ara, 162
paternalism, 38, 41, 62–63, 167, 269, 272–73, 274–79
patriarchy, 279
Penn State University, 92
Person, Chuck, 18–19
Philadelphia Phillies, 53
Pierce, David A., 29
Pipkins, Ondre, 178
Pitino, Rick, 4, 18
Pittsburgh Pirates, 48–49
Plonsky, Chris, 63
Plonsky, Chris, 63, 282, 283, 291
Pont, John, 159
Power Five conferences: 6, 12, 26, 28, 29, 31, 33, 69, 70; game attendance, 76; basketball arenas, 76; donor contributions/endowments, 73, 75; facilities, 80; fiscal health, 79–80; institutional/government support, 75; media rights, 75; royalties/

Power Five conferences (*continued*)
licensing/advertising, 75; stadiums, 76; student fees, 75; ticket sales, 73, 75
Power Five football: 10, 11, 37, 72, 89, 96, 97, 98; expenses/revenue, 73; player compensation, 79, 81–82; player exploitation, 73; race issues, 73; revenues, 77–79; television/live streaming, 77
Power Five men's basketball: expenses/revenues, 73; game attendance, 76, 77; player compensation, 79; player exploitation, 73, 81; race issues, 73; revenues, 77–79; television/live streaming, 77
Power Five universities, 95
premium seating, 2
Professional and Amateur Sports Act (PASPA, 1992), 12n3
professionalism: 1, 24–26, 28, 70, 99, 172, 200, 272; and NABBP clubs, 39
profit-athletes, 82n2
Pryor, Terrelle, 171

Quinn, Robert, 171

racism, 12, 32, 151, 158, 160, 283, 315
Radovich v. National Football League (1957), 46
Radovich, William, 46
Raley, Dan, 159
recruiting, 8, 9, 17, 18–19, 21, 22, 63, 69, 200, 202, 209–12, 217, 231, 250–52, 266, 275, 284, 298, 299–301, 308, 309–10, 312
Rickey, Branch, 46
Ridpath, David, 170
rifle, 72
Robertson v. National Basketball Association (1976), 54
Robertson, Oscar, 54
Robinson, Jackie, 43
Rockne, Knute, 9, 10
Rose Bowl, 30, 156, 157, 170
Rosen, Josh, 164
Rosenberg, Michael, 27
Rothstein, Jon, 180
rowing, 72
Rozelle Rule (NFL), 54, 58
Rozelle, Pete, 54
Rutgers University, 80
Ryan, Nolan, 63

Sack, Allen L., 70, 76, 162
Sanders, Bernie, 138
Sanders, Deion, 59
Schooling, Joseph, 29
Schwartzwalder, Ben, 157, 158, 160
Scott, John, 160
Scott, Larry, 165
Seattle Seahawks, 29
SEC Network, 77
Seitz, Peter, 55, 56
Sewell, Rip, 49
sexism, 151
Seymour, Harold, 39
Sherman Antitrust Act (1890), 41
Silve, Mike, 69
Simmons, Ted, 55
Simms, Chris, 171
Sixth Street Partners, 2
skiing, 72
Slaughter, Sheila, 88
Snyder, Brad, 53
soccer, 88
social media, 3, 92, 94, 139, 164, 166, 170, 197, 211, 213, 316
social media activism, 164, 165
Southall, Richard M., 165
Southeastern Conference (SEC), 2–3, 4–5, 80, 82n3
Southern Methodist University, 169
sport participation, 38
sports apparel contracts/sales, 7
sports labor disputes, 38
sports marketing, 38
sports media, 38
St. Clare's Hospital, 131
St. Louis Cardinals, 53
Stansbury, Rick, 22
Starr, Kenneth, 148–49, 192
Staurowsky, Ellen J., 24, 159, 161, 163
Steelberg, Ryan, 6
Stern, David, 58

Stuart, Helen, 90
student loan debt, 43, 44
Student Right-to-Know and Campus Security Act (SRTKA, 1990), 100
student-athlete (term), 89, 93, 94–96, 97
Sun Belt Conference, 5
Super Bowl, 4, 5
Sutherland, Jock, 156, 157
Sweeney, William F., Jr., 17
swimming & diving, 72, 73, 88
Swinney, Dabo, 190, 291
Syracuse Eight, 157–58, 159

Taylor, Charlie, 4
tennis, 72, 88
Thought Equity Motion (TEM)/Wazell Digital, 6
ticket sales, 2, 5
Title IX, 12
Title IX, 12, 60, 136, 190–94, 201, 202, 203, 204, 206, 214–19, 229, 254n10, 267, 291
Title VII, 136, 203
Toolson v. New York Yankees (1953), 46
track & field, 72, 73
Trump, Donald, 31
Trustees of Columbia University (2016), 131

US Department of Justice, 18, 19–20, 22, 23, 32, 33
US Ninth Circuit Court of Appeals, 26, 30
Uiagalelei, DJ, 209
Under Armour, 7
Underwood, Brad, 4
Underwood, John, 160
United States Military Academy, 5
United States of America v. Chuck Connors Person and Rashad Michel (2017), 17, 18–20
United States of America v. James (Jim) Gatto, Merl Code, Christian Dawkins, Jonathan Brad Augustine, and Munish Sood (2017), 17
United States of America v. Lamont Evans, Emanuel (Book) Richardson, Anthony (Tony) Bland, Christian Dawkins, and Munish Sood (2017), 17
United States v. International Boxing Club (1955), 46
University of Alabama, 8, 178
University of Alabama–Tuscaloosa, 103
University of Central Florida, 30
University of Illinois, 7
University of Indiana, 29
University of Louisville, 17–18, 92
University of Maryland, 80
University of Massachusetts-Amherst, 5
University of Memphis, 5
University of Michigan, 98, 179
University of Mississippi, 80
University of Missouri, 81, 164
University of North Carolina at Chapel Hill, 23, 92, 98, 171, 181
University of Notre Dame, 5, 10, 80, 103
University of Oklahoma, 164
University of Pennsylvania, 140
University of Pittsburgh, 156, 157
University of South Carolina, 241
University of Texas, 8
University of Washington, 159
University of Wyoming, 159
US Ninth Circuit appellate court, 93
US Supreme Court, 45
utilitarianism, 264, 265

Valiant MGMT, 304, 305
Veritone Digital Hub, 6–7
video game licensing, 42
volleyball, 72, 88
Vourderis, John, 18, 19

Wake Forest University, 157
Waldrep, 122
Walters, Norby, 170
water polo, 72
Weiler, Jonathan D., 165
Western Kentucky University, 22
White v. NCAA (2008), 174
White, et al. v. National Collegiate Athletic Association (2008), 48
Wicker, Ken, 20

Wilken, Claudia, 26, 61, 93, 105
William V. Campbell Trophy, 177
Wilner, Jon, 5
Wilson, Marvin, 165
Wilson, Russell, 29–30
Wirtz, Arthur, 46
Wolfe, Tom, 164
Women's National Basketball Association, 71
World Cup, 5
World Hockey Association, 48
World Series, 5, 45, 58
wrestling, 72, 88
Wright, Harry, 39

Yale University, 167
Yankee Global Entertainment Holdings (YGE), 2
Yost, Fielding, 168
Young, Logan, 169
Young, Nick, 62

Zimbalist, Andrew, 180